Penguin

REMEMBERING
WEARY

Margaret Geddes was born in rural Victoria in 1949 and grew up in the shadows of World War II. Four of her mother's six brothers went to the war and two died, one on the Burma–Thailand Railway.

For *Remembering Weary*, she travelled to the UK, Ireland and Thailand as well as throughout Australia and drew on her experience as a journalist with the *Age* newspaper.

Margaret lives in Melbourne with her husband, Dick Barnes, and their two children.

REMEMBERING
WEARY

MARGARET GEDDES

Penguin Books

Penguin Books Australia Ltd
487 Maroondah Highway, PO Box 257
Ringwood, Victoria 3134, Australia
Penguin Books Ltd
Harmondsworth, Middlesex, England
Viking Penguin, A Division of Penguin Books USA Inc
375 Hudson Street, New York, New York 10014, USA
Penguin Books Canada Limited
10 Alcorn Avenue, Toronto, Ontario, Canada M4V 3B2
Penguin Books (NZ) Ltd
Cnr. Rosedale & Airborne Roads, Albany, Auckland, New Zealand

First published by Penguin Books Australia Ltd 1996
This edition published by Penguin Books Australia Ltd 1997

1 3 5 7 9 10 8 6 4 2

Text copyright © Margaret Geddes 1996

All rights reserved. Without limiting the rights under copyright
reserved above, no part of this publication may be reproduced,
stored in or introduced into a retrieval system, or transmitted,
in any form or by any means (electronic, mechanical, photocopying
recording or otherwise), without the prior written permission of
both the copyright owner and the above publisher of this book.

Cover photograph by Quentin Fogarty
Typeset in 12/17 Jansen by Post Typesetters, Brisbane, Qld.
Printed in Australia by Australian Print Group, Maryborough, Vic.

National Library of Australia
Cataloguing-in-Publication data

Geddes, Margaret, 1949– .
Remembering Weary.

Includes index.
ISBN 0 140 26970 3.

1. Dunlop, E. E. (Ernest Edwards), 1907–1993. Burma-Siam
Railroad. 3. World War, 1939–1945—Prisoners and prisons,
Japanese. 4. Surgeons—Australia—Biography. 5. World War,
1939–1945—Medical care—Burma. I. Title.

617.092

In memory of

Stan Burke

2/10 Field Company RAE

who died in Thailand in 1944,

aged 25

Contents

Acknowledgements

I WOULD LIKE to thank Alexander and John Dunlop for their co-operation and for permission to reprint their father's letters.

Thank you to Valda Street for her assistance in locating Sir Edward's friends and associates and for her boundless encouragement; to Sue Ebury, for her help and for her book *Weary, the Life of Sir Edward Dunlop*, which has been a constant source of reference; to Professor Richard Lovell for his support and to the Anti-Cancer Council of Victoria for coming up with the idea for this book in the first place; to Bill Haskell for his guidance and time; and to the late Des Trowell, who was always keen to help.

Thank you to all who passed on Sir Edward's letters, in particular Vera Marquis and Rowan Nicks, and also Lerida Delbridge, Dr Jim Donaldson, Keith Flanagan, Martin Flanagan, Stanley Gimson, Bill and Alice Griffiths, Bill Haskell, Adrienne Holzer, Dr Tom Kemp, Dr D. Ronald Kilgour, Pamela Menzel, Cliff Moss, Sir Benjamin Rank, Mavis Ryan, Margaret Spinney, Alec Young.

Thank you to all those who gave up their time to speak to me or gave me permission to reprint their articles: Patsy Adam-Smith, Melvie Barter, Fred Barnstable, Judy Bierwirth, Eve Brunner, 'Blue' Butterworth, Dr John Colebatch, Natalie Delbridge, Lerida Delbridge, Dino De Marchi, Dr Jim Donaldson, Hugh Dunlop, Winifred Dunlop, Dr Frank Engel, Clive Fairbairn, Jim and Doreen Ferguson, Keith Flanagan,

Martin Flanagan, Quentin Fogarty, Rod Gabriel, Sir Archibald Glenn, Dr Nigel Gray, Dr Mildred Green, Shirley Hah, Bill Haskell, Dr John Hayward, Merryl Hince, Adrienne Holzer, Hester Hopkins, Gert Hutchins, Betty Jeffrey, Louise and Stewart Joy, Tim, Heidi and David Joy, Rajah Kannan, Bill and Phyllis Keitley, Paul Large, Michael Long, D.G. Macleish, Dr Davis McCaughey, Vera Marquis, Robert Marshall, Pamela Menzel, Cliff Moss, Father Gonzalo Munoz, Dr Phillip Nathaniel, Rowan Nicks, Stewart Noble, Joan Palmer, Ray Parkin, Sir Benjamin Rank, Mavis Ryan, Margaret Spinney, Vivian Statham, Les Tanner, Freda Thomas, Jean Lloyd Thomas, Barbara Todd, Cecil Tulluch, Gerry Twomey, the Hon. Tom Uren, Bill Wearne, Mollie Woodhouse, Dale Wright.

In Britain, thank you to Jack and Helene Bridger-Chalker, John Donovan, Professor Hugh Dudley, Stanley Gimson, Bill and Alice Griffiths, Dr Tom and Ruth Kemp, Dr D. Ronald Kilgour, Eileen McCarthy, Harold Payne, M. Steele-Bodger, E.W. Swanton, Sir Laurens van der Post, Alec Young.

In Thailand I thank Professor Thira Limsila, who arranged for me to meet the Dunlop-Boonpong scholars, the scholars themselves, Professor Kasarn and Thanpuying Sumalee Chartikanavij for their hospitality, Kannikar Prayoonhong, Boopa Krishnamara, and Kanit Wanachote, who enabled me to visit both Hellfire Pass and my uncle's grave at Kanchanaburi.

For assistance with photographs, thanks in particular to Quentin Fogarty and Dale Wright.

Thank you to the *Age* newspaper for permission to reprint articles by Les Tanner and Quentin Fogarty, and to Blackwell Science Asia and Robert Marshall for permission to reprint Weary's obituary which appeared in the *Australian & New Zealand Journal of Surgery*, Volume 64 (1994) Pp 24–26.

I am grateful for permission to publish extracts from *Little Sticks* by Alan Dunlop, Acacia Press, 1985; *How You Take It* by Charles Hopkins, Neptune Press, 1985; *The Things to be Remembered* by Archie Glenn, published privately, 1991.

My research was assisted by Betty Jones in Benalla; Colin Smith, archivist, Royal Australasian College of Surgeons; and Frank Prain, the *Age* library. Thank you.

Thank you, also, to the editors, Sandy Webster and Linda Ristow, the designer Sandy Cull and the staff at Penguin Books.

And thanks, finally, to my husband, Dick Barnes, and daughters Lauren and Anna.

Introduction

GREAT MEN ARE in danger of being lost beneath the accolades we heap upon them and Sir Edward 'Weary' Dunlop was a great man. My aim in *Remembering Weary* has been to present 'Weary' as the man he was.

When I began these interviews, I expected reticence from Sir Edward's friends and colleagues. Instead, I was struck by their generosity and candour. Sir Edward's faults have been aired as freely as his virtues. As the surgeon Robert Marshall suggested, without his foibles, he would have been unbearable.

I was keen to speak to women as well as men. Weary is best known in the masculine context of his wartime experience, yet he was a man who enjoyed the company of women. His friend Rowan Nicks spoke of his and Weary's delight in female conversation, and concluded gleefully, 'No footy!'

During his wartime captivity, Sir Edward conscientiously wrote up his diary. In peacetime, just as conscientiously, he would write his letters. His friend, Jack Chalker, recalls that when he was staying with him, Weary would sometimes begin his letters at 1.30 a.m. Several times, during the interviews, letters were mentioned and I have included some of them. It is wonderful to hear Weary's voice amongst those of his friends and colleagues.

Sir Edward's life was so large that inevitably there are omissions here. To those who have been involved in these areas, they will seem like gaping holes. Time and space have been the constraints. I have deliberately kept the section covering his experiences as a prisoner of war to a minimum since this area has been covered so well elsewhere.

Sir Edward 'Weary' Dunlop touched the lives of many. One image that remains is Rajah Kannan's of the young student members of the Melbourne Council for Overseas Students sitting in their meeting, wondering who the old man was. 'Eventually we all worked out that he was a fair dinkum guy. Everything he did, he believed in.' So many of his actions were done quietly, away from the glare of publicity, which he nevertheless enjoyed. He was a paradox – a much-loved man, in popular demand, who, in his private life, was lonely.

This has been a rewarding and often exhilarating project. In writing about an inspirational figure, I met men and women who were themselves an inspiration. He was remembered with great joy and Ruth Kemp spoke for many when she said, 'I just wish Weary were here to enjoy hearing us talk about him.'

1

FROM ERN TO EDWARD

Sir Edward 'Weary' Dunlop was born in Wangaratta on 12 July 1907 and lived on the family farm at Major Plains in north-eastern Victoria, before moving a short distance to Summerlea on Sheepwash Creek near Stewarton. **Gert Hutchins** *knew Sir Edward, whom she still calls Ern, when they were children and he called in to visit her in Shepparton on the weekend before he died. Gert and I sat at her dining-room table and looked through her mother's photo album.*

MY MOTHER HAD the camera. Some of the photos – well, I'm eighty-two, and they were taken when I was a little kid. Some are starting to fade. She used to do the old sunlight ones, you know you used to print them in the sun? Leave them so long, then take them out. This is Toby, the Shetland pony. Ern gave him to me to learn to ride on. And that's Star, who I acquired after Toby stumbled with me and fell. He was getting a bit old. Ern used to ride him to school, flailing him along. He used to jib, he didn't want to go to the school, it was too far. Ern used to flail him with a stick, and of course the kids used to call him Ornie Windmill. Toby got going though.

My parents visited the Dunlops all the time. We were family friends before we went to live near them. Because I was only two or three years old, and Ern was about five years older, he and his older brother Alan took care of me. You see, they lived

on Sheepwash Creek and we lived directly opposite on Broken
River, on the other side of the Benalla road. It's now called
Ballintine's Road. We were only about half a mile apart.

Ern taught me to ride. He was a good teacher, very patient.
He practically lived over at our place, every chance he got,
'cause he and my mother were so friendly. He told Valda, I
think it was, that my mother was the first woman he ever fell in
love with.

Mum was an auburn haired, outward-going wild person, a
bit like himself. They challenged life to the limit. You know, she
swam the Broken River in full flood, and that river really hikes in
full flood. And she challenged herself to swim it. She was a very
strong woman – she didn't pass it on to her daughter. (laughs)

She and Ern idolised each other. He was the apple of her
eye. My mother lost two children within two days of each other
from diphtheria, and the eldest one was a boy. I was three
months old at the time, so that left me an only child. The boy,
I think, was very – you know, beyond his years a bit. The little
bugger, he was only two years and ten months, but she said he
was always a jump ahead of everybody else, and I think she
took Ern under her wing and made a fuss of him in place of
her son.

We turn back to the photos.
That's the Broken River down there.

That was my swimming hole. (*She shakes her head slowly.*) I
would never have let my kids go down and swim alone in a river
– it was shallow but there were deep holes.

She turns to a photograph of the two Dunlop boys on horses.
Mum and Ern used to go hunting – possums and rabbits and
whatever. Mainly possums at night. You know how you can see

them in the moonlight? And of course it was good money for possum skins. They would enjoy that and they used to share in the profits, I think.

My mother could shoot better than most men. She came from Dunolly. I think her father was a woodcutter, it was in the goldrush days. She and her brother were both auburn haired. They were going up the street and they must have teased this lady and she poked her head over the fence and said 'You little so and so's, you ran through hell with your hats off.' She was horses over logs or fences or whatever – that sort of woman. And Ern was that sort of boy. He'd do anything. We had a row boat on the river and my mother used to make drum nets – you know, get bicycle hoops or a round hoop of iron and a door on one end that you open and a funnel on the other end for them to go in, and she used to supply them and ourselves with fish. And of course Ern used to love that, getting into the boat and off down the river.

Do you remember Ern's mother?

Oh, yes, she was a marvellous woman. She was tall and very receptive. I don't know whether it was because she never had any girls and I was a girl and it was vice versa with Ern and my mother, or whether it was just a mutual friendship. My aunt used to dink me over there on the back of the horse to see Mrs Dunlop. She was more of a lady than my mother. I mean she was more of an indoor person, my mother was an outgoing person. I always hoped I'd grow up and be a lady like she was. I sort of classed her like a pin-up. You know how if you ever went to Ern's house, you'd be received as though you were a real friend? Well, that's the way she was. She received you – she'd welcome anybody.

So you were made to feel special?
Yes, that's the way it was. She saw to it that they studied a lot. Alan always said 'Our storybooks were our dictionary.'

Do you recall how you amused yourselves as a child?
We didn't know what games were. You know how they used to say in those days, run outside and play? Well, who did I play with? The animals. More horses than anything. If the boys were there, we'd make harnesses for the two cattle dogs out of string or rope or anything we could find. Yoke them up in a sledge or something. They gave me a couple of pet lambs and we'd get the dogs to pull the milk down to feed the lambs. I had a couple of pet curlews and we used to dig worms for them, but you could never get them, the curlews always got them first. They were very quick. We used to ride around the paddocks and look for wildflowers. That was good sport. We'd see how many different wildflowers we could get or count or whatever. There used to be beautiful wild peas, nice mauvey wild peas, buttercups and harbingers of spring. That sort of thing. But kids wouldn't do that now. When Ern was a kid, he used to operate on frogs down at Sheepwash Creek – I don't know what he did with them after he'd operated either. Whether he stitched them up with horse hair, let them go or just put them out of their misery. Perhaps he wanted to see what made them croak.

We moved to McCallum Park and I used to ride my bike into Benalla every day but the Dunlop boys, who were at high school then, used to stay in Benalla with their aunt. They'd go in Monday morning and come home Friday. If they were on the road when I was going in I'd ride in with them, but always on a Friday, we'd ride home together. Sometimes one of their uncles would be in the town with a spring cart – you know how they used to load it up with a bag of sugar and a bag of potatoes and a bag of flour – so he'd pile the three bikes up on top of this and we'd sit up there in that spring cart. We thought that was great.

Ern became a very close friend and a hero to me for another reason too. I used to get held up with a chappy on my way home from school – I'm not mentioning any names – and if it wasn't for the boys I might have had a terrible disaster there. A young man. Ern spoke to him – what he said to him, I don't know.

Did that stop it?
Well, if there was nobody about, it didn't. I never ever told my parents, because I didn't know what he was talking about, but he tried to get the bike away from me and I'd pull it and he'd pull it and I'd run away at last and he'd throw it down and I'd wait, stand back, and when he got sick of me, he'd move on. Then I'd grab the bike and go. Friday nights I was safe because the boys used to ride with me. In the finish, Mum started to drive home behind me and then pick me up when I got past this particular spot. I used to wonder, What are you doing in the town? I didn't ever say it to her but I thought, I wonder what you're doing in the town today, you should be at home milking, you know, because it was that time of the day, it was cow time.

Somehow or other the boys must have got through to Mum, through their parents, I think. I know Ern did confront him.

Ern was supposed to be a farmer, but my mother said to me when I was about six I suppose, that Ern was going to be a doctor. So whether he confided something to her or not, I don't know. She was always very interested in medicine – she had a thick doctor's book and I think she just about knew it backwards. You never knew what my mother was into. She said, 'Ern will be a doctor one day.' I wasn't very impressed. (laughs) I reckoned he should have been a farmer.

Tell me, could you see the boy inside the man?
Oh, yeah, he hadn't altered. No, just as wild as ever. He couldn't stand anybody to pass him on the road. If he'd take you into the theatre or something, he'd edge them out of the way so that he could shoot through and get in front of another bloke. Going over to a Scottish dinner one night, this big car came along and cut him off at the roundabout and he did the lolly and took off after him. I said, 'He's bigger than you, Ern' and Ern said, 'A bigger bastard than me.' Fortunately he turned off or we'd probably still be chasing him.

Alan Dunlop was twenty months older than his brother Ernest. In 1985, he published Little Sticks, *his memoirs of their shared childhood. This incident takes place on their property at Sheepwash Creek, Stewarton.*

ONCE AT A quarterly Tea-Meeting, Mother as part of the evening's entertainment, sang 'The Rosary', and was profoundly rebuked by the Home Missionary for singing 'that song'. Mother held her ground and silenced the enemy guns with the statement that she believed that all music was good.

The gentleman in question sometimes visited us merely to keep in touch with the flock, and generally brought his wife with him for an outing. At such times she was very much the grand lady among the peasants. One Saturday we boys returned from our hunting of rabbits in which our dog Joker had assisted by scratching out the bunnies and throwing black earth back at us as we stood behind him. Like two young primitives we returned home to be asked in cold, disdainful tones by the visiting lady what we were going to grow in the gardens in our ears. We made no retaliatory comment, but our pride was deeply hurt. I thought of the incident as just another of those things which had to be endured, but not so proud Ernest, who found the insult insufferable and quietly and secretly plotted a revenge. Relations were further damaged when the missionary's son killed the pet parrot, which we had found injured and nursed back to life.

One day when we went to town, Ernest suggested that we should buy some crackers, an idea which would never have occurred to me. We had our own money which we had earned, so we bought several strings of cheap inchlong crackers, but E. Edward made a much bigger investment in a large triple-bunger. We played with the small ones at home, and had much aiming practice, but the treble-bunger was hidden away until I had almost forgotten it.

Next time the man of religion and his wife came and were having afternoon tea at the small table covered by Mother's best crocheted tablecloth, the big gun, the treble-bunger, was brought out while our parents and the visitors were pleasantly conversing. I had no idea of what was about to take place. The big cracker was carefully lit and dexterously thrown right under the table near the feet of the seated quartet, where a violent explosion occurred, and as the thing shot out to explode again a few feet away, there was a hurried uprising from the table and four pairs of startled eyes, as the thing again danced away for its third and final explosion well away from the adults, leaving sparks everywhere and a sulphurous smell in the air.

I have always admired the great aplomb with which Mother handled the situation. When all were standing in shocked surprise, smiling divinely, disarmingly, Mother merely said, 'Oh those boys,' and distracted attention to her tablecloth, which after inspection she found to be miraculously undamaged. I have always felt that she understood the reason for the attack, and must have been rather sympathetic to our cause, for the matter ended there, and strangely enough neither of us was rebuked or punished.

LITTLE STICKS, THE STORY OF TWO BROTHERS,
by Alan Dunlop, Acacia Press, 1985

With neither son keen to settle on the farm and driven by his own problems with allergies, James Dunlop sold the farm in 1922 and the family moved into Barkly Street, Benalla. **Mavis Ryan** *grew up in Benalla and knew Weary Dunlop by repute long before he became her doctor in 1946. Her parents were friends of Alice and James Dunlop.*

MUM USED TO associate with his parents, who I called Aunt Alice and Uncle Jim. When they came into Benalla, Aunt Alice used to have her afternoon soirees and things like that, if that's what you call them. And my Aunty Nell was a brilliant pianist and she used to play for them. I presume Mum went to them because they were very friendly.

What do you remember of Aunt Alice and Uncle Jim?
I don't remember much except that Aunt Alice was very gracious. She was a lady – a beautifully soft-skinned lady with white hair when I knew her, and Uncle Jim, he had lovely skin, too, and he had white hair. But he had the most ferocious temper, which Ern inherited. Crikey, did he ever. Alan was a little bit different, the other boy. They were as different as chalk and cheese in many ways.

Was the move from the farm to the town difficult?

Well, I don't know that it was. I think it would have been a real Godsend for Aunt Alice, because, from what I heard, she used to have a kitchen right out in the sun, and I think it was galvanised iron, and she used to cook there all day. Now Benalla and Stewarton and Major Plains, all round there, it can be 100 degrees at midnight. It must have been absolute hell for her in that kitchen. And the boys, well, they slept in tents, hail, rain, shine or snow. I think the main house, from what I could gather, was just the two rooms: eating and sleeping for the parents, and the boys were outside and so was the kitchen.

It was the same as far as my family household was concerned in Benalla. They had a big room outside and – this again has been told and handed down to me – where my Aunt Heidi used to cook. She was the one that stayed home and cooked for the family. She used to cook all day there and Uncle said he just couldn't understand how she never collapsed, because he said it was like an oven. Because of course they had the big wood-fire ranges and things like that.

That sounds pretty tough, even for the country in those days.

Well, it didn't sort of hurt them. (laughs) It toughened them up. Aunt Nell married George Dunlop – that's Hughie's mother and father. She used to say that Ern would get up and he'd run on the frosty grass in his bare feet and he'd run on the hot dirt, and she said it didn't seem to worry him. He worked for Mr Say, the chemist, and I think it was Mr Say who saw his potential and he sort of advised him to take up medicine but that, again, is just something that has been handed down to me. So that was his beginnings. Very humble, and I don't think he ever forgot them. He was never a snob.

Hugh Dunlop spoke to me in the sitting room of the Ascot Vale nursing home in which he lives. He is full of admiration for his cousin, though not for a moment does he see himself as inhabiting the same world.

MY FATHER WAS Weary's cousin. I was about four or five when we came to Benalla. My father had a horse and dray and we started a milk round. I come from a very humble background, actually. I remember Ern's mother and father very clearly. They were very keen Methodists. Aunt Alice was fairly religious – a good-living woman, mind you. There are Christians and religious people, and you'd class her as a Christian. Uncle Jim was all right, but he used to panic a bit. If he heard somebody had started chaff-cutting, or something like that, then he'd be all aflutter until he got his men out.

What was Weary like then?
He was a very humble man and a very brave man in my opinion. I don't think he ever altered much. You know, they wanted to keep him on the farm and send only Alan to be educated, but they talked Uncle Jim into letting Weary go as well.

Was Ern held up as an example for you, 'You should work hard and go to university like your cousin Ern'?
No, I went to the 8th grade in high school and then we had to go home. We had a milk round and it was Depression days. They couldn't afford to do it, anyhow.

It was a fairly big deal that Ern was allowed to go on then?
Oh yes.

So there wouldn't be many farmers that would send two boys on?

No, that's right. I often think about what a loss it would have been if he had stopped home on the farm, a man with his skill and brains. 'Course, we'd have never have known actually.

What sort of farm did Weary's people have?

It was mixed farming I think. Mostly wheat farming and things like that. I don't think Weary minded the country so much but right from the early days he had some medical desire.

As I was leaving, Hugh Dunlop added one last comment.

There's one difference between us, he had brains and I haven't.

In 1924 Ernest Edward Dunlop began an apprenticeship with William McCall Say in Benalla. **Alan Dunlop** *describes his brother's early endeavours in his book.*

RETURNING HOWEVER TO the conclusion of our secondary schooling, and our embarkation upon our careers, while I was undergoing my final battle with Physics, my brother was the first to be launched upon the stream of work-a-day life. It was an interesting, novel sight to see my brother come home on the run, for lunch, and lightly vault over a chest-high gate with his right hand on the topmost woodwork for support. Ernest Edward was then a tall, slim young man of more than six feet in height . . .

W. McCall Say, to whom E. Edward was apprenticed, was well-qualified, being the son of a very early Pharmacist in the town, and he had sent Bill to England to receive a first-class training, resulting in a high degree of efficiency.

He was active in municipal affairs, and when the Queen visited the town in 1954, Will Say received her as Mayor.

His young apprentice aged sixteen, received study material from Melbourne, which he readily understood and memorised. He had only one serious barrier to overcome. It will be difficult for those who know him today to realise that throughout childhood, and at this stage, E. Edward was most painfully shy, when confronted by unusual situations, such as being photographed at school. This shyness welled up when he was called upon to go to Mr Say's counter, to attend to the many and varied needs of the customers. Some of the requisites asked for were embarrassing to a young man brought up innocently and genteelly, fresh from country life. Mr Bill Say came round one night to tell Father he doubted that my brother would ever succeed in the profession because of his great shyness.

LITTLE STICKS, THE STORY OF TWO BROTHERS

In 1932 Winifred Erlandson married Alan Dunlop, and Ern was best man. **Win Dunlop** *was happy to talk about those early days, though she said on the phone, 'I don't think I'll be able to help you much.' We sat on the porch of her home in Dandenong and she thought back.*

ALAN AND I met at Melbourne Teachers' College. He was in residence of course, but I was a day student. I went up to Benalla quite a lot. They were wonderful people, his mother and father. Always doing something for somebody else. You know, that kind of person. Looking after people and giving.

What I mean is, they weren't well to do. They were

reasonably comfortable but they didn't have a lot of money. But they'd give things away, they'd leave themselves almost short of things because of what they gave away. Generous.

When the boys were at high school, they were living out at the farm and the two boys went into Benalla and stayed with their uncle and aunt, the Guppys. But by the time I knew them, the Dunlops had sold the farm and moved in and bought the house in Barkly Street.

Tell me about Alice Dunlop.
She was really a wonderful person. Gracious and generous, loving. And a happy person. And so was Jim, too, though he was different. He was a kind of solid man, you know.

I think Alice and Jim were a very good couple and they were very happy together when I saw them. They'd been married for years when I first met them. She was sickly. She had a lot of trouble after Ern was born and I think it was Aunt Lil who took Ern, the baby, and brought him up for quite a while. In those days I think a lot of woman had trouble with childbirth and the like. I know my own mother had trouble also, rather similar. It was depression. But I was a twelve-pound baby, to start with, that didn't help. (laughs) And I think it may have been much the same with Alice and Ern, I'm not sure.

She was never very robust, as I remember her, but she kept going. She'd be going in all that heat. I've been up there when it's been terrible and she'd keep going, doing things. She didn't give way. She had a strong will. Probably passed it on to her son.

I liked going around the country, and they'd take me travelling. We'd have a picnic out this way and a picnic somewhere else and go out to look at some dam, and round and about. Jim was the one that always instigated all that kind of thing. They didn't have a car, they had a horse [and buggy], you see.

And what are your first memories of Ern?

The first memories of Ern I really have are of a person who studied and studied and studied. He had brains but he also put in a lot of hard work. He seemed to work all day and most of the night. He wouldn't even come out and associate with the family really, his mother would take him in meals, and he just kept on working. But you see, he got to the top of everything. He topped the Pharmacy College. Strange to say, Ern was our best man, and my bridesmaid was at Pharmacy College the year before him and she topped it. So the two names are one below the other on the board. (laughs) It only hit me later on. He did brilliantly there but he really studied and studied.

Was he a solemn young man?

Oh, no, he wasn't solemn. If he came and talked, he could talk about anything really. But he didn't. He just didn't spare the time.

It must have been very hard.

It was difficult. They were very happy that their mother and father had gone and lived in the town rather than them having to board with the relations. That was a happy situation for them. Not that there was anything wrong with their relations but they were missing their parents, I suppose.

It must have been when he was doing medicine that he used to stay with cousins down in Carlton, near the Exhibition Building, and all his spare time he worked in a chemist shop in Collingwood. His mother and father couldn't pay for his medical course.

His two aunts, Lil and Vi, had both been World War 1 nurses and Lil had a nursing home in Elsternwick. It was Lil who helped him through his studies. They were great people, both. Aunt Vi went as a CMS [Church Missionary Society] missionary to Tanganyika and she was there for about fifteen or twenty years.

Were they a religious family?

Well, they went to church regularly. But I wouldn't call them religious. They weren't holier than thou or anything like that. They were just nice ordinary people but they were church goers. The Dunlops were originally Presbyterian but when they were out at Stewarton, there was only a Methodist church so they went to the Methodist church and when they went back to Benalla they continued with the Methodist church. But the two boys, as soon as they grew up, they became Presbyterians. So it was a bit tangled really.

Were they well read?

I don't think they read a great deal, I wouldn't say that. They were more ... They had visitors. They had people coming to meals. They liked people, people coming into the house and the like. The house in Benalla, do you know the old house in Benalla?

I think it's gone now.

Oh, it was there the last time I looked. What a shame. It was a nice old house. You know, a weatherboard house with a verandah across half of it and down one side. And they turned the one side into a sleep-out because it was terribly hot up there in the summer. Dreadful. I remember being up there one Christmas and it was 117 degrees. I had two little boys, there were bushfires all round the place, Alan had gone off fighting bushfires and I said, 'Look I think I'd better go home', and I think they were glad to see me go because of the two little children in that heat.

Did Weary go back for Christmas?

Sometimes. Not often. No, I think he worked. He had to earn the money and he didn't go home much.

Benalla would have seemed a lot further then.
Oh yes, and there was the cost of the fare. That was something to consider in those days. It's 120 miles from Melbourne.

You went to Ern's engagement party in 1940?
We had the engagement party without Ern there. He was overseas, you see. That was the first time I'd met Helen. We went to the home in Toorak Road which was actually the Ferguson home then.

What do you remember of Helen?
She was very pleasant. I suppose she was quite brainy but she was very pleasant and very easy to get on with. We were living out in Ringwood at the time and she'd come out there. We were in a very ordinary house and so forth. What I mean is she didn't put on any style or anything like that, she just accepted us as we were and was quite interested in what we were doing. I had both boys then. Jim was born in '34 and Rob was born in '37.

Did you go to the wedding?
No, I didn't. I parted from Alan in '41. I came here to Dandenong then. I was a teacher, you see, and they were absolutely desperate for teachers. Anyone who could stand up and hold a piece of chalk, they'd appoint. They appointed me to the Dandenong school so I came. I actually came for something like ten weeks and stayed thirteen years in the same primary school.

I did see Ern after that on odd occasions. But there was a rift. Actually I was rather indignant and I said that I was going to stand on my own feet and do without the Dunlop family. And I did. Alice and Jim were very good to me even when Alan and I had parted company. They used to come down to Melbourne and make a lot of fuss of me. Of course I had the two children with me, I suppose, but they were really very good and they never seemed to blame me. I was always welcomed.

Did the boys maintain a relationship with their grandparents?

Oh yes. They used to go up and stay with them. Alan would take them up, you see. They didn't have a car when I first went up there, they had a utility. I can remember going out in the utility. Jim had some kind of a business in Benalla. He used to go out installing some kind of gas lights in farmhouses. They would manufacture their own gas. So that's probably why he needed the ute.

You know, I don't think they had a horse. They didn't have the land to run a horse. Oh, I'm a bit hazy. (laughs) Look, it's nearly 70 years ago.

Were you aware of Ern's change of name – when he became Edward?

I think it was Helen who wanted the name change. If ever he wrote to me, he always just signed his name 'Ern', and no one in the family ever referred to him as Edward. I think he took the name of Edward about the time he was married. Whether he took it or Helen took it. No one in the family ever recognised it though.

How did he and Alan get on?

They were two very different people and I have an idea that Ern didn't seem to have much time for Alan. They lived different lives, they lived different social lives even, and Alan was a bit difficult at times. I found him difficult, too, you see. He was difficult. Whereas Ern was so outgoing and easy. But they did drift apart. They didn't have much to do with each other at all.

You can take the boy out of the country but you can't take the country out of the boy. Edward Ernest Dunlop bought forty hectares (100 acres) of untamed bush at St Andrews, a hilly area north-east of Melbourne, in the late 1950s and later purchased a further eighty-one hectares (200 acres) five kilometres away at Smith's Gully.

*Until 1970, managers came and went, then **Bill** and **Phyllis Keitley** took over the property. In 1982 the land at St Andrews was sold and the Keitleys retired to the mountains. They live now in a cottage in Noojee.*

PHYLLIS: We first met Sir Edward twenty-five years ago when we came down to manage the farm for him. He'd had a very unfortunate run with managers in the past, they'd treated him very dishonestly and unkindly. When we came and he found that he could trust us, everything settled into place very nicely. We loved it there.

BILL: But I had been in contact with Sir Edward many, many years before that. He operated on me for a diaphragmatic hernia at the Royal Melbourne Hospital way back in 1951. Then we didn't contact him again until 1970 when we answered an advertisement for a manager in the *Stock and Land* and we met him at his house in Toorak.

PHYLLIS: He had a remarkable memory for faces because he remembered having seen Bill about twenty years before. He said, 'Yes, I remember your face.'

Did he enjoy the farm?

PHYLLIS: He loved his farm more than anything under the sun. It was his sheer joy and delight to relax up there.

BILL: We lived on the farm, and he used to come up practically every Sunday to have a look at it with Lady Dunlop. He didn't seem to come up so often after Lady Dunlop died. He was always busy lecturing or overseas or one thing or another.

PHYLLIS: Occasionally he came out to the farm to spend one or two nights, and it was a revelation. He just delighted in getting into the most ragged old trousers he could find, tied up with a piece of telephone cord, and an old coat that nobody would countenance and a pair of shoes that fell off his feet and he was so blissfully happy.

Did he help you on the farm?

PHYLLIS: Occasionally, if we were haymaking or whatever, he'd hop in and do his bit. One year, he came out to help us cart hay, the poor dear man. He had just bought the Toyota –

BILL: Landcruiser –

PHYLLIS: – and we were carting hay at the time. We had finished baling, and he and Alexander took the Toyota out. Bill had made a crate specially to fit it and it would take 70 bales on the back of a ton truck. So he filled it up and sailed off blithely to take it down to the stack and the next thing we knew –

BILL: – He'd tipped the Landcruiser over on its side. Instead of straight down the slope he'd gone down sideways, and of course it was pretty top heavy with the load of hay on and over it went.

PHYLLIS: He said to Bill, 'Look I've come down there with the tractor many times and it hasn't rolled,' and Bill said, 'Yes, Sir Edward, but the tractor has a much lower centre of gravity.' So he said very gravely to me afterward, 'Well, I've learnt a lot about centre of gravity today.' His son said he had no right to be driving at all because I believe he'd wedged the tractor between a couple of trees on previous occasions. (laughs) Poor old Sir Edward.

Did you know Lady Dunlop?

BILL: Oh yes, she used to come up with him.

PHYLLIS: She was the most sympathetic person I have ever met, I think. She was wonderfully sympathetic. She was a very lovely person. He was devastated when she died. They were a husband and wife but they were really . . . he used to call her Chum. 'Come on Chum, it's time we were going home.' So he really felt it.

Does the property have a name?
BILL & PHYLLIS: Gumbarwil.

PHYLLIS: Which means 'headache'.

BILL: That's right. An Aborigine name.

PHYLLIS: He said he bought himself a headache when he bought that place.

BILL: It was nice country as far as scenery is concerned but it wasn't very good from a quality point of view.

PHYLLIS: It had been very neglected. He said to us, Look all I want is someone to take a bit of interest in the place and we certainly did. Loved that farm. When it came to auctioning it, the auctioneer said it was the showpiece of the district. We built it up from flat fences, stones lying round the pastures by the tons. I'd hate to think of how many stones we collected. We lost two stone, both of us, in the first six months. Bracken so tall that you couldn't see the big 65 tractor when I drove it into it.

Was Sir Edward proud of his cattle?
PHYLLIS: Oh yes. He was very piqued once though. He had bought a Brangus bull which is an Angus/Brahman cross which makes it just a little more fizzy than the Angus and we didn't ever really trust that bull. You'd keep an eye on him. He accepted us because we were always around and handling the cattle. But Sir Edward went down one day, opened the gate and went through and the bull sort of looked at him and put his head down and was going to go for him. Sir Edward said, 'So I gave him a hit over the nose and got through that gate as quickly as I could.'

What was it you most liked about Sir Edward?
PHYLLIS: As far as I was concerned, the genuine interest he took in everything one did or said. If you weren't well he was the first to spot the fact and do something about it. If you had something pleasant to share he was as pleased as though it happened to be his own personal affair. It was his genuineness, I think.

What did you find frustrating about the man?
PHYLLIS: (quiet laughter) He'd forget things. You'd mention something to him, 'This is really important, will you remember this?' 'Yes, yes. No worries.' And the next thing you'd be on the phone a week later, 'Did you do or get or find . . . ?' Oh, well, you couldn't really hold it against him because he had so many irons in so many fires.
BILL: We appreciated the fact too that only just three days before he died we had lunch in his rooms at Parliament Place.

What was that last lunch like?
PHYLLIS: Oh, just like soup, sandwiches. A lot of laughter. He said, 'You know, at the rate I'm going, I could quite easily go on to ninety.'

That must be a memory you really value.
PHYLLIS: Oh, it is. No one would have believed he was eighty-six, he looked more as if he was in his sixties. One comment was made at the time, 'He was a legend in his own time', which he was.

Was he conscious of all that?
PHYLLIS: Oh yes, I think he thoroughly loved all the crowds who came out to see him, the newspaper articles about him. Oh yes, yes. He was proud of it but it didn't spoil him.
BILL: Didn't spoil him at all, no.

PHYLLIS: I read somewhere that the true greatness of a man is revealed by the way he can take praise and that man was a really great man because all the praise in the world didn't spoil him. The average person would have been so unbearably superior. I mean, he dined with kings and queens and emperors and duchesses and you name it, but he'd come home to our place and he'd sit down with us and eat with us during harvest there. And it was a long cry from Buckingham Palace. But there you are, he was just like that. He was able to mix with anybody and make you feel as though you really belonged in his company. He was really a remarkable man.

At the beginning of 1927, Ernest Dunlop left Benalla for good to undertake his Intermediate year at the Melbourne Pharmacy College. Then in 1929 he began the six-year medical course at the University of Melbourne and the transformation from Ern to Sir Edward was under way.

*When **Mollie Woodhouse** first met Sir Edward Dunlop, he was a young man of eighteen. Their friendship lasted a lifetime.*

I FIRST MET Weary at Pharmacy College. In those days, the girls and boys were separated. The girls sat on one side of the hall and the boys on the other, so I didn't really meet him immediately. But I've known him ever since. He was a country boy down here in the city and I think my family took pity on him.

Was he Edward then?
No, he was Ern in those days. Ern – a terrible name. I think he knew a few people at the college and that was it, more or less.

He had an aunt living here, I don't know how long for though. He was a bit shy – not that we were very much otherwise in those days. Still. He did very well. He did a lot of study.

Did you two go out socially?
Yes, my brother used to come with us, several of us used to go. He was my partner for my twenty-first, and that's a long time ago. He was a bit shy, he was not used to people in the city, I think. Do you know what I mean? They are different in a way, country people.

How did he look back then?
In a way he was an awkward looking young man, very tall and he filled out a lot in later years.

Were you surprised when he went on to study medicine?
No, I don't think there was enough in pharmacy for him, really. It meant a lot more study, but he didn't mind that. He wanted to be a surgeon. I used to go up to Ormond when he was there. They worked pretty hard the people there.

Was that where the Ern became Edward?
I don't know, but I always hated the Ern. That name. I really couldn't take it. Terrible name.

What did you do after Pharmacy College?
My father was a pharmacist and I was apprenticed to one of his pharmacists at one of his pharmacies. Then I went to relieve at a pharmacy for three months and I stayed for twenty-seven years, a bit longer than I intended. Weary was overseas for a long time then, but we were always friends.

Were you surprised later to hear of his heroism?
In a way, but he always had something behind him, you know, there was something there that made him stand out like he did.

On completing his pharmacy degree – and in his final year he won the gold medal with an average mark of 91 per cent – Ernest Dunlop went on to study medicine at the University of Melbourne. At the end of his first year, he was awarded a full residential scholarship to the Presbyterian university college of Ormond.

The industrialist, **Sir Archibald Glenn**, *now retired, and Sir Edward Dunlop met when the former was eighteen and the latter twenty-two years old. They both entered Ormond College at the University of Melbourne as freshmen in 1930.*

INITIATION WAS TOUGH but a wonderful introduction to the college and to our tertiary or adult life. Any status or privilege you had enjoyed at school was ignored and the country boys from Woop Woop such as E.E. (Weary) Dunlop were if anything treated a little (very little) more leniently. *The Blue Book*, the history of the college, had to be learned for the exam. All the students who were returning for the second or more years had to be addressed by their titles – Chief Justice, Doctor, Chief Engineer, the Rt Reverend and so on. We had to know all about them and, importantly, what number study they lived in. This latter point was quite important as one of the scum privileges was to answer the phone and promptly locate the person required . . .

We were allocated to a senior study to serve supper each evening as required and to generally be of assistance. It was also important to make yourself scarce at a moment's notice.

In hall at meals we had to sit at the end of the table and cut the bread and when called on had to toss a slice on the end of the bread knife so that it virtually landed on the recipient's plate. The cries of derision soon made you an expert. On Exhibition Night we had to produce a signed exhibit.

Mine was to call on the head of Taylor's Business College and get a written statement from him explaining what he meant by his advertisement describing it as 'the college that educates'. Weary had to collect Queenie the elephant's footprint from the Melbourne Zoo. Ted Wilson had to collect a bucket of horse manure in Sydney Road at the peak hour. Sol Green had to produce a dead bird.

On the last night of the initiations there was a wake. All the scum paraded, crocodile fashion, around the darkened corridors carrying candles and singing the dirge:

> *Did you ever think as the hearse goes by*
> *That it won't be long before you and I*
> *Will be going along in the same black hack*
> *And we won't be thinking of coming back?*
> *Now old Miss Brown went by last week*
> *The worms are eating her damsel cheek . . .*

The procession ended in the common room where we all had to lie on our backs while the seniors took our candles and practised eye drops with candle grease into our navels. This was known as a Naval Engagement. It sounds painful and terrifying but in fact the candle grease is quite cool at the time of impact. The final act is to have a large teaspoon of asafoetida, which is the most evil-tasting potion you can imagine. Its main use normally was in prescriptions for malingerers who expect their doctor to give them a cure.

At the end of these proceedings initiation is officially at an end. After cleaning ourselves up, the seniors who we have served invite us back to supper. The title scum is dropped and we are accepted into the life of the college.

THINGS TO BE REMEMBERED *by Archie Glenn,*
a private publication, 1991

SIR ARCHIBALD: Weary and I first met as freshmen at Ormond College and we went through the initiations together. Initiations were much more rigorous in my days and although a lot of people said they were cruel in some way, I think they have got the completely wrong idea.

The whole idea of initiations at Ormond was to make you get to know all about the college and its background, the people who had been through it and what they stood for. They were also to help you get to know all the people who were in college with you and it succeeded marvellously in that. Unless you got 100 per cent in the exam, you had to do a supp. so you really had to learn about the place you were living in, like a family. It was marvellous that way.

It was during the initiations that Weary was given his nickname and it stuck to him all his life. It seemed to suit his personality. He was a great lumbering chap with a slight stoop even then, which got more noticeable as he got older.

Weary was great. He loved every minute of it and he always entered into the spirit of it. We got to know each other very well, and of course our lives came quite close in many ways. While we were in college we got to know the Fergusons – that was his wife Helen's name of course – and we used to go to their home in Parkville for supper on Sunday nights and things. They were very hospitable people, marvellous people.

Later on, Weary was invited to a party at the Fergusons when they had moved out to Toorak, and he arrived on the wrong night. Typical Weary. They said, 'Oh, don't worry, stay for dinner with us anyway', so he stayed and of course that was where his association with Helen was forged. Through turning up on the wrong day.

Weary was always very charming. When he was taking the girls out, the mothers thought he was courting them I think, at times. That's absolutely true. I know one case where the mother was a widow and she fell for Weary in a big way. (laughs) I won't put any names to that. I think the girl knew, but he was a great diplomat and he handled the situation very well. I think the younger one was always the one in his sights, but getting along well with Mum was part of the deal.

Living in college was a great advantage as a student. If you lived out of college, you had all the travelling, you've got home chores and things like that. You are spared all those things if you live in a college and you can fit in a tremendous lot.

Weary had a fantastic physique. While he was in college, Ormond didn't have anyone to run the mile in the intercollegiate sports, so he said, 'Oh, I'll train for the mile.' Usually mile runners are slight, long-limbed people, but he came second in the intercollegiate mile, just through sheer doggedness.

And the university wanted someone to fight in the heavyweight intervarsity boxing contest and he entered for that and won. He got a blue for it because they couldn't knock him out. He took fantastic punishment and he could just battle on and battle on, typical of his whole life. Then he took up rugby and got into the Australian rugby team. Typical of his whole determined attitude. Of course he had, as I said, this wonderful physique.

I think Weary found that these other activities gave him a rest from his study. Medicine is a very intensive thing, you've got to memorise so much. Some of the medical students just sat in their study, day after day, trying to remember all the things they had to know. They didn't have time to do anything else, those people who had bad memories. Weary was blessed with a very good memory. He also had a great power of concentration. He could read a book while all hell was breaking loose around him. You know how noisy a place like that could be at times, and he'd be sitting there reading a book.

He came into college older than the average. He was four years older than me, but it was not something I was conscious of. Not at all. He was just Weary, right from the word go.

We were at Ormond during the Depression. No one had cars, and you had to make your fun on the spot. No one had any money, so we used to sit and chat, and there was a great cross-fertilisation between the disciplines. At supper parties there was always a cross-section of the disciplines. It became a custom that at about 10.30 at night, you'd get a bit weary of swotting and you'd go and put the kettle on and you'd issue invitations at the last minute. The conversation was interesting. You often hear that when men get together the conversation develops into the lowest ebb of quality, but I didn't ever find that.

We played a joke on Weary once. I was an engineering student and we'd done a town plan and while putting a colour wash over it I saw that the paint water looked like cold tea. We heated some of this up – it was a terrible thing to do, we might have poisoned him – and we put it in Weary's cup for tea and he was telling a story and he kept taking sips of this tea and every time he'd take a sip everyone laughed, and he thought his story was going down well. Afterwards they said it just showed how rotten our tea was. He noticed in the end when the laughter got too much.

Weary was a great mixer. He came from the country and I

think country people have that more highly developed sense of equality. Not so much equality as understanding. Life's tough in the country, particularly in those early days.

It didn't surprise me that he did achieve so much in the war because he was that sort of person. He was always exceptional, I think. He just excelled in everything he did. He was very well liked around Ormond. He was such a very gentle giant.

After we left college we used to run into each other regularly at Ormond things. Later on, of course, he came and lived next door to us. He lived in Toorak Road and we lived in Heyington Place and our houses backed on to each other, and of course the families became great friends and the children saw a lot of each other. He was probably a little bit remote from his children, you know. He was always busy, terribly busy with his medical work and his work with the ex-prisoners of war, and I think his children suffered a little bit as so often happens.

And Helen too. She was left alone with the boys and the boys were bits of devils, I remember, at one stage. As I said, our houses backed on to each other and a tennis court ran along our back fence. One day the older boy, Alexander, had his younger brother John hung up by his feet from the tennis court fence and John was crying out blue murder. My wife went out and said, 'Zander, stop hurting him,' and John called out, 'Don't worry, Lady Glenn, I rather like it.' (laughs) Like his father.

Dr Frank Engel was also a student at Ormond College and I asked him to recall Weary Dunlop and the college in the early 1930s.

THE ORMOND COLLEGE of 1930, the year in which Weary Dunlop entered it, was very different from the college of today.

There were only 120 resident students, compared with over 300 now. They were all men, whereas Ormond has been co-educational for some twenty years. There were, however, non-resident women students, as there were also non-resident men, who attended college tutorials. There was the Ormond Women's Association which had a room on the ground floor, and a newly inaugurated Ormond Women's Students' Club, and a women's intercollegiate tennis team. But for the rest, it was a very male environment.

It was usual for all students to stay in residence for the duration of their academic courses. The majority came up straight from Scotch College and Geelong College. Weary was an exception as he came from a high school and a country one at that, and as he had already done pharmacy, he was three or four years older. He was one of twenty-nine freshmen in 1930.

The first six weeks of first term were dominated by the initiations. These were taken very seriously by the student body. While there were elements of buffoonery and ragging, even fagging, with the strong message that freshmen were 'scum', the predominant purpose was educational. The *Ormond Chronicle* of 1934 records Weary's comments on the initiations: 'He traced the life-history of the student entering Ormond; how he receded down the animal scale during his first six weeks in college and then slowly rose again to self-respecting manhood with the passing years.'

Weary quickly became not only a part of the college, but an outstanding member of it in sport, leadership and academic success. He was heavyweight boxing champion of the university, a leading rugby union forward (with blues for both sports), winner of the intercollegiate shot putt, the chairman of the general committee of the Students' Club, and one of the ten–fifteen college men who attained first-class honours in successive years.

Rugby received a boost at Melbourne University from Queenslanders coming to study medicine, several of whom lived in Ormond. Weary was soon not only a convert but an outstanding exponent. His prowess and popularity resulted in a rapid increase in the number of Ormond men playing rugby, so that, in 1934, the *Chronicle* could state that 'the prestige of the college as the stronghold of rugby within the university was fully upheld'. Weary himself was in the university team, the captain of the Victorian team and an Australian Rugby International in those years.

For all his size and strength, he was a gentle giant. On one occasion, when four of us, including Weary, were playing tennis, we suddenly saw cushions flying out of his study window on the first floor. Rushing up there, we found another student enjoying himself by messing up the study for some now-forgotten reason. Weary was very annoyed, but all he said was, 'If you were bigger, I'd hit you!'

He was an eager and cheerful participant in all aspects of college life, including various student stunts and the common room dances. The *Chronicle* of 1931 has a photo of him dressed charmingly as a fairy and striking a suitably sweet pose prior to joining in the University Commencement Parade through the centre of the city. He was a natural and very popular leader. He was in danger of being idolised as a Rugby International, but he remained unassuming. His dry, even wry, and quietly expressed sense of humour kept him level-headed, as well as endearing him to his fellows. I do recall, however, that his speech had the tendency to inaudibility which marked it in later life.

Already in his student years, he was the physically strong, intellectually able, dexterous, quietly humorous, kindly and caring man of generous spirit which he proved to be throughout his life, whether in city hospital, prisoner-of-war camp, or in professional or personal relations. And he called forth, unwittingly, the admiration and friendship of his fellows.

*When I spoke with **Sir Benjamin Rank** at his home in Mt Eliza, we were surrounded by the paintings which take up much of his time since his retirement as a leading plastic surgeon.*

When did your association with Weary begin?

We were in the same year, and right from the time he joined the medical course, we were close associates and friends. I started at Ormond College a year before he did. He didn't come in till his second year. Then we were residents in the hospital together and overseas together and so on. All our lives we've been close friends and associates. Of course Weary was older than I was, not a lot.

When he first came to Ormond, he was a big strong fellow, he had great physical strength, stamina, endurance. He came from the country of course and he was a little bit of an outsider. He wasn't in the public school group and I think he felt a little bit out on account of that, you know what I mean. Most of us had been to school together, if not one school then another, but he was a country boy. He shared a study next to me with a fellow called Charles Hopkins who came in the second year from Queensland. Charles Hopkins had a big effect on Weary. He helped him, he got him sort of tuned in with the mob, so to speak.

Charles introduced him to playing rugby, for example. Weary was good at those sort of sports, rugby and boxing. It was all physical stuff. He had great stamina. He was not an athletic person but his strength and endurance were his great advantage.

In study, he'd be up until two o'clock in the morning

studying then the next morning he'd be up again. He had that sort of capacity, endurance and so on. But he studied hard, he read furiously, he was good at his academic work. We marched along together. We were mostly in the honours class all along. We graduated the same time. He had a good academic record.

Ormond appears to have played a very special part in Weary's life?
It did, it did. It introduced him to the professional group life, you know what I mean? He owed Ormond a lot and he always recognised that.

Of course the name Weary – he was anything but – but that had nothing to do with him getting the name. Of course, he wasn't initiated the same time I was, he was a year later. But they'd say, 'What is your name?' 'Rank.' They'd say, 'Cab rank, Cabby,' so your name would be Cabby for the initiation ceremonies. So with Weary it was Dunlop, someone'd say, 'Oh, Dunlop tyres, call him Weary.'

Now, nobody ever kept their initiation name. Weary is the only one who did. There's a certain thing in that too. I shouldn't say this but as a kid he was always Ernie Dunlop and I think he thought it was a bit country, Ernie. He never liked it and he always said Edward Dunlop. And he stuck to the Weary, so it was Weary Edward Dunlop.

Was Weary a prankster?
He took it and gave it. Living in college then had a very homogenising effect on the group. I've been looking at my photo album of the student days at Ormond College when we used to go camping and things. For the 1931 Melbourne Uni Commencement we were dressed up as a lot of harlots or women. There were about eight of us. Weary was dressed as a

fairy – anything more stupid and unfairylike you couldn't imagine. He had a little wand and so on. There was one picture of the group, and it's rather interesting three of those people are knights of the realm. George Lush, Weary and myself. We went into the city on this truck but we had to get back the best way we could. Weary had to catch a tram, but he didn't have the fare. He wouldn't think of something like that.

In the academic world, he was better at some subjects and I was better at others. We went parallel pretty well. There was nothing personally competitive. I was always better at form, I always have been, all my life. That's why now I'm retired, I'm painting. He was more in the chemistry/physiological side of medicine.

When we were students, to do well you had to have an English fellowship of surgery, anything else was considered second-class. The English college used to run primary exams out here, they sent them out every few years, and Weary and I sat the first part of our Master of Surgery in our final year as students and both passed. That was right at the end of my college career. Then we went into residence together. In Melbourne we were junior residents, and three were selected as senior surgical residents to go a second year. He was one, I was another. We were pretty parallel.

Was life as a resident a tough one?
Oh yes, we worked hard. It was Depression years. We didn't have any money and we'd walk down to the hospital rather than take a tram. I can remember we'd get the penny-halfpenny cable tram rather than the twopenny one. It was like that. I got five shillings a week from an older sister of mine who was working in the city. I'd take her laundry down. And he was the same. We lived on the smell of an oily rag. Not as they do now.

*At Ormond College, Weary shared a study with **Charles Hopkins**, a young medical student from Queensland. In his foreword to Hopkins' autobiographical account of those days Weary wrote:*

I ARRIVED AT Ormond College, Melbourne University, in the second year of the medical course across the sheep tracks of north-east Victoria and the Victorian College of Pharmacy, rather apprehensive, a little older than most, and feeling my country school unorthodoxy.

I found myself paired in rooms with another stray piece, a grave responsible youth with tow hair, even more bleached by the North Queensland sun, clear frank blue eyes, and a shy flashing smile. His accent bespoke his English public school sojourn at Berkhamstead. He had a faintly hesitant way of speech with slight pauses, and talked of an enthralling tropical world of North Queensland. His most profane exclamation was 'strike!'

He had musical tastes and played the violin. My first impression was of an incarnation in the flesh of an impeccable character in English schoolboy literature called David Blaize.

He proved a most generous, forbearing, and congenial study mate or 'wife' who constantly revealed new talents. Whilst not a heavyweight, and one of the cleanest of sportsmen, he played with great spirit as 'hooker' or 'rake' in the fiery front row of the rugby union scrum, always playing a bit above his weight.

After a brief time he cajoled me into forsaking the Australian football game for rugby union – a game I took to with unearthly joy and gusto as though predestined. . . In his reflective writing about life in the Army, Hopkins advances the observation that if something were needed to be done well, get an Englishman, if it was to be done promptly, get an Australian. It occurs to me that if I wanted something done both well and promptly, I would think of Hopkins.

How You Take It, *Charles Hopkins, Neptune Press, 1985*

Dr Charles Hopkins died in Melbourne in 1992. **Hester Hopkins** *spoke of Sir Edward and his relationship with her husband.*

CHARLES GOT TO know Weary at Melbourne University. They shared a room and they were both up against the same sort of difficulties at Ormond College. They were with a very talented group of people.

One summer holidays, Weary went up to Dunk Island and met all of Charles' family. Charles was one of four brothers. When they were just teenagers, Charles' parents allowed the four boys to sail up a hundred miles of Barrier Reef on their own – it was very treacherous, you had to know it, so they were very used to sailing. Very used to it.

Charles had a choice of either going to university in Sydney or Melbourne. He thought Sydney had a more commercial attitude – he preferred the atmosphere in Melbourne. He felt, and it's still true I think, that money means much more to them in Sydney. Whereas here, specially that group, they were just all for helping civilisation really. They were an extraordinary, talented group and they all had that broad, generous desire to just help the community. They were missionaries, really, in their own field.

Charles must have been able to lead Weary to a certain extent, although Weary was always the big man who everybody knew about, and Charles was very small by comparison.

Charles was a real gentleman but whether he was a gentleman in the way they wanted at Ormond, I don't know. He had polio when he was a small boy and he had a very bad back. He used to play all this rugby and everything but I mean, he'd be a different picture from Weary. It was he who persuaded Weary to take up rugby and he saw what Weary could do. I suppose when they went through college they were pretty close.

But in 1982 Charles was bashed up when he went to investigate a break in at his Mornington surgery and it took everything away from him. I think he felt later in life, he never said this and he never showed it, but I feel he probably felt, you know, Weary was the famous big man and Charles was sort of a nobody in his own eyes a bit.

I don't know. Weary was still very close to Charles who wouldn't have wanted recognition like Weary, but I think he perhaps felt he wouldn't want to be a nuisance to Weary. Weary had such a very full life. So had Charles until he was bashed up, though in a different way.

In his book Charles Hopkins wrote of his initial impressions of Ormond:

AFTER DINNER ALL the freshers had to line up in the common room in pyjamas and dressing gowns with a towel round our necks and perform tasks which to tell the truth I thought were rather silly. The seniors would ask us questions from a book we were all given on the history of Ormond College, and if we didn't know the answer we had to pull our trousers down and receive a flick on the bottom with the towel round our necks.

This went on every evening for three weeks, and at the

end of that we still had to wait on the seniors at supper and sit at separate tables in the dining room.

This had the effect of dividing the College into annual watertight compartments. Nobody could make friends outside his own year – which I thought rather contrary to the idea of a 'college'. Melbourne University was known as 'The Shop', and it was not regarded as a special, privileged place. Nor was there any consciousness of the community or the outside world. I had chosen to come to Melbourne rather than Sydney because the Sydney graduates I had met in Townsville had appeared a rather mercenary lot. I had hoped to find more idealism in Melbourne and I was disappointed. So I remained a Queenslander.

HOW YOU TAKE IT *by Charles Hopkins*

Dr Mildred Green *studied medicine alongside Weary Dunlop at Melbourne University and attended tutorials at Ormond College. She then did a year's residency at the Melbourne (now the Royal Melbourne) Hospital.*

Halfway through this interview, conducted in front of a blazing fire in her Hawthorn home, we took a break for a cup of coffee. 'I'm sure coffee is addictive, I enjoy it so much,' Dr Green said. She was concerned she might be wasting my time. 'I don't think I've got much to contribute, just that Weary was always brilliant, and removed because of his brilliance.'

WE HAD A small year in our final year in 1934 – small, but it was a very high standard. We had this coterie of ten or twelve really brilliant people and we all benefited from the contact with them. The main brains in our year came from Ormond College. There were odd other ones but really it was that Ormond group who were brilliant, and Weary and Benny Rank were two of them.

When I say they were brilliant, I mean it. But Weary was so diffident. He was always sort of, not belittling himself exactly, but putting himself in the background. And yet he did believe in himself, in a way. It was his shy superstructure. But Weary was always very gifted, obviously.

Did Weary work hard, play hard?
Well, yes because he had a university blue in football, wasn't it?

Rugby.
Rugby. Of course.

And boxing.
That's right. Amazing, isn't it? Weary was a rugby player of note. But also, he was so controlled. He seemed a very gentle man because he was completely controlled. It must have stood for him later on, I think. There was always this contrast. You felt there was a fire underneath his calm. He was also deeply resentful at the same time about certain things, injustices, and I always felt he was very resentful about them but he was detached from expressing the intensity that he felt. Of course it came out later in life, didn't it? Sometimes you'd be talking to him and there'd be a pause in the conversation, and you'd think these strong feelings could just burst out, but they never did.

Did Weary stand out because he had already done a pharmacy course?
No, a lot of them did pharmacy first, it was quite the thing in those days. They would save enough money to put them through the medical course because their families couldn't do it.

My father did the same thing. He lived over the pharmacy and did the night work and was a medical student during the day. He could be pulled out of his sleep. The people used to call up the chemist much more in those days.

Was there much rivalry within the Ormond group?

I think it was more of a camaraderie between them than a rivalry. They had excellent tutorials and they helped one another. I attended Ormond for tutorials. We didn't really mix with the students, we just went along to a tutorial and that was it. The conversation and discussion of the people round you in those tutorials can set the tone. There are all sorts of ways brilliant people can lift the level of the group they are in. It makes a huge difference because it's not only personal studies, it's the clinics. There would be eight or ten of us in a clinic and we would ask questions of the honorary. Well, Weary and Benny Rank would put forward the right questions at the right time and they would lift the whole tone of the clinic. The questions that were asked were so much more stimulating and opened things up more.

You then went on to the Melbourne Hospital with some of that group. Was there a similar camaraderie between those doing residencies?

Yes, there was, because we all had meals together. John Bolton was at the Melbourne when we all turned up as residents. He was the senior resident. We would discuss things with one another in the corridors, we were bursting with wanting to talk. It was really terrific, because we were very busy – we didn't get much sleep the whole time we were there, it was very stimulating. You had a day off once a week and you'd go home and sleep. It was fearful.

It was a tremendous experience, the resident year. Afterwards, within a year or two, they started to put the residents on shift, so that they could get enough sleep. But we just worked. We worked day and night sometimes. It really was quite something. And we were doing it because we were learning all the time, we were stimulated all the time and we were happy to do it but we didn't get much sleep.

And not much money?
Well, it was put up for us. We were the first people who got 100 pounds a year, so we were in clover. We had a bedroom in the hospital.

How many of you were there?
The number twenty comes to mind, I'm not quite sure why. Usually the tops went to the Melbourne and then you got jobs if you could.

Were you tempted by surgery?
I think everybody's tempted by surgery. It's so dramatic and constructive. Easier than medicine. Medicine's a much bigger subject, much more complicated and you go on learning it all your life. Surgeons have got some very neat handiwork but they don't have a high level of anxiety. You do a hernia or something simple like that, they recover and they're home in a few days. They're relatively simple, but with medicine you've got to think of everything.

Were you aware of the former Ormond student, Sir Thomas Dunhill when you were a student?.
My parents went through medical school with Jack Dunhill, Sir Thomas's younger brother. He died during residence. I will

never forget Mother telling me of the tremendous waves of grief that went through the hospital, through the residency staff, because they loved Jack Dunhill so much.

Tom went to London and did very well and had a society practice and was in another world, really. A lot of the graduates from here would see him when they got to London and he would see that they got a hospital placement and this sort of thing. He was a point of call – particularly for the men.

Women didn't have these entrees. We had to set up our own. But we never accepted that it was a closed shop. My sister and I never accepted that men and women were different – we were raised by a woman doctor and I guess we just kept our eyes on the ball. We felt we would get where our abilities took us, and we never felt excluded, because we were going places. We never bothered about the discrimination if there was any, we just coped with it, and then of course there's less of it. If you go looking for trouble, you find it. And if you tackle the job confidently and you're a competent person, well, you'll get on well with your colleagues, there's no problem.

Was Weary supportive during your student days?

The habit of the day was a bit stand-offish. He was with the Ormond group and they were so self-sufficient that they could be polite to us and it really wouldn't matter to them if we existed or not. They had perfect manners, and that was all you needed then. I think that we were simply treated as colleagues. Perhaps a little at arms-length because it was easier to talk to the fellas, but by and large they accepted us very well by that time. My mother did medicine at the turn of the century so there had been women in the area for a couple of decades by the time I started.

So it was a case of 'all chaps together'?

Well, it probably was, but we were real people, we existed, and if some people didn't want to talk to us they went down the corridor, and if some people did want to talk to us, we'd talk. You just make your way with what's about. The Ormond mob really kept themselves together. They were brilliant, they were men with men's interests in sport and things and we were just in the environment. We didn't matter to them really, but there was no persecution, they were very polite to us.

Was there a snobbery attached to Ormond?

No. I suppose they were snobby days but not at university. At university you took people for their own value. Snobbery was old fashioned.

Tell me, was Weary good looking in those days?

Yes, he was. He was distinguished. He was obviously of high quality and therefore demanding respect and so on, you know? He always had this. It's this I think of when I hear that he infuriated the Japanese. Because he had that dignity, he was sort of unsinkable. And it must have been maddening for them. It wasn't only his size, it was his bearing.

Was he a leader amongst the Ormond group?

They were a group of leaders, so they went on together. Weary and Benny stand out but there were a number of other gifted people. And they helped one another to excellence. They were the leading lights in our year and it was a bright year.

Dr John Colebatch met Weary at the Melbourne Hospital in 1936 and struck up a lifelong friendship.

I FIRST KNEW Weary when we were both senior residents at the Melbourne Hospital and he was twenty-nine and I was twenty-seven. We were both older than the other residents. Weary was working on the surgical side and I was working on the medical side. He was tough, physically tough, handy and quite indefatigible. That's really why he got the name Weary, because it is the exact opposite of what he really was – like calling a red-headed boy Blue.

We were good friends in that we had so much in common. We were on duty, we were on call all hours. The only other doctor on the resident staff who was of comparable age to us was a man who had suddenly been promoted mid-year to medical superintendent, John Bolton. He became a physician and his special interest in medicine was blood diseases, as was mine. He became a close friend. The fourth member who became close, though he was younger in age than all we three, was Benjamin Rank, the plastic surgeon. He was more mature than most youngsters are for his age and we made a good happy quartet of friends.

Weary was well into rugby when I got to know him. He already played for the university and I saw him play a game at the MCG for Victoria. Shortly after that he was captain of the Australian team. That is one example of people having recognised his ability, his outstanding ability, after minimal contact with him. He was chosen to play not just for the university, not just for Victoria, but for Australia, when rugby was a game played by those in Sydney and Brisbane.

He was physically terribly active and quite tireless. When we were all doing study for surgery or medicine postgraduate degrees, we all did a lot of reading after hospital work, and hospital work was very concentrated. Weary would do a day's work, operating with his master surgeon, and once the operations had finished and his ward rounds were finished then he'd go out to rugby practice, at four or five o'clock. Then when it was too dark to play any more and they had finished their practice, the rugby players would like to adjourn to Hosey's Hotel for a T-bone and a beer. It was not uncommon for him to arrive back at the hospital at about eleven or twelve o'clock at night. We'd have been there trying to study for exams, with the help of a little beer now and again. I remember him coming in one night and saying, 'Oh Coley, what about coming and having a drink?' 'Oh,' I said, 'I've just had one with John Bolton.' 'No,' he said, 'I mean outside, we'll go outside.' And if you said yes, you'd probably go out and be with him for a couple of hours. He was indestructible and indefatigable.

*One person to remember his fleeting brush with Weary Dunlop in pre-war Melbourne is **Rod Gabriel**. The retired Melbourne pharmacist was a prisoner of war in Ambon during World War II, and, he later worked with Weary in the Ex-Prisoners of War and Relatives' Association.*

WEARY WAS ON the staff of the Children's Hospital in Melbourne and he was one year, maybe two, ahead of my brother John. Anyway it was October 1937 and I drove up to the Children's Hospital to pick up John. We were going to Sydney for our holidays, you see. I whipped in and picked up John's bag, and coming out, I looked up and saw a bucket of water coming from the top floor. I said, 'Who's that silly bugger?' and John said 'That's a fellow named Dunlop.'

On Weary's 80th birthday, I reminded him of that. I said, 'Fortunately for me you were well in need of target practice.' He said, 'In future I'll make certain that I do a bit of pre-training.'

In September 1937, Ernest Edward Dunlop graduated as
Master of Surgery. On 24 May 1938, he set sail for England,
working his way as assistant surgeon on the SS Ormonde.
He was thirty years old. The purpose of his trip was straight-
forward: he wanted to pass the College of Surgeons examination.
But for Weary, like many Australians of his generation, going
to England was also 'going home'. England remained the 'old
country' and London was the centre of the universe.

Once in London, Weary took up residence at London House,
a postgraduate residential college for students from the British
Empire, in Bloomsbury. He also caught up with a number of his
colleagues from the Melbourne Hospital.

SIR BENJAMIN RANK: Funnily enough, having done that first
part of our Master of Surgery before graduation, Weary and I
could then go straight to the second part. And in our second
year as residents, we did this. I was lucky. I passed and Weary
didn't. He stayed on in Melbourne another year. I went on to
England then, so we spent a year separated. But when we
came to do the English fellowship final, the first time I sat, I
failed and he passed. And I had to do the second year. We were
neck and neck in that sort of way but there was no ill-feeling.

We were socially associated because he knew my wife. As a
matter of fact, he was a groomsman at our wedding in London
in 1938. John Colebatch and Jack Bolton were too. The bride
was unattended but I had three attendants. They'd been to a
luncheon earlier and while I was changing my clothes to go
away, they'd been to the local pub. They came down to Victoria
Station and gave us a hell of a send-off. Rowdy. People wondered who these raucous kids were.

DR JOHN COLEBATCH: I went to England six months before
Weary and we both lived in London House.

When you go overseas you like to have the names of a few people you are strongly recommended to study with. You often make arrangements by letter before you go. Weary had an introduction to Sir Thomas Dunhill, who was very important to him. I went to the hospital which was most favoured for medical postgraduate work and that was the London Hospital.

We used to go sometimes on day trips together out of London. Most things we did together were in London House. I was engaged when I went away. I told my fiancée she'd better come over. We were together for a year before we got married at All Hallows Barking by the Tower. Weary was my first choice as best man because I'd known him for a whole year in Melbourne before I went away.

He took me and got me thoroughly drunk two days before I was married. I had never been so drunk in my life as I was that night.

Dr John Hayward was a year ahead of Weary Dunlop at Melbourne University and, like Weary, graduated with a Master of Surgery in September, 1937. We spoke in his sitting room in East Melbourne.

IN THE 1930s there wasn't a College of Surgeons' examination in Australia, and the highest degree you could get was Master of Surgery at the university you trained at. If you wanted to be a specialist, you had to go to England or America, or both, and most of us went to England. That's how we both got to London. I went over before Weary but our times overlapped. Various hospitals ran courses for the FRCS examination. I did the Barts' course. When I got my degree I was interested in chests, and I went to Brompton Chest Hospital. Weary was interested in general surgery. There must have been two or three dozen of us dotted around various places in London at any one time, certainly about twenty anyway, and I heard on the grapevine that Weary was in London, browsing around somewhere.

At Brompton, and I suppose at the other hospitals too, payment was very, very small – £100 a year plus keep – and there was no official leave at all. If you went out of the hospital, you had to arrange that somebody else in the hospital was on call in your ward while you were out. Even if you only went out to get a haircut. All the time I took off regularly while I was at the hospital was every second Sunday. I thought I'd damn well take that and I'd fix it up with somebody and do a cheap trip. We only got about two pounds a week, so you couldn't go far on that.

I had a friend in Cambridge, and he and some other students had organised with students from Heidelberg University to share a ski hut on the Austrian Alps, just over the German border. It was jointly owned by these two student bodies. I got a phone call from Brian saying something had come up, and would I like to take his place? Would I like to! I thought, Heavens, I don't know if I can get away, but I said, 'I'll ring you back.' Then I thought of Weary floating around London somewhere so I rang various people and I soon got in touch with him and asked if he would take my job for two weeks.

'Oh, yes,' he said, 'I think I might be able to do that.' So I said, 'I'll ring you back after I fix it with my boss.' Old J.H. Roberts was my chief and he said, 'That will be all right, if you think Dunlop will be able to manage.' I was sure Weary would manage. (laughs) If he couldn't, nobody could. Although he didn't know anything about chests specially, he was so bright, he'd be a jolly good assistant.

That's how I got my trip to Austria. It was all most interesting because we arrived there at the time of the Hitler's move into the Sudetenland and the Germans were very, very hostile at first. But that's another story.

The day I came back, I reached Brompton in the afternoon and Weary had to leave after lunch so I didn't even see him face to face. But I did hear from Roberts that he had very much enjoyed Weary's company. I think that is the way he put it. And the ward and theatre sisters liked him too. He was just that sort of person.

Professor Richard Lovell first encountered Weary when he was a student at St Mary's Hospital in London. He met him again in 1955 when he came to Melbourne to take up the position of Professor of Medicine at the University of Melbourne.

MY ORIGINAL MEMORY of Weary is in 1939 at the outbreak of war – from September 1939 and the next three months. I was a fifth-year medical student in clinical years. When the war was looming, London was divided into sectors with each of the teaching hospitals designated to act as a casualty clearing station to deal with air-raid casualties.

A wedge went out to the periphery of London and the peripheral hospitals were designated to receive the casualties that had been patched up and dealt with initially at the central London teaching hospitals. The medical students at St Mary's had been asked to indicate which hospital they would like to work in at the outbreak of war and some said they'd like to work in this or that peripheral hospital, and I was in a group with four or five of my close friends who elected to stay at Mary's.

So on September – it was probably the first or the second – the plan for the medical defence of London, as it were, was put into operation and those of us who'd elected to stay at Mary's moved in and lived together with certain members of the staff and surgeons to help deal with the casualties in the private patients' wing which had been emptied of private patients.

The medical staff appointed under what was called the Emergency Medical Service consisted not only of some of our honorary staff at Mary's, who were our teachers, but also staff from other hospitals. The additional staff that came to Mary's at that time, and moved in on the days just before the third of September, included Weary Dunlop, who then was a young surgeon doing his postgraduate period in the UK.

My memory of Weary really is in relation to teaching because although war had broken out – well, because war had broken out – most of the staff had absolutely nothing to do. The raids didn't happen, so there was plenty of time to fill. One of the positive things they did was to teach our group of students who'd stayed at St Mary's. They taught us in the few remaining wards that were left open and particularly in the outpatients.

It's in the outpatients that I really have recollections of Weary and my memory of him is of a tall, gangly sort of character, who spoke in a very soft voice. He had absolutely no sense of time in teaching in outpatients. If a patient came in who was interesting from his point of view and was a case to be taught on, Weary would just go on and on, regardless of any other patients that were left and with absolutely no conception of when outpatients should end. Actually, there was no hurry to end it because there wasn't a lot to do after it had ended except walk over to the Fountains Abbey pub. This was the St Mary's pub where the students and their teachers used to foregather every evening at about 5.30 for a few beers and continue very often the sort of tutorial we'd had during the afternoon.

It was a very intimate association, a very unique association between teachers, many of great distinction, and students. The team also included Arthur Porritt – he was the surgeon in charge of the whole hospital under the EMS scheme to deal with these hypothetical air-raid casualties. Alexander Fleming, of penicillin fame, was the microbiologist who was left at Mary's and he used to come over to the Fountains and chat, and other teachers used to come over, so we were very privileged students. Weary was really under no incentive to hurry to end the out-patients' sessions.

The other feature that I remember about Weary was that to me as a young student he was a strange surgeon because he always carried a stethoscope and he actually used it. I'd never seen a surgeon carry a stethoscope or use it. I think this reflected Weary as I saw him then, which was that he always seemed interested in the total patient, whereas so often in surgical outpatients someone might complain of a pain in their ankle and they wouldn't really undress, they'd just be asked to pull their trouser leg up and take their shoe and sock off and the surgeon would examine the ankle. Weary always took a full medical history, as it were, and examined the whole patient before he got down to the site of complaint, which was a very physician-like sort of approach.

As I say, there was practically nothing for these members of staff to do during this period of the phoney war, because they had a virtually empty hospital awaiting casualties that never turned up. A large part of the population of London had been evacuated and people weren't encouraged to come and use what was meant to be a Casualty Clearing Station, so they didn't have a clinically busy life at all – they had plenty of time to play rugby football.

In the occasional conversations Weary and I had over many years after the war, we always used to reminisce about Mary's, and Weary's chief memory was always about how he'd been incorporated in the rugby football team. Mary's was a very keen rugby school, largely due to the influence of the dean, Lord Moran, who prized rugby football above all other human activities, and when the war broke out, as far as Moran was concerned, the Mary's football team must go on as the top hospital team in London. It didn't matter if the war came and went, the rugby football went on, and he obviously identified Weary early as automatically a new member, an excellent member, of the St Mary's rugby football team.

Weary used to say that he kept on trying to join up and go to war with the Australian forces. Lord Moran was the administrator of St Mary's sector at that time, and it was he who determined who should be disposed where in the sector and there was no way he was going accept Weary's resignation to go to war, because it was much more important that he should stay and play rugby football for St Mary's. Weary, one could reflect perhaps, would never have been 'in the bag' [captured] and had the subsequent war story that he had if he had been allowed to join up when he wanted to.

Dr D. Ronald Kilgour, a retired gynaecologist living deep in the New Forest, was a house officer with Weary at the Hammersmith Hospital in England in 1939. They worked together in the Emergency Medical Service at St Mary's, Paddington, once the war began.

WEARY WAS THE house officer for Professor George Grey-Turner at Hammersmith while I was a house officer on the gynaecological side. We were kept pretty busy, then quite suddenly we were informed that we were to be moved to St Mary's Hospital, Paddington, just before the outbreak of war.

Did Professor Grey-Turner influence Weary's career?
Professor Grey-Turner was the professor of surgery at the post-

graduate medical school and there was no doubt that he had a great influence on Weary's professional career, largely over major oesophageal operations, which Weary eventually carried out with great success.

What was life like at St Mary's during the four months Weary was there?

Most of the senior staff had been moved to peripheral hospitals to be able to work in safety and away from the possible bombing of London. That left at St Mary's the younger members of the honorary staff, like Arthur Porritt and Reggie King. The actual amount of routine surgery in the first three months was very limited because patients tended to be sent to the peripheral hospitals for treatment.

Those months when Weary was at St Mary's – it was a very impressionable time for all of us. Here we were, relatively young men, coming in contact with some of the giants of medicine in Alexander Fleming, Arthur Porritt, and others who obviously had a big influence on us. And the great beauty was that these men were so approachable. Whereas in peacetime days they were revered as gods and you went rather humbly in front of them, once war came along you were able to talk to them with great ease and perhaps have a drink with them at the Fountains Abbey pub across the road.

They were living in. All the medical students and qualified doctors working at St Mary's for the first months all lived in the private wing, where we each had a room. I can remember Weary coming into my room early one morning with a telegram which he'd received from Helen saying that she would wait for him to return to Australia. It was quite a moving thing for Weary, I can remember that quite well.

Did he talk about Helen?

Not really to any extent. I knew that he was engaged to Helen Ferguson but more than that I knew nothing.

Weary was best man at Algie Jackson's wedding during this period.

I can remember a little about that wedding. As far as I remember, Weary got hold of me one day and said, 'Look, Algie's getting married.' Weary being the best man, he said to me that I'd better come and form part of the wedding party.

That's about all I can remember about it. That's not because of the large amount of liquor we may have had, but it's so far back, I really can't remember.

What was the relationship between the students and the staff at St Mary's?

The students were treated as pals, as equals. I used to teach them obstetrics, for the final examinations which took place I believe in December of 1939. That was the first examination that they were taking. I taught them obstetrics and gynaecology, others taught them medicine and surgery. Weary was involved in that. We had sort of little classes, maybe twenty students at a time.

How many classes were held across the road at the pub, at the Fountains?

No, there was no time for that when you were in the Fountains. You couldn't hold a glass of beer and a piece of chalk at thesame time. The Fountains was only twenty feet across the road from St Mary's Hospital and we did all drink there together.

Did Weary have a reputation as a drinker?

No, not at all. He enjoyed going to the pub with the lads but in no way would you say he overindulged. He was a sober chap. To start with I think the thing about Weary was his stature. But he was also an approachable person, easy to speak to and easy to understand. One of these people who would help you if you wanted any help. He really was what I'd call a loyal good friend.

Weary joined the Australian Army in December 1939 and I joined the Royal Navy as an RNDR Surgeon Lieutenant in September 1940. My first appointment was to an old 5000-ton cruiser based in Singapore. I lost touch with Weary then. In 1946 an article by Albert Coates about prisoners of war and hospitals in the Far East mentioned a Dr Dunlop and it was only after some years that I realised that it might well be Weary.

I had a brother who was a medical officer in the RANC. He had been in Singapore and he acted as an anaesthetist to Albert Coates in Sumatra. My brother sailed with a number of Australians from Padang, in Sumatra, in a small twenty-foot native boat. They had the idea of sailing to Ceylon. Unfortunately they were struck by a monsoon on the voyage and were swept onto the Burma coast, where they were caught by the Japanese. One man was swept overboard, another died of illness and my brother died a few months later of dysentery in Rangoon jail, where they were all imprisoned. I heard all this news after the war ended.

I got in touch with Weary again in 1987, which seems an awfully long time to have waited. It was about the time he published *The War Diaries of Weary Dunlop* and that was of great interest to me, having lost a brother in that area and also having served in the Royal Navy during the first two years of the Japanese war.

Were you conscious of Weary's Australianness in pre-war London?

Well, obviously he had an Australian accent, but then I had the accent of a Scotsman. Mind you, Scots accents vary a bit, perhaps Australian ones do too. We never had any difficulty understanding each other, especially as Dunlop's a Scots name.

When we met in that pre-war year, we were concentrating so much on our future and the war came along as an incident in life. It changed things completely.

13 January, 1987

Dear Ronny,

A man named Lissenburg was it seems with your brother Hugo when he died in Rangoon gaol after that magnificent attempt to escape by sea.

He rang me today and gave me your address. This removed a doubt from my mind, as I wondered whether you were the one whom Sir Albert Coates thought had perished at sea.

My last queer memory of you was at Algy Jackson's wedding to Muriel with that astonishing coincidence about the church which I selected by sheer chance.

Well at least both you and Algy survived the war although I haven't heard anything of him or Muriel for many years.

I am still practising in Melbourne though moving rapidly towards 80 in July.

I have travelled overseas a lot down the years, with a lot of interest in Asia from Japan to India, and also in England and Europe with the International Society of Surgeons and the James IV Association [a select society of 100 surgeons].

Last year, it was Thailand, Paris and England with a brief call on Switzerland and Holland.

I have a book published here rather raffishly labelled 'The War Diaries of Weary Dunlop' – Java, Burma Thailand Railway which surprises me by being a best seller. The third reprint is being run this month. Thomas Nelson do not seem to have much of a sales connection with the UK but it is likely that when they establish a sales base that I shall pay a visit.

The BBC are considering a TV documentary when I go to Thailand in April and I may go on to England then.

So much for me. My dear wife Helen has the wretched Alzheimer disease. Two children – one doctor, one engineer. What of you? I am glad that you are surviving.

With affectionate regards

'Weary' E.E.Dunlop

Dr Tom Kemp *was a student at St Mary's Hospital Medical School, Paddington, when he first met Sir Edward in 1939. They became team-mates in the St Mary's rugby team and remained friends for life. Dr Kemp went on to captain England in rugby union in 1948 and was president of the Rugby Football Union from 1971-72.*

I THINK MARY'S was probably unique. After the First World War, Sir Charles Wilson, who was later Lord Moran, became dean. What a lot of deans did was to select a student on his or her particular qualifications and so on. But Lord Moran set out to fill the medical school along the lines of the Rhodes scholars, with a third intellect, a third character and a third sport. It was the scholar/athlete ethos, and this he did quite brilliantly.

So they said, 'We'll have a few scholars with brains coming out of their ears and we'll have a few footballers and a few musicians, a few this and a few that,' and when I went there in the '30s, they had a mixture that melded together in quite a remarkable way. The whole school was full of vigour in all sorts of directions, certainly including sports – Lord Moran was a fanatical rugby enthusiast – but also in drama, music and medicine. There were quite a number of these all-rounders who were becoming professors and leaders of the profession, and this obviously fitted into Weary's idea of life.

At the beginning of the war, we students ceased to be in digs and the private patients' wing was virtually emptied. Everybody was a bit scared about bombs and things and we were housed at the hospital. The community was very close – we went to the same pub and we ate together and we talked together and it didn't take long to discover that Weary had played for Australia. He played for two or three months with Mary's. I was merely a student when we played together and as soon as I qualified, I moved on to Harefield and he moved on to the Middle East.

The senior consultants and the doctors all seemed to collect in a pub across the road from Mary's. The students used to go there as well and somebody would announce that he was going to give a tutorial on the hormones or something, so all the students, with their pints of beer, would listen to this quite brilliant exposition of some medical subject. It was very vigorous. But these were people who were all very, very bright and had nothing to do because London was evacuated.

There were people like Fleming there, too, discovering penicillin. It really was a remarkable place, a happy ship. Everybody seemed to pull together and in the evenings the doctors and junior doctors and senior consultants and the students would all eat together or play poker together. We were all waiting for the bombs to drop, but not many did during that phoney war period.

I recall learning a lot from Weary in snippets, not formally, more like a tutorial on some simple surgical techniques. Once Weary asked if I had a spare pair of socks. He got these socks and he said, 'Now imagine these are the intestines. There are various ways of sewing up the intestines – you can either have them end to end, in which case you stitch like this. You can have them end to side, or side to side, and this way you stitch like that.' So he used a pair of my socks and did all the stitches the surgeons would do when they are anastomosing [joining] pieces of intestines. And now that is just about the only bit of surgery I remember.

My main memory of Weary was on the football field. He was very big and he used to run with knees up, rather like a horse, and his elbows sticking out, ploughing his way through crowds of people. He ran at the opposition with great determination. He averaged about a try a game. His strengths were as a forward, a very powerful forward. He was quite a fast runner, but it was this sort of high stepping thing which made him so difficult to stop. You'd get a knee in your face or an elbow in your side. He played with tremendous vigour – the sort of character and determination and that he used to fight the Japanese. He was about thirty-two then.

He was very popular. There was a gap between my group and his group – we were students, and he had already passed his mastership of surgery and fellowships. But in a way that gap was filled, I suppose largely by him. He'd drink with us and talk with us and make us feel that we were on the same level, and I'm quite sure as a prisoner he made everybody feel they were on the same level, too, and if the Japanese got a bit stroppy, well, he would stand up to them on behalf of all his prisoners.

In rugby union, both sides are trying to win but the object of the game is for both sides to have fun. Weary played it with determination, but he was quite big enough to see that enjoyment of life was the object of the exercise. Lord Moran was very anxious to keep Weary at St Mary's so that he could continue to play rugby. We were sorry when he left, but he wasn't getting the kind of surgery that he wanted at Mary's and he was very keen to be part of the war.

2

WEARY'S WAR

In January 1940, Captain Dunlop, VX 259, of the 2nd AIF, who had turned down the offer of a staff job at St Mary's Hospital, began life as a Medical Officer with the Australian Army Medical Corps in Jerusalem, Palestine. He was appointed acting Deputy Assistant Director of Medical Services to the ADMS, his former teacher in anaesthetics at the Royal Melbourne Hospital, Colonel Clive Disher.

His first task in Palestine was to assist in the preparation of the 2/1st Australian General Hospital at Gaza Ridge, and for the next two years Weary Dunlop found himself involved mainly in administrative matters, supervising evacuations, purchasing medical supplies, inspecting hospital sites, with paperwork and more paperwork.

On 6 June, he and Helen Ferguson announced their engagement and in July he was promoted to the rank of Major and became a Deputy Assistant Director of Medical Services. On 26 March 1941 he landed in Greece, as the AIF Medical Liaison Officer to British troops, and assisted in evacuating the wounded.

In June, at his request, he joined the 2/2nd Casualty Clearing Station in Tobruk, as second-in-command. It was during his six weeks there that he began to develop his ideas on forming a mobile field hospital. Back in Palestine in August, Major Ewan Corlette, a physician, and the surgeon Major

Arthur Moon joined the 2/2nd CCS. In October Major Dunlop received the authority to create the mobile surgical unit.

*In 1940, sisters **Gerry Twomey** and **Jean Lloyd Thomas** met Captain E. E. Dunlop of the AAMC in Jerusalem, where they lived with their family. Their father, the Australian agriculturalist Gerald Gustaph Masson, was employed by the British Colonial Service.*

I met with the sisters at Mrs Twomey's home in Melbourne to talk about life in Palestine during those early years of the war.

JEAN: In 1939 when war broke out, I had finished school and I was in Palestine. I was going to do domestic science at a place called King's College in London. Then the war hotted up.

GERRY: I was in boarding school in England at that time. Then in 1939 Mum and Dad decided to let me come home for the holidays. I normally would have gone to somebody in England as a paying guest, but I think they realised that the war was very imminent. I came out in 1939 and I never went back. The war broke out while I was in Palestine. Mum and Dad decided to keep us together as a family.

JEAN: There was a place called the Fast Hotel in the middle of Jerusalem. The government leased it as a R & R [rest and recreation] place and the Comforts' Fund ran it. My Dad was a convivial sort of person –

GERRY: That's where he met everybody. Dad was at Gallipoli and my mother had met him over here when she was a nurse in the war. They were married in Jerusalem at the end of 1918. He was known as Gerry Masson of Jerusalem.

JEAN: We used to give afternoon tea with cakes and scones every Sunday. There were crowds from generals down to privates, nurses and troops. We lived in a small house, a bungalow, and we would have every chair around the wall and cushions on the floor. Many a time we sort of rustled up something on toast, scrambled eggs or something, for the one that overstayed – not their welcome, but the time.

What are your first memories of meeting Weary?
JEAN: He came in after a rugby match, hot and sweaty. Tousled, full of beans. Interested, I think, in being in an Australian household. He had met my father, who went out of his way to entertain Australians. Took them around the country to various sites – sites of battles – and he probably took Weary on the same things.

What was Weary like then?
JEAN: Oh, he was charming and good looking and tall and impressive.
GERRY: In fact a very eligible bachelor. (laughs)

And how old were you then?
GERRY: I was sixteen and Jean was twenty when we met him. He was tall and he was a rugby player so he was quite sturdy. He had a slight stoop.
JEAN: Probably from going through doors and bumping his head.

Did he seem English to you then, or Australian?
GERRY: Well, perhaps Australian but a bit of an Anglophile.

Was there some hostility between the English and Australian troops?
GERRY: The Australians were paid so much more than the English.
JEAN: It was like the Americans coming to Brisbane.
GERRY: Exactly the same. They had Peter's ice cream and all that sort of thing, a lot more parcels. It was all brought in. The

Australians used to get so many socks, and instead of bothering to wash them, they'd throw them away, whereas the British troops had very, very little.

JEAN: They lived on a shilling a day, and their wives got some allowance.

Apparently Weary felt hostility from some British officers.

GERRY: I reckon the difference is that those people were permanent army. They belonged to the regiment. The Australians were all sorts, and ninety per cent of them were voluntary and therefore had no attachment to a regiment. In Britain the regiment is in their blood because families have been in the regiment for generations. And then these people came who thought they knew everything, taking over, swishing their money around, that sort of thing, do you see?

I can remember seeing troops in the third storey of the Fast Hotel throwing their change down onto the street and the little Arab boys scrabbling for it. You'd never get a British soldier doing that because he couldn't afford it.

JEAN: In the bars they could hardly afford to have one beer, where the Australians would –

GERRY: – well, let's be quite honest, I was quite ashamed of their behaviour because they just got tanked and looked it and behaved it.

Did Weary Dunlop stand out when you met him?

JEAN: Yes.

GERRY: He just had a way with him. You couldn't really put your finger on it, I suppose.

JEAN: A presence.

GERRY: He had a presence, yes.

So you weren't surprised to hear of his wartime experiences?
GERRY: Not a bit. It seemed to follow on.

Tell me about meeting him again after the war.
GERRY: He looked Dad up after the war. I think he even came to see them in Sydney, and we saw him quite often when we were living in Malvern. Another time I remember, years later than that, after I was married and so forth, and my son Peter was at Scotch. We were at a parents' ball and he came over and asked me to dance. I felt like a million dollars. (laughs) I did. I was in seventh heaven.

From the Middle East, Major Dunlop went to Greece as AIF Medical Liaison Officer to the British troops, arriving there on 29 March 1941. The Greek Army surrendered on 23 April and the evacuation of the Allied troops began the following day. In the meantime, in Northern Africa, the siege of Tobruk had begun.

On 24 June, the Benalla Standard *reprinted as an article a letter written by Major E. E. Dunlop to his parents on 8 May. Under the three-tiered headlines, reading* Tense Days in Greece – Difficulties in Evacuation – Letter from a Doctor who Escaped, *it continued:*

Grim memories of trying to drive through mountain passes at night, with roads torn by mobs and choked with endless convoys moving with little or no light, are recalled by Major E.E. Dunlop, son of Mr and Mrs J.H. Dunlop, of Benalla, in a letter dated 8 May, in which he describes his experiences in Greece.

Major Dunlop states that he had had no real opportunity for writing until a judicious sneeze while he was swimming in a little bay on the Island of Crete gave him a middle ear infection which was aggravated by sleeping in his clothes in the woods and on a destroyer. Finally he got back to his base feeling rather miserable, and was popped into hospital. He added that he felt this was a pity as he was thoroughly enjoying a wild and untrammelled existence.

'Greece was rather an amazing experience altogether, seemingly packed with years of living. During the last two or three weeks one only seemed to sleep in snatches now and again and dug some food out of a tin when there was time. I lived a good deal on the roads towards the last, and saw something of the annoyance of unopposed air action by the enemy. It was disconcerting to have your car chased like a hare by enemy planes, machine gunning and bombing, and it was not much more pleasing when you left it if the ground happened to be bare.

Burnt by Tracers

Some things seem funny in retrospect. My batman and I were getting badly machine gunned on a bare spot of ground, when suddenly he yelled, jumped to his feet and ran 100 yards to some low crop. When the rain of bullets ceased a bit I caught him up and found that a tracer bullet had scorched his posterior, burning a hole in his pullover!

I have some grim memories of having to drive through the mountain passes at night, with roads torn about by bombs and choked with endless convoys moving with little or no lights – it was a difficult business. Heaven only knows how many were injured by rolling down into the gullies and ravines. I had one car wrecked by overturning downhill, and lost my Man Friday with an injured forearm. I also had two other narrow squeaks of similar nature. I eventually felt more happy about the risks by day!

Not even tiredness and strain could dim the superb beauty of Greece in April – I don't think one could imagine anything more beautiful in this world. I specially recall one or two scenes which, somehow, brought enchantment too strong to be disturbed by any thought of war's hideous destruction, or even that flinching from death or capture which sometimes creeps into consciousness.

Superb Beauty

From the dim blue shadows of early dawn, threading one's way along a mountain road amid forests of pine and olive groves – the whole universe seemed to be in separate shades of lovely blue from the shiny darkness of the tarmac road, the sea, the atmosphere, and the great ring of surrounding mountains rising tier on tier. Gazing across the pale eggshell blue of the sea to the Island of Salomius, with its rambled mountains delicately etched in blue, the intervening great gulf in the atmosphere was full of delicate, drifting strata of mystic lakes. The golden radiance away to the left quickened, and suddenly the beams of the rising sun caught the drifting fleece of the clouds, changing them to a dazzling gold, and the dim faint blue of the quiet sea sparkled with life. The old gods of Greece surely walked there often.

I shall feel sad about Greece as long as I live. Poor in resource, practically starving, with most of their country in ruins, the people had no reproaches to offer the country on which they staked so much. Rather, they led us to believe that in some way they had let us down, and invested every Digger and New Zealand soldier who had fought and suffered for Greece with an heroic aura.

The Greeks Help

Our headquarters in Athens for the last day or so was simply surrounded by masses of people begging to be taken away with the British troops, to fight on – so heartbreaking when it became doubtful if there would be enough shipping to get our own troops away. Yet they did everything possible to help us escape. Evacuations may be interesting experience, but they bring a bitter humiliation, to which death might be preferable by many. Byron's words seem still apt:

> *The mountains look on Marathon,*
> *And Marathon looks on the sea.*
> *Musing there an hour or so,*
> *I dreamed that Greece might yet be free.*

Most impressive I found the attitude of the Greek hospitals to our wounded. I stayed on till what was to be the last night of the evacuation in the hope of getting all possible wounded out of the country, and spent a last strenuous day collecting up all who could stagger or be carried to my lorries to reach the beach. Without drugs or dressings, practically, and with very little food left, the devoted medical staffs gave their all, and devoted nurses wept over the wounded and petted them in a pathetic way. No thanks would be accepted. "It was our duty," they said. Some of these nurses were delightful people of the highest social strata, speaking fluent English and French. All had given up their cars, and many their homes, few knowing the fate of their immediate relatives. It was rather heartbreaking, and one tried not to look at the poor devils too severely wounded to be taken away. A number of medical officers had to stay on to look after the wounded and be captured –

a rather dreary outlook. I did volunteer, but felt a cowardly relief at being ordered to escape.

A Close Call

As it was I cut things fairly fine, and was the last of British HQ to leave Athens, I believe. I got a rather frightening telephone message at the last, and had a nightmare drive lasting all night, eventually getting across the Corinth Canal to Morea a few hours before it was cut by German troops. There was a nasty moment on the way when the car rolled into a bomb crater and stuck firmly on the edge of a precipitous slope, with one front wheel sticking out into space! Of course, the darkness hid all this until one got out with a torch. It took much sweating and digging and the muscular efforts of a party of Greeks to get the car back on to the road. Finally I was so tired that I found myself nodding over the wheel almost oblivious to the consequences.

With the dawn there was much ditch hopping while merry German aviators strafed the roads, but eventually I found a party on the beach with whom to take pot luck. An amazingly beautiful day was spent for the most part lying up in a little flowering orange grove, surrounded by cypress trees and mountain slopes ablaze with flowers of all sorts, notably giant Californian poppies, yellow marguerites, little white daisies, and so many other unknown ones.

Anxious Waiting

I read a little book of poems in a detached sort of way, watched enemy planes making hell over the little port below and the roads on all sides, and considered climbing the mountain to an ancient fort which towered on the cliffs above, without raising the necessary energy. Occasionally I went to seek information as to the possibility of the party getting off, which seemed still in doubt; but I was only machine gunned for my pains. Eventually, to our relief, we found it was to be that night, and after an ordered but very tense night march, fraught with a good deal of suspense, we were aboard a little wooden caique threading our way past burning shipping, and I suppose harmlessly over mines. Then a pleasant surprise – the steel sides and devastating efficiency of a British cruiser. I drank a pot of beer and went to sleep in a chair, still clutching the pot, not to move until our anti-aircraft guns thundered into action at 7 am. Good fun now, being able to hit back, and a destroyer also mopped up a submarine.

At Crete

Crete! A mild untrammelled island with an entire absence of galvanised iron and modernity. First experience – a march eight miles along dusty roads, sweating profusely while the great mountains rose above, freely covered with snow. Flowers blazed enchantingly everywhere, and the sea kept popping into view admirably blue and calm. But, Lord, how difficult for masses of troops, many of them in hopelessly mixed formations, practically no blankets, no transport, and rationing haphazard. Some of the wounded suffered bitterly indeed.

I spent some days feeling rather lost, with no longer any headquarters to take an interest in my doing, living like a beachcomber and sleeping in my one uniform. I felt rather indifferent, and like a character from *As You Like It* until the calamity of my ear. A discerning staff officer realised that I was having a pretty rotten time, and suddenly got me off. Now I feel a rather deaf old gentleman, pestered with carbuncles and things, but with hope in the future. Perhaps I shall really and truly leave the staff for a while now and go to some unit. The AAMC has suffered some knocks of late, and we left a number of fine chaps in Greece, killed or captured so we have few enough to cope with the work.'

Milton 'Blue' Butterworth came to Australia from England in 1938 and enlisted in Sydney in the Australian Army in October 1939. He had served in Tobruk before he met up with Weary in Greece, in April 1941. Weary's role was to see that the Allied wounded were safely evacuated.

We spoke when Blue came down to Melbourne from his home in Woy Woy, New South Wales, for the unveiling of Weary's statue in St Kilda Road. Blue has told his story so many times it comes tumbling out in a rush, almost word for word in parts to previous tellings. It's a series of moments, frozen in time, and a query like 'How many days were you in Greece?' is met by the answer 'You know I can't tell you that? A few days. Not long.'

Blue almost apologises for his enthusiasm. 'I do go on about Weary, I used to drive people crazy,' he told me. At the conclusion of our interview, he pressed his hand to his heart. 'No baloney,' he said.

I HAD MY twenty-first birthday in the Western Desert. I wasn't with Weary then, I was with the 2/1st Infantry Battalion. We got word that the Germans were on their way in and we did a forced march. I had my boots and socks on for 72 hours. Not only were they on for that long but they weren't my regulation socks and they got saturated. I got trench foot.

They put me on a train for three days and I ended up in this English hospital. Then all the wounded started to come in and I felt a bit guilty that I wasn't wounded. I volunteered to give up my bed and I went back to Daphni, which was a suburb of

Athens, and that was our first camp. All the ex-personnel were there and I became one of them.

Then right out of the blue, the commanding officer just tossed me a bunch of keys. He said, 'You can drive Butterworth.' Now I kid you not, I had never driven a car. I'd had a go in a ute, and a six-wheeler Morris. I had no licence and this was the first column controlled, a 1941 Chevvie, Brigadier Owen's staff car. I was told to report round to corps headquarters, which was in Daphni. Around I go and an officer came out with his aide-de-camp and said, 'Car all right?' All I knew about a car was it needed oil and water. I got the groundsheet out, spread it on the deck and went off to sleep alongside the Chevvie. At about half past two in the morning, 'Hey Blue, Blue.' It was a little fellow called Peewee, out of my regular battalion. He said, 'Everyone's gone. They're all gone.' He said, 'There's a fortune. They've just left everything in their tents.' I said, 'Go away.' He said. 'Come on, we'll make a fortune.' I said, 'Go away.' (laughs) Anyway, I got off my groundsheet and I went and there it was, they'd left everything. They'd gone, they'd flown the coup.

First light, they all came streaming back. I think it was a false evacuation. All the trumps – what I call the trumps – they never told me. And then it was, 'Butterworth, your services are no longer required here. See the quartermaster, pick up iron rations and report to a Major Dunlop in Force Headquarters at the Acropole Hotel.' I pulled up thinking, cripes, who am I going to meet, what's he going to be like? At Athens at that hour of night it is very busy, believe you me. Up I go and knock on the door and an English brigadier answered. I told him who I was and he called out, 'Dunlop, your driver's here.' I could hear this soft voice asking, 'Where's he parked?' I said I'd found a park right in front of the building. 'Tell him to go and wait, I'll be down there shortly.'

Over there they drive on the right-hand side. The curb is

approximately eighteen inches from the pavement. I'm sitting
in the car and – no licence – my steering wheel is up against the
curb. And when I look out, there are feet this big and a big army
great coat. I said to myself, 'Shit, he'll never get in this car.' And
he just came around, introduced himself, I introduced myself
and from that very moment, I tipped that we're going to be
right – first time I met him, you know?

He said, 'Right, do you know the King George Hotel?' We
went to the hotel and he said, 'I don't want to make it look as if
I'm on the move.' So very gently, he got what he wanted and he
left other gear there. And he left a tip. And away we go. We took
off going north. Everybody had started to come back and we
were going north. It's pitch dark and I had had hardly any sleep
the prior night waiting for this other major. Weary said,
'Butterworth, I'll relieve you, you must be tired,' which I was.
'You're straining your eyes because of these blackout conditions.'

All the big stuff was coming back. The English army. And
next, the car's over, ditched, like that. 'Oh,' he said, 'shit, have
you got a trenching tool?' And there was one in the boot of the
car. I got it out and I went to take it and he just said, 'Give it to
me'. He spoke so quietly, he said, 'What I want you to do is . . .

And I'm trying to work out, what is this fellow? I had him
as Intelligence, everything bar a doctor, and he stripped and he
gave me a little pencil torch with a purple globe in it – a doctor's torch – and asked me to hold it for him. That's when I
thought, This bloke must be a doctor. When he stripped and he
started digging (he shakes his head), I thought, Jesus!

Well, he dug the car out and we took off. We stayed with
the car that night in the olive groves. The next morning I'm
looking for him and there's this Stuka [German plane] and he
was circling. We were gone. I thought, I wonder where the big
fella is – I christened him the Big Fella, or the Chief – and I shot

along and there he was, sitting there with his steel mirror, shaving. He said, 'Get yourself out of the way, get out of the way.'

We were coming back along the way we'd travelled the night before. Where we'd been, you'd have thought a bobcat or a mini-bulldozer had been in there. He was so strong and powerful.

We went to Kephissia and I'm talking to a Scotsman and he said, 'Do you think you'll get away?' I said 'I don't know mate.' He said, 'If I write a letter to my wife, will you post it for me when you can?' I said, 'OK.' He gave me a bottle of beer, 'cause everybody was taking all their alcohol – they didn't want the Germans to get on to it. The next thing I'm paged. 'Private Butterworth, report to your car immediately.' Over I go and Weary's sitting in the car and he says, 'Right, don't panic. I've got the message that the Germans are on their way.' So there was no panic – I just forgot the roads and went straight over all the gardens. (laughs)

This road into Athens, it was a beautiful road, a five-lane job, and the sun was in my eyes and with my slouch hat, I couldn't see, and the big fella said to me, 'Knock it off' and took his peaked cap off and put it on my head. We pulled in at the front of force headquarters and he told me to wait. Out he came after awhile and he said, 'The bloody idiots. They've burnt the gear, they've set fire to everything.' Down in the kitchen, they'd burnt papers that he'd wanted. He told this corporal to abandon his post to come with us, because it was futile him staying there, and he wouldn't. No, he said. He'd been told he had to stay there and that was it.

So we're taking off, full speed ahead and next thing a Greek with mule and cart, loaded with boxes of apples came out and I clipped him, just a clip and he was over. I was going to stop and Weary said, 'He's right, he's right, keep going.' We arrived in Daphni and there they are, burning all the payroll, the Australian Corps' payroll, in drachmas, boxes and boxes and boxes of drachmas, so the Germans couldn't get them, you see. He came out and said, 'Right, we'll catch up with the convoy.' So we took off and we caught up with the convoy. We were the last in the line. It was dark and the colonel called out, 'That you Dunlop? The Brigadier's waiting for you.' Weary said to me, 'Right, pull around,' and the next thing, we're in a hell of a hole. The car was on that angle. Half the road had been blown away. He said, 'Are you all right?' I said 'I'm all right.' I'm hanging on to my column. And he said, 'Try and reverse' and I just tried. Now the only things that would hold us were the bomb crater and some boulders – that's the only thing that the car was on. He said, 'Give it another go,' and he got out of the car, and he's standing in the crater, on the side of the hill. Now if that car had rolled, I'd have gone, he'd have gone.

In the finish I said, 'No Sir, no, I won't do it.' So he said, 'Shit.' He came around and the next thing, a voice said, 'You'll have to abandon your vehicle and get in the convoy.' Weary very nicely said, 'I don't know who you are or what you are but will you please fuck off.' And I thought, Ah, there's no doubt about him. (chuckles) And then the convoy's gone. And it's quiet. You can hear the sea lapping below, then in the distance, you could hear this singing. The Greeks capitulated before we did. They'd been ordered to get back to where they came from as quick as they could, and they're all singing when they came around the corner. They got hold of the car and next thing, the Chevvie's back on the road. Weary was trying his bit of Greek that he'd picked up and a bit of Latin and a bit of this, a bit of you name it. I had Woodbines, Capstan cigarettes, Players cigarettes, in the glovebox. I just gave them the lot and away we go. Eventually we caught up with the brigadier and the brigadier and his valet were asleep. Weary, trying to find where he was, kicked him, stumbled upon him. The old Brigadier didn't like that.

Then we were off down to a place, Nauplion, down below Argos. A troop ship had gone aground coming into evacuate and they reckoned the harbourmaster or someone else had sabotaged it. It had only just been beached when we came over. We were in a yard with a camouflage unit with pigs and chooks and everything and these Stukas were going over when I sighted Weary's tin hat, his helmet. Away I went and there he was, sitting on the sea wall, doing his notes. I said, 'You better have this Sir.' He said, 'Get to blazes, what are you doing here?' With no nerve, you know. He was fantastic.

We came off Nauplion on a wooden barque. It was absolutely crowded, to the point of danger. So many people up the riggings and everything. And there's a ship aglow that had been bombed. You could feel the heat of it. We went straight past that to the HMS *Calcutta*. Officers to the right, NCOs to the right, other ranks to the left. And you went through the blackout curtains. The next thing, we got cocoa – the British Navy – and then it was on. At first light they started bombing the convoy, and Weary's missing. He was up on deck. He came down afterwards and he told me that there was definitely an area where the Germans could get at it. He was right. Not that day but in her next voyage, off Crete.

We went to a place called Canea and the order was evacuate. So we went to Suda Bay. By the way, I had refused to abandon his gear. I'd been ordered to do this and I said, 'No, no.' I think that's why Weary and I got on so well.

Next thing, red tape came along and said, 'Dunlop, he can't go with you.' Weary said, 'I want him to go with me.' 'He can't go with you and that's an order.' So that was an order and he slipped me a thousand drachma note. Well, it was better than it going up in smoke, wasn't it? (laughs) And we said goodbye.

The goodbye was a temporary one. In June 1941 Major Dunlop was hospitalised briefly in Alexandria, Egypt and discharged himself to make his way to Tobruk. Three weeks later, he and Private Butterworth were reunited. 'I knew if I was alongside of him I was right,' Blue Butterworth said. 'There was a bloke up there listening, saving him. He loved him. This is the feeling.' In January they set sail for Java on the Orcades.

The Orcades, the fastest ship in a convoy that was to take the Australian Army's 6th and 7th Divisions from the Middle East to the Asian theatre of war, set sail from Port Twefik on 1 February 1942 with 3400 men on board. Once in Java, Weary Dunlop was promoted to the position of temporary lieutenant-colonel and then temporary colonel, a rank he didn't take up. In Bandoeng he established the 1st Allied General Hospital, which continued to operate until almost six weeks after the capitulation of Java on 8 March 1942. After the surrender of the Allied forces in Java, Weary's family received the following letter:

UX 259 Major E E Dunlop
2/2 Aust CCS Abroad

My Dears
Java – sorry to say I cannot write more than a line. I am well and happy and this is a lovely country.

Things are not so good and I leave you to the papers for the rest. God bless you both and watch over you. Do not worry about me – remember that I am happy and have no fears.

I think I outlined my affairs to you adequately before and there should be some £800 to my credit (including deferred pay) if the worst comes.

But anyway all my love and cheer Helen up a bit, won't you? Chin up my dears.
Ern

On 18 April, Weary and members of the 2/2nd Casualty
Clearing Station were marched off to Landsopvoedingsgesticht, a
cramped penal institution designed for Javanese criminals, where
they spent the next six weeks. They were then shifted to No. 1
Concentration Camp No. 4 Tjimahi, where they spent two weeks.
    On 14 June they were marched to the larger Bandoeng
camp, which was situated in a former army barracks. Lt-Col.
Dunlop had been the commanding officer at the first two camps,
and at the suggestion of Lt-Col. Laurens van der Post he
continued as commander of the allied troops. In November, the
Australian troops were moved to Makasura, a camp near Batavia
(Jakarta), and then by boat to Singapore and to the prison camp,
Changi, where Lt-Col. Galleghan challenged Dunlop's authority
as a non-combatant officer over combatant officers.

Among those on the Orcades *with Weary and the 2/2nd*
Casualty Clearing Station, were the 2/3rd Machine Gunners.
Keith Flanagan *was a gunner from Western Australia. Since*
his retirement in 1985, the former journalist and actor has
made the promotion of Weary Dunlop, and the values he
believes Weary represents, a top priority. We spoke at his home
in the hills of Perth.

WE WERE ON the Orient liner, the *Orcades*, the first and fastest
ship out and the only one that didn't get back to Australia. When
the Japs came into the war, Curtin recalled the 6th and 7th
Divisions and the initial idea was that they were going to go to
the Netherlands' East Indies – Sumatra and Java – and hold the
Japs back there. But we were very much amateurs against the
professional Germans and Japanese. We were machine gunners
and the army's Movement Control put us on one ship, with our
machine guns, transport, stores and kitbags on another.

ABOVE: *Ern (left) and brother Alan, wearing the Deerfoot costumes their mother made for them (courtesy Gert Hutchins)*

RIGHT: *Weary with his pony Jock, 1918*

TOP: *Lilian Steen, Gert Hutchin's mother, on her horse (courtesy Gert Hutchins)*

BOTTOM: *Weary was best man (second from right) at his brother Alan's marriage to Winifred in March, 1932*

OPPOSITE PAGE: *Dressed as a fairy for the 1931 Melbourne University Commencement Week prank*

HONOURS GROUP

E. Cohen   J. R. A. Glenn   A. H. Norman   J. A. Lyne   A. R. Lobban   E. R. Love   C. McT. Hopkins   E. A. H. La
R. M. Green   T. C. Adams   E. E. Dunlop   D. F. Lawson   R. M. Campbell   B. K. Rank   G. Thirkell

TOP: *Ormond Honours Group, 1932, which includes Archibald Glenn, Charles Hopkins, Benjamin Rank and Weary (third from left, front row)*

BOTTOM: *The rugby player in action with Victoria against the Waratahs (Weary second from left)*

LEFT: *Cholera Isolation Area, Hintok (drawing by Jack Chalker)*

BELOW: *This article in the* Australian Women's Weekly *greeted Weary on his return to Australia in October, 1945 (courtesy Australian Consolidated Press)*

Vol. 13, No. 19   60 Pages   October 20, 1945   SYDNEY   The Australian Women's Weekly   17

British and Japs called him "King of the river"

By MERTON WOODS

TOUGH, ulcer-scarred men coming home from the horror holes of Thailand tell, with shining eyes, of the selfless devotion and heroism of two Australian doctors.

● These two doctors are big (six feet four), thirtyish, Lieut.-Colonel Ernest E. ("Weary") Dunlop, surgeon from Benalla, Vic., and Major Ewan Corlette, of Orange, N.S.W.

● For his magnificent care of sick and dying soldiers during the two and a half years at the Thailand jungle horror, Dunlop is known to Japanese and Britishers alike as "The King of the River."

● The boys whose lives he saved simply and reverently call him "The Christ of Thailand."

● Both Col. Dunlop and Major Corlette have been officially recommended for an honour to mark their service to Australia.

● They carry the unofficial recommendation of all their men, that there is not an award the King can make that is too great for them to receive.

● Col. Dunlop and Major Corlette, after two and a half years in Thailand, are still in Bangkok, working with Recovery Allied Prisoners of War and Internees.

MAJOR EWAN CORLETTE, affectionately called "Slapstick of Kwanki River" by the men whose lives he helped to save. He and Dunlop are still in Bangkok

COLONEL ERNEST DUNLOP, "King of the River" to British and Japanese alike. His bravery and skill saved scores of men from death.

A.I.F. surgeon and his physician worked miracles for prisoners in Thailand

LONGING FOR NEWS, ex-prisoners of war flock to the post office on the wharf at Darwin, which handled 1400 telegrams the day before the troops berthed, with 200 men aboard.

FIRST AUSTRALIAN NEWSPAPER seen by Spr. A. B. Miller, Newcastle, N.S.W., after his release was the Army News. He relaxes in a hammock on the voyage home.

PICNIC at Darwin for L/Cpl. T. A. Wing, Cronulla, N.S.W. Pte. R. S. Davis, Yackandah, N.S.W.; Dvr. L. A. Windross, S.A.; Cpl. J. P. Dooley, Sydney; Pte. J. Ashton, N.S.W.

ABOVE: *Weary and Helen (Ferguson) were married on 8 November, 1945*

RIGHT: *With Helen when he was made a companion of the Order of St Michael and St George for his outstanding service to medicine in April, 1965 (courtesy Age newspaper)*

TOP: *The consulting room at 14 Parliament Place. The examination couch is visible through the open door*

BOTTOM: *605 Toorak Road, Toorak, on the day of Weary's funeral*

ABOVE: *Bill and Alice Griffiths outside Buckingham Palace on receipt of Bill's MBE, 19 November, 1977*

RIGHT: *Valda Street at work at 14 Parliament Place*

Weary was with the 2/2nd Casualty Clearing Station. I think there were about eighty of them aboard. Weary had been in Greece, Crete and Tobruk, and he was equally heroic there. People forget that. He'd got this mobile hospital unit together – they could put it up in twenty minutes – and he had all this captured Italian equipment. They were put on the ship with one Regimental Aid Post pannier – that's a wicker basket – with a few bandages and aspirins.

We got to a place called Oosthaven, to the south of Sumatra, and the machine gunners, those who didn't have rifles, were given old rifles out of the ship's armoury (some say some were stamped VR but I don't know about that), Canadian Ross rifles from World War 1, bayonets (and of course there was nothing to put them in so they had to wear them thrust through their belts, pirate fashion), and some were even given stout sticks. And this is to go ashore and stop the Japanese thrust!

There were about 2500 of us. We got off the *Orcades* onto the tanker *Van Spillsbergen* and pulled up by the wharf and we stood there, shoulder to shoulder with our full packs on for hour upon hour upon hour. It came nightfall and messages were being flickered on the clouds from searchlights. Hurried conference followed and they said the Japs were only a few miles down the road – they'd already taken Palembang – so we were to get back on the ship. Of course, the ship was in darkness. We got on this tanker and they found a pilot who would take us out, only on condition that not a word was said, because he had to pick up the throb of the blacked-out *Orcades*. Then somebody flickered a torch and we got on. We got to Batavia, which is now Jakarta, and we were off the boat, on the boat, off the boat, on the boat – they didn't know what the hell they were doing.

I found out later that there was sort of an argument going on between Curtin and the war cabinet and Wavell, who was the commander of the American, British, Dutch and Australian forces and had his headquarters in Java. The war cabinet wanted us back because we weren't just soldiers, we were specialist soldiers, and we had our role to play. Curtin wanted us back because it was essential for the 7th Division.

Wavell wanted us there because the Dutch had been promised some support and we were it. The final denouement came when Curtin sent an unwise cable: What are your plans for these men? Don't forget, Wavell's got the whole weight of the world pressing on his shoulders, everything had been shot out of the sky and so he said 'That means they're under my command', so we were off the ship.

Three weeks later we were in the bag. First of all, though, we guarded the Kemajoran aerodrome at Batavia, and then we went out and fought an action at a place called Leuwiliang. That was the only real action that was fought in Java. That was the first combined American-Australian thing. It was fairly brief, only a couple of days, then we withdrew with the theory allegedly being that the *Perth* and the *Houston* would pick us up at Tjilatjap and we'd get back to Australia. That was what we fondly believed. The *Perth* and the *Houston*, of course, sailed into this convoy that actually landed the Japs that we were fighting. They went down very gallantly, the *Perth* firing practice bricks at the last – that's all they had left.

Within that three weeks, Weary went to Bandoeng, which is in the middle of Java, and he established what they called No. 1 Allied General Hospital in a Bandoeng school. They scrounged stuff from off the wharf, from everywhere, and the Dutch helped magnificently. They had Dutch 'helpsters' and they treated about 1300 sick and wounded in those three weeks. They brought Bill Griffiths in there and Weary saved his life three times over. Weary called Bill 'that legend of British pluck'.

In March 1942 a bomb blast left British Royal Air Force driver
Bill Griffiths *blinded, with both hands blown off and one leg*
badly injured. He was taken to the Allied General Hospital in
Bandoeng where there were doctors and nurses alike who thought
it would be kinder to let the young man die. As the commanding
officer of the hospital, the newly promoted temporary Lieutenant-
Colonel Dunlop determinedly kept him alive.

I spoke with Bill Griffiths at his home in Blackpool.

WHEN I WAS blown up, he was not far away, fortunately. I
would have certainly died, within minutes, had it not been for
Weary because I was picked up and dropped off and he attended
to me on the operating table. So that was number one – he
saved my life straight off there, you see.

This was all amid the confusion and chaos of being a prisoner of war in Java. The following day a Japanese guard came
in, saw me and got his bayonet out to kill me on the spot. Weary
stood in front of him and said, 'No'. So there's two occasions,
two successive days, where he saved my life. That was my introduction to Weary.

And then, of course, we were prisoners of war.

I was in the same camp as Weary for quite some time. He
used to come and talk to me. Of course, he was a busy man – it
was a very big hospital, amid all the casualties – but that was
Weary, he seemed to make time and have time, in his very
relaxed way, to come and talk to me at the bedside. Watch my
progress.

Did you ever want to be allowed to die?
Oh yes, oh yes, oh yes. I didn't want to live really, it was too awful
for words – blind without hands. With these injuries, you see, as a
young man I could not envisage life at all, living like this. But

Weary used to come and he'd say, 'You'll be alright, it will take time.' He was a comfort then. He really was. I was only a kid, I was 21. And Weary, when he came to the bedside, just his voice there, 'Well Bill, how are you this morning?' It was a great comfort.

He used to instil a bit of optimism in me. He said all wasn't lost. And there was something about him that gave me hope for the future. As calm as could be was Weary, and he sort of transmitted it to me ever so quick, as soon as he'd come. I felt more secure in every way. And that went on through life. Up till his death, actually.

There was a certain magic when he was around, somehow. Just the thought of him being around. Even in thought now. I often think of Weary. I get great strength from it, just from thinking about him. What would old Weary have done – any awkward situation, any difficult situation, feeling down, whatever, just think of Weary and I'm right. You see? It's someone to look up to.

He seemed to be completely unflappable, he really did, and he used to have a little laugh. He used to laugh from the inside, really. He loved his bit of fun, he used to have his little jokes. He was the complete person. He had the common touch and obviously he was a very cultured, highly educated chap, skilful surgeon, and he was one of the lads as well.

When the war ended, the very first day, a message came to me that Weary had survived. He was in Thailand, I think, but he had survived and he wanted to know how I was, how I felt at that moment, and he passed the message on that he would see me as soon as he could. I thought, Isn't that marvellous? A man like that, a surgeon, and humble little me, sending this message that he wanted to see me as soon as possible. Obviously word had got through to him that I'd survived and his message said how delighted he was that we'd both survived.

Bill Griffiths' survival in the camps and his remarkable post-war rehabilitation are recorded in his book, Blind to Misfortune. *It includes a letter from Sir Edward Dunlop to Professor Sir Ludwig Guttmann of the rehabilitation hospital St Dunstan's, written when Bill Griffiths was voted Disabled Sportsman of the Year in Britain in 1969.*

I MAINTAINED MY belief in man's unquenchable spirit and intelligence which could open doors even if he seemed imprisoned by darkness and helplessness. Further I promised a Court of Enquiry if anything happened to Bill within my hospital!

. . . His subsequent career, with his successful entry into a transport business, and the remarkable way he has triumphed over such formidable disabilities, you must know, for the man is a legend. . . So I am utterly thrilled that the flickering candle of life I cared for in Bandoeng has come to burn so much brighter than I could have imagined. He is very much your protegé and admirer so I congratulate you too.

After capitulation, **Keith Flanagan** *made two escape bids, the second ending in the death of one of his fellow escapees and the incarceration by the Japanese of the remaining three in a civilian jail.*

WE HAD STILL another escape bid planned. We were going to cut through the little thin bars of this cell and we were going to pull them back. We were then going to go over a barbed wire fence, over to a fourteen-foot wall with a standard light burning, and somehow throw a rope around it. Oh! You know, it wasn't until later years that I realised it would have only ended in being bayoneted, or if they thought it stupid enough or rash enough, to beheading. And two days before we were going to go, they shifted us. All I can think was that somebody up there thought, Oh God, it's like shooting fish in a barrel.

They sent us to Bandoeng. This is where Weary was the camp commandant. I didn't realise quite the stature of the man then. Bandoeng was this mixed camp of various nationalities, various services, and if we had stayed there and things had remained the same, I and all of us would have come out of it educated men. They were the halcyon days because we had camp concerts, we had brains trusts, we had some very intelligent men there. I remember Laurens van der Post reading poetry on a poetry reading night and crying. Moved, you know.

At the concert, the theme song was 'Time On My Hands'. They had an orchestra, they put on plays, bloody good plays, and they had these classes, and you could take anything. I concentrated on Dutch and Malay, I'm afraid, because I still wanted to make an escape, you know. (laughs and speaks a few words of Dutch)

Weary was commandant over men of much higher rank than he was. There was van der Post, Nichols, but Weary was the leader. I think probably nobody wanted it, and Weary said, 'All right, it's mine then.'

*Another West Australian machine gunner, **Bill Haskell**, was in the Bandoeng camp. Bill Haskell, now a retired public servant, joined Keith Flanagan and me to talk.*

IN THOSE DAYS we just used to go out on work parties doing a bit of work here and there. It was play to what we had later.

On a Saturday, there was a sports field there and they used to play soccer and they had athletics. I was interested in sport and I thought, Oh, I'll have a bit of a run and I had a run and there was Weary with his loping legs.

Then I saw them having the shot put and the discus – they had full equipment at this place – and I thought, I wouldn't mind having a go at that. Being a proper mug, I got hold of a discus and I was trying to throw it and I can still remember Weary coming along, 'It's not like that, lad, this is how you do it.' He took the time to show me how to throw a discus and how to get the best out of a shot put, because he was a good athlete, he did all that sort of thing at university. But he was the camp commandant and I was just a mug private and he was quite happy to take the time. I didn't know who he was at the time.

Ray Parkin, a survivor from the HMAS Perth, *is the author of* Into the Smother, *one of the finest accounts of life as a prisoner of war in Thailand. He found time to sketch in Bandoeng and it was there that he made two lifelong friends, Weary Dunlop and Laurens van der Post.*

BANDOENG WASN'T VERY adventurous but we could have gone on to the end of the war like that, it was Shangrila. I did a lot of work up there. I thought, Yes, this will suit me, though I felt a bit of a bludger. We ten survivors from the *Perth* were the only navy blokes there. There's a difference between soldiers and sailors, you know, and we made sure that they knew the difference.

Weary had already become a bit of a legend. Everyone was so glad to be with him, they looked up to him. Although the officer quarters were separate – it was an old army camp and therefore it was arranged in that way – he used to come and mix with the blokes and of course we'd see him on the sports field. Although he was a doctor he was so much of a leader that he was actually put in charge. There were a lot of colonels and so forth and Laurens van der Post should have been the leader but if his identity was known, because of his previous subversive activities, he would have been for it. As a matter of fact, he was taken away and tortured once for three or four days or more, so they had to keep him under wraps, and Weary was made the camp commandant.

Weary was interested in the navy and when he found out there were some *Perth* blokes there, we formed a friendship. We just had the same frame of mind, as it were. No way of explaining it. In a way, he looked to us, too, because we were a group who stuck together and, after all, I'd been in the navy already for twelve years. We were used to knuckling down to things. There was a great feeling between the army and the navy. We'd been in Greece and Crete with them – we took them in and we pulled them out and we got ships sunk. Anyone who had served in those campaigns wouldn't say a word against the navy. We were the blokes that had pulled them out.

While I was in Bandoeng, I was sketching around the camp and I looked up one day and there's a bloke standing over me, looking over my shoulder. I'm painting a tree in front of me. I looked up and I could see he was a colonel. 'Hello. How do you do, sir?' It was Laurens van der Post and we became friendly then.

*When I spoke to him in his London apartment overlooking Chelsea, the eighty-eight-year-old writer, conservationist and philosopher **Sir Laurens van der Post** was still leading a busy and productive life. We talked about his priorities in life and he said, 'I feel almost as if I hate my writing because it takes me away from people.'*

I CAME UP with a very special little group from a place called Sukabumi, where we consisted mostly of chaps who tried to get away and not get caught by the Japanese. We came later into camp. I met Weary in a new larger camp which was being created at Bandoeng. It was full of people who had surrendered. Absolutely no option. They were soldiers who came and had no guns to fight with, airmen and people from the Battle of Britain who had no planes to fly. There were all sorts of groups and it had no cohesion or form.

On the first day, I remember the officers were paraded by the Japanese and they were booed by the men. That was the sort of spirit. It was full of nothingness in that camp. I thought this was a terrible thing. We can't face what's in front of us with this sort of thing going on, I thought.

I had with me a remarkable RAF officer, Nichols. We talked it over and said, 'Well we must somehow bring all this group together.' And suddenly, in the midst of this, we found Weary and his group. He had his medical group round him and remnants of the pioneer battalion who'd fought at Leuwiliang as a part of Blackforce under Brigadier Blackburn, who was a VC from the first war.

They had a sense of unity, this little Australian unit and we were immensely taken by them all, but particularly by Weary. I was the senior British military officer and the senior British officer of all was Nichols. Weary was a colonel. Nichols and I talked with Weary and I said, 'My own feeling is that whatever the structure of command the Japanese impose upon us, we have to obey, but one thing that we shouldn't allow to happen is that the Japanese divide us.'

I attested that we should have our own election from all the commonwealth officers there, our own commanding officer, and we elected Weary, unanimously. I said, 'It makes sense in what we are going in for. We will need medical care above anything else and we need someone who is interested in healing. We can't do better.'

So Weary was our own commanding officer, and we couldn't have done better. I don't remember any dispute about it at all, none at all, because it was the thing for us. The Japanese insisted on the Australians reporting specially, so they had Weary reporting for them as an Australian officer, Nichols reporting for the British, the Dutch officer for the Dutch.

The immense medical team that Weary had was really remarkable, they were lovely people, and in civilian life, they were doctors in all kinds of things. Arthur Moon, if I remember, was quite a famous gynaecologist. What he was going to do enlisted, I don't know. What was left of the Pioneer Corps that fought very gallantly at Leuwiliang really turned automatically to Weary as an Australian colonel, their commanding officer, had been removed.

Weary and I worked very, very closely together. We created our own educational system in the camp. I can't tell you how very, very sad we felt when, early in November, Weary and most of the Australians were suddenly banded together and marched out of our camp. It was a thing that we feared most in prison, breaking up, people going away. It was a great blow to us. By this time you couldn't put a knife between any of us, we'd become so bonded, and we hated to see them off. They were on the way to the Burma road.

The education program that was set up seems extraordinary.
My own second in command, Major Pat Lancaster, who was commissioned in Churchill's Old Hussars and had come from the Western Desert, he taught three Australians from the Never Never, who couldn't read or write. He had the junior

class and he loved doing it and they were so responsive.

We took people right up to university level and there were quite a lot of farmers, so we had an agricultural college as well. In a democratic army you get experts on every conceivable subject, you see. Our professor in classics was a don from Cambridge, Don Gregory. And the Australians particularly – this struck us all – loved the classics. They loved studying the history of Greece, the mythology of Greece. Gregory gave lectures under trees, everywhere, and they were absolutely packed out within hearing distance. They were so lovely and responsive.

You have described Weary as the Renaissance man.

Weary was, in the Greek sense of the word, a whole person. He was a many-sided person. Of course he was a doctor and a healer but he was also many other things. He was a man who had remarkable balance, who wrote extremely well, and was a very serious and a very profound person. But also he was very amusing and witty. I used to think of him very much as a phenomenon of the Greek, of the period of Heraperecles.

Of course we attach enormous importance to knowing him in prison. In fact, I think prison for all of us was a great university. We learnt things there that one couldn't have learnt in any other way. He had a sense of immediate realities and I think he played a remarkable political role in the area post-war in the refocussing of the western spirit in the Pacific, bringing it into alliance with the South-East Asian nations. He wasn't political at all, but through education, through what he did, he played a tremendous role and he was terribly important. I think what he's done will live.

We loved having him here in England but he really had a great sort of constituency in the world, even if people didn't personally know him. For instance, when the news of his death came through, almost immediately someone rang me from Canada who had been in Java in that period, so within about half an hour, I spoke on Canadian radio about Weary. There were enormous numbers of people all over Canada who picked it up and were grateful to know it.

I say constituency because one of the things we did in prison, we had a parliament. A commonwealth parliament. Although it was quite, quite serious, there was nothing we could do except discuss the common problems in the world as if we were the parliament.

Did the camps change the way you experienced life?
To survive in the camps one developed a kind of 'now' that was a kind of 'forever', which in a sense is not a concept but a feeling and an experience promoted by the great mystics. This was not a sense fragmented into past, present and future, because in a sense we had no past, we were cut off from it; we had no future, we were cut off from that; we had no power and we had to find the force to live, and the meaning, from somewhere else. That's why living that sort of way, it gave one the values that saw one through afterwards.

When we got back and we found the old battles being repeated, the heresies prepared, somehow we'd broken through into a new world. It is very interesting to me that in these remembrances we had here recently, there were people who wanted the Japanese to apologise and wanted money for what they'd suffered, reparations and that sort of thing.

I couldn't find amongst the people who spoke like that, one person who'd been with us. They were all from somewhere else. I couldn't find anyone who'd been with Weary. Of course they obviously had been imprisoned but where they were, I couldn't tell.

One understands people suffering and finding it difficult,

but I think that we lived in such a way that when we came out of prison, the experience was behind us. Completely behind us. People kept on saying to Weary, to me, 'It's wonderful of you to forgive.' And I think Weary's answer was the same as mine. That was: the question of forgiveness never arose, because it never entered that area. We dealt with it as it happened and it's in the past. But it taught us a lot of about the future. In that way it lived on.

Weary had a great sense of fun. He was fun to be with all the time. He enjoyed life and it was lovely and he was a caring person. I think from what I've heard from Ray Parkin and others, that if he hadn't cared so much about what he owed other people, he might still be alive. He got going much too soon after that pneumonia. He couldn't stop still. He had this strongly extroverted side, and he had to be active and he had to be doing, but he never lost his touch with his being.

He came to England after the war and he got in touch and after that he came about every two years and I saw him regularly.

Could Weary have found peacetime dull?
Oh no, no, no, no. Impossible. I don't think Weary knew what a dull moment was. He would have conveyed it to others if he had. I think he found peace a great challenge and very exciting. He'd never let peace just be a peace. Things happened when he was around. You know, he was coming over here when he died. It was all planned, we had the dates. We were heartbroken when he couldn't come again.

Did he find some sort of Buddhist faith in the camps?
No, I don't think so. I don't think he was a person for dogma or irrational concepts, but in his feeling and in his values he'd lived very much in a religious climate of his own. It was his natural

clime – without it being a dogma or something to shout about, he was just it. He experienced it and lived it. He was very sensitive. It comes out in his writing so much, it comes out beautifully in his writing. And why not? Great soldiers very often spoke well. Wavell was a very good writer, and his anthology of poetry, *Other Men's Flowers*, is still the most popular anthology in the English language of poetry.

Another quality Weary had – I don't think he ever felt a stranger. Wherever he went he was at home, and that is a great sign from life that the spirit is on course. It was lovely to introduce him to one's friends. Whether he was staying in a fashionable house in Scotland and going out on the hills with fashionable people shooting or in the camps, he was at home. And he was certainly always welcome. We all loved him very much.

The Australian troops were moved on from Bandoeng, first to Makasura and then by boat to Singapore, and Weary and his men went to the prison camp, Changi, where Lieutenant-Colonel Galleghan challenged Weary's authority as a non-combatant officer over combatant officers.

KEITH FLANAGAN: We were what they called the Dunlop Thousand, or the Dunlop Force. We were never a thousand, anyway.

We were to go with Weary to Makasura, that was a camp near Batavia, or Jakarta. Van der Post was a highly articulate, highly intelligent, highly educated man, and I remember the night before we left he made this speech and it was beautiful. The right sentiment, every word well used. Lovely speech. The one you've always wanted to make.

Then Weary got up – (laughs) he'd hate me for this – and

he was standing on one foot then the other. I don't know if he was blushing but he made the speech that you never want to make. There to my mind were two of the most notable men that I'd ever met, but the greater was Weary.

Then we went to this camp at Makasura. We didn't know it at the time but it was preliminary to getting on a ship and going to Singapore. I remember New Year's Eve. They had a piano there and they sang the dirtiest songs I'd ever heard in my life. They sang all night. They had an air force officer playing the piano.

Then we got on this ship and went to Changi in Singapore. That's where Weary had a run in with 'Black Jack' Galleghan. He tried to take command away from Weary and he refused. He tried to give it to Bill Wearne and he refused. Bill got an OBE for his work in Tobruk.

BLUE BUTTERWORTH: The men just took to him. There were a lot of officers like him, without doubt. We had some beauties, don't worry about that. The others – well, they didn't like him. They're dead now, but some, if Weary had come back and exposed them straightaway, what he thought of their behaviour, they'd have been drummed out. They'd have been stripped and thrown out. 'Black Jack' Galleghan especially. When we were in Changi, he treated us like . . . well, he christened us the Java Rabble. Oh yeah, the Java Rabble. He wouldn't give us rice polishings, which is the husk off the rice. Fortunately we did get it occasionally because that's what saved us.

I was there when Brigadier Blackburn signed the bit of paper that said, while the Dunlop Force were together, E.E. Dunlop was to remain in supreme command. Bill Wearne was a senior combatant officer, and he refused to take over.

You see, Black Jack reckoned that being a medico, Weary shouldn't be in charge of combatant men. But Bill, being a

Duntroon man, and he'd been on Wavell's staff at one stage, he said, 'No, that's the way it is and that's the way it's going to stay, as far as I'm concerned.'

Years later my wife, Lesley, and I were living in Manly. One Saturday morning I got a phone call from Weary, 'Helen and I are up here in Sydney at the Windsor. Come over for lunch.' I bought the paper and there it was about 'Black Jack' who'd been promoted to Brigadier, and I thought, You twerp, after what you did to us. So when we're having lunch I suddenly remembered it and I showed Weary the paper and he just shook his head. That's all he did. Oh yeah, he could have rolled a lot of them. He had it all down, too. All in the war diaries. He left things out, for the families' sake.

RAY PARKIN: When we left Changi – I was told this, I haven't seen the letter, but I don't doubt its existence – Weary said, 'My men arrived here without this and that and they have left in a similar condition.' In other words, you've done nothing to alleviate their condition.

We were in rags, virtually. I'd swum ashore [from the HMAS *Perth*] and all I had was a pair of small blue jeans shorts and then anything I could scrounge. Bandoeng was good but nevertheless we'd had to put up with certain deprivations. We'd been through the mill.

When we arrived at Changi, it was unreal, the conditions that these fellows were in. They were just soldiering on as if it was just another club. They all had regulation haircuts, they had uniforms still in relatively good condition. They hadn't been out on hard working parties, the things we'd experienced. They were still on parade. Broomsticks for guns and all that sort of stuff. Of course we met a lot of mates there, too, and they didn't think like that, they just had to go along with it.

Why do you think Weary failed to report Galleghan when he returned to Australia?
I think he found more urgent things to talk about. It wasn't worth the fuss. He was big-minded, he wasn't little-minded, and only if it had served a purpose would he have done that. But by the end of the war, you can imagine, he was fed up with it and possibly he didn't want to include it in the diaries if he did say anything. But he certainly didn't press charges.

Bill Haskell spoke of the state of mind of the prisoners they encountered in Changi.

THE BLOKES FROM Singapore, for an entire division to be taken prisoner, you know, they were feeling it. It was kind of light relief when they realised a boat-load of blokes from the Middle East had been taken prisoner, too, and I don't think they felt quite so bad about it. (laughs) Funny, isn't it? Because it's an awful feeling to be taken prisoner you know. No one joins up to become a prisoner of war.

On 20 January 1943, Weary and Dunlop Force, the 878 Australians under his command, boarded railway cattle trucks and began the long trip north into Thailand. On 24 January, in Ban Pong, they were herded onto lorries which took them to Tarsau, and they continued, finally on foot, to Konyu, where they set about establishing a camp on 25 January. Dunlop Force were the first Australians to arrive in Thailand.
Prisoners were being assembled in work camps up and down the 415-kilometre stretch along which the Japanese planned to build the Burma–Thailand Railway. The Japanese were

winning the war at this stage, but their ships carrying men and supplies to the Burma front were vulnerable. Their answer was to connect Bangkok in Thailand with Rangoon in Burma by rail. Australians had already arrived in Burma where they began creating cuttings, felling trees, clearing a path through the jungle. British, American and Dutch prisoners of war and Asian forced labourers were also put to work along the line. In the end the death toll stood at 13 000 Australian, British, American and Dutch prisoners of war, and an estimated 70 000 Asian forced labourers.

Work on the railway itself began in October 1942 and from March until October 1943, Weary Dunlop was based at the Hintok Mountain camp.

After the two ends of the railway joined at Konkoita in October 1943, the extreme pressure on the prisoners was relieved. For Weary, the end of the railway meant the end of Hintok camp. He left Hintok for Tarsau in October, then on to Chungkai in January, before stopping briefly in Tamuang in May. He then went on to the hospital camp Nakom Patom in June 1944, where he remained until the end of the war.

At the conclusion of the railway, some of the healthier prisoners were shipped to Japan to work in the coal mines and other industries. The remaining prisoners formed work parties to maintain the railway, build roads and bridges and other tasks. Allied bombing during 1944 and 1945 added a new danger to an already perilous existence.

Tom Uren, *the former federal Labor minister, was with Weary Dunlop on the railway for eighteen months. On Weary's death in 1993, he wrote the following tribute.*

HE WAS THE tallest tree in the forest. He was a light and a beacon of hope to his fellow prisoners of war in those dark days of 1943 and 1944 on the Burma-Thailand railway . . . He had served as a medical officer in the early part of World War II in Tobruk, the Middle East and Syria. When Australia was under threat of invasion by the Japanese in late 1941 and early 1942, Prime Minister John Curtin recalled our military forces stationed in the Middle East. One brigade of troops to which Colonel Edward Dunlop was attached, was diverted to Java.

Weary Dunlop was taken a prisoner of war on Java in early 1942. In late 1942, he was transferred from Java to the Burma–Thailand Railway via Singapore. I first met Lt-Col. Weary Dunlop on 26 January 1943, at Konyu Camp on the infamous Burma-Thailand Railway. I served for the next one and a half years under his leadership. The major portion of it being at the Hintok mountain camp.

The Japanese set out to build a railway from Bampong in Thailand to Moulmein in Burma to maintain the supply of goods and communications to the Japanese military forces in Burma. The railway was built because the Japanese were vulnerable to our naval attacks on their shipping lines. The Japanese shipping route went around Singapore and up the west coast of the Malay Peninsular where they were prey to British and United States submarine and air attack.

In Hintok mountain camp, where I spent most of the time while we were building the railway, Weary Dunlop's leadership made an awesome impact. He was an inspiration not only to our camp but to prisoners of war along the whole length of the railway line. Under Weary Dunlop's leadership we were living by the principle of the fit looking after the sick, the young looking after the old. And we collectivised our incomes. Our medical orderlies and officers were paid an allowance. The men who worked on the railway were also paid a small wage. This was a sham kept up by the Japanese to save face under the Geneva Convention.

In our camp the officers and medical orderlies paid the greater portion of their allowances into a central fund. The men who worked on the railway did likewise. Weary would send our people out to deal with traders to buy drugs and food for our needy and sick.

Although Australians tended to fare better and had a higher rate of survival than prisoners from the United Kingdom and other countries, not all Australian camps were like ours. Largely due to the efforts of Weary, the survival rate of other prisoner of war camps could not be compared with ours. Weary Dunlop's medical team was magnificent but the man was an inspiration not only to the medical people but also to the military officers who served with us. My experience serving under Weary Dunlop had an enormous impact on my life.

Even after the war, Weary continued to serve his former mates by imploring the government to understand the plight of the former Japanese POWs. He also built bridges of friendship with our Asian neighbours; with the Thais, the Malays, the Chinese and his wartime enemy the Japanese. He always looked forward. There was no progress in hate, he believed.

He was not only a great Australian, he was a great citizen of the human race.

BILL HASKELL: Weary was a shy bloke, you had to strain to hear him, but if you know you're in control of a situation, and you can control and instruct people, it's still very good if you can come over as being shy, he wasn't the bombastic type.

I think Ray Parkin summed it up when he said, 'Weary could get more from the men with a smile than an army of blooming colonels wielding big sticks.' The blokes would do anything for him. He just had that quiet, assured way. 'Do as I do, not do as I say,' that was Weary. He gave confidence. He looked assured and he was assured and he was just brimful of confidence.

RAY PARKIN:. He held us together with his morale. In the old language, you'd call him a brick. He'd put up with anything. Not long-suffering but enduring is perhaps the better word. When blokes would complain, just his example would shame you. He never preached a sermon on it, he was just doing it. It was that example.

When we shifted camps, he had much more than he could carry with his equipment and books. He'd be trying to carry the lot and blokes would say, 'Come on, give us a bit of this and a bit of that,' and they'd take it. A bit further along the track, you might find he'd picked up a bloke staggering a bit and he'd taken this bloke's pack. And he wouldn't do it to say, 'Look what I'm doing,' he'd have to do it surreptitiously, otherwise they'd be taken off him.

Was Weary the perfect person for that situation?
It's what Laurens van der Post and I used to call confluing – flowing together. I'd rather use that term. I believe it has a Chinese origin – they call it the togetherness of things.

When you say he was the perfect man – well, we all know he was nowhere near perfect, that's what made him real. No, he was a man for all seasons in a way, yet he was the man for this particular season. I can't even say he was a man of his time because really, he was a bit old-fashioned at heart. Well, what are now supposedly old-fashioned values, but I don't think the real virtues ever change with time. They're still the same, and the vices likewise. It's just that the vices become more popular and the virtues less popular, that's the only difference.

BILL HASKELL: When we did all that early walking and Weary had that thumping great valise of his full of stuff –
KEITH FLANAGAN: – 250 pounds.
BILL: And he humped it all the way.
KEITH: You see when we went into the jungle, we had our whole life-support systems on our back. We left our big kitbags on the wharf, so it was just what we could pack. Everything we had was to last us for three-and-a-half years. Weary had this officer's valise and sidepacks as well. The officer's valise was so heavy that only somebody like Weary could lift the damn thing. I think Blue helped him.
BILL: Blue wouldn't have been able to carry that.
KEITH: That had all his operating gear. There had been some criticism of an officer carrying a valise – seemingly with all his pyjamas and things like that – and of course what was in it was medicine and equipment.

It was at Konyu campsite that I started to get to know Weary. We went down there and we were hacking out these great bamboos to make huts. I already had dysentery on the way up there, and I had malaria. As far as I remember they only had the one bell tent, and that was the hospital and I was in it. I used to dream of cold rainwater and crystal jugs but all you'd get was the boiled River Kwai laden with bamboo smoke.

Then in the middle of the night a bloke went down, Private 'IXL' Jones, with a perforated duodenum. This was about midnight and there we are in the middle of the jungle, no lights, no facilities, nothing. That's when my morale sort of sank. I thought, Christ, what chance has he got? What chance have any of us got? And then they bundled us out of that tent and they built an operating table out of bamboo slats tied up with a bit of vine in the middle. They borrowed a hurricane lamp and a torch from the Japs and they rolled up the sides of the tent and built roaring bamboo fires and boiled kerosene tins of water. Then Weary emptied his valise which was so bloody heavy. There was all his operating gear, his anaesthetic, his books and Christ knows what. He operated on this bloke for about two or three hours, and in the morning the bloke was alive. They kept him on that operating table, and to make bloody sure he survived, they fed him on eggs and milk and everything they could get. Because he was a symbol, you know. Weary said, 'Well, it was not a great operation,' but it was in the circumstances. It was the sense of purpose.

I thought, Great, these people can handle these things. We're not alone. And I don't think things ever got quite as bad again. From that moment. Because you had somebody like Weary, and of course the other doctors too. My particular doctor was Arthur Moon. He was a beautiful man. I reckon he saved my life and he probably saved my foot. I call him a saint's saint. It was Weary who used to say that he shuddered when the Japs belted into Arthur Moon because it seemed somehow like sacrilege, you know?

BLUE BUTTERWORTH: At Konyu, there was no tobacco. We were smoking leaves, fine leaves, and blokes were starting to knock one another about. You'd get in a queue to get a bit of rice and a bloke would try to get in front or he stood alongside of you. It's not your so-and-so turn and bang, bang, bang.

So Weary got us all out on parade and he said, 'Right oh, you chaps, we're doing our best to get you tobacco. If you want to have a go at someone, have a go at me.' We all loved him for that.

And when he was giving a needle, when cholera came, they gave us all injections, and Weary used to stand there and he'd go like that. (He plunges an imaginary needle into his buttocks.) And you'd see blokes as big as Weary, wah. They'd fall over.

Was it that he didn't suffer pain?

No, it wasn't that. He did. Oh, they belted hell out of him. Oh yeah, they had him down. One time he didn't salute a Nip. The Nip was having a bath in a 44-gallon drum. They used to build a fire underneath and they had a wooden trestle inside the drum. You'd see the steam coming out of it while they were washing. Weary went by without stopping to bow to him and of course that's the worse thing you could do.

He put on a turn and he was trying to knock Weary over and, once again, Weary's boxing ability saved him a lot. They used to call Weary Doctor Number One. When he did his first operation in Konyu, the Nips on the guard really took to him, what a great bloke he was. Always Number One Doctor. *Ichimai.*

I would work on the railway – the batman part was done in the camps by older men, to protect them – then I'd go in and I'd be doing extra work because I felt that the shining light was there and it was my duty. I could be in the surgery, I had the run of everything, I could go wherever I wanted – just magic, you know?

In the early days when blokes started to die, they might have a post-mortem. Where we used to do that was a room, believe it or not, shaped something like a coffin and it had no electric light in it, only a little tungsten light. So I had to be there. I had the belt on and the battery and the head light strapped around my forehead. Because where the scalpel went I had to have the light on it.

You just got tough – till you saw your mates go. You'd go out to work, come back in and see the bed boards with bits and pieces missing and they'd been taken off and burnt. Then you'd go down quick smart.

Cliff Moss, the secretary of the Murray Goulburn Ex-Prisoners of War Association since 1973, is one of the 'Numurkah Mob', a group of young men from the Numurkah region who, in 1940, enlisted together in the AIF and were captured as part of the 4th Anti-tank Regiment in Malaya in 1942.

I FIRST MET Weary in Thailand in September '43 when I was shifted up to Hintok. There were several Hintok camps and God knows which one this was. But he was there at this camp and at that time there weren't many men that were fit to work. Very few. An awful mess, this camp was, mud up to your hocks and people crook everywhere.

I must say, when I first saw him I was very disappointed. I'd heard about what a wonderful bloke this Dunlop was and I'd never believed what they said. I thought, No man could be as good as that. I was on sick parade because I had a little bit of an ulcer on my foot, I was in the queue and he walked in. He'd been to some other camp, and this long, skinny, dreamy look-ing bloke came in and I thought, God almighty, this is surely not the great Dunlop, is it?

But there was one incident in Hintok that I was in and it was written in his diaries, and naturally his memory is not exactly the same as mine. Of course I had the complication of being sick. You were either light sick, where you were liable to do a few duties, or you were what they called heavy sick and you didn't work. If you were heavy sick, you didn't get paid but some of the light sick people could be sent to work. They used to line up every day and there'd be fifty or sixty or more. The Japanese guard Okada was in charge of the party. Dunlop spent a long time with Okada [Sergeant Okada, aka 'Dr Death'] and he had a lot of battles with him. Okada would say. 'I want forty men to go to work.'

Other doctors would be in charge of this parade and if Okada said these men had to go to work, that's about the number that went. They'd argue and fight with him but he'd beat them. This particular day, I'm on the thing and Okada says I want thirty men and Dunlop says, 'You can have ten. Don't be bloody ridiculous.' And they'd argue and fight away and Dunlop just didn't budge. He'd say, 'Ten men, that's all you're going to get.' Okada went into a long screed about what a shocking doctor he must be and how such-and-such a camp had all sorts of men and there were hardly any sick at all. My recollection of what actually happened then was Okada said, 'Why are these men sick?' Dunlop didn't answer that. He pointed to the cemetery, where there were several hundred graves, and he said, 'Why are those men there?'

Okada just walked away, that was the end of the argument. Just as simple as that. But no other doctor could do that. Ten men went to work.

BILL HASKELL: Weary was a man of the moment, one in a million. The construction of the railway coincided with one of the wettest monsoon periods on record. At Weary's camp at Hintok, it rained for 110 days of which forty-three were full wet days. The camp worked for ninety-three days without rest. It was at least four miles from the camp to the railway and we usually walked both ways in darkness through a sea of mud. The rail track was blasted through deep stone cliffs with cuttings connected by long embankments and in one section a huge three-tier trestle bridge was constructed from timber hewn on the site. The work would have been difficult for fit men, well fed and well shod.

You hear these days of men working their fingers to the bone, that it's back-breaking work, but you just cannot imagine what the blokes up there went through. Not only did you have the terrific amount of work but you had all the tropical diseases to contend with and you had brutal blokes who'd knock you down as soon as look at you. They'd hit you with anything they had. We were putting these cuttings through and they used to dynamite twice a day. It was gelignite, not dynamite, and there were casualties – they were indiscriminate the way they'd send these huge salvos of fracture up, and so there were constant injuries from that and people breaking down. Some poor devils wouldn't get back until one or two in the morning, but until the last bloke came in you could bet your bottom dollar Weary would be there. And he'd be trying to work out who he was going to get out of going the next day, as well as attending to them.

And then of course he had the cholera visiting him and that was work on its own. The Nips were dead scared of cholera and they consigned the cholera patients to what we called Cholera Gulch, which was away from the main camp, and they put them under a miserable tent fly, not a tent but a tent fly, water cascading down. Old Weary would be bent over administering to them, changing the drips.

Weary was both camp commander and doctor surgeon. He fought the Nips every day to protect his sick and he battled on even when he was ill himself. His fight against cholera was one of the epics of the railway. One of the other officers, Jock Clarke devised a still which produced distilled water for making the saline for intravenous drips. With this, the cholera death rate dropped from around 100 per cent to forty per cent.

Weary spent long hours in the cholera compound. I reckon that for a two-month period, he couldn't have got more than two hours sleep a night. The medicos were subjected to the full blast of the Nips' wrath and they were superb.

Major Bill Wearne was Weary Dunlop's second-in-command in Java and Thailand and he recalled the 'speedo' period on the railway at the Hintok Mountain camp when cholera struck, as the grimmest period of captivity.

Brigadier Bill Wearne retired from the Australian Army in 1964 and he spoke to me from his home in Buderim, Queensland.

I THINK WEARY understood the Japanese. I often wondered why they didn't really remove him and I think that was because they had great admiration for him, first as a surgeon and also for his general demeanour – his size and shape and intellect.

One of the things we tried to do was to not follow the Japanese pattern. Quite a number of our people said, 'Look at the way they treat their own troops, how can we expect anything better?' and Weary and I said, 'That's nonsense.' We tried to bend the Japanese to our way of living. It wasn't always possible but it was a worthwhile aim.

During those 'speedo' days of construction on the railway, we were trying to enable the troops to take as much rest as possible, not that we succeeded that well. And we tried to keep them fed, by bringing in extra eggs, fruit, when we could get it.

The Thais were awfully good at bringing stuff up the river and we used to pick up supplies when we could. They were encouraged by the Japanese, I think.

The Japanese are a peculiar people. We eventually got them to let us have quite a few young cattle in the camp. Before that our fellows would knock off the end of the line cattle that went through. They were horrible beasts, poor old scraggy tail-enders, but of course it was beef and we ate the lot. Except the horns, though I think we even boiled them up with the hooves. The Japanese eventually said they would buy the cattle for us. They said they were embarrassed by our actions.

Weary and I had a tremendous friendship. You had to pull together, those of us who stayed fit in particular. I was one of only one or two people who never got malaria. There was a grim sequence: you got malaria, you couldn't eat, you died.

Weary did get ill but he worked through it. We relieved him of any jobs we could and generally we relieved him of a lot of the routine administrative work.

But he was a man of great energy. He would be playing bridge until midnight and the Japanese would flog him because he had his light on. And he'd be writing notes, and hiding them wherever possible. That was one of the more hair-raising things. He kept his diaries, you see, and there was a penalty of death for that. Jock Clarke [Major J.E.R. Clarke] kept one too. I wasn't a diary-keeper. But it had to be done to include case histories, drawings, records.

Did you find out much about Weary and his background during those days?
No, very little. The time was spent in surviving and trying to help others survive. I don't remember discussing anybody's past. Some people could get terribly depressed. A lot of people really

couldn't face the fact that they might be living under these conditions for two years or more. So really, we lived very much in the present.

Mental strength played an enormous part in survival and that's what Weary had plenty of, you know. He was tremendously strong, physically and mentally.

He was the obvious choice, with his giant stature and his intelligence, for the position of authority in the camps. The aim of the whole operation once we were taken prisoner was to bring home as many men as possible. There wasn't any opposition to Weary as commander, except from Black Jack Galleghan back in Changi and that didn't amount to much.

It must have been appalling when cholera struck in June, 1943.
Oh, it was pretty grim. The early days were terrible, when our doctors carried out their operations in appalling circumstances and the men were so ill, and then the cholera arrived.

The fight against cholera was greatly helped by the production of distilled water, wasn't it?
Well, a still is a fairly simple thing to put together. Jock Clarke, who was a dentist, was the main operator and it was a normal still to distil water and alcohol. The alcohol was used as antiseptic, it didn't taste all that good. It was very much a team effort. The doctors we had were a very good lot. Ewan Corlette, Arthur Moon, Tim Godlee. They were extremely good. Weary just stood out because he was bigger, that sort of thing.

He was more or less forced into the leadership role. He would stand up to the Japanese and say, 'No, that's wrong. What you should do is this.' He couldn't stop them of course, when they were taking men out to work who were too sick to work. But he would try, as we all did.

Does the Weary Dunlop legend stem back to those bleak days?
He was highly regarded by everybody, there's no question of
that. He did the right things, and he took it further than that.
He did the most extraordinary things. In one instance, he
plucked these pieces of wireless from a truckload of vegetables
in front of the guards and rushed off at high speed screaming
out 'Medical supplies'. Anybody else would have been executed
on the spot. He acted so quickly. He saw the situation, saw the
radio pieces and acted, in a split second. That sort of thing.

Did Weary tempt fate?
I don't think so. I think he took calculated risks. He was no fool.

*The artist **Jack Chalker** was a gunner in the Royal Artillery.
He worked with Weary Dunlop in the camps, as a physio-
therapist and as an artist, documenting the disease and hardship
alongside the many ingenious attempts to overcome them.*
   *He and I sat in his studio overlooking the Somerset
countryside. He had put aside the portrait he was working on to
talk about the man to whom he dedicated his own book,* Burma
Railway Artist.

Did Weary's reputation precede him in the camps?
Oh, it did. My first working camp was in Konyu, up-country on
the railway. I'd been working in a labour camp in Singapore for
a few months, Havelock Road. Things weren't good – they are
not good in any prison camp – but they were a damn sight better than later because we had contact with the outside world,
with the working parties in town during the day. We could steal
stuff and we could make the odd contact, flog a bit of whatever
we could scrounge. But then we went up-country. We had a five-

day journey in cattle trucks. It was awful because a lot of people already had dysentery and malaria and we were crammed into those things, about thirty-two to a truck. Only a few people could sit down at any one time. It was for five days and five nights and it got pretty smelly, quite apart from the discomfort.

Then I marched up to Konyu. Again there were five or six appalling days when a lot of people fell out because they were ill. We got there and we lived rough and built the camp. I worked there for a while but went down quickly with dengue fever, malaria and dysentery – all the usual things that everybody had. I was pretty sick.

But then I went up to Hintok with these two Japanese. I think they wanted to lay a telephone line. That was the first whiff I had of Weary. Things were pretty tough there. It was a terrible situation for them, digging those cuttings which were absolute murder, and cholera broke out later. It was an Australian camp, the Hintok camp, and everybody talked about Weary not only as a friend but as a kind of godlike creature who fought like the clappers for everybody to try and defend them against all this nonsense. He was this rather good-looking, rangy, tall character. He was so nice, and obviously absolutely loved by everybody. That was what was so nice – people would have done anything for Weary.

I'd been doing some drawings in Singapore first of all. I had some records of the place there which I took up-country with me. And then I made some more in Konyu, during the time when I was sick. I was too tired otherwise when I was working. Then a Korean guard came in and found a whole load of drawings and we had a hell of a time for a couple of days. He tore most of those up except for two – one I use on the frontispiece of my book, 'Working Men, Konyu Camp, October 1942'. It's symbolic for me because they survived a pretty nasty two days, to say the least of it.

I got sick after a while. I had dysentery, and went down to Chungkai – heavy sick. There I met the Canadian surgeon Captain Jacob Markowitz, and worked with him, making some more drawings. I managed to get these through, strangely enough. I had a false bottom and sides to my little haversack and we carried some bamboo, the drawings were in that, it was rather like carrying this exploding bomb.

Marko was a wonderful, generous and delightful man. A brilliant man. He was the first of the experimental surgeons. The first man to make successful organ transplants in animals. He started taking the first of the legs off. I worked with him on that making surgical notes and records, because he was developing a new system of flaps for thigh amputation which were more comfortable. He had this kind of marvellous mind. It was a bit like a terrible form of *MASH* in some way because he had a beautiful Canadian voice. I remember the first leg amputation I saw. We didn't have an operating theatre, and he was sawing away at this leg on the bamboo racking, saying, 'Oh let's get it arf, it's better with it arf.' Of course the patient was conscious, because they had spinals. This was at the end of a hut, and two men came up and were looking with horror at Marko sawing away and suddenly the tourniquet broke and an enormous jet of blood shot up all over them. They ran off and Marko said, 'Well, that will teach them.' It was something dreadful but something terribly funny.

Then Weary came down and that was absolutely marvellous, because the sick camp was really in a state of chaos. People were piling into it. I think it was in the hands of an absolute idiot. Some dirty, utterly irresponsible, inane British colonel was in charge and Weary came down and really had to turn this man inside out. It was Weary who properly established Chungkai as a sick camp. He turned it inside out in no time. And then we began to see the measure of this man – his kindliness and unceasing work. He would work almost around the clock for everybody. He seemed to be utterly tireless, yet he had ulcers, he was often ill, but in no way allowed it to interfere with his work for others. You quickly got this message from Weary.

I then began to realise fully the importance of making records. It was Weary and Marko, but largely Weary, who woke me up to it. It had always been an indulgence that I wanted to record things. There were landscapes, there were camps, there were places that I knew, there were incidents, horrible and otherwise, that we got down on a small scale. But then we realised that it was important to keep these records, otherwise there wouldn't be any visual records at all. And so I began to work closely with Weary.

Weary was courageous beyond words in front of the Japanese. On one or two occasions he would actually quote Shakespeare to them. He was going to be beaten up, but to stop them he would quote Shakespeare or something from Homer in Greek. You just couldn't believe that anybody could have the guts and the presence of mind to do this in that situation where all it did was hold them up a little bit from knocking him about. They didn't like him because he was tall, and they made him kneel down to beat him up sometimes. He would come back into theatre and say, 'Oh well, they've done it again, Jack' and we'd wipe him down, and he'd just go on operating for the rest of the day. Just like that.

I think that it's difficult, really, to describe properly the hideous situations we all were in. He'd go to the commandant to try to stop this bestiality, try to get more medical supplies because there were hardly any, knowing full well that they'd probably knock him about, which they did. And to do that for us all the time was pretty good, you know. Nobody could do more. When you think about people being given VCs or any awards, he deserves about ten for what he did. It's a build-up but I do mean it, I mean it very sincerely. This is somebody that you just don't meet in this world.

In all the time I knew him, he obviously was as pleased as any of us are at praise. Fine. He was just a normal, natural person. But I saw no exhibition of him actually using it as a bravado thing. If there was any kind of bravado about it, I think he wanted to show the Japanese that he was not going to be mangled by them and destroyed by them, and that was a good thing because it was a good example to us. I won't say he was impervious to pain but I think that on the whole he had the mental capacity to stand pain more than a lot of people. He expected it and he accepted and rode it and got through.

What affect did his behaviour have on the men?

It certainly made me feel, an ordinary man – I was a gunner, I wasn't an officer – it made me feel, Okay, we mustn't let him down. If he can do this and he can stand this and he can behave like this then it's up to us to try and behave well ourselves, to get through this better, and to think positively. I think that was the key to survival, all the time, because once you began to think in a negative way you could just drop in a hole almost instantly, and there were a lot of people who did that.

I was originally going to do medicine, but I changed direction to do art. It saved a lot of lives, (laughs) me doing art instead. But I had this interest. I'd never seen people literally commit suicide mentally before. I was young, damn it all, I was only about twenty-two or twenty-three. The Tamils did this an awful lot. The physical conditions, clinically, were not sufficient for the patient to die but if they had dysentery and immediately believed they had cholera, nothing on the face on this earth would stop them and they'd die in about forty-eight hours. They'd just do it.

It happened to one or two British people. There was a man in our regiment who also sort of gave up. He had a bad ulcer. I'd had a bad beating up – they'd kicked a great big hole between my eyes and I couldn't see. I was put next to an Aussie who'd just had his leg off and opposite us, in the middle on these bamboo racks, was this chap in my regiment who wasn't very bright. He had a bad ulcer but it was granulating and they'd saved his leg and he would have survived.

He was sitting up and rocking, as a lot of those ulcer patients did – the pain, you just rocked and rocked – and in the night he was saying, 'Oh, I'm going to die, I'm going to die,' and I remember this Aussie getting up on his elbow, he'd had his leg off that day, and he said, 'Christ, mate, if you're going to die, hurry up and do it, I want some sleep.' And within about two hours this bloke was dead. I remember this Aussie saying to me, 'Christ, it's the last thing anybody ever said to him.' He was upset about it. But it was an interesting phenomena, because it worked and it worked so fast.

It's really only on reflecting back that you see the strange and very salutary effect people like Weary and Marko, particularly Weary, had on you. He was in the camp and it was getting better. He was organising, he was standing up for us, and you thought that in those conditions, there was a lot of hope there. That I think was a very precious thing under those circumstances, and a thing that so many of us remembered, particularly Australians, who were closer to him than I was.

There were many other wonderful doctors in Burma and Thailand. Why is Weary remembered so well?
Well, my experience was limited. Other people were doing marvellous things elsewhere, but Chungkai was the first of the big sick camps. They carried this terrifying load of heavy-sick people

pouring in, hundreds and hundreds dying at a time with these terrible tropical ulcers, legs rotting. It was Weary – also Marko but mainly Weary – who reorganised that camp so quickly and so well.

He had the ability to do his surgery and, at the same time, do battle with the Japanese, making repeated requests for help. It was a pretty heavy load. It wasn't just charm he had, it was a real caring attitude and a tremendous strength of mind and all of the organisational capability and the surgical capability. I think this is where he really shone perhaps more than anybody. And he did seem to care for most people.

It's an inexplicable thing. So many people responded to him so easily. And we knew he was sincere. There were other medical officers who were equally sincere and nice but who hadn't the charisma, hadn't the power, the energy, to cope with these things. They were superb when faced with almost impossible situations, but Weary seemed to power right through this terrible mess and make sense of it. And that doesn't denigrate the surgical capabilities of other people. There was Arthur Moon, for instance, and all sorts of Australians. In Nakom Patom, he was working with Bert Coates.

Somehow I was so grateful that I was with so many Australians. I enjoyed the Australians and I began to feel part of them. It was an impertinence in a way but somehow they would get things done, I mean actually working. It was always Aussies that would make some brew of something-or-other tea. I was with English friends but I so admired the Aussies and I learnt a lot from them. This applied also to the Australian surgeons, because that group of Australian surgeons working with Weary, they were damned good, and they were easier with us. You could talk to some of these fellows and there wasn't the kind of bullshit of the British Army – all those sort of things that inhibited the way people reacted to one another.

After the war, the Aussies treated me rather like a fringe Anzac, which was the nicest thing that could happen as far as I was concerned. It was a great privilege for me. Somehow my whole memory is of the Australians handling me so well. Led by Weary but with a team of people who could laugh and talk to you in an easy way. You could always go to them – that was part of the Weary ethos.

You went back to Thailand with Weary in 1985. You must have seen many changes.
There's a lot of magic still there but they've made it so commercial now. It's totally different. It's a holiday resort for Thais now. There are roads up there. It's so terribly different. When we were there, of course, it was virgin jungle and I think part of the reason why I survived was because I loved looking at it. It was full of the most beautiful birds, white ibis and the most beautiful huge blue kingfishers. It was full of monkeys, and cheetahs came up there. Tiger pug paw marks, and the most exquisite butterflies and lovely, lovely flowers. Those little round orchids which are still growing up there through the rail tracks. Those are nice memories. They're things that are lovely.

I can remember that march up. We were going through a great gully coming down off a hillside in thick jungle and we were terribly ill and terribly tired. But we looked up and down this gully, it was full of thousands of butterflies, the most beautiful butterflies, and these are lovely things to see, aren't they?

I had a friend who was a naturalist and also a friend who was a geneticist and they made the whole thing sing because there was so much to see, so much to look at, and I was new to this. I was a young man, I hadn't seen jungle before in my life, but then it all became rather wonderful so it wasn't all horrible.

It was a great asset to all of us in that sense, because it was full of beauty. And that river was lovely, not so much during the monsoon season – then it came tearing down – but in the dry season it was exquisite. Absolutely exquisite.

At Konyu, I crawled down to the edge of the river. It was the end of the monsoon, the rain had stopped. I was with another man and we lay there in the reeds and we watched this blue kingfisher diving for fish. It was heavenly. I can remember that hour or two there as being so lovely. Mind you, it was the release from the work, too. We were there on our own and nobody molested us. Just to hear the water going through the reeds, and these beautiful birds and monkeys who were hooting, and these gibbons. I remember it as one thing I would never have missed. It was beautiful – it sounds daft, but it was. I think it was the release – it didn't matter to me then whether we died or not. We were completely relaxed. He died the next day, he had diphtheria. I didn't know he had it, he was frothing at the mouth a bit, but I didn't know. It was magical. You leave a lot of yourself there.

Stanley Gimson, QC was a British officer and artist who helped Weary ensure the conditions of the camps were recorded. He now lives in the heart of Edinburgh and spoke to me over lunch at the club to which he used to take Weary for meals.

WE WERE IN Konyu British camp and the Australian camp was about a quarter of a mile upstream from ours. I remember seeing this very tall figure striding into the camp. At that time we were rather unfortunate in our own senior officers, they were a pretty disreputable-looking pair, and the camp was a gloomy one. Weary comments on this in his war diary, that he was a bit shocked by what he found. It was just good to see anybody who obviously had the energy and the drive that he showed.

I don't think I saw him again, other than a glimpse, until he went down to Chungkai, which was something like a year later. By that time he had acquired the tremendous reputation of being a successful doctor, and he came with the reputation of having halved the death rate at Tarsau. Whether that's mathematically correct, I've no idea, but he certainly had made a tremendous impact and the effect of his coming was simply to raise morale all around. Everybody was inclined to say, 'Now that Weary's here, things will improve.' And they did indeed.

I think that impression came from the fact that he was a stickler, first of all, for hygiene, which was so terribly important. The other thing was his awareness of the importance of mosquito suppression, to try and reduce the incidence of malaria. Everybody was conscious of this, and groups were formed with the duty of trying to eliminate standing water. Others were busy renewing the latrines, making them fly-proof, if that was possible and all sorts of things were going on wherever he was.

It was bound to seep through to the troops when he intervened with the management of cookhouses, saying that they could do better. He did have a pretty constant feeling that most things could be done better if people really put their heart into it, and as he appeared to be unsparing of his own time and energy, it all created a tremendous impression of somebody of a particular quality and professional standing who was working hard all the time for the good of the camp.

And in Chungkai, Weary really drove through a plan to increase the amount of pay, particularly of officers' pay, that was deducted in order to keep the hospital supplied as well as was possible. He got through to everyone that the first call on all funds that came into the camp should be for the hospital, and only when its needs were satisfied as much as was possible, should money be distributed to individuals. There had been a degree of contribution of pay from everybody right from the beginning. Of course the pay was pathetically small, as it was based on Japanese army pay, which was peanuts, but it was also subject to absurd deductions. About two-thirds of the pay was taken for housing, clothing and food, which was just sheer robbery. So there was some resistance to an equal sharing out through pay deductions, but that is more or less what Weary achieved.

Chungkai was about half British, quarter Australian and a quarter Dutch. It was a big camp. It eventually went to over 10 000 men, with a great many ill – perhaps two or three thousand in hospital, but many of the others would have been in hospital in any civilised set-up.

We did tend to congregate, drifting together whenever possible. In fact, the hilarious point about it was that we used to try and insist on our national differences. You would find an Englishman and a Scot arguing about something, and failing to agree, and then an Australian would come along and the Englishman and the Scot would then join together and say, 'Of course these hicks from down under, I really don't know how they work,' and at that moment a Dutchman might come along and the three English speakers would say, 'You know, they're weird people, these Dutch,' and then the next would be a Dutch-Eurasian and the man from Holland would say 'Oh, these are strange people.' And then the ultimate was when they saw a Japanese, and they all said, 'Really, there's no difference between us but look at that creature.'

Was the hatred for the Japanese a positive thing, a uniting point?
Yes, I'm sure it was. It was a distrust as much as anything. There wasn't much distrust among the prisoners, except for a few

individuals. I hazarded a guess that out of all the people there, only about one in 200 was quite unable to stop himself stealing or hogging food or acting in an anti-social way. It seemed to be about that number that couldn't keep out of trouble. Everybody else tended to co-operate.

The Australians were, in my view by far the best at looking after their very sick mates. They worked out rosters of hospital visiting and they visited at every moment they were free. There was always somebody going in. Whereas the British rather held back. I always thought we'd got into the state of mind that you didn't visit anyone in hospital unless you had a bunch of chrysanthemums or a bunch of grapes to take, but these hospitals were just . . . I think it was Weary who called it a medieval pest-house.

How did you get involved with Weary?

I had been working as a labourer on the building of the medical centre which included the operating theatre, and I was anxious to do an interior sketch once it was complete and in use. Eventually I went in and sat in the corner of the theatre while he performed an operation. Fortunately for me it took much longer than was anticipated and I was able to do two sketches of Weary operating. I'd been in before and drawn the interior of the theatre in detail and I superimposed the figures.

I showed Weary what I'd been doing and he always expressed an interest. The next time I remember having much contact with him was at Tamuang camp where Ray Parkin was. Weary had taken over Parkin's sketches in order to pass them on among the medical records and he introduced us and asked Parkin to show me what he had done. I was fascinated when Parkin's books came out to see that *Into the Smother* had a number of drawings which corresponded almost exactly to what I tried to record. The comparisons were striking – just the same scenes had appealed to both of us as something that was worth doing. *Into the Smother* is one of the most compelling accounts of what it felt like in the camps.

What was it that made Weary so popular?

It was his easy way, the fact that he had no side at all. He chatted away to everybody. He was very, very open in his relations. Plus the fact, I think, he went about deliberately encouraging people. Making light of their problems, inducing them to feel that things were being done for them, and that had tremendous force with men in this grim circumstance as most of us were. And of course the fact that he took part – if there was any occasion when we were allowed any form of sport, he was there, and it was thought rather unusual for someone in his rank and position to join in, to muck in, and all that made for popularity. The great thing was the way he boosted morale. We were very conscious of this at the time.

The whole impression I have is not associated with incidents so much as the effect of his presence, his presence and his attitude. And the fact that I'm sure no prisoner of war, nobody in the 10 000 in Chungkai, would have hesitated to go and speak to him, because his whole attitude to people was open and welcoming. I reckon if you had any great problem and you saw Weary about to pass, you wouldn't hesitate to say, 'Sir, can you help me?'

Among the doctors we had there, there were two distinct temperaments. There were those who saw every successful case, every case in which they achieved a cure or a partial cure, as an immense victory over tremendous odds, and were cheered by it. There were others who, if you'd probed their minds, would have said, 'Well, we may have saved ten but look at those we can't save,' and their usefulness was reduced by this attitude.

They couldn't convey what Weary conveyed, and that was hope – that you never know what's around the corner, and here we're having successes. It didn't matter how few. He was able to focus on them, whereas others with the best will in the world were just overwhelmed by the losses.

How did you preserve the sketches you made in the camps?

One of the big infantry regiments was going to hide its records and for that purpose they had managed to get hold of four bottles, which I think were French wine bottles from French Indochina, litre-sized. They had four but they only needed three. Major Tony Smith, another man who took a great interest in helping others, passed the fourth over to me, along with, to my astonishment, a rubber cork. I'd never have thought to find that.

So I rolled up all my regimental records, my diary and my sketches, and the wills which some of my friends wrote out, and letters home, which others wrote. I rolled them until they were about the thickness of a cigarette and poked them down.

They filled the bottle in two layers and then we put in the rubber cork, depressed a little down the neck of the bottle. They also had produced a piece of red sealing wax, so I sealed the top with sealing wax and then put a piece of mosquito netting over the top and then poured candle wax over the top of that and handed it to the major, who turned it over to the infantry regiment, and I knew no more.

When the war ended, I was about 150 miles away to the east and I decided that it would be foolhardy to try and go back. We didn't know if the country was peaceful, whether the Japs were wandering around, looking for trouble, and I thought it was better just to forget about the sketches. Then we were flown out to Rangoon. I was in hospital there on my birthday – I was the only person in this particular ward because I had malaria – and an officer walked in and said, 'Is your name Gimson? I think these are yours.' He opened the haversack and spilt out the contents of the bottle.

Alec Young is a retired art teacher, living in Milngavie on the edge of Glasgow. He is another who kept a diary during the war. He was in a Christian group in the camps with two of Weary's medical orderlies, and it was one of these men who put him back in touch with Weary in the 1980s.

MY DIARY WAS an ordinary, small diary, that I had been given as a present by a friend in Norwich early in the war. I had written practically nothing in it, but when we got on the ship I started writing, day to day. Right up from the end of August to November, when we landed at Singapore and went up north. Oddly enough I stopped writing at that particular point until the Japs started to bomb us. They bombed the airport and, of course, Pearl Harbor and I started writing again.

Well, by this time I'm writing in December, so I was practically at the end of the diary. What I did was when I got to the end I went back to the beginning and filled up all the spaces [between the lines]. When I got to the end a second time, I got some paper, cut it to size, sewed it in sections. I was fortunate in having been a battery clerk so I had access to paper. I added sixteen pages, thirty-two – multiples of four. I reckon there was about as much sewn in the diary as there was of the original. It is very confusing to read because it's in bits.

The other thing was pens. Being a battery clerk, I grabbed a gross box of nibs and I grabbed a container of ink powder. Well, the ink powder lasted me right through. The nibs didn't survive the complete imprisonment, although they went pretty far. What I did was I used the back of the nib – you can get a finer line. I was getting something like ninety-five lines to the page, so small that you would require a magnifying glass to re-read it.

We had instructions before we were captured to burn all our records but I copied out all the casualty lists and shoved them in my pocket. I copied them into my diary after I was taken prisoner. One of the things that met me when I got home was a letter from the record officer, asking me for my casualty list.

If the Japs had found my diary, they would have thrown it into the burner, but there was the suggestion that if you had written one and it was found you could be shot. I was never confronted with that, I never thought of it. I was scared at one or two points and I did a stupid thing, I put some oilskin around the diary and buried it for three or four days. When I took it out, the edge of the pages were affected with the damp so I vowed to myself, Well, I'm never going to do that again, and I didn't.

So how did you keep it?
Just between my trousers and the crutch here, I made a little pocket and it could only be entered from the inside. When I was standing to attention for searches or anything, I always kept my legs together.

Did you transcribe it on your return?
When I came back I typed out the diary. It took me about twenty years to do that. I'm no typist. I did it and duplicated it with carbon. I had to use a magnifying glass. My father typed some of it. I didn't really tell him much. I'm sorry now that I

sort of kept quiet on the horrors of prison life. We were almost commanded to keep quiet. We were more or less told to shut up and that it was not only discourteous but it was morally wrong almost to speak about it. You'd frighten the people at home.

I was in a small Christian group in the camps with Des Tarren and Don Thomas, who were orderlies in the Australian Medical Corps and with Weary in Nakom Patom. Through the years I've corresponded with both these men and Des Tarren visited us in 1981. It was during that time he spoke to me about Weary. He said, 'You know Weary kept a diary,' because he knew my diary is in the Imperial War Museum. He said 'You should get in contact with him. He'd be very interested.' So I did just that. From then onwards I had a regular correspondence with Weary, right up to a few months before he died.

29 July, 1986

Dear Alec Young,

I was very touched by your extremely generous gift of Ronald Searle's splendid collection *To the Kwai and Back*.

What a generous man you are! Even the stamps on the package are impressive.

Looking at those Japanese faces depicted by Searle gives me a shiver even today. Strange how the image has changed now that we have them as our best customer! That has become an Australian necessity.

I do hope that you are well and that on some future occasions we can meet and compare notes.

I am now headed into my eightieth year and find it a bit difficult to accept. I am still working as a consultant surgeon, but winding down. Still on many committees and multitudinous activities.

My dear wife Helen has the dreadful Alzheimer complaint and is totally dependent in a nursing home.

She comes to our home for a few hours a week, and I find things rather lonely in a large house mostly on my own. I do have a number of charity parties to warm the place up.

My war diaries are to be launched as a rather ambitious enterprise by Thomas Nelson in October. The Governor General will do the job in Queensland at a big POW reunion.

I really have shrunk from publishing my writings at that time – mainly a military record – everything seen black and white with no shades of grey. So I await the event with some apprehension. Maybe these things would emerge best posthumously. I suppose there will be UK promotion – but whether I'll make it personally in the near future I'm not sure.

Judging by the state of the Australian dollar and by my taxes and expenses, I need to pull my neck in a bit.

I feel rather conscious of the world in general being in a rather sick state, and wonder whether the rush of the Gaderine swine is nearing the abyss – maybe Revelations says it all!

Poor Scotland so victimised over the Commonwealth Games:- a blatant unwarranted injustice. It puzzles me that amongst all the monstrous injustices of the world that South Africa looms so large. I'm for the 'Iron Lady'.

Thank you most generous Alec.

In affection & admiration

'Weary' E.E. Dunlop

*At Tamuang, on the eve of his departure in a work party to Japan, **Ray Parkin** entrusted Weary Dunlop with his drawings*

*and diaries of his time in Java and Thailand. At his home in
Ivanhoe, overlooking the Yarra River, he pointed out some
dry-point drawings on the wall.*

HE BROUGHT BACK all my paintings and drawings and diaries
at considerable risk when I was sent to Japan, you see. And I got
them back in pristine order – the same as I'd given him. I
thought, What can I do to thank a bloke? There's no way of
thanking him. So I made these from the original drawings and
bound them up into a book with handmade paper and an
embossed leather cover. I gave it to him and he used to keep
them at home.

Weary and I used to talk about all sorts of things. When
Weary took charge of my drawings and diaries, he knew we
were due to leave the camp the next day and go down to
Singapore and then on to Japan. I'd taken all the stuff over there
for him and we sat and talked until well into the small hours of
the morning, about all sorts of things, and one of the things we
spoke about was Helen and Thelma. Of course, I was the senior
hand, I'd been married. (laughs)

I knew that he'd been a man of the world, he made no
secret of that – but he was concerned about whether Helen
would bother to wait for him. I said, 'Look, it'll be all right.' We
spoke about how close you get in a marriage. I said, 'Thelma
and I, we get to a situation where I'm you and you're me. And
we can't separate us. We really get that feeling, the inter-
penetration of personalities, until they're bonded.' Weary
brightened up considerably, but I think he wondered if he could
live up to it. And I assured him that it was only a matter of
practice.

From Tamuang, Weary and 500 heavy sick were sent to Nakom Patom, a huge hospital camp built to take 10 000. Weary spent the last fourteen months of the war here, working with the Chief Medical Officer, Lieutenant-Colonel Bert Coates. Visible from the camp was the dome of an enormous Buddhist wat, or temple, four miles way.

The English cricketing writer E.W. Swanton was a colleague of Weary's in Thailand and he wrote this recollection of their time together.

OTHERS WILL HAVE far better credentials than me to write about Sir Edward Dunlop's qualities and achievements as a surgeon. I will therefore confine myself to a personal recollection or two of the man whom I would rank, along with Colonel Philip Toosey of the Hertfordshire Yeomanry, as the two prime heroes of our captivity in Thailand from the autumn of 1942 to the Japanese surrender in August 1945.

We were in Kinsayok at the time of the worst 'speedo' on the Thailand-Burma railway in 1943 when one day I saw the tall figure of Weary standing to attention in the sun outside the Jap command hut. He was being punished probably for some imagined slight, or even for protesting too forcibly about the sending of grievously sick men out to work. There was a pile of bamboo lengths nearby and a Jap or a Korean – I can't remember which – picked up one piece and made to hit Weary with it. Weary snatched it before it struck him and threw it away. This happened again and again amid the laughter of a group of guards. Fortunately the assailant who was, of course, losing face minute by minute was ordered to stop and Weary was released. Such defiance as this might have led to horrible retribution. Luckily this apparently was an unpopular guard among his colleagues. Life with them was utterly unpredictable.

Later Weary and I both found ourselves down-river, first at Tarsau and then in the hospital camp, so called, in the shadow of the Buddhist temple at Nakom Patom. I there contracted polio, the damage confined by the grace of God to my left shoulder. Weary put my arm into a horizontal splint for a while, but the nerve had died, and there is no raising of my left arm from then to now, a minor inconvenience which only became tiresome when on the cricket field a catch came wide to my left.

Talking of cricket, if it does not desecrate the name, we improvised a form of it when the railway work became lighter, using a tennis ball soaked in water and a crude bat made by sawing a board to something like proper dimensions. The climax came with a 'Test Match' played before hundreds of Poms and Aussies at Nakom Patom with me and Weary respectively captains of England and Australia. The match was immortalised in an article by me entitled 'Cricket under the Japs' which appeared in the 1946 edition of the *Wisden Cricketers' Almanack*. (It is the Bible of the game, for those not conversant with it.)

England batted first and made a good score. Then

'With the Australian innings comes sensation. Captain "Fizzer" Pearson, of Sedbergh and Lincolnshire, the English fast bowler, is wearing BOOTS! No other cricketer has anything on his feet at all, the occasional flint being accepted as part of the game. The moral effect of these boots is tremendous.

Captain Pearson bowls with shattering speed and ferocity, and as each fresh lamb arrives for the slaughter the stumps seem more vast, the bat even punier. One last defiant cheer from "the Hill" when their captain, Lieut.-Colonel E.E. Dunlop, comes in, another and bigger one from the English when his stumps go flying.'

Yes, there were lighter moments, for those not too ill to enjoy them.

I toured Australia nine times in all after the war, and as the succession of MCC teams came to Melbourne, it was a joy to be able to renew my friendship with Weary. We talked not only of mutual friends made as POWs but also of those he knew as a postgraduate student at St Mary's Hospital in its palmy sporting days of the 1930s when he was a contemporary among others of that great all-round South African sports-man, 'Tuppy' Owen-Smith. Weary achieved membership of the famous Barbarians, and might well have won more rugby football caps for Australia if he had been available at the right time.

He and I and Helen, his adored and adoring wife, used to play golf at the Peninsula Country Club outside Melbourne. Those hands so precise with the surgeon's knife were much less so with driver and iron. He laughed as his ball flew off into the deepest rough: for him the game was just exercise and an unex-acting social diversion.

Weary's knighthood must have given deep pleasure to every POW and to those who met him medically in many coun-tries. It was completely characteristic, of course, that he was active in the cause of humanity to within a few days of his death. He was a legend of our times.

Jack Chalker credits Weary with saving his life by taking him down to Nakom Patok.

I WORKED WITH him in Chungkai and then he very kindly kept me with him. I mean I was sick but he took me down to Nakom Patom, the final base hospital camp and had I not gone down there with him, I'd have probably gone up-country again and I wouldn't have survived. I don't think so. Or I would have been sent on to Japan like a lot of my friends and half of them drowned. So that was a big move for me and I owe Weary that.

When we got down to Nakom Patom I worked very closely with him. Surgically and in practical terms. I ran the physiotherapy unit and did a lot of medical drawings there, a lot of medical records, quite apart from my own thing. He had a little sort of a stool rather than table, made of rough bits of wood with a false top to it and in that he kept some of my drawings and I kept the rest in my pack and in the ground.

I was once with him during one of the searches. We were sitting together, it was very hot and I was sweating like a pig, you know, I felt like rushing to the loo. He sort of looked at me and we knew exactly what each other was thinking, hoping everything was going to be all right. The Japs were tearing everything apart and it was all right, you know. I got a lot of strength from him. These are difficult moments (laughs) and it was lovely, you know. I remember these things about him so much, in those times. He would sort of look at you and smile and say OK, it's going to be all right, kind of thing. And you needed somebody to say that to you.

Tensions rose as the end of the war approached. The prisoners knew that the war in Europe had ended and presumed it was only a matter of time until the Japanese capitulated. But what would happen to them in the meantime was a matter of great speculation. Weary made plans that in the event of a massacre, selected prisoners – about 100 in all – would escape and notify the outside world. Finally, as rumours of the atom bombs reached the camp, on 16 August the camp commander

*summoned Lieutenent-Colonel Bert Coates and the other officers
and declared the war over, and said: 'The maintenance of
discipline is your own responsibility. . .'*

JACK CHALKER: Just before the end, Weary knew that we were
going to be shot. Nakom Patom was a very big camp, of about
7-8000 sick and heavy sick, and a large graveyard too, which we
were filling all the time. Down one side of the camp, the
Japanese had dug a huge pit with a big mound which the sentries
used to patrol and we knew this mound was going to be a grave.
An enormous grave. They'd put machine-gun posts in this.

I only knew by chance because of this little man, one of the
Korean guards, who was actually apologising for this situation. He
used to come and get a man in the hut to play him Japanese tunes
on the violin he had there. He was a generous little guard who
never beat anyone up and professed to be a Christian. It was very
strange. He was one of the nice guards and they were very rare.
He informed us that we were due to be shot. Anyway, we knew
what it was about but Weary knew before we did. He was organising, with Colonel Coates, I think, and with Major Moon and
others, a group of people he thought would be capable of using
primitive weapons. Weary had to keep that very close to himself.

We were going to be shot if there was an invasion of the
Malay Peninsula. The whole area was alive with Japanese
troops anyway. We didn't know then that some American paratroopers had been dropped into the jungle not so far from there
and other camps and these were the first people we saw about a
week after Hiroshima and Nagasaki. They came in.

There was a group of Chinese irregulars together with
some commandos and some paratroopers in the jungle nearby
and they came in about five or six days afterwards. That was the
first jeep I'd ever seen. It was all very strange.

Weary was hastily trying to organise medical supplies, and trying to get some of the desperately sick out, because people were still dying. He whizzed off down to Bangkok in a Japanese car he commandeered. He had a big fight for that. After about two or three weeks the Americans flew in a lot of food and medical supplies with Dakotas and dropped stuff into the camps.

Extracts from Weary's first letter to his parents after the surrender appeared in the Benalla Standard.

IT SEEMS INCREDIBLY unreal being free, and strangely enough, beyond scribbling a few lines and a cable, I just haven't had time for anything the last two weeks. I was immediately taken to headquarters to work on evacuation and it has been a fascinating and hectic job.

Now things are in hand and I can ease up. The place was in a fairly chaotic state, but now almost everyone is in from the outlying jungle camps and fairly well looked after. There is just too much in the last years to attempt to write about it all at present. It has largely been a trail of sickness and death. I began in a Java native gaol, where we lost all ranks and privileges, and were stripped of all things such as Red Cross etc, in fact, lucky to retain my head.

Commanded a large camp of some 2000 assorted nationals, instead of doing surgery and medicines, and finally was railroaded up to Thailand, via Singapore, in command of a bunch called Dunlop's Thousands, to work on the railroad construction.

We had a pretty tough time, with malaria, dysentery, starvation, ulcers and cholera and despite magnificent fortitude, nearly everyone was completely worked out or dead by the end of 1943.

By that time the human debris drifted in thousands to surrounding stables, called hospitals, without any equipment and practically no drugs.

I commanded a couple of these with some 2000 sick each for a few months. We gradually got things under control. Since then the Japs have been seeing the writing on the wall a bit, and we have had things a little easier.

For something over a year I have been working as OC surgical block of a huge hospital, commanded by Lieut.-Col. Coates, and have done a deal of surgery.

In fact have done surgery all over this country under unimaginable camp conditions.

I have been lucky in having a magnificent constitution. I have only had five days in bed in this country. Have had some twenty goes of malaria, but none the last nine months; some of the other prevailing complaints usual to the prevailing conditions and a rather nasty tropical ulcer in 1943.

You may guess there has been plenty of work for me, at any rate, and probably few medical men have had more opportunity of saving lives than we have had here. But why talk of nightmares, it is all over now and God's great world to wander in again.

Life may not be quite so promising after all these lost years, but anything is good now, and it is just a dream to think of seeing you all again as there hasn't been more than an odd letter over a year old.

I hope you are all well, and haven't been worrying too much. Please excuse this letter being mostly of me.

JACK CHALKER: Weary went down to Bangkok and formed an Australian headquarters there and he asked me whether I would go down and join him as him as a war artist with the Australian army, which I was delighted to do. If we could do anything to sort of repay him a bit it would be wonderful, so I went down to Bangkok and stayed there with him before he went back to Australia. We were completing the visual records at that time.

It was a great joy because it gave me then a chance to see Bangkok, to see something of Thailand in that old state, with these marvellous boats on the river. I lived first of all at the Australian headquarters in a school, it was really their Eton of Bangkok. We had an interpreter, Peter Jacobson, a nineteen-year-old German boy that Weary got in because he spoke seven or eight languages. He spoke immaculate English and French and as well I think he spoke Cantonese, Mandarin, Thai, and Abyssinian, fluently. And all he wanted to do was mathematics, which he found terribly difficult.

He had a very strange background because his mother was pure Aryan and had had him and a daughter who was then about eighteen and a very beautiful girl. His father was a Prussian who had been killed by the Nazis. She was an anti-Nazi journalist and she quite quickly married a Jew who was a very brilliant eye specialist. They subsequently had another son. They escaped with their lives and went to Abyssinia, of all places, and he then came on to Bangkok and set up as a very successful eye surgeon there. This boy was interested in my drawings. He said, 'Come and meet my father,' and he took me home.

So I came out of the camps after these four years and I sat there in their luxurious house listening to his mother, who was also a concert pianist, play this Beckstein grand with this exquisite daughter who looked like an angel. I was in tears. It was a sort of Alice in Wonderland thing that happened. They invited me to come and live with them and Weary said yes to this.

'Come in and we'll work together during the day and you can stay with the Jacobsons at night.'

There were paratroopers that took me in a jeep at night. There were lots of little internecine wars going on between the Chinese and the Thais – old scores, because the Chinese had been supporting the Allies and a lot of the Thais had been collaborating, and had to, I suppose. One of the paratroopers gave me a Stenn gun and I went everywhere with it. Weary used to laugh. I remember some bullets going through the sides of the jeep under my legs one night so we fired off a few rounds. They were terribly funny times.

I used to go with Peter Jacobson to an open Chinese restaurant in Chinatown. There was a big celebration, masses of Chinese and Thais on the streets, and a Thai policeman for some weird reason started firing. Bullets came in and went through an enormous mirror behind us and shattered it. There was glass everywhere and there was only Peter and I, all the rest were Chinese, and we got under the table while this was going on. It was like a western film. And when it was over, we got up and helped them sweep up the glass and then went on with our meal. The whole time there was like this. I know that Weary used to enjoy this. Blue was there – that's when he knocked off a couple of samurai swords. During the first week Blue said, 'Jack, would you like a Samurai?' And that was about three in the morning. I wish I'd taken one of them. I said, 'For God's sake Blue, we've been told not to cause a stir. We could have another war break out here.' The Japanese were still riding about in Bangkok with their arms and their samurai, in the best cars, yet at the same time we were collecting war criminals. It was a completely upside-down world.

It was wonderful working with Weary and once again he just worked solidly, tirelessly, all the time to get people back, to get records made and everything else. He wanted me to come back to Australia with him – which I would have loved to have done because we still had a lot of work to do, there were a lot of drawings I wanted to finish for him – but the British Army wouldn't release me. Everybody else had gone home by then, so I was sent up to Rangoon, flown up in a Dakota, and then brought back by ship with a few remnants.

BLUE BUTTERWORTH: When we got the word that we were free – fantastic! And on my birthday, 25 August, Weary and I came out of camp. Weary had been out before but I came out and we went into Bangkok, to a college that had been the civilian internee camp, and we took over the bombed building. I became Weary's batman, driver – though I had no car at that stage – and ration officer. He said to me, 'Right, get some lights, get some tucker,' and I took off and I ran into this lady and her hubby. They thought I was part of the occupation force because by this time I'd got jungle greens on, and when I told them that I wasn't, they cracked a bottle of wine they'd been saving for a million years. I was elephant's trunk, I was blotto. I didn't come home. When I got back it was, 'Where the hell have you been?' And I told him. He never roused. He'd been there in the dark and I got waylaid.

One day I'm over in the civilian camp – all cups of tea, it's a real different set up – and there's a bloke there in shorts, brown as a berry, and he was English. He said, 'They tell me there's a fellow by the name of Dunlop. He must be a great fellow from what I've heard about him.' I said, 'Would you like to meet him?' and they became good friends. That was Lieutenant-Colonel Clague. He died with typhus. Weary was always upset about him. He'd gone through all the war, endangering his life, parachuting into places, gliding into places, he was involved in the rapid recovery of Allied prisoners of war and internees.

In Bangkok, I knocked off this place and there was this beautiful surgical kit, all red velvet lining, all the surgical instruments that a surgeon would need. We had this car and while we were on one of our escapades someone took the battery, so it wasn't mobile. I thought, I'll get back in the morning and bring this gear to Weary. Like an idiot, I told him about it. I said, 'I've got a nice present for you.' When I went back – gone. And you know what? I suppose twelve months after we came back he said to me, 'I wish I'd have got that.' He reckoned it cost him a mint setting up in surgical gear after the war.

We were the last plane to leave, and we shot down to Changi, and we were in 2 Half Moon Street, and Weary's there relaxed, starkers. A motor bike pulled up – it was Lord Louis Mountbatten's front rider. Lord Louis wanted to see Weary. All the boys had been talking about Weary so he requested that he see him and they became the best of mates.

Weary and I parted on the plane at Mascot. I said, 'Oh well, sir, it's been nice being with you. I'll see you one of these days I hope.' He said, 'Really son, where are you going?' I said, 'This is where I enlisted, this is where I . . .' He said, 'You're coming to Melbourne with me.' I said, 'No I'm not. I have three people out on the tarmac waiting for me.'

I didn't know that Weary had got off the plane in Sydney until much later. He didn't want to attack that reception down in Melbourne. He knew they were there.

Next time I saw him was at his wedding to Helen, on 8 November. Of course he had me fixed up with a job. Brigadier Stevens, who worked on the Melbourne council was there. 'By the way,' he said, 'I'm told you're a bricklayer. You've got a job.'

I've often thought, What if I had of stayed? Hundreds of blokes said, 'Why the hell don't you go and live in Melbourne?'

But I said, 'No sir, I'm going back to Sydney. I've got all my friends there that I met before the war, I want to stay there.'

In other words, I just wanted to paddle my own canoe.

Ray Parkin spoke about coming home.

EARLY IN THE WAR, Weary was one for adventure. When he got to Greece – Blue Butterworth can tell you about what he was like in Greece – he was accident-prone, doing the most stupid things. It was Biggles at work. But when he became prisoner and we got mixed up in the real things, he got to the core of life, which went beyond Biggles. This was when he got to his more Buddhist type of thinking and he rethought his Biggles image of life.

And then when he came back to life here – a lot of POWs saw life back here as unreal and superficial. We'd been facing something very basic. Whether we realised it or not, it was life and death and the real things all the time. However we reacted to it, we were still facing those fundamental things. You see, you were never sure – it might sound like overdramatisation now – but you could never be sure that you would be alive the next day. That's true for those fighting, too, but up there we were non-combatant and yet you still couldn't be sure of being alive the next day, either from disease or ill treatment. We were living on that knife's edge all the time.

I'll tell you a little anecdote. My wife had been living with my parents, and of course the day I got back it was open house. I'd grown up in Ivanhoe and all the neighbours poured in to welcome me back and all the rest of it, and amongst all these people, I was set back. You are a little bit bewildered, because you don't know what to say or what they expect of you, and I was sitting back in a chair and the local butcher came alongside and he started to talk to me.

I was very relieved. He wasn't asking me many questions, he wasn't very interested in what I'd been through, apparently. He was telling me how tough it was back here. 'Oh,' he said, 'you've no idea what it was like during the war. Even tea was rationed.' And I said, 'Oh yeah.' He went on, you know. I said, 'Gee, I'm glad I wasn't here.' (laughs) But that was his attitude. He really believed it. When you come back to that – people just don't realise. I worked down on the waterfront after the war. They have a wonderful saying down there, 'You can't educate a mug,' and it's true. It's no good trying.

When we came back, some people wanted to know all about it, but all they wanted to hear were the horror stories, how terrible the Japs were and what was the effect. Well, I couldn't tell what the effect of it was on me until quite a number of years later.

On Weary's return to Melbourne, **Helen Ferguson** *wrote to her friend,* **Margaret Gibson.** *(Margaret Gibson was 'Peggles', one of Weary's friends, and a patient for life.)*

19 October, 1945

Dear Peg,

On this the most momentous day of my life, I can scarcely hope to give you the sort of coherent approbation that I feel is due to you for the lovely way you arranged my room with flowers, for the gorgeous box of lilac and rhododendrons, for the gin, cigarettes and chocolates – for all this I'm too deeply indebted ever to make amends. All I can say is that I shall remember your amazing kindness.

Miss Gurner drove me to Essendon but on arrival there

a call from the Brigadier came at once to say that Weary was coming on the later plane arriving at midnight. So I had to return.

In the end General Burston sent me an army staff car. The plane arrived at exactly midnight and I fainted into his arms to find him <u>exactly</u> the same, not at all grey, wonderfully well and amazingly English.

We came home in the staff car – had a family reunion here – drinks then coffee etc. till 3.30 a.m. Got to bed at 4.15 a.m. no sleep at all. No plans yet but he is off to Benalla tomorrow and I don't think you can meet him till he comes back.

I saw Jack Few at the aerodrome early in the afternoon and he too, I thought, looked astonishingly fit.

Ever so much love and for your thoughtfulness Peg, so very many thanks.

Helen

On 16 August 1945 Weary Dunlop wrote the final entry in his war diary:

There will be strenuous and exciting days working to get the last of these maimed and damaged men on their way home. I have resolved to make their care and welfare a lifelong mission.

On 20 October 1945 the Australian Women's Weekly *featured Weary and Ewan Corlette under the headline* British and Japs called him King of the river, *and for the first time Weary was publicly dubbed the 'Christ of Thailand'. The following year, he became president of the Ex-Prisoners of War and Relatives' Association.*

Weary Dunlop was a war hero, renowned for placing himself between an enemy bayonet and an injured man, rather than for storming the enemy barricades.

ROWAN NICKS: I think the war made Weary and that he was terribly lucky. It made of a nice Australian, a fine Australian, a great man. The prisoner of war experience brought out in him things that he never dreamed he had – all that feeling and his intense compassion for people.

The heroic mantle sat comfortably about Weary's shoulders, and after the war, he continued to build his reputation – as a surgeon, and through service to the prisoners of war and the community. The men of Dunlop Force ensured that his reputation spread.

BLUE BUTTERWORTH: Some of the blokes say their doctors were just as good and there *were* good doctors. As I've said to one of them: 'Why don't you start all this then, talking about your doctors? Why wait until Weary's front page?' Weary didn't ask for kudos, for accolades. He didn't go for that sort of thing. We're the blokes who did it for him. And he deserved it.

I heard one bloke running him down once, saying he'd heard from a mate that Weary was no good. I said, 'Listen old mate, your cobber must have been a bludger, he must have been coming the raw prawn.' Because some of these big fellows would try and put on an act, you know, 'Oh, my back,' and Weary did catch up with a lot of malingerers. That's about the only time I've heard anyone say anything bad about Weary.

KEITH FLANAGAN: After I retired in 1984, I went to Weary and said, 'To me you represent the "old-fashioned" virtues like honour, courage, compassion, devotion to duty, but in you, they come in a charismatic package. We are putting you on the shelf like any other product, because this is the modern age and you've got to sell your product.' What we basically did was sell Weary. We didn't add anything to his virtues but I think we made a lot of people more aware of them.

And how did he respond when you said that to him?
Well, (laughs) you could never quite tell with Weary. He raised one eyebrow, you know? But he knew what I was on about and he knew that I wasn't on about creating an idol, or anything like that, but about publicising the things that he stood for. He didn't mind. He could see what was in mind.

Harold Payne, the president of the National Federation of Far Eastern Prisoners of War (FEPOW) clubs in Great Britain, met up with Weary, his Australian counterpart, soon after the war.

WEARY WAS AN extrovert. We first met shortly after we got home. Weary travelled a hell of a lot and I have been involved in the prisoner of war movement in this country right from the very start. In fact I helped start it all up. We always liaised and met up. He used to come to a lot of our reunions. I also met him when he came over to do some of his lecture tours. You could never tell where he was. One minute he was here, the next minute he was there.

He was at one time federal president of the Australian Prisoners of War Association and also he was connected with the Melbourne association that was for prisoners of war and their families. On my trips to reunions out in Australia – I think I went to four or five of them – I always linked up with him and we spent a lot of time together. We exchanged a lot of views between our two organisations and a lot of his views were very similar to mine. But he did something which I could never do, and that is because of his Hippocratic oath. I don't know if I could operate on a Japanese. I must say that I'm a rotten swine – still, there we are. Weary was a rather remarkable man and something he did, which was very lovely, was devote a lot of time to the Thai medical profession, with the Weary Dunlop-Boonpong Exchange Fellowship and other things like that.

My wife reminded me of a time, and this is rather unkind, when I was having a meal with him and he was carving a joint of beef. I said, 'Weary, thank God you never operated on me.' He was making a bugger's own meddle of this piece of meat. That was the way we could speak to each other. We had a wonderful rapport.

We had a large reunion of people at Blackpool in 1987 to give overall thanks for all he did. There was no 'them and us' for the POWs – you were a sick person whether you were an Australian or whether you were a Pom. The Australians were wonderful – I'm blowing their trumpet now – because they were volunteers. That's something that people are inclined to forget.

I have devoted all my spare time to the Far East POWs, and the ex-servicemen as a whole, as a way of saying thank you for being allowed to come home. It's my hobby, you might say – I don't play golf. Sir Edward always put POWs first, particularly his Melbourne boys, and there are some who would have bent over backwards for him.

We had a friendship where if we hadn't seen each other for a couple of years, we'd continue the conversation. It happens in the POW fraternity. If you were a POW, then that was a season ticket.

***Is it because Weary was an extrovert that he came to
prominence?***
He didn't go seeking hero worship, don't let me give you the
idea he went seeking it. He was just able to accept it. His public just built him up and up and he fell in line. Quite a few doctors came home and went into their shells, maybe because
they'd seen so many terrible things. Being a non-medical man,
I have always made it very clear that everybody would be much
better if they spoke about it and got it off their chest. Our motto
is worth quoting: 'To keep going the spirit that kept us going'.
That's what it's all about.

***Betty Jeffrey** is the author of* White Coolies, *the story of the
confinement of Australian army nurses by the Japanese in Java,
published in 1954. The ship on which a group of Australian
army nurses were evacuated from Malaya a few days before the
fall of Singapore, was bombed and sunk. Twenty-one of the
fifty-three survivors were massacred, and the remaining
thirty-two were taken prisoner. Twenty-four survived the camps.
They make up a small but important component of the
Australian prisoners of war associations.*

I MET WEARY after the war with the Prisoners of War
Association. Weary was president and they made me vice-president with another man. I said, 'If anything happens to Weary,
I'm not going to be president of all these fellows, they don't
want a woman.' 'Yes, we do,' they chorused. They are marvellous with me, I'm not a woman to them, I'm just one of them.

I had a lot to do with the association. I'm eighty-seven now
and I left when I was about eighty-three. I said, 'I'm going now,
I'm deaf and I can't hear what Weary's saying in any case.' They

said, 'Well, neither can we.' (laughs) He was just gorgeous. I loved him. Well, when I say loved him, you know what I mean. He did speak very softly and he used to chair a meeting and nobody would have a clue what he was talking about. The big fellow would stand there with his head down – (she mumbles) – how the secretary got notes, I'll never know. Then we'd go to another meeting at the Nurses Memorial Centre. Weary was patron and I was vice-president again. He didn't have time to be president, but he was always on the council of management. How he got round to earning a living as well as all that, I really don't know.

I was thinking this morning, he walked with kings, and he walked with the common people – and by that I don't mean the rude word, I just mean us, the people. He was exactly the same with everybody. He was a humble man. He came from the bush and you know people that come from the country are always the best in the land really, aren't they? They've got to be down to earth, and they are. They are very open and honest and they keep their feet on the ground.

Weary was a man of the world really, not only a man of Australia. He was always everywhere. You'd go to ring up and he'd be in India, or in England, or in Brisbane or in Sydney or in Perth. He was committed to everything but he did have time for the POW Association. He had a very big soft spot for them. Oh well, he knew them and understood them. He was one.

His driving was terrible. They tell me he always had two Mercedes because one was always getting fixed. I don't know if that's true or not, I think that's just a story. [He did, in fact, have two white Mercedes.] He could be a very slow driver. I only drove with him once and it was after a POW service at the Shrine.

Weary said, 'Come with me, I'll take you down there.' We were driving along and he said, 'Do you know where this place is that we're going to?' and I said, 'No, do you know where it is?' and he said, 'No.' It just got to me, we laughed and we laughed and we laughed, and he said, 'Well, we'll keep on driving, the fellows will come up soon, Flannery [an ex-POW who often drove Weary] will catch us up, he'll know.' In about three minutes there was a toot, toot, toot and a car came screaming past on the wrong side – because Weary was driving up in the centre of the road at about one knot an hour – and there's a car full of these fellows, all hanging out, motioning over the top of the roof, 'Come on, follow us.' He had utter faith in those fellows and they didn't let him down.

He was special. If he said, 'Come,' you'd come. As far as the fellows were concerned, there was great respect from every one of them. Great respect but they were quite at home with him. He was one of them. I think that describes him pretty well.

The Murray Goulburn Ex-Prisoners of War Association's annual reunion, held at Numurkah since 1949, has been a focal point for ex-prisoners of war throughout Victoria. When Weary attended the Numurkah reunion on the Saturday before his death, secretary of the association, **Cliff Moss** *and past-president* **Fred Barnstable** *were there.*

CLIFF: Weary first came up to Numurkah in 1954. In his early years he was sometimes overseas, but if he wasn't he'd almost inevitably be here. As time went on he was more regular. The great thing about him was he'd talk to anybody. As president of the association, he always responded to the toast to the association, generally with a great heap of stories about POW experiences. No end to them. And he never ever repeated himself either. I don't know how he avoided it.

FRED: Often he would say something about repatriation affairs and on this last one he gave a pretty serious speech, actually, for him.

CLIFF: Sometimes he rambled on but he had a lot to say this night and he said it very well. That's another thing he did, of course. If anybody went to him, trying to get a pension, he would follow it right through. He may never have known the bloke before. You'd get the file and give it to him, he'd read the whole thing. A mate of mine died here and we were trying to get his widow a war widow's pension. It was knocked back, so we sent the file to Weary and he wrote the most blistering letter in which he said, 'I'm surprised that doctor so-and-so takes this view because that's been outdated for donkey's years, it's based on assumptions in textbooks that are twenty years out of date, and other conclusions are completely out of accord with things that the Repatriation Commission has accepted for years.' That lady got her pension very smartly.

He'd come to reunions and some poor devil would be crook or his wife would be crook and they'd go and talk to Weary and he would stop and listen very intently to what they had to say. His wife used to describe these people as 'tie swingers', because that's about how high up most of them came next to him. He'd advise them what to do or he might suggest something else. But he'd give them just as much close attention as anybody going into his rooms. Exactly the same.

FRED: He was as open as a book.

What made Weary stand out, after the war, from the other doctors in the camps?

CLIFF: We were very well served by doctors. They were all conscientious and naturally some had more skill than others, but there were a lot of very, very good doctors. But the reason why

Dunlop got all the publicity was quite obvious. He was the boss of the POW Association here in Victoria right from the day we got home, from 1946 until he died. He was involved in numerous public organisations and he wasn't just a token figure there, he took part in what they were doing. He operated on all sorts of people all over the state of Victoria, not just ex-servicemen. And then all the things he did overseas with the Colombo Plan, where he was going to God knows how many Asiatic countries, to Ceylon, Thailand, Vietnam, India.

FRED: Even Japan.

CLIFF: He spread himself everywhere. I had a sister-in-law who was in hospital in Melbourne at that time he got the knighthood. She said other doctors there said, 'He's just a general surgeon, he's not a specialist. Why should he get a knighthood?' There was a lot of jealousy about it.

He used to get very annoyed with governments and government departments. One night, I don't know what had happened, the government had done something which wasn't in the best interests of ex-servicemen, and he was as wild as a meat axe. 'If I was to reveal some of the things in my files,' he said, 'the government would be very embarrassed. I put in submissions, they take no notice of them. There's young fellows there who don't know anything about it, they throw them away.'

FRED: Early on after the war he was a Department of Veteran Affairs' doctor and he told me himself that he was relieved of that duty because he was giving too many pensions to people he knew of or had connections with.

28 June, 1993

Dear Cliff,
Through you my thanks to your president J.P. Davis – and

the organising committee of yet another great annual Numurkah Reunion.

I was sorry to have to split my weekend between Sydney, Numurkah and Edithvale – plus alas some time on the road with engine bloody mindedness.

Well, it was in the fine line of tradition. Ray and Wilma both contributed well to a splendid function.

With thanks and best wishes

Yours sincerely,

'Weary' E.E.Dunlop

On his return to Britain after the war, the British aircraftsman **Bill Griffiths** *went to St Dunstan's Hospital where he worked to overcome the loss of his sight and hands. At home in Blackburn, Lancashire, he married Alice, a concert singer who encouraged him to develop his baritone voice. He and Alice have performed throughout Great Britain. In 1989, he sang at the 'Tribute to Sir Edward Dunlop' concert at the Melbourne Concert Hall. For many years, he has worked as a public relations representative for St Dunstan's Hospital. He and Alice now live in Blackpool.*

BILL: He came to see me when he came to England, probably a couple of years after the war, and he came quite unannounced. No letter, no phone call, nothing. He just turned up with his wife. Yep. Alice answered the door and he said, 'I want to see Bill Griffiths.'

ALICE: I thought he was selling vacuums.

BILL: It was a surprise, wasn't it?

ALICE: I had an apron on, I was cooking fish and chips. He said something and I said, 'I'm sorry but we don't need anything.

We're all right, thank you.' He said, 'But I've come to see . . .'
I said, 'Who?' He said, 'Bill Griffiths. I am Edward Dunlop.'
Oh dear, oh dear. His car was out the front. I said, 'Is your wife
with you? Bring her in.' It was very strange, the two men being
back together, looking at each other. They were so quiet. I
thought, Good gracious, talk or something, make some kind of
conversation. But it was very emotional. There was plenty
there, but they weren't speaking. And Bill looked so well, you
see, when Sir Edward had only seen him at his worst and from
then on.

BILL: It was absolutely so unreal an event. After all the experiences as prisoners of war, here we were in Lancashire and
Weary sat there talking to me. Marvellous. Absolutely. It's difficult to put it into words just now, how it was. We saw him
many times again after that.

*Stanley Gimson proposed the motion that elected Weary
honorary president of the Scottish branch of the Far Eastern
Prisoners of War Association in 1991. 'All our members who
were in Thailand remember him as an outstanding figure.'*

MANY YEARS AFTER the war, about twenty years I should
think, I decided I should go and speak to the Imperial War
Museum in London about the sketches I made in the camps.
They asked me if they could make photographic copies and
they also told me they would supply further copies as required.
So I thought, I'll send Weary Dunlop the photographs of the
sketches of the operating and the medical centre. I sent them off
and that started a correspondence.

My contacts with Weary have been mostly social but I did
correspond with him quite a bit about prisoner of war health

problems. I was for twenty-four years the chairman of the Pensions Appeals Tribunal here in Scotland and on one occasion we actually referred a case to him for his opinion. I had a feeling that the ministry would object but they didn't.

Your ministry in Australia is famous for saying of a deceased man that he must have benefited from the fresh air and exercise in the camps.

Our ministry was quite hostile to Weary on occasions.
Well actually, Weary did go a bit too far. He was prepared to say that any illness was probably due to captivity, and what I wanted from him on that occasion was some statistics and he had none. What he'd returned was an emotional appeal.

When you contrast prisoner of war existence with existence in a country at peace, I think the basis of his feeling was that it was so bad that those who say that a condition is not linked to captivity have really no right to say it. It was bad enough for the consequences to be unthought of as far as medical science was concerned. That was Weary's philosophy, and it was the general philosophy among prisoners of war. We tended to think that our constitutions had been undermined to a degree that we more or less thought, 'Anything may happen to me as a result. I've no idea what it will be, how it's going to hit.' The surprising thing is when you meet people fifty years afterwards and there's quite a turnout of hale-looking old men.

20 June, 1965

Dear Stanley,
I was deeply touched by your gift of the excellent reproductions of those splendid sketches you made in Chungkai and other regions during our jungle 'vacation'.

To say the truth, I did receive the letter you sent to Ray Parkin, but felt a little diffident about writing to take you up on the matter. Having received your warm and generous letter, together with the reproductions, I now realise that my diffidence was unnecessary.

Looking at the sketches I recalled sadly the Virgilian lines which run roughly

> *'Time removes all things*
> *even the memory'*

For I have been back at times in Thailand for Colombo Plan and other tasks and have journeyed to Kanchanaburi and Chungkai, and have viewed again the more accessible regions of the Kwai Noi valley. The great war cemeteries are etched clearly and are beautifully kept, largely bogus though they may be as an authentic repository of the remains of our friends who rotted away in life and in death or were burned.

The friends of many nations are scattered informally together – I remember Col. More asking me at Kanyu [Konyu] whether I would like a separate Australian section in the cemetery and how I said 'No thanks – we'll be quite happy to just muck in with you chaps.'

The graves are indeed moving and I thought of some old biblical fragment of a prayer that 'They shall hunger no more nor thirst any more neither shall the sun light on them nor any heat'.

But as to the layout of Chungkai camp and hospital – which I once referred to as 'an old civilisation' – the jungle has sprung up and choked it as it has largely swallowed the Burma–Thailand railway with all its suffering, the achievements, the inhumanity, the ugliness, and the heroism. And so it is, I suppose with most of us, that we returned from it with a godlike concept of simplicity, like fresh-minted coins from the fire. I wanted nothing of possessions to clutter me up whether material or human; but was filled with a fierce desire to travel light: for 'he that is light of heart and heel can travel on the milky way'.

But of course the jungle kept on growing, and though I have been around the world four or five times since the war and have crisscrossed the East – I do not travel light but have the worries and concern that go with a large consultant surgical practice, and numerous ties, not to mention a town house of nearly twenty rooms and large garden, my professional suite in the city, a cattle farm in the country, numerous staff and a gaggle of things which keep me poor. Thus we become so preoccupied all the time with things that we simply must do, that there is no time for the things we want to do.

I have a postwar wife Helen née Ferguson of a lengthy line of Scottish engineers who migrated to Australia before the turn of the century. She is a fervent lover of Scotland from that romantic city of yours all over and particularly the wild sweep of the highlands. She came with me in 1960 and we stayed with Mollie and John Bruce in Moray St and went driving around the north before we flew off to India for a couple of months of surgical travel.

I am now so very sorry that I did not make contact with you – and no doubt all over Scotland there are others. We have two boys, Alexander and John.

Ray Parkin is an exceptional man who remains physically and mentally largely as you knew him. The jungle of life has not choked him, and he has stored in him the artist's clear pictures of life in Siam as we saw it long ago. I was more moved by his book and the generosity of his heart than I care to say.

He has a delightful home and family, and the deep satisfaction of the creative mind which has found satisfactory expression.

Most ex-POWs have kept their end up and many like yourself have done splendidly. Your own is a proud record of achievement. The Scottish Bar has always summoned my deep respect, and indeed it has always intrigued me that the two races which seem to show the most avid love of learning are the Scots, and the Jews, not distinguished otherwise by a deal in common. Your many other interests must keep you very busy.

I shall write you down heavily in my overseas address book. Meantime I shall ponder your generosity and reflect upon my own inadequacy of reply just now. So far as your surviving POWs are concerned I have the enduring gratitude for the greatness of their generous hearts.

Life's energies are not unlimited and July ushers in my 58th birthday. My way of life does not spare the machine, but I have hopes that presuming full steam on full boilers I shall see Scotland again and renew an old and absorbing association.

Meantime we have in Australia the challenge of this great land mass which we occupy so thinly. I don't feel that our destiny will be entirely European surrounded as we are by the vast populations of Asia. I only hope that when our past is weighed that it will be conceded that we did work as much for the world as men can do.

My sincere good wishes and warm thanks.

Yours sincerely,

Weary

Vivian Statham, formerly Vivian Bullwinkel, *is the sole survivor of the massacre of twenty-two army nurses by the*

*Japanese on Banka Island on 16 February 1942. She was
imprisoned for three-and-a-half years. We met at her home in
Perth.*

WEARY WAS PRESIDENT of the Melbourne POW committee
for a long time and I served on the committee for a number of
years. Weary's reputation preceded him no matter where he
went or what he did. When we went to Numurkah, he relaxed
a bit and he talked about everyday things. He never talked
about the war, though. We never talked about the war.

***Those Numurkah reunions seem to have been very important
to everybody.***
They were. First of all, so many were able to get to them.
Secondly, really they were just ordinary folk in the regiment.
Weary was an officer, yet he was able to come to these boys'
affairs and just be one of the boys. I think they had respect for
Weary rather than the rank.

***When he was the main speaker at Numurkah, do you recall
his speech? Was he a good speaker?***
I wouldn't say so. He spoke in public lots of times, and you put
up with him because he was Weary. He wasn't a speaker. There
were lot of other soldiers who were more impressive speakers
than he was. When he spoke, he spoke just like an ordinary
bloke, very low and hard to hear, you had to listen, and when he
gave over to somebody else you were perfectly happy. But you
would have to say it was worthwhile.

He seems to have had a great sense of humour.
Yes, he chuckled to himself. He was so difficult to follow, but
you knew when he was laughing.

What was he like at running the meetings of the ex-POWs?
No good. But a man like that, he's allowed one or two faults.

*In 1977, Sir Edward Dunlop was made 'Australian of the
Year'. 'The Quiet Lion' is a tribute by the writer and
ex-prisoner of war, the late* **Donald 'Scorp' Stuart** *published
in the* West Australian *on 22 January, 1977.*

BANDOENG, JAVA, 1942. The barracks of the army of the
Netherlands East Indies were bursting at the seams with
prisoners of war. Australian, British, Dutch and Colonial
Dutch, from navy, army and airforce, we were a mixed bag.
Japan was not a signatory to the Geneva Convention con-
cerning POWs and we thought we knew what to expect.
We hungered for food other than the meagre ration of
dirty rice, we slept on concrete floors, we developed dysentery, but of course we knew it would be for only a few
months, three or maybe four.

The Japanese made the senior medical officer responsible for the good order of the Bandoeng camp, and in our
miserable condition we knew they had unwittingly done us
good. Lieut-Colonel Dunlop was a giant of a man, physically and in every other way, and the other medical officers
were of the same cast of character.

Interminable parades for counting, for checking out
work parties and often for no purpose except to harass and
humiliate us; bashing for trivial offences or for nothing
except the amusement of the Japanese and Korean guards;
sickness, disease, weakness of body and spirit, all these were
our sorry lot, and always Weary Dunlop stood tall, facing
the enemy on our behalf, while conditions worsened.

I was fortunate enough to be in the party that left Bandoeng for Batavia (Jakarta) under Weary Dunlop's leadership, and went with him by ship to Singapore, and by train, crowded as sheep or pigs in a saleyard to Thailand.

We built a railway from near Bangkok to near Rangoon in Burma, with almost no equipment, through jungles and across rivers, thousands of us POWs and enslaved Asian civilians, all of us starved, scourged, racked with malaria, dysentery, beri beri, pellagra, and the stinking tropical ulcers that ate a leg to the bone in a matter of days, and always Weary Dunlop and his fellow MOs stood up for us, were beaten, scorned, derided, and beaten again.

In the mud and starvation of those long months we looked back at Bandoeng as the Garden of Eden, while men died and were buried in shallow graves in hundreds, and in thousands.

Always guards demanded more and more of the sick and dying to join the work parties on their sacred railway to Burma, and always Weary Dunlop, quiet voiced, argued and protested and stood up against Japanese might, and we came to know that he was permanent, unchanging, devoted to his duty as senior medical officer and our leader.

His physical size was indeed the least of his attributes. Over 190cm and a heart, a spirit, bigger again. We came to know the meaning of the description 'a Christian gentleman'.

A great neurosurgeon, and with him two other great specialists, and no medical supplies. Whatever they had of instruments they and their orderlies had carried on their backs into the horrid jungles, keeping faith with their oath as medical personnel.

We sickened and died, we lost limbs eaten away by tropical ulcers in surgical operations under the most primitive conditions performed by the most skilled and dedicated of surgeons, and every day the cholera dead were burnt, the other dead were buried, and always Weary Dunlop gave us his strength and many of us were able to survive.

When despair and death reached for us, he stood fast, his only thought our well-being. Faced with guards who had the power of life and death, ignoble tyrants who hated us, he was a lighthouse of sanity in a universe of madness and suffering.

Thousands of men, middle-aged now, in Australia and across the world, when they read that Weary Dunlop had been named Australian of the Year, would have said: 'Yes I knew him in Thailand. He's the "Australian of many years". We'd never have got back home if it hadn't been for the MOs.'

The black Ambonese soldiers of the Dutch Army named him, in their Malay language, Singa Yang Diam. I agree. Weary Dunlop, of the great heart and soft voice, was, is, and will ever be, The Quiet Lion, in the hearts and minds of all who knew him in our three-and-a-half years of suffering in the prison camps of Asia. When we forget him we shall be dead.

Keith Flanagan was behind the 1985 Weary Dunlop Tour to Thailand, which saw a group of former ex-prisoners of war and members of their family and members of the media return to the scenes of their wartime ordeal. Since then there have been regular trips to coincide with Anzac Day.

KEITH: Those last words in the diaries – that he resolved to make the POWs' care and welfare a lifelong mission – what he said, he meant.

Many ex-POWs don't seem to have had much contact with Weary until the 1980s.
BILL HASKELL: Most of this prisoner of war business has emanated after the fellows retired. A lot of the fellows had to get back to health, then a lot of them were doing post-war reconstruction courses to qualify for particular jobs, and then of course most of them got married, had a family. You didn't have time to think about anything. You had to get back into a world that you'd left for six years, make your mark and get cracking while you could, and then really I suppose it was only when most jokers had retired that they were able to get around and talk.

Keith said to me one day, 'If we don't do something about Weary soon, nobody's going to know how great that man was. I'd like to take him back up and do a trip over it again.' That tour was the genesis of the Weary Dunlop story. There were journalists and cameramen and they started sending reports back about Weary and the importance of Weary.

How did the idea come about?
KEITH: I retired, I looked at Australia and I was distressed, like a lot of us. What the hell's happened to this place? I thought. The style of politics, there's no dignity, no stature. All the entrepreneurs, a hell of a lot of greed. So I thought, My antidote for the sick society is Weary Dunlop. I wrote a story of my own called *Every Dog His Day*. I was thinking of making it into a film – I've got grandiose ideas, you know – and I got in touch with Weary. Then I decided that this was a bigger story than mine, so I advocated this trip. It was called the Weary Dunlop Tour,

much to his horror, and we retraced the steps we had taken.

There were fifty-one of us, from all over Australia. When we started off, we met together in the hotel in Jakarta. Groups from the east and groups from the west, they came at different times. Weary was one of the earlier ones and I remember when the next lot came in, he made a little speech saying, 'I probably remember you better by your scars than I do your faces.' Then he said, 'Now I'll sing you a little song. "Sweet Fanny Adams".' It's about the lover carving the name of Sweet Fanny Adams: 'The woodpecker came and woodpecked away, and all that was left was sweet FA'. (laughs) He doesn't sing terribly well, but it just set the pattern. Everything sort of collapsed and we had this wonderful tour. It was great fun, great harmony, great rapport. I wrote to him and said I thought it was the most memorable two weeks of my life and he wrote back and said it was the same for him.

I think it is the most rewarding thing I've ever done in my life. I added a little something, I think, to the regard in which he is held, and that's important.

In 1986, a group of West Australian ex-prisoners of war with Keith Flanagan at the helm, were instrumental in setting up the Dunlop-Boonpong Exchange Fellowship, an exchange program for surgeons between Australia and Thailand.

2 May, 1986

Dear Keith,

I returned from Perth with a very full heart – feeling much like a prodigal son.

How extraordinarily kind people can be – one casts a few

crumbs of bread upon the waters of life, and heigh presto they return as currant loaves and magic buns.

All this I think stems from your own generous heart, and I find it hard to live up to the grand image that you conjure up out of my shadow.

I have always felt borne up on the shoulders of the men I had the supreme honour to lead, and their esteem coming in such a generous way means more than official honours or material rewards.

However we are all just a representative of others who support us like Arthur Moon, Ewan Corlette ('The Gangster') and so many others. May Australia not forget them.

I returned to a rather heavy accumulation of work and correspondence, and it may take me a while to write to all those who did so much for me during my stay.

I spoke to Lang Fraser this morning. He is interested in the projected launch of my book in Queensland as his son is in the Thomas Nelson Publishers.

Lord knows I am rather apprehensive about publication of my private records of those days.

Things were too black and white and no shades of grey.

I went to the Japanese celebration of the Emperor's birthday after my return. Note Hiro Hito, now eighty-five, is the only monarch to see Halley's Comet twice!

I told Lang Fraser that you would be writing to him again.

I am wondering about whether a book sale allocation is entirely adequate as a personal contribution. Maybe the book won't amount to much.

I am working up a Symposium here on 'Thailand Today' or some such title with co-operation between the Australian Asian Association and the Australian Thailand

Assoc's – and there could be some conflict in money raising since we will be having functions and approaching firms to underwrite the symposium. Further the wretched Dunlop name is diluted by appeal being floated here for 'The Edward Dunlop Research Foundation' for veterans and families to be housed in the Heidelberg Repat Hospital.

I feel that my personal contribution should be of the order of $1000 and that I had best make an initial response in this financial year when I get together with my accountant to cross the Rubicon again.

I am enclosing a letter to the Ian McFadgens who gave me a beautiful painted cup and saucer – no address. I hope you can lay your hands on it. 'Ian and Paddy'.

The Dunlop book of memories you put together with such remarkable industry and loving care will be treasured forever and forever, in the family or some hallowed spot.

My dear wife Helen grows steadily more sadly lost in a remote and crippled world of her own, and still has a sweet smile for me.

Please keep me informed as to the progress of the Foundation and how I can best help.

With love to you, Lynne, Liam and family.

Sincerely,

Weary

The Hellfire Pass (Konyu) Cutting, eighty kilometres from Kanchanaburi in Thailand, is a part of the 415-kilometre Thailand-Burma railway constructed by the prisoners of war and conscripted native labour in 1942-43. It is now a memorial to Sir Edward and to the men who constructed it. Sir Edward unveiled the first commemorative plaque at Hellfire Pass on

Anzac Day 1987. The Hellfire Pass memorial walk trail has been developed by the Australian-Thai Chamber of Commerce, the Snowy Mountains Engineering Corporation and the Australian government, with funds contributed by former prisoners of war. Some of Sir Edward's ashes were scattered between the rails at Hellfire Pass at a Memorial Dawn Service on Anzac Day, 1994.

CLIFF MOSS: It was Anzac Day 1943 when Australians arrived at Hellfire Pass. I built a little bit of it, and I went back in 1984. We were the first tourist party that actually got to it and the party included four or five of us that had actually worked on it. It was quite an experience. It was hot as the devil and of course it wasn't as deep as we thought it was. It's about 200 yards long. It's quite incredible, they built that line in twelve months.

FRED BARNSTABLE: We started on the Thanbyuzarat end of the railway at the end of October 1942 and the line was joined at Konkoita in October '43. There was a lot of maintenance work to be done on it then. The jungle has overgrown it now and it's as if nothing had ever happened in Burma. Hellfire Pass is now a memorial to Sir Edward.

BILL GRIFFITHS: When we went down to Hellfire Pass for the first time in 1985, Weary said to Alice –
ALICE GRIFFITHS: He said, 'Alice, I don't think Bill will manage these steps, they'll be too much for him.' And Billy said to me, 'I don't think Weary should go down those steps. They're too much for him.' (laughs)
BILL: And we both went down.

*The television journalist **Quentin Fogarty** accompanied Weary on a 1987 trip to Thailand and the following article was published in the* Age *newspaper on 11 July to coincide with Weary's eightieth birthday.*

IT WAS ALWAYS an ambitious plan, given the terrain, the debilitating heat and the age of the main participants. But there was a determined look to this band of old warriors. After all, they had survived the disease, hunger and mindless brutality of the Death Railway. And leading them once again, striding out in front in his camouflage trousers, was their former surgeon and commanding officer, Sir Edward 'Weary' Dunlop.

This stumbling journey back in time was supposed to have been a secret. The official itinerary called for a bus trip to some hot springs, or a day tour to a famous railway landmark, Three Pagoda Pass, on the Burma border. But a small group of veterans had their hearts set on retracing a section of line built by Dunlop Force – a torturous five kilometres along the jungle-clad slopes of Hintok Mountain.

If they were successful, they would then try to find the site of Hintok Mountain camp which had been their home during the infamous period when they were forced to work around-the-clock shifts, in appalling conditions, and at the height of the monsoon rains.

The organisers considered themselves to be in good enough shape to complete the journey and they didn't want to be held back by those who were not so fit. There was also the real chance that someone might collapse from exertion, or heat exhaustion, and that could place the party in a serious situation. The victim would either have to be carried out of the jungle, or someone would have to walk out to fetch help.

But it was obvious as we gathered outside the River Kwai Village Hotel after breakfast, that our planned journey was the worst-kept secret in the Kwae Noi Valley that day. A quick head count showed that we had a total party of thirty-eight – twenty-five former POWs, friends and family members, media and film crews, and a small group of hotel staff whose job it would be to carry water bottles and food.

By the time we had been driven to our starting point, Hellfire Pass, it was mid-morning. We estimated that the temperature had reached the high thirties, and was still climbing. An added burden was the oppressive humidity. It was like walking through a fine, warm rain.

Although the sleepers and rails were gone – ripped up by the British as part of Japanese reparation payments – the course of the line was still easy to follow. The jungle had reclaimed some sections but had barely made a dent on the cuttings that the POWs had blasted and scraped out of the solid rock of Hintok Mountain.

The cuttings remain as a permanent and impressive memorial to the men who built them. They have a sense of achievement, of pride in a place where it has been said that one man died for every sleeper. It is impossible not to be aware of the lingering presence of the young men who remained there.

Small clumps of bamboo and some trees had taken root, and there had been some minor rock falls, but the cuttings didn't present any major problems for our ageing band of time-travellers. But the gullies between the cuttings were proving a major obstacle. The ingenious wooden trestle bridges built by the POWs had long gone and our party was forced to scramble up and down rubble-strewn slopes. For many of the veterans, the rough inclines, with their thorn bushes and spiky creepers, were taking on nightmarish proportions, sapping the last reserves of energy and spirit.

The sun was now directly overhead and the temperature had climbed into the forties. Dunlop stopped to catch his breath: 'Fellows worked almost naked, real slave stuff. Men, in bare feet, clearing rocks, their feet like raw tomatoes and the ground as hot as hell. It was an exercise in Dante's Inferno.'

For those of us who until now had only read or listened to stories about the Death Railway, there was a growing appreciation of the physical conditions that had confronted these men more than forty years ago. Then of course, they were bags of bones, slaves, weakened by disease, hunger and brutalised by their guards. We could never know the full horror – that was something locked away in the hearts and minds of those who had experienced it.

Weary Dunlop was a tonic to us all, cracking jokes and making light of his obvious discomfort. He was an absolute ham, always conscious of the camera. Whenever he found himself under scrutiny by a lens he would straighten his back, pull back his shoulders and wipe the strain from his face with a smile. Many times as he passed by the camera crew he would deliver a little homily – he was a film maker's delight.

Although Dunlop out-ranked everyone in the party he was, for the purposes of this journey, only the titular leader. The driving force was Bill Haskell, a sixty-seven-year-old retired taxation officer from Perth. For years he had dreamt of returning to this place to pay homage, as he put it, 'to so many of the boys who didn't make it along the track here.'

As the journey progressed, Haskell assumed command. When he was last on this section of track he was a private. Now, here he was in charge not only of the entire party but also his former commanding officer as well as Dunlop's 2IC, Bill Wearne. Dunlop was more than happy with the reversal of roles. Only a few weeks earlier he had fallen down the stairs at his home, fracturing his wrist and collarbone and damaging his kidneys. The fractures were still healing and he was also suffering from a severe attack of gastroenteritis.

We were all grateful when a lunch break was called.

We were now about halfway along the Dunlop Force section of the track and a small group had already turned back. Bill Wearne suggested that everyone should call it a day and return the way we had come. Bill Haskell was in a quandary. He had waited forty-four years to fulfil his dream and he had tried to keep the trek secret to avoid the very problem that had now arisen. Whatever the choice, it was obvious there were going to be some causalities. Finally, it was decided that the party should stick together for the time being. Haskell's map showed a road a short way ahead and the plan was for those who were unable to continue to wait there, while the remainder attempted to complete the journey.

Dunlop, in spite of his seventy-nine years and obvious exhaustion, decided to soldier on. I don't recall exactly how many decided to stay by the roadside. All of my energies were being directed towards completing the journey. Note-taking seemed quite irrelevant. But I do recall that a Thai cameraman gratefully sank to the ground. Although we didn't know it at the time, the cameraman was suffering badly from heat exhaustion.

On leaving the road, the going became particularly tough, with a steep climb up a rock-strewn slope. That climb finally robbed Dunlop of his reserves of energy. A short way farther along he faltered. Something deep inside told him this was the end of the line. It was a touching scene. Dunlop, on the ground, with Bill Haskell standing above fanning him with a handkerchief, and then wiping his brow.

It didn't seem an appropriate time to explore his feelings but he told me later he was bitterly disappointed he couldn't go on. 'I was suffering from heat exhaustion,' he said. 'I had lost a great deal of salt and water over the previous twenty-four hours because of the heat and the gastroenteritis. I was just rubber-legged. You can go on saying "left leg, right leg," and I had done that so often during the war when I was full of malaria and so forth. You can talk to your legs and keep going.' Only this time Dunlop's legs were not answering.

We left Dunlop and a small group by the side of the road and headed back into the jungle. I had decided that if these old fellows could keep going, then so could I. Out of the original party of twenty-five former POWs, only four were still standing and we had about one kilometre of the line to complete. Finally, we made it to Compressor Cutting, so named because it was the only cutting on this part of the track that was excavated with the help of compressors. For Bill Haskell, it was an emotional moment: 'It is a place with a lot of memories. You have mixed feelings in a place like this.' And then Haskell paid tribute to Dunlop and Wearne, his voice sharp and crystal clear in the silence of the cutting.

'When you look at the likes of Weary Dunlop and Bill

Wearne back there, they were the mainstays of our camps. You hear so much about our medicos and you cannot say too much about them. But you look at a bloke like Bill Wearne – Bill was responsible for maintaining crews and he copped everything. But he is a soldier, he is a soldier from the word go. Those two are really compassionate men and I think that is the story. I just don't want to –' And his voice trailed off. The emotion of the moment became too much for this former private in the 2/3 Machine Gun Battalion. Fighting back the tears, he turned away and walked along the cutting. He wanted to be alone. All thoughts of continuing on to find the mountain camp were forgotten. It was mid-afternoon, still stifling hot, and we were keen to retrace our steps and meet up with Dunlop and the rest of the party.

On reflection, it was probably a foolhardy adventure and there were times when I was concerned that the railway might belatedly claim another victim. Although Dunlop agreed that some of the party should not have attempted the journey, he didn't place himself in that category. As far as he was concerned, he was simply the victim of a particularly bad bout of stomach problems and a couple of annoying fractures that were taking too long to heal.

Later, beside the hotel pool, I was amazed at how quickly the walking wounded picked up in body and spirit after a couple of cold beers and a refreshing dip. They are certainly tough old coots, these remnants of Dunlop Force.

3

14 PARLIAMENT PLACE

On his return to Australia in 1945 Weary and Helen Ferguson were married at the Toorak Uniting Church on 8 November. Helen wore a dress of pale green Thai silk brocade that Weary had brought back from Thailand.

Weary's first professional task was to write articles for the British and Australian medical journals on the clinical lessons learnt from his experience in the camps.

After his demobilisation in 1946, he was appointed honorary surgeon to the outpatients at the Royal Melbourne Hospital and the following year moved from rooms in Spring Street into a suite of offices he shared with G.R.A. (Bob) Syme on the fourth floor of 14 Parliament Place. In the same year, he took up a position lecturing and examining at Melbourne University and began tutoring at Ormond College. His practice as a general surgeon grew and he operated in a number of Melbourne hospitals as well as several hospitals in country Victoria. His sons Alexander and John were born in 1947 and 1949.

The ambivalence expressed by some of Sir Edward's colleagues regarding his surgical skills was not shared by the patients I interviewed. Their trust in him was absolute. One patient is reputed to have said: 'If he asked me to chop my head off and replace it with a button, I'd do it.'

*The surgeon **John Hayward** and Weary Dunlop assisted each other in the operating theatre in the post-war years.*

AFTER THE WAR Weary Dunlop was more nearly indefatigable than anyone else I've known. He was physically tall, well built, amazingly strong. Mentally he was top grade in all subjects, never missed a trick. In mind and body he outclassed most of us and he knew it.

He only needed about five hours' sleep a night, and during the day a catnap of about five minutes between operations was enough to recharge his batteries. I always knew when he was overtired and he hadn't got his five hours' sleep because he'd just get slower and slower in the operation, but he'd still go on doing it. Right till the last stitch.

Weary and I got together in late 1946 or early 1947. We worked together on oesophagectomies. The oesophagus is an in-between organ, it goes from the neck to the stomach through the chest. The chest surgeon is used to working in the chest, a general surgeon is used to operating in the neck and below the diaphragm. General surgeons were frightened of the chest right up to that time. Before the war, when I was at the Brompton Chest Hospital, chest surgery was just developing, and operating on the lung itself was just beginning.

Being a very adventuresome surgeon, Weary didn't like being stopped on any job, he liked to do the whole thing and not be dependent on anybody else. But he needed help on the oesophagus and I was not so competent as I would like to be in the upper abdomen. I don't remember how we got started, but we decided that if either of us got a patient who needed an oesophageal operation, we'd each tell the other one and arrange it so that we'd work together. We agreed that if it was my patient, I'd be boss – because it's no use working unless there's a boss – and if it was his patient, he'd be boss.

Therefore at the Royal Melbourne Hospital, if it was my patient, it was done in my operating theatre with my resident and my team and Weary assisting, and if it was his patient it was done in his theatre in his time and I would assist. It worked very well, and we both learnt from each other.

After the war, when we all came back, we were stony broke. We had no patients at first, we just had a practice address. Then patients began to come along in a small dribble. It was usually over a year before your practice would do more than pay for itself. You never got any real income at all. The work at the Royal Melbourne was purely honorary. You even had to pay for your own transport there and back, and you were not paid a halfpenny. So life was a bit difficult, but it was easy then to arrange to do these operations together. This became more difficult as our private practices grew. By 1950, it was getting hard to arrange, and by 1951 we couldn't organise the times any more. But by that time we could each manage without the other, so our association in oesophageal surgery fizzled out, not because either of us wanted it to stop – we enjoyed the time together.

I always got on very well with Weary. There were many people who didn't, and there were many senior to him who hated him (laughs) because he didn't bother to cultivate them. He could have if he'd wanted to, like he twisted Thomas Dunhill and Dixon Wright around his little finger in England.

When young and up-and-coming he could cultivate the esteem of seniors with consummate skill. After the war, when he had 'come' and was 'up', he did not bother any more with that sort of behaviour. He was never rude, never arrogant, and he never tried to get anything for himself. While he was working, the patient was the only thing that mattered. Nothing else, not even the time. The people with whom he got on well with were usually equals and people under him.

He was a good teacher as far as I know. His students liked him. His residents liked being with him, though some didn't like the many long hours of operating and him being late. Nobody liked his unpunctuality, but you just had to put up with this foible, and the reason he was late was he concentrated on caring for previous patients and he forgot the time.

He hated talkfests and administrative meetings that produced pages of agenda and achieved little. He was a man of action, not talk. He never aspired to or approached anywhere near the high administrative positions such as president of the Royal College of Surgeons or the honorary staff of the Royal Melbourne Hospital. He just didn't want those jobs.

The administrators over him were driven mad by him, and you couldn't blame them. Weary chose to turn a blind eye to it. He was an old devil. He was always late for operations. I'd worked out his average lateness was about forty minutes. You can imagine how difficult it was for the anaesthetists. If you were booked to start at two o'clock in the afternoon, then the patient would probably get some mild sedative at twelve o'clock and then their final injection at about half past one or twenty to two, so that they'd be nicely, quietly sedated, in a 'don't care' frame of mind and not frightened when they're wheeled into the theatre. Of course if the surgeon is forty minutes late, that previous injection will have worn off and the patient may worry, saying, 'Why am I delayed?' Usually the anaesthetist knew and would give the patient a little bit more sedative while waiting in the anteroom to the operating theatre.

I was a surgeon who, if my operation was booked to start at two, it started at two. Two o'clock meant that I would be there not later than ten to two, to give me time to get into my operating

boiler suit, cap and mask and start scrubbing up while the anaesthetist started the anaesthetic. But when Weary was the surgeon,
you never knew when he would be there to start, and you didn't
dare start until Weary had appeared in person on the operating
floor. When he got there he was as quick as lightning, getting
changed and on the job.

One day I was called about a patient in another private hospital. Something had gone wrong and they wanted me to look at
it. It wasn't very urgent, I could have left it till after the operation,
but you never knew with Weary when the operation would end.
If I was operating I'd know, Well, that will take me from about
two o'clock until five o'clock, and then I will have time to call at
the hospital and be home in reasonable time for dinner. With
Weary I couldn't do that. The other hospital was on the way, so
I called in and fixed up what was there to be fixed up and then
arrived about thirty minutes late. Who should be there to greet
me? It was the one and only time that Weary was early and in his
operating suit before I arrived. I don't know how much earlier
than me he was, it might have been only five minutes, but he was
changed and he was dying to appear there before me, you see.
With a grin from ear to ear, gloating over me, he said, 'You're
late.' (laughs) I called him a bloody old bastard, or something like
that. 'How did you get here so soon?' But he never said any more
and I didn't either. And the next time, he was late again as usual.
I've never known how he knew to choose that day to come early.

He was usually late with consultations as well as operations.
He often worked in his rooms until ten o'clock or more at night,
and then he would do his rounds, sometimes it was midnight when
he was doing his ward rounds, before he got home. And then he
was awake by five and sometimes he'd see his wife at breakfast time,
but he'd often left for the day's work before she was up.

My wife, who died three years ago, knew Helen, who told

her that sometimes she didn't see Weary for days on end, because she needed her eight hours sleep at night and she'd go to bed at the time you normally would go to bed, at ten or eleven at night. She had her dinner fairly late, normally, between seven and eight, and she had a hotbox on the sideboard to keep his dinner warm. She said, 'I'd know he's been home because the dinner would have been eaten.' Helen accepted it. She was a wonderful woman, marvellous, and Weary worshipped her. Really. Oh dear, it's very sad he managed so little time to show it.

In surgery, once Weary determined on a course, nothing would make him deviate from it. He'd work out what he thought was the right thing or the best thing that could be done under the circumstances, and that he would do. He was indomitable. The most indomitable person I've ever met.

To a fault?

It depends on how you look at it. After all, what is wrong? Right and wrong are very often very difficult to fathom. Is it wrong to operate on incurable cancers in the hope that though you won't cure them, you'll make the rest of life better for the patient? Some would say yes, some would say no.

There are a lot of questions to which there is no definite answer, there is no truth. Nobody knows what the truth is. It perhaps may be found later on. There were so many things in surgery, at that time, that we understand better now. Now we know far more and there are better indications to guide us on what to do and what not to do. But we're still groping with cancer. What is the best? Well, you don't know. You need some indomitable, courageous surgeons like Weary to find out. And he always kept careful records, so that if things didn't turn out well, it was recorded. This helped to know what to do, what not to do, another time. You see, he was learning all the time and most of his patients survived and did get helped. They may have died in the long run but they had better deaths, or better ends to their lives, than they would have had without that surgery. And they all worshipped him.

He was sticking to his moral precept: my patient, my staff, myself. This was his variant of the priorities followed by knights who went to war in the days of chivalry: 'My horse, my men, myself'. He told me this when we were working together shortly after the war. He kept to that during his whole surgical life – you may say *too* much. I think he did it too much in respect to relations with his family, his own family. I think it was unfair to them. He gave too much of himself away and didn't keep enough for the family. But it's very difficult. Any surgeon who is very, very busy and very, very devoted to his work doesn't have much energy left when he gets home at night.

A long time ago Weary told me that he made a vow while he was a POW in Thailand, that if he survived the railway he would care for his prisoner of war mates for the rest of his life, and this he did. Many brought their troubles to his house in Toorak Road, and when they came, those with not a penny to bless themselves were still received at the fine house as honoured guests. He never changed, never changed.

He spoke quietly, he never opened his mouth unless he had something apt to add to the conversation. He was never rude, never spoke ill of others. If asked, the worst he might say of another would be something like, 'I doubt if what he or she is doing or saying is appropriate or wise, or the best way to tackle the situation.' He would never run anybody down.

He was never pushy or offensive. He played rugby until well into his forties. In company he was the life of the party, full of interesting and amusing tales. He had a wonderful command of English. Exactly the right words for any situation flashed at once into his head.

He never was aggressive or arrogant, never. He very rarely lost his temper, but by Jove, if he did. This story was told to me by Weary, so I've only got the little bits that he told me. He was driving along the road – if you've ever been driven by Weary, you'd only do it once! (laughs) I went once. Never again. He disobeyed all the road signs and everything else and took all sorts of risks and always got away with it. This time, he'd nipped in front of somebody and stopped at a traffic light. So there was somebody behind who was very angry. A young man. Much younger than Weary anyway. That's why Weary was rather proud of his effort. This was when Weary was in his seventies.

This chap got out of the car behind and Weary had his driving window down and the man came and told him what he thought of him and, bam! The punch broke Weary's nose, but Weary, like a spring on wire, opened the door, which then knocked the man back, shot out of the car and gave him a couple of punches in the chest, got back in his car and drove off. He told me, 'I gave him a shirt-full of broken ribs.' I am sure that is exactly what he did do. He never picked a fight, but if you picked one with him, beware. You'd come off second-best – twenty-second best. In that case, he knew he had been naughty but he was secretly pleased with himself nevertheless.

He didn't give up operating until he was made to give up because he was losing his skill, and he never seemed to realise that he was not the surgeon of his younger days. The hospitals became reluctant to give him beds and theatre times for his patients, and finally he was advised to stop operating by the Royal College of Surgeons.

I suppose it was very hard to tell him. If they'd told me, I could have talked to him. But I didn't know what was happening. I'd retired and was not hearing any surgical gossip. When I thought I wouldn't like myself operating on me, I stopped. I was sixty-six then. I continued part-time work until I was seventy-five and giving medical opinions in Repat, but not treating and operating on patients. I don't think anyone over seventy can do difficult surgery as well as when younger.

Poor Weary, that was a sad end to his surgical career. He practically had stopped because, as I said, hospitals failed to have beds and theatre times when his secretary rang for them. But when I spoke to him, after I first got a whisper of it and asked him why didn't he retire as I had done, he said, 'I can't say no to my patients. They say I want you to do it, nobody else, and I can't say no.'

In his latter days some people thought he displayed his medals at special functions like a peacock enjoying the limelight. I think that's wrong. He did not care about *gloria mundi* for himself. His motive, I think, was to please the organisations and their people who had bestowed the medals, and also those who were basking in his reflected glory. He did like people to be happy in his presence but his happiness was all in their happiness.

If you forgot his lack of punctuality and not doing enough for his family, he was just the perfect Christian really. Everything he did was to try and help somebody. He just liked doing his duty to please others and was only pleased to be pleasing others. It was misjudging him, I think, to believe he liked parading, peacocking. He liked to do his duty and, now he was a knight, he had to continue to consider others first. That was his motto, which he followed faithfully unto death.

Mavis Ryan spoke of her memories of the Dunlop family in Benalla, and then moved on to talk about the doctor/patient relationship she had with Sir Edward. She consulted him first when she was twenty-six and living in Traralgon.

WHEN I WASN'T getting any better, Mum said, 'Oh, I think you'd better go down and try to see Mr Dunlop. They say he's a marvellous doctor.'

He seems to have been more than just a doctor.
Oh yes, he was. I can't explain it. It was a close relationship, I guess, but you also knew just how far you could go. I knew where my borderline was and I knew I wasn't to step over it. I think those that did might have been in strife.

So where was your borderline?
Well, I hadn't been married long and Jack and I had a row to end all rows. I didn't have anybody to turn to, so I rang Ern up. I was crying my heart out and I said, 'Can I come in to see you?' And he said, 'Oh, I'm terribly busy today, what's the matter?' I said, 'Wo, wo, wo,' you know how when you're crying, no one can understand you. He said, 'Well, look, how long will it take you to get in? I'll wait for you here.' So I went into the surgery but by the time I got in there, I thought, Well, what am I coming in here for? I'd sort of got over my scot and my desolation, but when I was telling Ern about it, I broke down again, and I said, 'My marriage is a complete mockery. I don't want to go on,' and the tears were falling. He said, 'Now steady down now, and tell me all about it. Just sit there and go through the events.' I told him pretty well everything that had been said and he got a bit of a shock, I think, because it was such a ferocious battle.

Then he said, 'Now dry your eyes,' and he gave me some very good advice which stood me in stead for many a day. But I knew that as I'd been to him once in a case like that, I couldn't make a habit of it in the future. He gave me such good advice that I knew how to manage it next time. That's what I mean –

you might have got help once, but you wouldn't go back. Or you couldn't go back, because it was just not there.

He was my husband's doctor, too. When Jack first went to him, he said, 'I've got more patients than I can deal with at the moment. If you don't want to give up drinking and smoking, don't come back, because I've just got far too many.' So when Jack came back to Traralgon I said, 'What are you going to do?' He said, 'I wouldn't give up a man like that. I'll give up my smokes and my grog,' and he did.

Jack suffered from emphysema, and my sister and I used to beg him every year to get the flu injection. Jack was adamant, because he was an Irishman, and he said, 'I'm not going to have that bloody flu injection, I don't care what the old fella says.' So he stomped off up on the train to see Weary. About twelve o'clock the telephone rang and he said, 'I'm over at the chemist. Weary sent me over to get the flu injections.' I went in to see Ern about a fortnight later. He looked at me and his eyes, I've never seen them twinkle so much. They were just absolutely electric blue and I said, 'What's up?' He said, 'Jack had his injection, didn't he?' And of course that brought peels of laughter.

He had a wonderful love for Lady Helen. I only stood on the perimeter of it, I'll admit, and yet it was there for you to see. There's one episode I can never forget as long as I live. One day, he came in and he put his hands on my shoulders and he said, 'My wife is dying.' I got a dreadful shock, I didn't think I'd heard him correctly. He sat down and picked up the phone and in front of me he made all the arrangements for the church service and the burial. Then he turned to me and you could see the devastation it was going to have on him.

He did everything he could. He told me that he took her to Tasmania – apparently they had friends there and Lady Helen loved going over. He said, 'I took her over there in the hope that just something might spark recognition,' but he said there was absolutely nothing. He also used to take her every weekend to church, just the same as they always did, and he'd take her for a drive pretty well every day of the week. He'd put that time aside, but nothing sparked that little point that he was looking for.

You could tell the desperation that he was feeling, that he just couldn't help her in any way. 'You know Mavis,' he said, 'all she wants to do is sit in the chair and sing to herself and rock.' I could have cried for him. It's a shocking thing. If ever there was another love like that, whoever is the recipient of it will be very, very special.

Lady Helen was a beautiful lady. I met her only once, and that was when she didn't know who I was. I took some orchids in one day, because we grow orchids, and Valda said to me, 'It's Lady Helen's birthday today. We'll wrap them up and you can write a card.' Ern wrote me a lovely letter back again, thanking me for the orchids. He said she really appreciated them but that writing a letter was now beyond her.

Once Lady Helen had died he was different altogether. He was just as compassionate but he had a – oh, what shall I say? – a drive. He was in everything. I don't know how Mrs Street ever kept up with him. I used to read in the papers that he was down at Aspendale or he was up at Numurkah, and I thought, Oh no, it's too much. He just drove himself on and I don't know why.

As your surgeon, did he ever lose his temper?
I was in St Andrews Hospital and he'd inserted catheters in various parts of me and he said to the nurse, 'Now rinse those tubes out with water, don't let them block up.' When Jack came to pick me up I was out cold, so he went round to tell Ern and Ern rammed on the hat and tore off in front of Jack. I was in a

bit of a mess by the time he arrived because all the tubes were blocked up. He got hold of them and he ripped them out and absolutely stormed at the sister and this other lass. 'I told you to rinse these out with water.' 'Oh, it wouldn't go in.' 'Course it would go in. Look.' And he just shot the needle in the tubes and squirted it all through and it came away. Then he threw his hat on the floor and stomped on it, and flew off in such a storm that he forgot the hat. Here's this little tweedy thing all squashed on the floor and one of the nurses said to me, 'Sir Edward's left his hat behind, I'd better run after him with it.' I said, 'No fear, you leave it where it is. He'll be back before long.'

It wasn't five minutes and he stormed back into the ward, and made a swipe at the hat, and missed. (laughs) He looked across at me and I wasn't game to laugh, I had to stay absolutely serious. The second time he picked it up and away he went. The poor old hat used to get a bit of a bashing I think, one way and another.

One day, he said to me, 'Don't call me Ern.' I said, 'What am I going to call you then? You've always been Ern.' He said, 'Call me Weary.' I don't know if I ever did call him Weary. I don't think I called him anything. That was another time when I knew how far I could go.

When I spoke with **Sir Benjamin Rank** *he produced the letter reprinted below. 'I was looking back and I found this,' he said. 'I've never read this or shown it to anybody but it does tell you our relative relationships, as it were. This was written by Weary after I had written to congratulate him on the 1977 Australian of the Year award.' He read the letter aloud, then gently folded it and looked up. 'We were different but it's funny, he spent the time and he wrote that out. It's a lovely letter. That's Weary.'*

20 January, 1977

Dear Benny,

Of all the people to have around on the receipt of an 'Australian of the Year' award you would disconcert me most, because I regard you as the outstanding ornament to our profession in our contemporary times.

You have been the complete surgeon and have filled our great offices with distinction and now move with great maturity into the role of senior statesman and a greatly respected administrator, author, orator and counsellor.

It might be a simplification to say that in contrast I have had an easy passage by spilling out the charm. In truth I have strived and agonised over my profession but I lack some essential political fortitude to pursue any political goals against opposition of others. I need to be persuaded to run for any office. I recall with amusement that I once stood against you for the chairmanship for the Royal Melbourne Hospital staff with not the faintest desire or expectation of winning but because Paul Jones persuaded me that there should be an election! No contest.

It was then that the college was run by rather spiky characters in my day like Henry and Julian Orm and after Bill Hailes' death, I decided on a life outside the snakepit. This may be gutlessness. I only hope that it is perhaps more a sensitivity and awareness of a lack of gifts in the field of politics.

I have often felt that those who denigrate would say just one of those birds pushed up by a lot of war nonsense operating with knives and spoon. That aspect was irrelevant. In the time of war I found a gift of insight, discipline and example that could control and influence large forces of men of several nations. I made no capital of this and in fact the high honour recommended by Mountbatten and later by my force commander foundered on 8th Division jealousy, and the Labor Government.

The stubborn devotion of the men I served has won the later recognition of a less heroic nature.

For the rest, I have turned out a volume of work which no one is going to accomplish today and it at least reflects an efficient mastery of most of the standard operations, while suffering brickbats in the high mortality areas of innovation, sweat and endeavour.

Why all this telling of beads? Certainly not self-adulation. Yours was one of the significant letters amongst the flood. It is I suppose a sort of apologia from one who has done so little to raise his profession when confronted by one of such stature. In short it would be more fitting of course if the recognition came to you as I hope it will anyway.

But again not relevant. That which we are, we are.

I shall endeavour to make our paths cross before very long. It was a delightful dinner party out at Vine Street.

Our love to Barbara – if you can get to the end of the dissection.

The TV program! I never seem to see these elusive things, but my thanks anyway. You would handle it superbly.

Love from us all

Weary

*After the war, **Sir Benjamin Rank** was a consulting plastic surgeon at the Royal Melbourne Hospital, where he was a colleague of Weary Dunlop's. The Colombo Plan, to which Sir Benjamin refers below, was established in 1950 at a meeting of*

*Commonwealth foreign ministers in Colombo as a co-operative
scheme to assist the economic development of Commonwealth
members and dependent territories in South and South-East
Asia. The recipient countries could request aid which included
loans, grants, technical advice and assistance and training. By
1954 the USA and Japan had joined as donor nations, and the
recipient nations included most of South-East Asia.*

I WENT FROM Britain to join up in France and then to the
Middle East. Then, after seven years away, I was posted to a
hospital within walking distance of our family home in
Heidleberg. Extraordinary. I met Helen then, she was with her
mother.

I was on the next ship to Weary's, an American ship bound
for Burma, but the captain refused to take his ship in. He said, 'I
won't take a ship with all these people on it through the straits
without air support,' and he wouldn't. We went round and round
and round in the bay for a while and then he said, 'We're going
south.' We were the first ship from the 6th Division to get back
to Australia. That's the fortunes . . . it's just extraordinary.

Were you surprised to learn of Weary's wartime pursuits?
Weary could do what other people couldn't do. And he did.
Lots of prisoners of war never came back and Weary coped with
it.

And after the war?
After the war it took him a little while to get adjusted, you know
what I mean. To get his practice going. After we got back from
the war, he was sort of getting organised.

I was involved in Colombo Plan activities right from 1951,
early on. In fact, I was the test pilot who introduced it into

medicine. The Colombo Plan wasn't in the matters medical then except in the field of tuberculosis control, because TB was very rife and they were sending cases down to me from Japan and Singapore.

I went right to the top and banged on Casey's door [Richard Casey, then Minister for External Affairs] and as a result I went to Singapore and Malaya. Anyway after that, I wrote a long report, and they said they wanted a neurosurgeon, I think, so they changed the Colombo Plan and that was the genesis of it. Of course a lot of people then went. When that sort of work was embraced in the Colombo Plan arrangement a few years later, Weary started doing the same sort of work as I had done. Weary was always interested in Asian affairs, rather related to his Thailand experience.

One of the things about Weary, time didn't mean anything to him. The clock didn't worry him. He was generally always late. No concept of time. And he'd go on until three o'clock while everybody was sitting out there waiting. It was the same with his family, I think. Poor Helen. She'd wait at the evening meal and Weary would turn up at eight o'clock and he'd have a couple of people with him. That sort of thing. No concept of time.

My wife Barbara played golf with Helen quite a lot. Weary played golf but he hit like hell. Always in the bush . . . but he never lost his ball. He always had a pocket full of balls. He'd come out and say 'Found it.' He was not good at that sort of sport at all. Or tennis. He was as clumsy as could be on a tennis court.

I think Helen had a hell of a time really. There was a time when there were a lot of Government House functions and we were always invited of course, knights of the realm, so to speak, and poor Helen could hardly stand up, she was that tired. And of course she eventually couldn't cope.

He didn't look after his family really. It wasn't that he wasn't good, he just didn't give them any time. He would over-commit himself. That's why he didn't get on in the professional world. He gained recognition for his contributions and he was on a lot of foundations but that was all related to his POW experience. He was never on any hospital committees or College of Surgeons' committees or anything like that. He wasn't active in that sort of way. Part of it was, I think, because of the time he was away – he had to catch up a bit. But also he was never any good at that sort of thing. He was not a good committee man. He'd forget to come or he'd come an hour late, and people don't take that.

We had one extraordinary example here. The person over the road is a Rotarian. He came and said to me that Weary was coming down to address a charity function over at the village school and would I come? Black tie job and all this. I said we would, and blow me down, I was getting dressed and the man came and he said 'Benny, Weary is not coming. Would you come and speak?' I said, 'Oh, for God's sake.' So I did and I went and did what he was going to do. He might have been sick or something, I think he probably was, but he hadn't told anyone, you know what I mean? He didn't think of these things. So this is why he was never . . . his effort was very individual.

Then he'd write you a very nice letter after it.

Was he a man who enjoyed his fame?
Oh, yes, he loved it. Albeit a sin to covet honour, I think Weary loved getting up in his medals and that sort of thing. We were members of the Order of St Michael and St George together. I was senior in that order to Weary, but he had other honours, and he would always come with all his medals. What's more, when he got a higher honour of the same sort, he wore them both. Covered

in medals and rightly so. Oh no, he enjoyed that. He was not completely isolated and egotistical. He liked praise and he liked to give praise. Render unto Caesar the things that are Caesar's.

Vera Marquis and I met one winter's evening at her South Yarra home. As Weary's former secretary, Vera Hart, she was wary that her observations could be misinterpreted but we agreed that the real man was far larger than the myth created around him. 'And what I've said to you, I've said to him,' she said. 'None of it is ever meant to be derogatory at all. It's said with affection and with truth.'

I ACTUALLY GO back to 1954. At that time, there was quite a feeling about married women working. It was the days before the pill and prospective employers thought, Oh, you'll probably become pregnant and then they'd have to replace you. It really annoyed me that sort of attitude.

This agency said they had a job with some surgeon and I said, 'Oh, I don't have any medical background,' and they said, 'No, he wanted someone with very strong secretarial skills.' So I went along to this interview and I remember them saying how famous he was and, coming from Sydney, that meant nothing to me.

I had the interview, and I should have known then what I'd be letting myself in for. He kept me waiting an hour. It was a Saturday morning and I really thought I had the wrong address. I was standing outside his rooms thinking, Will I wait or not, and in came this giant of a man who was 6'4" and 16 stone. He had this bag and an armful of x-rays and he was trying to unlock the door and raise his Homburg, because he always wore a Homburg then, and then of course he dropped everything and said, 'In you go.'

I had to wait while he tried to get his office ready. He decided he'd better put the blind up and he yanked it so hard the thing came crashing down and hit him on the nose – I didn't really know whether to laugh or whatever – and then he thought he'd be very efficient and take some notes and found that his fountain pen didn't have any ink, so he had to fiddle around and get the ink bottle out and there was this great big blot over everything. And with that he threw the pen down and said, 'I'm making a terrible impression, aren't I?' I burst out laughing, and he laughed.

But the thing that made me really take the job – he asked if I was looking for something permanent and then he said, 'No, no, I retract that, because there's nothing permanent in this life.' And I thought, I could work with that, someone with that sort of attitude. And so I started.

I had planned to have a week's leave in-between jobs and I got an urgent telephone call from him because his other secretary had walked out. I hadn't realised that no one until that point had lasted longer than a month with him. He was so difficult. Everything was in the most dreadful mess and there was no one there to ask and there I was, my first day, and I had no medical background whatsoever. So the hard road started.

It was a tremendous challenge because I'd always been on top of jobs. My former employers had said glowing things about me and I knew that I was good at my work and there I was confronted with this chaos. It was the height of his practice. Most surgeons have one public hospital appointment but he had three and we had to fit patients in wherever we could. The hours were very long and Saturday mornings were always worked. And he was extremely difficult because he would never explain anything and he could be terribly bad tempered because he wouldn't suffer fools.

He was wonderful to his patients, they absolutely adored him. Because of the fact that he had complete disregard for time, probably as a result of his POW experiences, he could be maybe three hours late. You can imagine what that does to other surgeons who are waiting and so I would do all these devious things, like telling him that he would be starting an hour earlier or something. I got caught once, and I must admit I just denied it.

But those first three weeks were really very rugged. And then one terrible day I couldn't find him and I had something difficult. I knew he was at St Andrews so I rang the receptionist there and said, 'Look, I think he's really still in the building and I'd be really grateful if you could make some discreet enquiries,' and she said, 'Hang on, I think he's coming out of the lift.'

So she smiled sweetly and beckoned him over, and of course he loved women who smiled sweetly at him, and she said, 'There's a telephone call, a nice young lady on the other end.' In getting to the phone he had this great big wooden box which contained his gastroscope and instead of putting it down he tried to pick up the phone without letting go of it and in so doing, he dropped it.

And so of course, his mood changed and then he discovered it was me at the other end and the language he used would have shocked a navvy. I was really furious about that so I banged the phone down in his ear, and it was one of those big black old phones, so if you thudded that down it really would hurt your eardrum. I was so angry. He got quite a shock. I don't think anyone had ever done that to him in his life. All the POWs used to call him 'Christ of the Burma Railway'.

By the time he got to his next destination he must have calmed down so he rang me, and I was still fuming. I said, 'I just want to get one thing straight now Mr Dunlop, I'm not used to being sworn at. As far as I'm concerned, no job is worth it if I have to put up with that sort of nonsense. I don't think you're God, I just think you are another member of the human race.'

There was a stunned silence. Then, 'Oh honey, what penance can I serve? Can I walk a tightrope for you?' I was still very angry, and I said, 'Well, quite frankly Mr Dunlop, I think the tightrope would be better suited around your neck.' And with that he laughed, and I sort of calmed down. But from that point on, he was terrific. He never ever had another outbreak like that, he never ever swore at me again.

So that was the start, and I broke the record because I stayed there for five years. We had this really great relationship but when I started my family and moved to Sydney, of course I had to resign from my job. That was in 1959.

From that foundation, he remained my closest friend. I saw him just a few days before he died. He was the kindest person that I've ever known and he became such a wonderful friend. My daughter is his goddaughter. He's probably got quite a few godchildren. But he was always there.

When I was working for him, he'd break out once a year and disappear and when he came back he'd test the water. He'd throw his Homburg into my office and if I kicked it out, he knew that he'd gone too far and then he'd do a very cowardly thing. Because I'd have all the patients' records, he'd wait until I either went to the loo or went to the door and he'd run out and pick up all the patients' records and run back with them. So he could then come in and get the patients himself, which he always liked to do anyway and the patients just loved that.

After work on Saturday, he used to drive me home and he wouldn't even say 'have lunch with us' he'd just turn into 605 Toorak Road. I really thought it was an imposition. If I'd been Helen I wouldn't have wanted anyone else coming in. And then sometimes he'd fall asleep in the chair so I would just tiptoe out and order a taxi and get myself home.

I think Helen adored him. When I knew them, her mother was still alive and he used to call Mrs Ferguson Tossie which was short for La Tosca and she adored him. I used to think, Gosh, poor Helen, she could probably never sound off about him because her own mother would come to his defence. I used to think it was a very difficult life.

But he was difficult, he really was. He had a great capacity for sleep. All the time I knew him, he'd have these catnaps of five minutes, ten minutes, whatever and then be really refreshed. He was as strong as an ox, he had wonderful health. He could thank his parents for that, growing up in Benalla. A lot of Benalla people would come in. His name was Ernest Edward but the brass plate just said Mr Edward Dunlop and of course he was Weary to his close friends. But the farmers would come in and they'd say, 'Good day Ern,' and of course I just used to love it. (laughs) And he knew the effect it would be having on me, and he'd take them off and look back and poke his tongue out at me.

I adored him like most people, but the warts and all were there. He had all these other wonderful qualities but boy, he sure had his share of human frailties as well. Occasionally he'd say, 'Honey could you drive me down to the Melbourne Club?' I'd say 'Oh all right, but it's conditional.' He'd say, 'What? What is it?' I'd say, 'Well, there are two things. Don't you dare sit in the back seat and the other is don't you dare engage me in conversation with the other drivers.'

He was a terrible driver. If he was telling you a story – and he had loads of stories – that he wanted to finish before he got to a destination, he'd drop the speed down to about five miles an hour and he'd be sitting out in the middle of the road and you'd be abused. I used to slink down, trying not to be seen, because it really was so embarrassing. People would be horning him, yelling at him and he would be just oblivious to it all and continue on his way.

It was probably a pretty unique relationship, I guess, because we knew each other so well. Warts and all for us both. Valda and I both agreed we survived with him because we were strong people. That if you weren't, you would not have been able to work with him. He was very demanding. And also, because he gave so much to patients, he really expected everyone else to do the same.

In later years, he had an accident up at the farm, at St Andrews, a pretty bad one. Valda rang me and told me he was in Freemasons hospital, and it had been a while before he was found – a fractured femur and cracked ribs and he was really pretty knocked around and he was really very depressed. She said, 'Would you go to cheer him up? You're one person who can cheer him up.'

On my first visit at the Freemasons I was escorted down, and I went back a week or two later and I got such frosty reception from the nursing staff. I thought Oh-oh, I wonder what he's up to. No escort this time – it was, 'Oh yeah, his room's down there.' I went in and I said, 'What have you been up to?' 'Oh,' he said, 'I went out last night.' I forget what it was, it was some dinner he wanted to go to. I said, 'You can't treat the hospital like a motel, they'll kick you out.' He thought it was terribly funny.

The next thing, there was a little knock on the door and it's one of his patients – a dear little old lady. So she came in and she sat down and the next thing he's writing a prescription. And I was thinking, This is going to be good, she's going to be settled in for the afternoon because he can't escape, so I said, 'I've got to go,' and I went over to give him a little kiss goodbye and he whispered, 'Don't leave me. Please don't leave me.' And I said, 'I've got to go, bye bye.'

I rang Valda and so we had a really good old chuckle about that. It served him right. Not only was he turning the hospital into a hotel, he was turning it into his consulting rooms. No wonder they were getting jack of him.

Did the publication of the diaries in 1986 raise his public profile?

Oh, it did. He wasn't really quite forgotten when I was working for him but he was something of the past. It allowed a younger generation to know something about it. I think the diaries should be standard reading for all high school and secondary students, I really do.

The state funeral really was an incredible occasion – to have brought the whole of Melbourne to a halt. When the cortege was coming out, there was this poor old digger who was in his uniform with all his medals and he collapsed just as it came up to that particular pew. It halted the procession and it went through my mind, that I wouldn't have been at all surprised if the lid had lifted up and he'd popped out and seen to him. (laughs) And Valda said the same thing later. It wasn't an irreverent thing, it was just typical of him.

One of the lovely parts of it all was how the Dunlop family insisted the first few pews were reserved for the ex-POWs. That meant that Keating and co had to sit behind them. I thought, what a pity he's missing this, he would have loved it.

I was probably one of the last people he operated on. I got breast cancer about eighteen years ago and he was seventy when he operated. I had this infinite care and attention with two visits a day in hospital, seven days a week. No other surgeon would do that. But he did that for all his patients.

There were some friends who were a little bit surprised that I wanted him to operate because of his age and one asked me, 'Why did you go to him?' And I said, 'Well, the operation, I believe, required great skill but it didn't require great stamina, and it was the after care – I knew that I would have that kindness.'

When I asked him about breast reconstruction, he was against that and he gave me the reasons. Other lumps appear, it reduces your chances. A year later, I consulted a plastic surgeon and I told Sir Edward I was going to do it and he was great. He said, 'Look, it's your decision.' The requirements for the reconstruction were two things: that the pectoral muscle hadn't been damaged, and there had to be sufficient skin in the flap. The plastic surgeon said it was a beautiful job and she didn't have to say that.

I wouldn't have consulted him when I was working with him, added to which I was very healthy then. But that barrier had been removed and I continued to see him as a patient after my operation. I firmly believed up until the time of his death that he was the best diagnostician in Melbourne. I used to say to people, 'Well, look, if I had something serious the matter with me, I know that he would be able to diagnose it correctly, and he would then be able to refer me to the best person.' Added to which I would have engaged him to keep an eye on things during the operation. So that's how I viewed him.

I guess if I was asked what I learnt from him there were two very big things. One, I think that I learnt courage from him. He and Helen invited me to the premiere of *The Bridge on the River Kwai*. He was very upset with that film. Watching it was a very emotional experience for him. It was meant to be based on his life and his experiences in Thailand and there were a lot of inaccuracies, and he was a stickler for accuracy. There was a reception for it afterwards and we didn't stay. Afterwards we went back to 605. It was winter and it was the first time in my life that I had drunk cognac and he wanted to have this talk. He had something that he really wanted to tell me, and I can remember these words very well after all these years. He said, 'There's one thing that I want to say to you, honey. As you go through life, and you probably will get your share of traumas, just remember, they will either make you or break you, there is no middle road.' And I remembered that all my life. I've never forgotten those words.

The other thing was his letter writing. He would be perhaps two hours late and we would have an overflowing waiting room, to say nothing about urgent calls and everything else, and he would come in and he wouldn't say a word.

This is before we moved – my office was the kitchen. Talk about ergonomics, you know, I'd sit on a stool with the typewriter on a bench and he'd sit on this garbage tin, this great big garbage can in there, and he'd be oblivious to anything, and he'd be writing, and I'd be yelling, seething, until I learned that what he was doing was the most wonderful thing.

It could be a letter of condolences to the family of a patient who'd died, it could be a thank you letter, it could be a letter of congratulations, and it would all be in his own hand and he'd even address the envelope. And that would be done. That really was the right thing to do.

If you're running two hours late, what's another five or ten minutes? But the important thing was how the recipients of those letters felt, to have had a letter – and they'd be beautiful letters – and he did that all his life. The timing is important. There is no point in getting a thank you letter a month after an event. It was his sense of priority really. I never knew anyone with the timing he had.

He really was unique – a very important part of my life. I

feel I have been pretty privileged to have had the experience and the friendship. The friendship above everything.

*On 30 June, 1980, Sir Edward wrote to **Adrienne Holzer** of the Anti-Cancer Council of Victoria.*

30 June, 1980

Dear Adrienne,
I was concerned to hear of your father's sudden death today. Such things always leave a great void as well as the immediate grievous loss.

A parent is such a reassuring link between past and present, and somehow we never fully resolve this during our lives together. You will need a little time to get over the shock, and tend family needs.
With my deep sympathy.
Yours sincerely,
E.E. Dunlop

***Professor Richard Lovell** renewed his acquaintance with Weary Dunlop when he took up the chair of medicine at the University of Melbourne, where Weary was a lecturer in surgery, in 1955.*

AS THE YEARS went by, I heard and learnt more about Weary's capacity and activities as a surgeon. I think I'm left with the abiding impression that my early judgment was right, that Weary's outstanding strengths were that he was an absolutely first-class doctor who was always deeply interested in the whole patient and everything about them, their friends and relatives, what their illness meant to them and so on. I suspect it was this capacity to see people in the whole and take trouble to understand them apart from the acute surgical problem that they presented, which made him singularly designed, as it were, to cope with the sorts of problems he had to cope with in Thailand.

Weary at one stage became chairman of the medical staff at the Royal Melbourne and I remember that when he took the chair for his first meeting of his year in office he said there was nothing so inevitable as seniority. The chairmanship of the staff used to tend to go to people roughly in order of seniority.

He was the most terrible chairman. I think we used to meet at 8.15 p.m. or something like that. Of course in those days everyone would have been rather tired and a number of people would have taken the opportunity to go their club and have quick dinner and a few glasses of wine before the meeting, so people tended to arrive in a rather relaxed mood and time meant nothing to them.

But even having said that, it meant even less to Weary, because at about ten o'clock you would still be dealing with business arising out of the last minutes. Weary seemed to have no volition to get ahead with a businesslike meeting – again there was a sense of timelessness. This may well have been one of his tremendous strengths in coping with situations like Thailand, where it was important that someone should have no sense of time and it helped their innate obstinacy because they didn't have any sense of dealing with anything accept the problem that was immediately confronting them.

It is a component, in a sense, of a good doctor, because a good doctor consulting with a patient should have their attention totally focused on the patient and on nothing else. And if the particular patient in front of you is time-consuming, it's a great advantage not to have a sense of time, because the patient must be aware that you are in no sense looking at your watch, you're just there for as long as you need to be there to cope with the patient's situation at that particular moment. There was an up side in terms of direct personal relationships with patients, and a down side – it's a socially undesirable trait.

My picture of Weary was that he was absolutely, quintessentially a non-committee man – he was a loner. My picture of Weary is as a loner, not wishing to have other people influencing his decisions and perhaps being relatively intolerant of having to sit and listen to and join in some consensus operation. So it doesn't surprise me that he didn't contribute in any committee-like activities anywhere with any enthusiasm. I think he was very much his own man.

Freda Thomas started nursing at St Andrews Hospital in East Melbourne in 1950 and retired in 1980. She was seventy-seven when we spoke, yet she seemed much younger, perhaps because she was sharing a house with her very lively and alert ninety-five-year-old mother.

WEARY WAS ONE of the foremost surgeons. He was a general surgeon, he covered a wide range. He wanted to help his patients, that was the attitude. Even something he had perhaps done before, he would deviate from the original. He would think I can help him or her if I did that. He'd think about it a long time and then implement it. He was a capable practical person not just a dreamer or a delegator, and he liked people, he liked people very much. I think the war was an extra in his life, about which so much has been written. Take that right out and you still have quite a worthy, capable wonderful person.

When he was accorded a *This is Your Life* and Roger Climpson came, they weren't too sure how to get Weary to be in the right place at exactly the right time, because, you know, he was often late. Heather Dunlop, his daughter-in-law, was working for him then and she rang me up and said, 'You know you're having a birthday next Tuesday.' I said, 'I just had one ten months ago, I don't want another one.' 'Oh well,' she said, 'I'm afraid you're getting one. We've got to get Weary there at eleven o'clock and the only way we'll get him there really on time is to say they're giving you a birthday party and that it's got to be at eleven.' I thought, Cripes, I'll have to have another birthday.

He arrived at the hospital and he looked around and he couldn't see any birthday evidence because we had a little staff room. He looked in first thing, nothing there, and I trailed him off to see a patient, just so that the cameras would come out of the right door at the right time. He really was surprised. He stood stock-still. He just couldn't believe it. And when Roger Climpson approached him and said, 'Sir Edward, this is your life', he just stood there, and he looked like a great big . . . he looked like a great big penguin! He clearly was surprised, so we achieved that. He had big feet and a sort of long coat and if he got into one of these 'Mm' looking into the middle distance moods, he always reminded me of a penguin.

Sir Albert Coates, the surgeon, and the resuscitationist Dr Drevermann and Dougy Donald were all in the war with him too. They all worked at the hospital. They used to bait one another, in a friendly way. They were great friends but they'd put things over one another, like most smart groups do.

He had so many strings to his bow. We had a patient for ten o'clock surgery who had her pre-operative medication and at quarter to four, she's still waiting. But the theatre staff's day was often planned around this possibility. He got on very well with the people who knew him, but if you had a new theatre sister, well, of course you'd have chaos. But that's why our centre was one place he liked to work, because we were all used to him.

His day had so much in it. You couldn't expect to be on automatic switch all the time. Then of course two things could go amiss. Or it could take longer, be more difficult. I think that he was inclined to have ten minutes shut eye in the car occasionally. That's a tale out of school.

He used to come out of the front of St Andrews at twenty past four on a Friday – you know the traffic, and it was a one-way street there – and Weary would come out the wrong way and turn right. You see, it's only two car lengths off Lansdowne Street. A smarty, I got up at five one morning going up to the country, and I thought, If Weary can do it on a Friday, I can do it on a Sunday morning. I dead-heated with a carload of police, and I waved them on, all the time blaming Edward, thinking, Well, he did it, why shouldn't I?

He would appear at ten to eleven at night when everyone was asleep. 'They're asleep,' you'd say. 'Very creditable,' he'd say, 'you must be nursing them well.' But he'd still go in and put the light on. Several of the patients, you know, the laying on of hands was important to them. They really did think he was magnificent. He had one dear old lady, she was terminal, and so long as Weary would come . . . and he knew that and he used to come.

That's why he was often late. He would come in and sit with them and listen – he would let them talk to him for at least five minutes. It didn't matter what it was about. I think this old lady in question, I think her husband had been a friend of his, and it wouldn't have troubled her had he come in the middle of the night, Sir Edward was there and that fixed the day.

Were you very aware of Weary's knighthood in 1969?

The day his title was announced, he came downstairs with the Homburg hat held to his left breast, looking sweet, and I said, 'Ah, Sir Edward Bear.' Wrong thing. You see, you had to be cuddled if you were Edward Bear. (laughs) Then he put his hat down and went and saw the patients and one of my friends got a daffodil and stuck it in the band of his hat. When he came back, he picked it up as if he didn't see it and he went down to the next floor. We rang to see what happened and it wasn't there when he got there. We think he ate it. Oh, he could be a trick, you know.

At one stage St Andrews had the head of the clan from Scotland come over and Edward came in, in his kilt, and he had the two boys with him, too, all in their kilts. Well, did he make history. Everyone was following him up and down the corridor but he knew he'd make a sensation and he loved it.

He was a bit of a trick. If he'd had more time, he'd have been a greater trick. If he hadn't the war thing, I think he'd have been even more of a personality. He sort of thought he was observed because of that, if you know what I mean. But occasionally he'd lash out. He arrived one day in a new suit and a new hat with a feather in the side of it – it was just when feathers were in. He came by and I saw him and said, 'Mm, Tom Piper.' Remember the Tom Piper pudding tin with the little red fellow with the hat with a green feather? He gave me rather a queer look but away he went. About a fortnight later, I was speaking with some specialists and someone else quite important from the Royal Melbourne Hospital. Weary shuffles right over close to me and says, 'Mm, Tom Piper,' and away he goes. They said, 'Wasn't that Dunlop? What's the matter with him?'

Apparently the day before he'd been to the supermarket with Helen and he'd come upon that little pudding tin with

Tom Piper on it, and the pennies had dropped. He knew that I'd lunged at him, you see. He'd woken up. I said to him, 'What did you do that for? Everyone wondered what the heck you were talking about.' And he said 'Mm, saw him on the tin.' (laughs)

Did he operate for too long?
Many of us perhaps thought that. It was getting too much for him, I think. He was tired. He was very 'with it' but physically it was a bit much. He was working still to some extent when I left in 1980. Not a lot.

Did he ever bring his sons into the hospital with him?
His kids were little when I first knew him. He used to leave them sitting in the car. He brought one to the floor one day, sitting there, writing all over the papers. He said, 'Has my Dad gone home?' I said, 'Oh, he wouldn't go home and leave you.' He said, 'He left me at the Mercy last week.' I had nursed his wife and his mother-in-law so the family knew me very well. Helen was a bit like him. I think they understood each other. She was a dear.

He had a great fondness for the royal family. Very keen on Her Majesty, the Dowager Queen and he was always invited over to Government House when she was here. Once, he was late getting there and tried to deviate amongst the heavy traffic, whereupon a young policeman said, 'You can't go in there.' 'I think I can,' he said. 'I think Her Majesty would be disappointed if I was late.' Tricky.

He was very proud of the fact that the Queen Mother knew him and he was invited over to Balmoral and things like that. I think he enjoyed that. But not so much, I felt, for the glory of it, as the fact of what it proved – a little boy from the back of

Benalla, to get to be known by the Queen is really quite . . . I wouldn't mind knowing old Liz myself!

Did he speak about his wartime experiences much?
For months he wouldn't mention it, and then something would trigger him off and he would say, 'I remember when we were in Changi . . .' What he'd tell you wouldn't be a great thing, just incidentals. He might have dwelt on it himself but he certainly didn't bore you with it.

In the war, he was the right man in the right place at the right time. He was good professionally, and he knew his responsibility about keeping diaries. How he kept those diaries, I don't know. Even if he was sick, he kept his diaries very well. Well, it was a war record, and he realised that. As I say, he was a practical person.

The Melbourne surgeon **Robert Marshall** *worked alongside Weary in the operating theatre from 1953 to 1963, assisting in almost all his major operations during that period. He is at once one of Sir Edward's greatest fans and most lucid critics. The obituary he wrote for the* Australian and New Zealand Journal of Surgery, *which closes this chapter, is recommended by supporters and detractors alike as a fair and accurate account of Sir Edward's surgical career.*

HE HAD A lot of tremendously good characteristics, and I admired him immensely, but that didn't blind me to the fact that he could drive you crazy on occasions. Like all fellows with very strong personalities, there's always a flipside, and the flipside to him was that he really was an impossible fellow to work with. His absolute total disregard for his own or anybody else's comfort or convenience led him to behave in a manner that, I don't know, a lesser man just wouldn't have got away with. He would habitually be two hours late for operating appointments. God knows what he was doing. A lot of the time he was late because he had spent so much time doing whatever else had to be done, but you couldn't say that was the case at eight o'clock in the morning.

He would book operating sessions at eight o'clock in the morning and he'd quite frequently turn up at ten o'clock. Let's face it, if you're two hours late for something there's no point in giving excuses. All you can do is say 'I'm sorry'. But Weary wasn't one to say he was sorry, he would just sort of pile in and say, 'Well, let's get going,' and that was the way it went.

Was he just oblivious to time?
He *behaved* as if he was oblivious. In fact, he was a very smart fellow. He was one of the most intelligent men you could ever meet. He couldn't possibly have not been aware of the effect he was having, but I don't think he cared – he thought there were more important things. This was the other side of his personality, which not just I but everybody found intensely irritating. As I said in the obituary, in turns we were instructed by him, stimulated, infuriated and exhausted.

He'd just work himself into the ground, except that he never let it appear that he was working himself into the ground. But he really did, and I think he did it almost deliberately, in the sense of provoking other people, as if to say: 'I'll just show them a thing or two. I'll just prove that we can work until we drop and if they complain, well, to hell with them.'

One of the things about Weary, I learnt quite early on, was that one should never get into a drinking session with him because, as a matter of honour, he would drink you under the table. In everything, even the smallest things, he cultivated this air of indestructibility. It's not that he was a liquor-head at all. I can't imagine anything worse from Weary's point of view than being drunk. But he had to drink and remain upright while everybody else fell under the table.

Everything was competitive with Weary. He had to be the best at what he was doing, he had to succeed at what he was doing. He couldn't stand the thought of failure and this drove him on, with sometimes excessive zeal, to doing operations with disastrous results – with the best of intentions – because he just had this built-in compulsion to get on with it, to survive.

His surgical persona was interesting. He used to do these enormous marathon operations. He was capable of doing the most beautiful surgery, but it often wasn't beautiful. He had a bit of a visual problem, I think because of a vitamin deficiency during the war, and I don't think his eyesight was all that it ought to have been. He could get into trouble operating because of that, and he would get problems arising that would then take hours and hours to get out of.

There are very few operations in surgery that should take longer than two or three hours, you see, but Weary would not infrequently go on for six or seven hours. This was usually because there had been some mishap and he had to get himself out of trouble. There was a correspondingly high mortality rate in those particular patients.

I think that Weary had remarkable and admirable persistence, a very good keen brain and keen surgical judgment – his judgment was excellent. But I must admit if I had had one of these terrible conditions myself, it would have been a nice idea to have had Weary say what was to be done and then get somebody like my friend Graham MacKenzie, who's a beautiful surgeon, to actually do the operation.

A very interesting conversation happened one day, with

Gordon Stanton, his anaesthetist. Weary was doing an abdomino-perineal resection for a cancer of the rectum. He did the top operation with me helping him, then went around to the bottom end and did the lower operation, again with me helping him. The whole thing took about three or four hours, maybe even longer.

Now the customary way is to have two surgeons – one doing the lower end, one doing the top, operating simultane-ously – and the whole thing's over in an hour or an hour and a half. I've done many such operations with colleagues. This was at the stage when I was about forty, I suppose, and nearly at the height of my powers. I flatter myself that I'm a deft and good surgeon – others will tell you whether that's true or not. I flatter myself that I was a better operator than Weary in the long run. But we'd done one of these and it had gone on and on and on. Gordon Stanton said to him, 'Weary, have you ever thought of doing these combined? Why don't you get Bob to do the lower end?' And Weary looked at me and he looked at Gordon and he said, 'Mm, of course if you've got two surgeons of approximately equal ability, I suppose there might be something to be said for that, but really I prefer to do the thing myself.' (laughs)

I thought, You . . . how dare you! But this was a different era, I didn't say anything. I just thought, Well, God. I looked at Gordon and raised my eyebrows and he raised his eyebrows. It was Weary's patient, after all, and he was entitled to treat him as he saw fit, but that was an interesting measure of his attitude to those around him. He had an absolutely overweening belief in his own ability, as you might imagine. He was proving it all the time to himself.

Gordon and I used to laugh about this. 'It just shows what he thinks of you,' said Gordon. 'Well,' I said, 'I console myself that it's not just me, he thinks that about everybody, whether it's justified or not.' He had absolutely monumental self-confidence. He thought of himself, I believe, as the best sort of colonial Englishman and a cut above everybody else. I don't mean in the sense of being worth more, because humility was also a characteristic that he admired, and if anyone had said, 'You're a conceited bastard', I'm sure he would have been deeply offended by that. Except that that's how he behaved.

You got the impression that he was performing, somehow, to an invisible audience, probably of himself in his own head. He was behaving the way he believed he ought to behave – *noblesse oblige*. As I have got older myself, I have recognised my own motivations more clearly, and also other people's motivations, and realised how often people do things because that's what they think they ought to be doing. Indeed, there's nothing wrong with that, this concept is called a sense of duty, if you will.

Do you believe he continued to operate for too long?

Yes, there's no question of that. He was still operating when he was seventy-seven, you see, and he was incompetent by then and he had to be stopped. He didn't get to the stage of one surgeon I once worked with who went mad and killed people. It wasn't like that at all. It was just that he couldn't come to grips with the fact that he was getting on and was too old. And, well, he was never as good as he thought he was, but it was only when he was seventy-five that he was really bad. He should have stopped.

He was very much a one-off. He was so idiosyncratic in so many different ways that I slide away all the time, from comparing him with other people. He was really quite unique, nobody else was like that. There were other good surgeons, and terrific surgeons and bad surgeons and so forth, but there was nobody who had this sort of overwhelming, total personality that Weary had. He would just ride roughshod over anybody. I'm glad I never had to fight against him. In the ring for instance, it would be diabolical. He was intervarsity heavyweight boxing champion. Just imagine: you would hit him and he wouldn't take any notice.

Did he leave much time for his family?

Helen was a most loyal wife, but I think Weary didn't have enough time in his life to spare much for his family. He couldn't have. He used to work twenty-four hours at a stretch, on and on. I did too for a while. All successful surgeons have this problem. I'm very conscious of the fact. Nowadays I try to make up for the neglect I might have shown my children. For ten years I never took a holiday. I was never home. I'd get home at eleven o'clock at night half the time. I retired partially at the age of forty-six and since then have taken a couple of months off a year. But Weary worked all his life, you see. Weary's boys would have suffered from the 'Important Father Syndrome' in a very big way: this overwhelming fellow was their father. For instance, one of the things that got me about Weary, he took one of his sons' appendix out one day, one Saturday morning. I found out about this later. Apparently his son woke up, he had a pain, and Weary put him in the car, took him to St Andrews hospital, rang an anaesthetist and took his son's appendix out.

Now, it's difficult to explain to you the enormity of that – I will not treat my family, I won't even examine them. I very particularly have a very good general practitioner. My daughter got appendicitis, but I called in our general practitioner, a very good chap, and he said, 'Well, she needs her appendix out, who would you like me to get?' I said, 'I have no opinion in the matter, I'm sure whoever you get will be excellent,' and he chose a man who was a friend of mine. But my point is that doctors really ought to distance themselves from the treating of their families, unless there is no one else around, in which case they have to. Weary didn't and I think it was very revealing about the man. I might say that his son was fine, but I disapproved.

Weary has a lot of vehement detractors.
There were a lot of them about, and a lot of them didn't know Weary very well. Orme-Smith for instance, the then senior surgeon at the Royal Melbourne Hospital, was terribly bad-tempered, much given to throwing instruments, and very much disliked, I might say, by many of his juniors. He was storming up and down one day shouting, 'You might be the Christ of Changi but you're not God Almighty in this hospital'. Weary did infuriate many of his colleagues.

What was Weary's response?
He'd just absolutely ignore it.

You chose to include Weary's foibles in the obituary you wrote.
I did spend a lot of time writing that. I rewrote and rewrote and rewrote, trying to get it right – to present him as a whole person, not as a stick figure but as a human being. As I say, he was vain, he was egotistical, he was absolutely abominably rude in his disregard for other peoples' convenience, and unfortunately he rubbed a lot of feathers the wrong way, particularly among his more senior colleagues. There were some of them who couldn't stand him, they thought he was an upstart and a mountebank.

A lot of people are very reluctant to criticise anybody even in the mildest terms because they figure it's likely to be taken in the wrong way. I suppose some of the things I say are open to that, too. You could take them the wrong way and say, 'This is someone who is being awfully pernickety and can't give a man the credit for being a great chap.' But I think if you knew Weary at all, you'd have to come down on the side of saying he was a most extraordinary character, that his sterling qualities were just pure gold, but that he was a very hard man to live with and he made some pretty bad boo-boos because of those very sterling characteristics. In fact, if he hadn't had these character defects, you might say he'd have been unbearable. You couldn't stand it, I think. So there's something to criticise. But it's strange, isn't it?

Sir Edward's former patient **Margaret Spinney** *and I spoke in her unit overlooking the Wattle Park golf course. She showed me some of the photos she has collected of Sir Edward. In one he sits next to her on the couch, his hand resting on her knee. She laughed and said: 'I could show you a dozen photographs of him sitting beside someone, his hand resting on her knee.'*

WHEN I FIRST went to see Sir Edward I was only twenty-five or so, but I had to strain every muscle to hear him. When we got to know each other, I said, 'For God's sake, speak up.' As he got older, he learned to speak more loudly and when he got angry, you would have heard him from Warrigal Road.

How did you come to go to him?
I have a very peculiar right leg, and after I had my daughter it started to play up quite dramatically and my GP referred me to Edward Dunlop. Coming from New South Wales, I'd never heard of him so off I trotted. I waited and literally waited and waited. At times, later, I sat in that waiting room for four hours. The waiting

room was always packed and it was always freezing cold. On one occasion Weary said, 'Come on through, the steriliser is on and it's warmer in here, dear.' And there was this steriliser bubbling away. He still had that when he died. The same steriliser.

What were his rooms like in the early days?
Well, not quite as tatty as they were at the end but still pretty ordinary. Parliament Place was where all the specialists were then. Eventually of course it ended up Weary was the only person there. The whole place was derelict. Valda had found rooms for him at Anzac House, and she said, 'Sir Edward, if you up and die on me after all the trouble I've gone to finding these rooms for you, I'll be very cross.' And he did. (laughs)

Did things change over the years?
There were much the same chairs, the paper was peeling off the wall, it was grubby and dirty and derelict. On the bell it said 'Ring the bell and wait', and somebody had stuck with sticking plaster 'and <u>wait</u> and <u>wait</u> and <u>wait</u> and <u>wait</u>', and Valda left it there until after he died. He was on the first floor. I wouldn't have got in the lift for a million dollars. It used to clunk and rattle and creak. It was really pretty awful.

Was he oblivious to all this?
He didn't like change. You see, nothing had been done to the house at 605 Toorak Road since the Fergusons bought it, and the ballroom there had the original curtains. The kitchen was exactly as it was when the Moores built it. Not one thing had been changed. Melvie, his housekeeper, loved it. She was as happy as Larry out there. It was a huge room, 1930s table and early Kooka stove. No dishwashers or any luxuries like that.

How did you go from being a patient to a friend?

Well, we always had a good rapport and when I went into antiques, I did a bit of work for him, mainly valuing Helen's jewellery. Of course she was starting to be a bit odd, and a lot of it was missing. He didn't know if she had hidden it or if it had been stolen, so he gathered up what there was and I valued it and he put it in the bank after that. Then after Helen got really sick and was in hospital, we started asking him to dinner. We had asked him to various other things over the years, but he loved coming to a house just for dinner. We always made it a party. You were always looking for an extra man and he was a very good one to have. He was free and available.

He seems to have had an enormous amount of charisma as an older man.

Yes, terrific, and I don't remember it when I first knew him as a younger man. He was probably about forty-two then. Weary became more stooped as the years went by. My husband Bob is pretty tall, and we were in Valda's office one day when Weary came in. Valda, who calls a spade a spade, said, 'Well, Sir Edward, there's somebody you can't look down on.' And immediately the shoulders went back and the head went up. I reckon he grew about five inches.

Over the years I knew him, he became a very important person, where he'd just been an important doctor. I feel some sadness that his war efforts have been so publicised and not enough has been said about what a brilliant surgeon and doctor he was. He wasn't just a surgeon, he was a doctor. I would not have this leg if it wasn't for him. Eventually he just became my doctor. I went to the GP for unimportant things and I saw Weary every six weeks regularly right up to the end. He understood and he gave you confidence. I always said to Bob, 'If you go to Weary feeling sick, you always come out feeling so much better.' And you did. Bob used to drive me in and wait in the car, towards the end –

Not for the four hours.

No, not for the four hours. Actually once Bob had an appointment with him and he had to wait. He waited two hours, got up and said to the lady on reception, 'I'm sorry, I'm a busy man. I don't have time to sit here and wait all day.' The phone rang at about eight o'clock that night and it was Weary. 'Oh Margaret, may I speak to your husband?' and he apologised profusely for keeping Bob waiting. I was furious because I had been kept waiting so long and so often and I thought Blimey, all the time I've sat there he's never apologised. He made an appointment over the telephone for Bob for ten o'clock the next morning and Bob walked straight in.

Did he visit you frequently when you were in hospital?

Of course. I was in the Freemasons on one occasion, I'd had a very nasty operation. Bob and my daughter Prue came to see me and in walked Weary. Bob and Prue scuttled off and he sat down in a chair. This is still when he was talking very quietly and the chair was over there and the bed was over here, and I was tired, because it really had been a horrible operation. Not fun. He was mumbling away over there and I said to him, 'For goodness sake, speak up, I can't hear you. Or bring your chair up.'

Well, he stayed until after eleven until eventually I said, 'Have you got a home to go to because I'm tired and I want to go to sleep.' He said, 'Oh yes, dear, I'll see you tomorrow.' He gave me a pat and off he went. And the night sister came in and she said, 'Mrs Spinney, we're very tolerant in the Freemasons with visiting hours, but you do realise it is after eleven, would you mind asking your husband not to stay so late?' I said, 'That was Sir Edward Dunlop, and I wish you'd ask him not to stay so long.'

He refused to admit to pain himself, and yet he was so sympathetic towards you if you were in pain. I suppose he went through so much during the war, he became impervious. He fell over on the farm once and broke his hip and was in hospital. And he got up and went to a reception for the Japanese Ambassador with crutches and then he got a taxi and went back to the hospital and went to bed.

He seems to have enjoyed his honours and he certainly had an amazing number of letters after his name.
Oh, incredible. Absolutely incredible. And when something else cropped up, he'd say, 'So that's another one . . .' But everyone said he was so modest – he really wasn't. He had a tremendous ego, and he loved all that, he really loved it. The night of the 'Tribute to Weary Dunlop' concert in the Concert Hall was very emotional but he adored every minute of it. He enjoyed it, loved it. Always whinged that he didn't have any money, and then of course when he died he cut up quite well really.

As far as patients were concerned, I don't think he would have ever turned anyone away if they couldn't pay. I've sat in that waiting room and looked at people and thought, You couldn't even afford the tram fare. And up to the time he died, I was only paying $28. It cost more to take the poodle to the vet than for me to go and see Weary, and I got practically all of that back.

But he didn't give much away. If you were in hospital, he would always come with a bunch of flowers that he had picked out of the garden, he hadn't gone to a florist and bought them, and that was lovely. Sometimes when he came to dinner he might bring a bottle of champagne or a bottle of wine, but not often.

He was always having car accidents. It was never his fault of course, it was always a stupid idiot's. I only drove with him once and Valda refused to drive with him. He bought an Audi which had all those things new cars have on their dashboards but I don't think he could work out what they were about. The car soon looked as if it had been kicked around. At Parliament Place I used to walk past the car and bring the keys up when he left them in the ignition. But he was a remarkable man and I miss him still.

Do you?
Still. At first it was devastation. What will I do? Where will I find a doctor? He always listened patiently and you weren't on a conveyor belt. I miss just seeing him.

13 June, 1984

Margaret my dear,
All your actions have style and charm. I love the yellow roses and the highly animated card to match.

I have been nailed, plated, and screwed into line and whilst unable to bear much weight on the shattered thigh bone am fairly active on crutches.

I've been out to a dinner party at the Regent, and last night went to a reception in Toorak by the new Nippon Consul general, and then home to 'case the joint'.

I should get home next week and should soon resume some activity in practice. I am sorry about the cold. Please let Valda know of anything with which I can help – prescriptions etc.
Warm and affectionate regards to you and Bob,
Sincerely,
Weary

*The surgeon **Michael Long** considered Weary Dunlop both a
friend and mentor, dating back to his days as a medical student
at the Royal Melbourne Hospital in the early 60s. A resident of
Benalla, Michael Long was at the heart of a community project
to erect a statue of Weary in the town. This is an extract from
an address he gave to the Benalla Memorial Appeal Dinner on
the 15 September 1995.*

I KNEW WEARY first when I was a medical student. I was
about twenty-three, he some thirty years my senior. I was naive
– excessively so but developing an interest in people. He,
slightly stooped, quiet, almost inaudible with interminable
pauses, a continuous warm smile. An endless flow of patients.
They had a vast spectrum of complaints – some grave, many
dying. I was struck by his concern and his industry and by the
fact, quite simply, that his presence and interest had a uniquely
reassuring and beneficial effect on these people. Behind his
back we joked that with Weary, at least the patients died with a
smile on their face.

He was a good teacher but one had to hug his heels and
lean forward to catch the endless pearls that flowed forth. He
insisted we attend his operating sessions – long affairs, beginning late, for he was always late, and then often sauntering on
towards midnight and beyond. In between operations he would
dictate notes in excellent English to a secretary who would
magically appear in cap and gown at the precise moment.

They sat at one end of the operating room, oblivious to the
clearing and setting-up going on around them. Occasionally he
would recognise we were rather bored, fearful students . . . As a
student I had little direct contact with him, except I can recall
the first occasion when I was caught alone. In my isolation and
nervousness, I bumbled my answers but he continued to take an

interest – spent time with me, talking and teaching cancer in the oral cavity and throat . . .

Time meant nothing to him. He often began late and was invariably diverted on route throughout the day. But as I was to learn later, if he was to meet someone important – Mrs Ghandi, Louis Mountbattern, a friend, or even the Queen, he was most particular about timing.

A litany of motor accidents, related somewhat to his inattention to motoring detail, were scattered throughout his life and were one reason why he was late. I recall one operating session where he explained as he made the first incision, 'Funny thing last night, when I left the car I had to push the door upwards to get out!' He had rolled the car yet again!

Surprisingly, his profile at the Royal Melbourne Hospital was low. Little was said of his war record. He did not serve on committees, either at that hospital or at the College of Surgeons. There were other seemingly high-profile types – effective in a way – good surgeons . . . at least they thought so. Politically they were powerful, rather frightening men. Now, in retrospect, they pale in significance.

On graduation my peer group were attracted to work with the rowdy, high-profile types, but I had an overwhelming desire to work with Weary and I believe, in my year, I was the only one requesting to do so. I am sure, like all of you, I have moments when some irresistible force leads me in a direction which I know to be right. It happens to me all the time and I marvel at it . . . somehow these decisions are right or lead to the correct process, although it may be a bit painful en route. And so, onward with Weary . . .

I joined his unit, Ward 7 North at the Royal Melbourne Hospital, where a rather domineering and intimidating ward sister was somewhat more frightening than Weary. Imagine my surprise when on my first afternoon off, still hard at work, a phone call came. It was to be the first of many, beginning with a long pause, heavy breathing and then, characteristically, 'It's Weary here. I'm going off to shoot rabbits, have you finished your work?'

I recall I had a plaster to apply and some other jobs. However he picked me up in his Bentley at the Royal Melbourne and we set forth into the countryside north of the city and shot rabbits. Would I teach his boys how to skin them? Of course, for at least I had great confidence and skill in dealing with rabbits. The lesson proceeded on the back steps of his house. Over dinner, he regaled with stories and jokes, food, much too much alcohol for me, and then at some impossible hour he drove me back to the hospital residence.

Gradually it dawned on me, I had a friend. I joined a very young group which he set about inspiring and he maintained his interest in us until his death. Others, such as Bob Dickens, the orthopaedic surgeon, and Brian Buxton, the cardiac surgeon, were early members. But later the list was extended. This infectious interest in the young has caught us, for each of us, I believe, has continued to take on the young, hopefully to set examples and act as mentors.

In due course I was taken to dinner with opera singers, introduced to famous people here and there and always included. Dinner at his house was a lively affair, interesting people, endless jokes – with me, the youngest I suppose, spending an inordinate time in the kitchen, helping the cook, waiting on table, and so forth. Always, however, he would indicate for me and any other young people to stay behind and laugh, joke and share into the wee hours.

Yes, I had become a friend and I was aware of a powerful bond between us. I realised though that I was not alone in my friendship. His friends were everywhere . . . We were part of a vast group, all made to feel by this warm man to be someone special and important.

Operating sessions were long and horrific – operations often not previously attempted. He had the largest experience of operating on the oesophagus, that is, the gullet, in through the chest. The modern operating room is something like the cockpit of an aeroplane but we knew little about resuscitation and I remember once we had an intravenous going directly into the heart! Another time, I am sure the patient had been dead for an hour before we stopped operating.

Technically Weary may not have been as good as some . . . but it was well known that his proposals for management were always first-class and up to date. He continued attending surgical meetings at the Royal Melbourne right up until the time of his death and would participate actively in discussion, invariably ending up with some rather prolonged story. We used to joke it would be good for Weary to state what should be done for a patient and then for some younger technician to do the job. And so I sailed through surgical training and work as a surgeon, marked as one of Weary's men. This support continued until the day of his death, when I know he was enquiring about me.

We travelled extensively overseas together, India mainly, and I realised how effective an ambassador for Australia he was. Our first trip to India found us stopping for some reason on the runway in New Delhi where we clambered out of the aircraft, hundreds of us. I was staggered how, in the semi-gloom and the mêlée of people, someone, an Indian, walked past us saying, 'Good evening, Sir Edward. Good trip this time?' Our bags were carried ceremoniously on heads before us and we were treated royally, but Weary was determined to remain at the airport for our six a.m. flight. To the utter bewilderment of our helpers, he lay quietly on an airport lounge, placed a Homburg over his face and was immediately asleep! Soon, he was snoring loudly – a feature of his sleep. Shops were set up around this sleeping giant and this bizarre sight kept me awake with laughter. In India I rebelled at having to share a bed with him. There was a shortage of beds! Invariably he would contract gastroenteritis and be indisposed much of the night.

I became a sort of aide-de-camp, organising and guiding him, helping with arrangements. I flew him about parts of Australia and remember it was difficult to shoe-horn him into an aircraft. One visit to the Western District, Willaura, I believe, had Weary guiding me into the wrong field, but eventually we sorted it out to land beside the state school where numerous children were lined up waving flags. He performed the operation with me assisting and we floated back to Melbourne.

His good humour was legendary, but he could become uncontrollably angry with bureaucracy, particularly at the Royal Melbourne Hospital. With me he only showed irritation over one thing that I can recall. In commercial aircraft, he would never tilt his seat back, but would sag forward, mouth open, glasses askew. On numerous occasions I would attempt to alter his centre of gravity by adjusting the seat back. He would awake with a jolt, obviously irritated by my efforts, refusing to have the seat altered. Within no time he would be asleep again – the same disorganised posture.

Curiously, on reflection, at the Royal Melbourne Hospital, I knew little of his wartime experience and he did not seem to talk about it initially. Quite suddenly, one day, as we sat together in the front of a bus – Helen, his wife, somewhere at the rear – driving from Acapulco to Mexico City, did it come out, some eight hours of it. I am not sure even if he mentioned his diaries, yet plenty of that detail was included. It was on that trip, for the first time, I realised the extent of his wartime experience.

I would go to his home where students and others from

Asian countries were frequent visitors. He would go out of his way to help them. I was staggered by the number of Japanese visitors, and recall the Japanese students staying upstairs at 605, so I learned a good deal about forgiveness, he practised it every day and had this wonderful ability of being able to review a situation and his part in it. I learned how all types of disputes, whether interpersonal or international depend in a large measure on this seemingly simply manoeuvre. He gave more and more time to the veterans and would do anything for them – operate, listen, fight their battles, take an interest in their families. He was very much in demand and effective. In all this we learnt a good deal from him about giving.

We knew his faults – driving, lateness, possibly his family, where Helen and the children saw little of him. It is alleged that Helen, in frustration, once made an appointment to see him in his rooms!

I knew little of his Benalla roots until one day he asked if he could stay on the farm. That was the first of a number of visits, and I can recall on one occasion how he and Helen slept on a mattress on the floor in our cottage. We would loan him the farm utility for his ventures to Goorambat and Benalla. The children were used to answering his radio calls for help – he was lost and they would direct him home!

Increasingly, however, I realised the importance to Weary of his association with Benalla. I heard endless stories about his exploits as a student, attending school at Stewarton, and how he was propelled into the Benalla High School. Increasingly he would return to this district to open this, or speak at that, or simply to see friends and it was clear how firmly established were his roots in this district.

Pamela Menzel, *née Cockerell*, *began work with Weary at 14 Parliament Place at the end of 1968. She gave up the position with Sir Edward when she married in 1973 and she left Melbourne twelve months later to live in Western Australia. 'That's where I felt rather sad,' she said. 'My family didn't get to know him as I did, which would obviously have been very enriching.' We spoke in her home in Perth during a brief respite in Perth's hottest heatwave for years. 'I'd usually see him when I went back to Melbourne for Christmas. He used to make comments about the pioneer spirit and so forth.'*

THE MAIN THING I used to find with him was his wonderful gift with words. He could always find the right word to say to people, he had a wonderful vocabulary and just a wonderful way of expressing himself. Because sometimes people, they can feel it but they can't always express their feelings on paper the way that he used to. He really was incredible. He used to write wonderful letters and he would include little drawings.

He was a Cancer and I was reading a book about star signs recently and it said Cancerians have a gift for writing and like deep-seated leather chairs. His deep-seated leather chair in the main consulting room was absolutely threadbare, because he used to love that chair. He used to sit there and have his little snoozes.

On one occasion he'd been out to lunch, with Lord Casey to the Melbourne Club. He and Lord Casey, like a couple of naughty schoolboys, would go off and have their lunch together. They'd always walk back up from the Melbourne Club and I used to laugh because the two of them had quite a spring in their step and they both had an eye – if there was a nice lass walking in front of them they used to quite appreciate it.

On this occasion there were no patients for the afternoon and the sun was streaming through in the back room. Quite often he would think about a case and he would ponder over it, so I would sit and draw little daisies while I waited, but this time I suddenly thought I'd drawn a few too many daisies and I looked up and he was sound asleep. I just sat quietly and suddenly this beady eye looked over the top of the glasses to see if I'd noticed. I pretended I hadn't and he cleared his throat and said, 'Would you read back that last paragraph please? I think I'll rephrase that.'

I remember the first time Jack Flannery [an ex-prisoner of war who drove Sir Edward in later years] appeared on the doorstep. With his broken nose he really looked a bit of a sinister character. He had these little mannerisms, the thumbs up, and he'd shift his weight from foot to foot as if he was bit punch drunk and he always had an open-necked shirt and rolled-up sleeves. He used to quite often call in with a rabbit or some fresh vegetables. I've got Jack Flannery's mother's rabbit recipe in my book. Jack liked to keep in touch and he used to ring and say, 'It's Flannery, the canary. Where's the boss?'

Sir Edward was always getting little gifts from this one and that. They used to bake biscuits and cakes and we used to munch away, always increasing the waistline. They were so generous and kind, all the different patients.

And very patient patients?
Yes, very patient patients. (laughs) One patient, Peg Gibson, was going to spread a rug in the waiting room and have a picnic one day.

He used to visit his patients when he was going to the Melbourne Scots, in the full dress with his kilt and velvet jacket, and he'd do a little sword dance for the nurses, just to give them a bit of a thrill, a bit of a break from the routine.

Did you work on Saturdays?

Usually. On one occasion he arrived at 11.30 a.m. and wanted to buy a hat at Henry Bucks. I drove around the block until he had bought the hat and we went back to the rooms and settled down and then I had to leave. I can still see him. When I said I had to go, he said, 'Go? What do you mean go? Go where?' I said, 'I'm very sorry but I've got arrangements made.' 'Oh well,' he said, 'if your social life's more important than me, you go. Off you go.' And I said, 'Yes, well, I will. Bye.' I really think he thought I would stay. But I did feel very guilty.

Sometimes he would get a little bit hard to handle and you used to think Oh, you are naughty. But in most cases you couldn't help but forgive him because he really was just so sweet.

I gave up working with Sir Edward when I was about to get married. Bruce said, 'You can't have both of us, you've got to choose one or the other.' He held Sir Edward in great esteem, too, but he just knew that he was very demanding, so I gave up the job. It was a shame because I did miss the patients – they become so much a part of your life, you can't help but wonder about them all. Being the sort of surgeon that he was, with cancer, it wasn't as if they came in for an opinion and surgery and then that was it. They kept coming back for follow ups and then they also treated him as a family doctor and therefore they would perhaps come to him not always for surgical matters, but for all sorts of other things as well.

He demanded a lot but he gave so much and that's just the way he was. He was a wonderful person. He spoils you for working for anyone else. He really was an inspiration. At the funeral they said, 'Seize the day' and I regretted that I hadn't answered his last letter. But you have to grab every opportunity and I think that's one of the lessons he's taught an awful lot of people, that you have to make the most of every moment and do what you can.

20 October, 1969

Dalat South Vietnam

Dear Pam,

So nice to have your letter and to hear of your cheerful doings. Tasmania has a sort of intimate charm. I am so glad that you have found some interesting jobs by the wayside.

I am having a couple of days up in this mountain resort before disengaging from Vietnam and commencing the homeward journey.

It is like the mountains of the European alps, the air is crystal clear, and tingles on the skin. 'The long light shakes across the lake . . . and the wild cataract leaps in glory'.

This old Dalat Palace Hotel is one of those massive buildings contemporary with the Victorian age, with lofty ceilings, dark heavy beams, enormous French windows looking on the lake and terraces flooded with light flanked with pines and gay poinsettias.

The servants are efficient, decorous French speakers but the plumbing leaves much to be desired.

It is largely filled with 'weekenders' of which the main body is composed of Americans, accompanied by girl-friends largely Vietnamese charmers. An American plastic surgeon – my colleague in Saigon – is rooming with Anne, a ward nurse, and they have kept me company between love making, for alas Je suis si seul!

The salient impression is of quietness, for all Vietnam screams on the eardrums with the roar of Honda Lambretta, Suzukis and the eternal chatter and din of war. The only sinister note is the heavy papering of windows against mortar and rocket blast, and the fact that last week a bus load of passengers from the airport was ambushed on the mountain road.

Two days ago I flew up to Song Be, the capital of Phuc Long province on the Cambodian border where the people are nearly all Montagnards. This is an area of strategic hamlets where some four villages are brigaded together with fortified perimeters – all within the zone of protection of the central fortress area of Song Be headquarters.

The country is pockmarked with the huge bomb craters of B52 raids, and the central fortress area of Song Be is a P.C. Wren effect of concrete pill boxes, crisscross trenches, sandbags, mortars, claymore mines and massed barbed wire.

They have some very heavy guns as well as the automatics. The effect of the 175 mms firing (7-inch shells) is positively ear shattering.

The mountain peak of Song Be Mountain is one of two twin sentinel peaks on the border and Song Be river with its rapids sweeps right around the fortress area.

The Montagnards are dark skinned. Curly haired. Slender, graceful and delicately featured. They adopt gay coloured skirts and heavy bracelets and anklets and wear large bamboo ear pieces in the lobes of their ears which are enormously enlarged, and when free of bamboo long like straps. The females go magnificently bare busted, but are a little shy of photography. I thought that it would be in the best 'gung ho' tradition to try to induce one to have her photograph taken with me, so that I could claim that she was my girl friend – but alas no luck!

The Montagnards are not nomadic like our Aboriginals, but go in for some mountain slope agriculture. The men are natural mercenary soldiers rather like the Sherpas.

In four days time, I shall be starting for home. I can't really believe it – until I see you across our desk – and Shirley twirling on her foot, 'Already it is 9.36 sir!'

Dear Pamela be kind to your perverse and wandering boss. A shadow has fallen on the mountains, the blue lake is grey, the darting swallows have gone to rest, as have most of my weekend friends – 'to leave the world to darkness and to me.'

Love
Edward

Fred Barnstable of Numurkah was one of the many POWs from country Victoria who beat a track to 14 Parliament Place.

I WAS A PATIENT of his for the best part of three years. I had what they first thought was a cyst in my finger, but they got the pathology back and my doctor said, 'I've got bad news for you.' In the meantime he'd been in touch with Sir Weary Dunlop, and Weary had already booked a bed in St Andrews hospital for me. At nine o'clock on the day of the operation, they prepared me and drugged me and took me up in the lift on a stretcher. I lay there from half past nine in the morning until half past four in the afternoon, and every time I started to come out of the dope, they bunged more into me. (laughs) I was just laying there. Somebody come along and grabbed my hand, and I opened my eyes and it was Weary. 'That won't be too much, it shouldn't be too bad,' I heard him say. Wheeled in. Out to it.

I saw him for checks afterwards and he said, 'You know I bloody nearly lost you Fred, on the theatre table. You had an attack of asthma.' That was in 1965. Anyhow, he saved my life.

So you must have been one of those patients who was meant to be operated on at 10.30 and Weary didn't turn up till 4.30.

That's right. Lying on this stretcher outside, watching other patients get wheeled in. God, that was a long day, I'll tell you. When I was in St Andrews, he'd come to see me every day but it was sometimes three or four o'clock in the morning when he'd arrive because he'd been operating in another hospital. He'd wake you up. I often wondered how a man of his stature, a big man, could keep going with very little sleep.

On the Sunday I was there, two of my brothers arrived down to see me with my wife, Flora, and I'd just finished my dinner and they walked in and about an hour later Weary came in to see me. Weary said to me, 'Are you partial to whisky Fred?' I said 'Yes.' He turned to my eldest brother. 'Go and get your brother a bottle of whisky.' Well, Sunday night that bottle of whisky just went down like that. Every nurse and sister came to me and said, 'I've got a very sick patient . . .' Monday morning, I'd only had about three or four nips, but the bottle was empty.

I had a beaten track down to see him and I had to pay all my travelling costs so I had a talk to him about this and he gave me a five-page report as to why I suffered a melanoma of the ring finger. Anyhow, I got before a Department of Veterans Affairs Board and there were three doctors, and the chairman who was a solicitor, and they opened up the meeting and started asking questions so I produced Weary's five foolscap pages of writing and the president of the board, he started reading it and he just folded it up and put it aside. 'Irrelevant,' he said.

GERT HUTCHINS: Mike, my husband, came out of the army with ulcers, peptic ulcers. It was from having dysentery. He was in the Middle East and New Guinea. For twenty-four years they told him, you can't operate on a peptic ulcer. I used to be up all night and then I'd be doing half his work in the daytime. The kids, too, had to do a lot of work. I went down and I had a talk to Ern about it and he said, 'Tell your doctor to send him down to me.' Our doctor said, 'Oh, I can give you a referral but I can tell you now, he won't do anything.'

So Ern put him up on the surgery table and he said, 'Lord, man, that's nearly ready to erupt and if that happens you've got one chance in a thousand.' Mike had reached rock bottom, and he'd suffered for twenty-four years with that. He'd swallowed gallons of medicine and thousands of pills and he took belladonna until he nearly went blind. Mike said, 'What do you do about it?' And Ern said, 'Operate, of course.' And Mike said, 'I was told you can't operate on a peptic ulcer. They told me at Heidelberg and they've told me at home.' 'Well, that's rubbish,' he said, 'I've done dozens of them.' So that was the first relief he had. Just like that.

In 1969, Weary Dunlop went to Vietnam as the leader of an Australian medical team. His second-in-command was the surgeon **Paul Large**, *who remembers their sojourn with mixed feelings.*

WEARY WAS A very stimulating person, as you know. A man who had, I'd say, few close friends but a lot of acquaintances. Everybody knew him. My major contact came with Weary in Vietnam. I went to Vietnam three times, and the second time, in 1969, he was in charge of the team. He was from the Royal Melbourne, I was representing the Alfred, but the team was drawn from various hospitals.

We were volunteers and we worked for the Vietnamese civilian hospital. All their doctors were put into the army because of the shortage of manpower and there were a number of Australian teams in various places.

I went to a place called Bien Hoa, about 15 miles north-east of Saigon. It was an industrial town, very vigorous and a huge military base. At the hospital, we staffed the surgical side and the Vietnamese staffed the medical and we were extremely busy – we just went hammer and tongs – so there were quite a number of strains on people. We had our own nurses there, who worked the operating theatre in the daytime, and in the recovery room until three or four at night, and so the strains on them were very considerable. They worked very, very hard indeed.

The war was going on. It was exactly the same each time I was there. There were rockets, oil tanks set on fire, ammunition dumps. In the daytime, there'd be distant rumbles, bombing and every night the whole countryside was alive with the war. There were flashes and bangs and bombs. The place where we worked was rocketed several times. We got a certain number of injured civilians, the occasional Vietnamese soldier, some American civilian personnel, not with war wounds but with things like burns, and of course we got the local Vietnamese. A lot of traffic accidents as well, because it was a military base. We also treated the usual sort of diseases everybody gets plus a number of tropical things.

To give you some idea of the workload, every Monday morning I would visit an outpatients department where about 100 people would come. At least. On that second time, when Weary was there, I did almost 500 operations in the three months, and I couldn't work the last few weeks because I got dysentery. The load was spread amongst everybody. Nurses as well. Everybody. People talk about stress, they don't know what stress is.

Weary could be great fun. He was very friendly, very

outgoing. It was great to be with him, but he wasn't very good at that particular job. He was unable to delegate and he rather ignored things. When the girls had trouble, he ignored them. I think his attitude was he really wanted us all to go away, and on one occasion, the girls revolted.

I don't know how much you know about Weary, but he was the most unpunctual person you could possibly imagine. He'd be going to operate at say ten o'clock in the morning and he'd arrive at two. It was chaos. Then he'd do a gigantic operation, inappropriate to the situation we were in, and come six o'clock he'd knock off and our girls, who'd worked all day, were expected to spend half the night looking after his patients. The girls used to come in crying. They'd get upset and they'd come and talk to me about it and we'd go and talk to Weary. We didn't make much headway. He was absolutely tireless and I think he was unable to conceive that other people might get tired.

Weary took on really impossible things as a surgeon and when you do that you're going to get a lot of disappointments. As I said, some of the things he took on in Vietnam really were not appropriate. He was doing huge operations on very advanced cancers, when the people were going to die, and it was really inappropriate to put them through this major repeated surgery. When you're just there for three months, you can't go embarking on things which will take perhaps a couple of years or so. He couldn't help it. He had to do something but it didn't work out.

When he was eighty, the College of Surgeons gave him a dinner at the Melbourne Cricket Club and he was delightful. He made a wonderful speech and in this speech he made the comment that there were no anaesthetists present. And he was dead right. There *were* no anaesthetists present. It brought the house down. There were no anaesthetists because they were just driven mad by him, his lateness and irregularity. We all knew why. He was extremely frustrating. He loved that party, he really enjoyed himself.

We had anaesthetists of our own in Vietnam but we also had Vietnamese anaesthetists, two of them. They weren't doctors but they had been trained and they were pretty competent at it and we had a riotous occasion once when one of these flatly refused to give anaesthetic for Weary. Weary had made uncomplimentary remarks about him and this chap understood English perfectly well. (laughs) So from then on, he refused. I think in the end it was patched up, but it took a little time. We all had to get around and soothe this chap's ruffled feelings.

I don't know whether you've ever read a book called *The Anatomy of Courage*? [The author, Charles Wilson, was the dean of St Mary's Hospital when Weary was there, and went on to become Lord Moran and Churchill's doctor.] That describes Weary, though it's about the First World War. It describes the man who had no regard at all for his own safety and no regard at all for other people and he was a VC.

In Vietnam, when anyone came or went, they'd have a party for them. Now, Weary had hollow legs and there were others up there who had hollow legs as well. The day I arrived, they had a party. Someone was going and I was coming. This was my second trip there, and I knew the war. The war was there, it didn't go away, and to my horror, I heard Weary at about eleven o'clock saying to one of the Vietnamese interpreters that he'd take him home. We quickly ascertained that the interpreter didn't live in the town, he lived out in the jungle.

So I got at Weary and said, 'You mustn't do that because you're going out into uproar and God knows what could happen to you.' You see what I felt was he was Australian, right, and if anything happened to him there would be a huge uproar.

What was he doing it for? We had found the interpreter a room for the night. I was the second-in-command of this job and I thought I had persuaded him not to go.

The next morning what does he tell me but, 'I took that interpreter home and do you know, I was fired at.' I said, 'Of course you were fired at. You shouldn't have done that. Look, if anything happens to you, what's our position?' But he was delighted that we learned about it. What really pleased him was that we all worried about him and were concerned for his health and safety.

Another occasion, he didn't turn up for work, and two of us thought he might have been ill or dead so we broke into his room and he wasn't there. We had to repair the breakage, of course, and then Weary turned up. He'd been wandering around a rubber plantation – rubber plantations were notorious hide-outs for Viet Cong, but he wasn't afraid of anything.

Weary didn't really make the team toe the line. I don't mean with a rigid routine and discipline, but to see to it they didn't break the curfew, they weren't running around the town at all hours and this kind of thing. He didn't bother about it. One night I was on duty and at two a.m. I got a call from the American military police to say 'We've got some of your people in Bien Hoa Hospital.' At two o'clock in the morning! I said, 'This is the Australian medical team' and they said, 'Yes, we know and we've got your people in the hospital here.' Three Australians had slammed a motor car into an electricity pylon. You see, Weary once told the team not to worry about the curfew. That's how these lads were painting the town rouge at two o'clock in the morning and slamming into a pole. But you had to worry about the curfew – a trigger-happy military policeman, an American or Vietnamese, might see a car hurtling around and shoot at it. Those are the things that really he could have done better, but I think he had a mind-set and he was more concerned with more important things than the trivial activities of team members.

Did Weary make a point of treating Viet Cong?
We all did that automatically. That was a medical principle. No doctor would ever treat people differently. We treated them according to their medical priorities.

Was Weary calm under pressure?
Yes, he was. He would never get rattled. The only time I saw him upset was when the nurses, and justifiably, tackled him about the way he was working. He was a bit rattled and a bit upset. I remember his words. He said, 'I am an important man doing an important job,' and brushed them off. He was very, very upset. You know, Weary wasn't overt in his modesty.

Did the problem resolve itself?
He didn't change. I suppose he might have briefly, but not basically. And yet he was fond of the nurses and, like me, they all liked him. (laughs) Of course it's all subjective, we all see it in our own way, don't we? I personally wouldn't have missed going there for anything. I really loved it. As far as Weary goes, I think he really loved being there. I don't want to give the impression that Weary didn't do his share of the work, because he did. He got around but he wasn't dashing off all the time.

But he did have problems with the nurses?
Not all the time, he had these difficulties when he was operating. I think his attitude to them was rather aloof. It goes back to the fact that while he wasn't unfriendly or hostile, he didn't establish a good rapport. I enjoyed his company, although he drove us all slightly mad. But even when we had arguments with

him, and quarrels, we all respected him and we all enjoyed his company. He was a very gracious man and he always found the good in things. I took him to the airport and I felt a real pang when he left. I didn't think I would, I thought I'd be pleased, but I really felt a pang.

Professor Hugh Dudley, *the inaugural Professor of Surgery at Monash University from 1963, returned to Britain and took up a chair at St Mary's, Paddington, in 1973 and now lives in Strathdon, in Scotland. He chose not to be interviewed about Weary Dunlop, and instead wrote the following piece.*

ALONG WITH MOST everyone else in Australia, I knew Sir Edward. We first met when I came to Australia as Professor of Surgery in 1963. My acquaintance with him was a nodding one, in that he moved in different circles from me. However, in 1969, when I was on my second tour with a surgical team in Bien Hoa, in what was then South Vietnam, he came to take over from us with a new team based mostly on the Royal Melbourne Hospital. Over a period of about two weeks, before I went off to join the 1st Australian Field Hospital in Vung Tau, we worked together.

There was no escaping his charisma and his ability to get on well with almost anyone (which includes me). I did not think a great deal of his surgical judgment or technical surgery but this is perhaps unfair from one such as myself in his late forties looking at the performance of one by that time in his sixties. He tended to operate through too small incisions and his objectives were not all that clear in the heat of the trauma of emergency surgery. However, everyone was devoted to him.

Thereafter he and his wife continued to be kind to us. This was perhaps best exemplified by them throwing a great party at their house for us when we were about to leave to go to London. This was such a spontaneous gesture that it took us quite by surprise and we will always remember it.

While I was at St Mary's I used to see him from time to time, particularly because a former colleague of his, and for a time of mine, was Tom Kemp of rugby football fame. Through Tom I would hear when Weary was in town and usually managed to meet him.

He remained always the same – courteous, urbane and enigmatic. Although I enjoyed his company and his unrivalled experience and felt at ease with him, I felt that there was an inner core that it was impossible to penetrate and which made him different from virtually every one of my other acquaintances. I value having known him and his personal signature on the copy of his *War Diaries*.

*Irish-born nurse **Eileen McCarthy** worked with Sir Edward for five years from 1976 in his rooms in Parliament Place. Formerly of Queens Road, Melbourne, she has now retired and lives in Raglan, Wales, across the green from her brother and his family.*

ABOUT THREE DAYS after I got off the plane from England in 1976, I saw this job advertised by an agency in Collins Street so I went along to see them and they sent me on to Sir Edward. I had actually retired when I got the job. I went out to Australia to retire but I couldn't sit still.

There are several little stories I remember, like the nursing sister who thought she had breast cancer. Sir Edward had to go to Government House for a dinner and there he was all dolled up in his Scottish tartans and full regalia. After he had been there for a little while and had his dinner, he rushed off to St Andrews where the sister was, marched through the corridors to the sister and he said, 'I knew you would be worried, so I've come back to tell you that you're perfectly all right, there's nothing wrong with you.' I thought that was absolutely wonderful. These are the little things that I think endeared him to people and also gained their really very deep regard and respect. He was a great man but he was a humble man, that's the idea I got.

One fellow nearly killed him by throwing a big ink well at him. You see, the insurance firms used to send people around who were claiming compensation and he used to test these people. One day he had a bad-tempered man in and Sir Edward was just watching him. He'd do that. He'd be making little notes and all the time from under his bushy eyebrows he'd be watching everybody. This fellow suddenly picked up the inkwell, a solid inkwell, and threw it at him. You can imagine how good his reflexes were because he just dodged. Oh yes, he had quite a lot of escapades. The fellow thought he wasn't going to give him the money obviously. You couldn't fool Sir Edward.

You never knew what was going to happen next, that's why I think it was so interesting. Sometimes the waiting room would be full of patients, and I used to think, What on earth is this man doing? I would peep round the door and, you'd never believe it, he'd be fast asleep. Having his forty winks.

One man he worked with on the drug and alcohol foundation, said to me, 'Do you know, I felt so sorry for him the other day. There he was, this poor old man, having forty winks while we were all talking and then I got the fright of my life when someone said something, and he jumped up and said, "That's not right." And there I was thinking he was so tired that he'd gone to sleep.' I said, 'Don't you believe it. Even in his sleep he can hear what you're saying.' (laughs)

He had a great deal to do with cancer, and the alcoholics and drugs people. He was always trying to save them as well. (laughs) I think he had quite a few missions in life.

His patients used to come there and sit for hours, hours on end. It just shows what faith they had in the man. There was a lady who used to come from Sydney every year to see him. He took a cancer out of her throat the size of a tennis ball. One day I was sitting doing some accounts there and he said, 'Come, come, I want you to see this.' So I trotted in and this lady was there. He said, 'Look, Eileen, just look at this hole. I'm saying now, I never thought you were going to get over it.' He had removed this cancer from her throat and there was a hole there, but she used wear a sort of thick necklace and you'd never know that anything was wrong with her, she was as right as rain. I believe when he did operate on her he sat with her all night because she kept dragging the bandages off her throat. He sat there all night with her. I think that's wonderful, because he was quite a great man in his profession, there's no getting away from it.

I think he suffered quite a bit during the war. I know the Japanese thought the world of him after the war but they certainly put him through quite a lot of indignities. I have an idea that a Japanese consul came for treatment while I was working with Sir Edward. I often said to him that I was surprised he treated him. He said, 'Well you know, you must forgive people, Eileen.' I said 'Oh, Sir Edward, I know what I'd like to do to them, never mind.' 'Ooh,' he said, 'you mustn't let that Irish paddy of yours get the better of you.' I said, 'Huh, it wouldn't be an Irish paddy, it would be outright murder.' (laughs) There you are.

*The cartoonist **Les Tanner** first met Sir Edward after being*
rushed to the Cabrini Hospital, haemorrhaging from a
cancerous larynx, in 1972 when he was forty-five years old. By
his own admission, he later sought unnecessary appointments
with Sir Edward just to cheer himself up.

FROM THE MOMENT he first came on the scene, all panic just
disappeared. He'd breeze in any time of the day or night, you
never knew when he was coming. I can't really describe the
presence of the man, but he exuded a feeling of 'Don't worry
everything's all right, Jesus Christ is here.'

He was a terribly easy man. There was none of the arro-
gance or imperial righteousness that you get from most surgeons. He took a bit of a shine to me, possibly because he was
also interested in sketching. He wasn't much good at it himself
but he admired it in others. I've never known anyone I've
trusted so implicitly – probably a story you are going to hear a
thousand times. It's hard to talk about him without going into
fairy land.

When I went into the Epworth for a minor operation, he
said, 'Did you bring a drop of the grape shell with you?' I'd
never heard of that expression, and I said, 'What do you mean?'
He said, 'Did you bring any drink,' and I said, 'No, how dare
you suggest that? No, I didn't.' So he told the charge sister that
I was to have 100 mgs of brandy every night.

He'd do some bloody outrageous things. I had a tiny little
lump on the end of what could almost be a piece of string, sticking out of my skin. I said, 'This worries me,' and he said, 'They
are a bloody nuisance,' and it felt like somebody had stubbed a
cigarette out on my belly. He'd just snipped it off with a pair of
scissors. He had these terrible jokes he'd tell you. His favourite
one was about a little boy at school with his teacher in a low-cut

round-necked frock and the kid says to the teacher as she leans over to correct his spelling, 'Gee miss, I can see both your lungs.' He'd tell me that while he was peering down a hole in my neck to see my lungs. I suggested he get a new scriptwriter or at least some new jokes.

Like when I said to him that I had this drinking problem he said, 'What? Have you got alcoholic constipation?' I said, 'What do you mean?' He said, 'You can't pass a pub.' Well, it was that sort of corn-balled joking, aligned with a very beautifully modulated voice, very quietly spoken. They say he used to recite poetry while he was operating, and he was forever quoting Browning. He had the air of the commanding officer who would go in the trenches with you. I certainly had no regard for officers, having been in the army myself, but he inspired a feeling of implicit trust. I've never known it with anybody else. Literally, whatever Weary asked me to do, I would do. If he'd said stop drinking, I would have, but he never did. He would tell you to ease off, or 'your liver's a bit large' – that sort of practical talk.

From 1972 until he pretty well retired from active surgery, I used to invent symptoms to go and see him, just to talk to him. He was tremendous charmer, particularly with women. He loved women, he loved their society. And of course his wife developed Alzheimer's. But he was, I don't know – like you'd like your uncle to be or you wished your father had been like.

He went out of his way to always keep me informed of what was going on and we mixed with him socially a bit. He'd turn up at the oddest places. At a dinner party in St Kilda, he kept falling asleep at the dinner table so we got up at eleven and left, but he apparently came to life and chatted on until three o'clock in the morning. I don't know if it was judgment on us!

I always called him Sir Edward, but everybody else called

him Weary or Sir Weary. He had the most bizarre set of patients, everything from old diggers to little Greeks, whatever, and always, always, always an Asian assistant. His theatre nurse was Singapore-Chinese, his anaesthetist was Indian.

He was notorious for his bad driving, and I went in one day, it was the first time I'd ever seen him shaken up. An umbrella had fallen down between his legs and he'd rammed the back of a car at the lights and he was cursing himself.

The energy of the man was tremendous. He'd put in a full day of surgery then he'd be off to a dinner for one of his ventures. I used to make him scones. For his birthday I took him down two dozen of the bloody things.

Farewell to a Man Whose Compassion Touched my Big Toe

He shook my big toe with his fingers and said 'How do you do Mr Tanner, my name is Dunlop.'

I couldn't have cared less if his name was Michelin but he exuded confidence. He was a big man, huge in fact, an attribute I am normally wary of, having had slight acquaintance with police and sergeant-majors who gloried in length.

I was to my mind, being prepared for the funeral slab having just lost great gouts of bright red blood in a sudden haemorrhage at work while I enjoyed, if that is the word, my second-last cigarette.

I had been rushed to hospital by the associate editor, Creighton Burns, where I was pursued by a lady wanting my medical fund details while I trailed blood from my wheelchair.

Meanwhile, my wife and a friend were gouging the name of the best surgeon in Melbourne from a medical acquaintance.

He came up with two names, one of whom was in Ireland, and Weary Dunlop who wasn't. There was now a fight behind the scenes as to whose patient I was, which Sir Weary solved with patient charm or, if he had been Irish, 'malarky'.

I came to know his Celtic malarky over the following years. He had an unshakeable belief in getting things done. Not how they got done, but done. He was a bit of a lair.

He was always well-dressed but there was always a bit of dash – the tie or handkerchief in his top pocket were tiny storm warnings of the unexpected. The flags of a man self-possessed.

I was only ever a patient when I knew him, one of his countless beings whom he thought he could 'do something for'. For me what he did was remove a cancerous larynx, shake his head sorrowfully when my liver enlarged but otherwise imbued me with hope. At one stage I sought unneeded appointments with him just to cheer myself up.

I was included on a panel in a *This is Your Life* and met behind the scenes some of the people he had saved, influenced or worked with.

One doctor said, 'He was the last of the all-over surgeons. He could operate on your earlobe or your toenails and anywhere in-between.'

He seemed to favour my big toe which he always shook on hospital visits.

What else? I only ever saw him lose his temper once. He had made for me a tube that slipped into what is called a stome which is the hole they leave for you to breathe through after larynx removal. The sister in the ward was having trouble inserting it and was bossily chiding him about it. He turned the shade of red that spells danger and plopped the tube into place. I forgot his precise words but he did call her Madam. It was the filthiest word I have ever heard.

By Les Tanner, the AGE – 3 July, 1993

Valda Street was the last of Sir Edward's secretaries – the last but by no means the least. Years after his death, she remains a point of contact for many of Sir Edward's former patients and the prisoners of war who continue to grieve his death.

At her tearooms, Valda's Treet, in Warburton, she has an alcove dedicated to Sir Edward, with photos and drawings on the wall, and some of the old consulting room and waiting-room furniture. It's an arrangement which provokes some discussion. 'I'm standing in the kitchen and hear people come in and say "Oh, Weary Dunlop, I used to have lunch with him,"' Valda said. 'It's amazing the people who knew him personally and went to dinner parties at his house. Incredible.' What percentage do you think did know him personally? 'Everyone. (laughs) Everyone had met him once at least.'

I WAS WITH Sir Edward for fifteen years. I started in 1978, and when I finished I had something like twenty-eight weeks holiday owing to me. He was seventy when I started and every year I kept thinking, Oh, he won't go on forever. I thought, Sensible people retire soon after they're seventy and so I'd go without holidays because he'd tell me how busy he was. At Christmas time he'd say he needed me there at a certain date and I'd think, Oh, he's an old man so I'll do it. All those years later and twenty-eight weeks holiday!

When I first started we tried dictation, but it was hopeless. You couldn't hear him because he had a soft voice and he'd be constantly rummaging through papers – all you'd hear was this crackle of paper, and so he'd write things by hand. Everything was written in draft form. Pages, pages, and then you'd have to transcribe it and type it out. He was constantly writing.

He wrote little notes all the time. I went to the petty cash box one morning and it had a little note in it: 'Sorry honey, stole your money.' (laughs) He had a really good sense of humour and he was so clever with words. Writing to people, he'd often write little poems and he was good at a verse to match the occasion, too. It's my great regret that I didn't write down all those little sayings. He had one for every occasion. From the really simple little things like: 'When I was young and full of hope, I washed my face with Velvet soap, and now I'm old and there is no hope, I wash my face with any soap.' He used to sing that to me I can't tell you how often, and I said, 'I know there's no hope.' But then he could quote great lengthy bits of Homer. People like the journalist Martin Flanagan could bring it out in him, and he would just talk for a whole afternoon, quoting all these things.

When you're there, you take it all for granted. I didn't know that this man that I worked for was going to have a statue larger than life and be on 50-cent coins and stamps. I mean, I just thought he was some nice old man, like my grandfather. I really didn't think he was ever going to be as famous as he is.

I think towards the end of his life, when the diaries came out and he accepted every invitation, that secretly he probably knew all this was going to happen. He'd love it, absolutely love it. He would think that statue in St Kilda Road was wondrous.

And what do you think of it?
I think it's terrific, but on one really cold Tuesday last year, I was in Melbourne and I was coming into the city on the tram, and

it was late in the afternoon and freezing cold and the tram conductor was telling everyone about this statue. I'm sitting there and looking out the frosty windows and here was this poor old man over there in the park, in the half dark and the cold, and I thought, Oh God, why didn't they put a coat on him? (laughs) It was so sad, I thought. He just looked sort of old and cold. But I do think it is so like him. I'm not sure what's going to happen in years to come when children that are young today are going to look at it and think, Who's that old man?

I've heard that you used to threaten to tell his life story.

One day he was sitting on a rickety old chair at work really annoying the life out of me, and I said to him, 'When I write the real Weary Dunlop story, warts and all . . .' and I'm here to tell you that this look of terror came over his face and he leaned over and he said, 'You'd better bloody not.' I mean, he seldom swore. Even now, when someone phones to ask if I will speak somewhere, I think there'll be a blue flash from heaven and it will be him and I'll be struck dead. I practically feel disloyal talking about him because I know that he really was a very private person and he certainly wouldn't like anything 'warts and all' to be told. So you can rub out anything that is sort of warty.

But he's in danger of being so close to a myth that he really needs some warts.

And we all have them, everyone has them, but we are inclined to think that some people are different. That was one thing that used to amaze me: you are inclined to think that a person in his position would be absolutely positive and confident and never have any insecurities. But he'd write something and often he'd come out and say, 'Do you think this sounds too tough?' He needed a second opinion, just wanted someone to confirm that if he was writing a report about someone, he wasn't being too tough on them. I thought, Well, they aren't any different to us really.

You said once that if any patient or admirer gave him anything, he had to keep it.
Oh yes, and he had to display it. That's why the rooms looked like the dog's breakfast, because we'd have all these little ornaments of the Parthenon from Greece and something from Turkey and gifts that people would bring in, and he'd take off his shoe and hammer another hole in the wall and about a cupful of cement dust would fall out of the place. Behind everything that covered the walls in Parliament Place, there was a hole big enough to put your fist in.

And he was a hoarder. Oh! When I went there, there were piles of magazines and things. You can't imagine what the place looked like. It was pretty awful when I was there but it was ten times worse when I started. If you moved anything, he would know you'd moved it and he got so angry. I'd stack stuff in plastic bags and stick it under the examination couch in the back surgery so if there was suddenly a performance whereby he wanted something, at a pinch I could find it because I would leave it there for six or twelve months.

Did Sir Edward sleep at work?
He would come out and sit opposite me and I'd be typing and he'd just fall asleep, writing a prescription or something. He would go to sleep in a second. All he'd need was ten minutes or so and I would often wake him. And I'm sure he believed till the day he died that I didn't know he was asleep. If you woke me up, I'd be jumping around and looking absolutely startled. He never did. He was cunning. He would wake slowly and lift his

head and he would peek around to see what was happening. Of course he was Superman. He would never want to be seen doing the wrong thing.

There was the wonderful day in Parliament Place, it was the April before he died and it was a warm autumn day. We only had these two elderly lady sisters sitting in the waiting room. I was in my office and the sun's streaming in and it's getting warmer and I'm getting sleepier, and he was in his office. He was equally quiet. I thought, If he doesn't take those patients in, in a minute I'm going to fall asleep.

Anyhow, he eventually came out and took them in and closed the door. Everything was quiet and I nodded off. I wouldn't know how long I was asleep but I woke up and realised where I was and thought, Fine, I haven't been caught. I sat there and fifteen minutes went by and I suddenly realised there was no noise coming from his office. Half an hour later, there was still no noise. Not a sound. I was beginning to worry. I thought perhaps the patients had been and gone and I'd slept through it, so I went and had a peek through the keyhole and couldn't see anything. And I was really just at the stage where I was panicking, thinking, What on earth am I going to do, when suddenly the door opened and these two little mice came into the office. These two little women. I said, 'What on earth have you been doing?' They said, 'Oh, Sir was asleep and we didn't like to waken him.' So Sir was asleep and the secretary was asleep – the only people awake were the patients.

Was Sir Edward concerned about his appearance?
Oh yes, very much so. He was always on the scales, he was terribly conscious of his weight. Before he went home for the last time, he hopped on the scales. He was a massive man with a massive chest, and hardly a wrinkle. He used to have a knack of

sweeping his hair that was covered in some sort of hair cream which was supposed to change the colour and make it grow, and he'd have it swirled around over his bald patch.

Was he vain?

Well, he was, I think. Mind you, you'd never think it when you saw some of the things he'd turn up in. He didn't believe in anything new. I suppose he, like me, thought that every year was his last year and he wouldn't get the use out of it.

I mean, the man just ran that place so economically. He was generous if he was at a function and he'd always have to be seen to buy something. I used to say to him, the one thing I would never want to be is famous. If someone says, 'We want to have a portrait of the current governor and we need $200 from all the head people in Melbourne', you can't be the one who says, 'I can't afford it', you just have to mark your cheque and send it off.

But in running his home and his office, he was really frugal. Absolutely unbelievably frugal. Mind you, so was Lady Helen. All the years I worked at Parliament Place, it was never painted. He would never maintain anything. That's why they had such problems in selling the house, because it had never had a thing done to it. But then on the other hand, he was involved in things on a different level and he didn't have time to think about those things.

What do you mean?

To a certain extent he was incredibly naive. An innocent in many respects, unaware of the things we take for granted. They were all just too small or unimportant. He didn't have time to even think about them. I spent my entire time sort of protecting him. And he could cut himself off, you know, he had this ability. For example, if it was 110 in the shade and I was absolutely falling about from heat exhaustion, I'd go in and he'd be sitting there with his heavy coat on, all rugged up and red in the face and writing, and I'd say, 'Sir Edward, it's 110 in the shade. Why don't you take your coat off?' 'Oh, if you don't think about it, you won't feel it,' he'd say. That's exactly the way he thought: if you don't think about it, you won't feel it. That's how he went through life. The afternoon sun would come streaming in that room and it would be boiling and he'd be there writing all these reports. Never stopped.

The rooms have been described as absolutely freezing in winter, too.
Well, don't think about it, you won't feel it, dear. It was a two-bar heater and I'd have it on when he came in, in the morning, and then he'd turn it off. Or turn one bar off, certainly. I used to put the steriliser on, thinking it might heat up the little surgery.

One thing I've heard about repeatedly is his lateness. I've spoken to –
Everyone. (laughs) But the thing is, he was impatient of anyone who was late. He would describe people and he'd say, 'Oh, God, that woman, she's never on time'. I'd think, How can you say it? He was famous throughout the country, and as for the poor nursing staff, I don't know how they put up with him.

And the anaesthetists.
Exactly. He wouldn't worry. It was this tunnel vision – he was doing something and he wouldn't get rattled. Even if you had a room full of patients and the temperature's 100 and everyone's getting toey and snitchy with the staff, he would still give the patients the same time and he'd be bowing and tapping and

comforting them and wouldn't hurry, wouldn't be seen to be trying to get them out quickly. And he would then go into the waiting room and say, 'I'm sorry, dear, I've got this problem', and they would excuse him.

He had the knack of turning a deaf ear, and that was really how he survived. If he didn't want to hear, he didn't hear it. On the other hand, he was very aware of everything that was going on. I well remember the day a patient came in, not long before he died and said 'How long have you been here, Valda?' I said 'Oh, I don't know, fifteen or sixteen years, but we won't talk too loud because Sir Edward would die if he thought he had to pay me long service leave.' And this voice roared from the back surgery, 'What makes you think Christ would forget his crucifixion?' (laughs) Of course he knew how long I'd been there, he knew precisely. He really was so astute. He only gave the appearance of being weary and away with the pixies. I could give as good as he gave and I really believe that if you stood up to him, he'd respect you deep down, I'm convinced of that.

You must have had some tumultuous times.

We certainly did. I'd stick it out and fight him to the death, and I'd usually win. He never did anything wrong. Ever. It was never his fault, it was always his staff, and you'd hear him telling patients things. Well, one day I was so incensed, I went in, in front of the patient, and I said, 'That is not true', and he just laughed. He laughed and he was forgiven, but he knew not to do it again.

He would get away with murder, he was an old devil, absolutely. Anyone who worked for him will tell you that. He used to have dreadful tantrums if he couldn't find a paper and he couldn't find it because he lived in such confusion. He carried this little basket in and out every day, and it had all his papers and invitations. Half of them were out of date and he'd usually lose the top ten anyhow, just walking up the driveway. It was like a wind tunnel and so the top ten would blow away. Occasionally some poor soul would come in thinking that they'd just won first prize in Tatts by finding some letter that he'd written in the driveway.

I remember one night I'd just got home from work and he phoned me and said, 'Oh a terrible thing's happened. I've lost the money.' One night each week, I'd give him all these envelopes and there'd be one with the housekeeper's money, one with the housekeeping, one for the cleaning lady. They were on the top of the basket when he went down the drive and they blew off, and when he got home, he didn't have the money. But someone looked after him, because I ran across the Fitzroy Gardens, fearing for my life in the half-dark and there they were in the driveway. Just amazing.

There was the very humane and compassionate side of him, too. He really had an incredible relationship with his patients, and the more I think about it, the more I realise that his patients were not only his patients, they were his friends. It was his patients who knew how much tax he paid, what his rates were, because he told them. That's the sort of thing you usually tell your friends, and it's very difficult to charge a friend. He didn't want to put them to additional expense, so if he was going to do some sort of procedure, he'd be careful to explain that they would get most of that back from their medical benefits. He was generous to the extreme in doing things for war widows, to get pensions and this sort of thing. You know, the way he was with the POWs, he was just fantastic. I find it terribly moving. (Valda begins to weep and apologises.) It was so moving. And the way they spoke of him. I could shake him till he rattled but it still really moves me. He was so beautiful to them. When you listen to all those old fellows and the stories they tell, it's just incredible. I think he gave them strength, many of them. He sort of gave them strength to keep going, and then I'd feel really guilty because he'd drive me nuts. And old patients that came in, he'd drive them round to St Andrews or drive them wherever they had to go. It was just incredible the time he'd put into them, the effort he'd go to, to look after them.

How would the working week begin?
On Monday mornings, you'd hear the old Mercedes and then he'd come tumbling down the drive and he'd have this big flower basket full of flowers. Half the camellias that he'd bring in would be spent before they even got in here, but he'd always bring in this enormous basket of flowers and there'd be petals and leaves all over the place. Similarly when he used to visit his patients on Saturday, he'd always take them flowers out of his garden. He loved to be able to take them to the patients. They'd say, 'He came in with three red roses,' and it just meant so much to them.

He had a white cat called Neige and he always wore a navy blue suit and he'd come in and it would be covered with white hair. He wouldn't ask me to brush him down if he was going out, he'd just back up to me and hand me a brush. When Neige died, I said to him, 'Next time, make sure you get a navy blue cat.'

If he was going off somewhere, I'd make sure he had sand-wiches to take, and he'd be running so late that he'd stuff them in his pocket, without paper, without anything. I'd look out and I'd see him going across that little park in Parliament Place with that little tiny hat on his head and he'd be scoffing these sand-wiches. He'd hop on the tram and go down to the city – that's if he wasn't terrorising the motorists. He was always having car accidents, and it was never his fault. 'The umbrella rolled out from under the seat and went under the clutch,' or under the something or other. That came out a dozen times. After one particular accident, I phoned the guy from the RACV and I said, 'Can't you do something to stop this man?' Because it seemed such a tragedy that a man like that could end up injuring someone. He said, 'Well Mrs Street, if you can find a doctor who'll write a certificate stating that Sir Edward Dunlop is unfit to drive, then that's all we need.' And who would do it? No one. Absolutely no one. In those last five years, whoever phoned and wanted him to attend something, I'd make sure that they picked him up and brought him home, and people were happy to do that.

He was a really very private person and you really didn't know what he was thinking. He wasn't a man who was close to his family, I don't think. He wasn't into cousins and aunts and uncles and keeping in touch. Not at all. Perhaps because he didn't have time. I think to a certain extent his family suffered because he was always busy doing other things. And so they went off and did their own thing because he wasn't there. But then at the end of his life, those last five or six years, when it would have been nice to have your family around, when he'd slowed down, there wasn't any family. And so for that reason, he gathered speed in accepting invitations. He would accept every invitation. He was a people person, he had to have people.

Was he a lonely man?
Oh, I think he was desperately lonely. He used to say to me how the boys had had the best education and he'd taken them overseas, but what they really wanted was to have him there every night, not just on holidays when he could take them to New Zealand or climbing in India. I think that as the years went by he realised his mistake. Too late. To me, he was a very lonely

figure. That's why he stayed in the rooms every night till really late. He couldn't bear to go home to an empty house.

You were able to notify Sir Edward's trustees of his wishes for his burial, weren't you?
After he came back from a funeral once, we were sitting down talking about it and I said to him, 'Now, you really should tell me what you want in the shape of a funeral, while you are fit and well.' He said, 'No, no, no.' I said, 'No, come on, you should tell me.' And so he did. He told me he wanted to be cremated, that he wanted half his ashes to go to the farm and half to be sprinkled on the Burma-Thai railway, so I made a note which I took home and put on my noticeboard with the date. I think it was March 1983. When he died I looked at the noticeboard and there it was.

In the time you worked for him, he went from being a busy surgeon to a living legend, didn't he?
He stopped operating at seventy-five and his patient numbers reduced, so it was convenient for him to find other activities. He was able to accept all these invitations and be seen here and there because he had the time and he made sure he was available. He always knew precisely how many committees he was on. He belonged to something like forty-three associations. I said to him one day, 'That's nonsense', and he sat there and wrote them all down. He knew precisely how many. Some were such vague things, overseas things that he had almost nothing to do with, but he listed them.

He also had a huge number of letters after his name.
Oh, and you had to have them in the right order or he'd have a stroke. And not only his but other people's. It was terribly

important, and I was such an ignoramus. Whatever new honour he got, he couldn't stop showing people. If anyone came in, he'd take them into the backroom to show them this medal. He was so proud of it – that was really the country boy in him. He'd have them all in this little backroom where he'd tapped holes in the wall and hammered them all in.

But it was a gradual process. I was never really conscious of anything much changing from when I went there to when I left. It's only since he's gone that I'm suddenly conscious of this great man.

This obituary by **Robert D. Marshall** *was published in 1994 in the* Australian and New Zealand Journal of Surgery.

. . . Every nation needs its idols and Weary filled the bill perfectly. The climactic deeds during the war that made him a folk-hero occupied only four years of a very long lifetime and, although his military career had ended in 1946, he was given a military funeral forty-seven years later. During the service there was little mention of the surgical work that occupied the greater part of the next thirty years of his life. He was, however, a Fellow of the Royal Australasian College of Surgeons and an Honorary Surgeon at the Royal Melbourne Hospital, Repatriation General Hospital, Peter MacCallum Clinic and the Royal Victorian Eye and Ear Hospital for more than twenty years, as well as having a very large private surgical practice. It therefore seems necessary for posterity that an attempt be made to appraise his purely surgical achievements and set them alongside the overwhelming 'Christ of the Burma Railway' image, which was to become his public persona and make him an Australian icon. The writer was Weary's assistant for ten years from 1953 to 1963, assisted him at most of his major operations during that time and is therefore well placed to comment on his surgical career.

Surgeons are men before they are surgeons, and they practise their craft according to their lights and their personalities. To understand Weary Dunlop as a surgeon, it is first necessary to understand the drive that made him the man he was and which made him almost a demigod to the prisoners of war he commanded. His surgical career on the other hand, although it made him many friends, also produced detractors, some of them vehement. It seems strange at first sight that a man of Weary Dunlop's stature should have been so little involved with the Royal Australasian College of Surgeons after the war. He never served on the State Committee, much less the Council, despite serving on and presiding over innumerable non-surgical committees. He had few close friends among his surgical colleagues, particularly his seniors, and he also stood apart from the mainstream of hospital politics. Why did he choose to direct his prodigious ability to organise and to lead mostly into fields outside his chosen speciality of surgery? The answer can only be sought in his personality and attitudes.

Most of us manage to present a more or less consistent image to the world, although the mask sometimes slips. Weary never varied; he never faltered; he behaved at all times as the very epitome of the best type of British gentleman. His chosen model was Sir Thomas Dunhill, with whom he worked in London before the war, but it could as easily have been an empire builder like Clive of India or

Cecil Rhodes. He was a staunch Anglophile and royalist all his life and, only a few days before his death, he commented that he was glad the republican debate would not come in his time. From early youth Weary assumed the sterling virtues of bravery, stoicism, fortitude and unflinching will. He could never ignore a challenge and would die rather than be beaten. He was a huge, slow, affable, shambling bear of a man who spoke slowly, courteously and calmly. He seemed the very personification of his undergraduate nickname but, in the true Australian tradition, the label 'Weary' was no more accurate than 'Tiny' would have been. His apparent slowness concealed a mind like a steel trap . . .

He was the ultimate individualist. He had an inexhaustible fund of self-confidence and an unquenchable belief in himself; this made him impatient of authority in any form. He was a great leader, but a poor follower. He was indefatigable and indestructible; he simply ignored his own discomfort or tiredness and expected that those around him would do the same. He knew that he was blessed with exceptional strength of mind and body and felt compelled to use these talents for the benefit of others. He really had no choice but to follow what he perceived to be his bounden duty; he lived the life of *noblesse oblige*. These personal qualities were tailor-made for the man who was to command 'Dunlop's Thousand' during the war and so defy their Japanese captors that he became a legend in his lifetime.

Weary was, of course, only one of the Australian doctors who spent the war in Japanese prison camps. 'Bertie' Coates, Kevin Fagan, Alan Hobbs and others were also prisoners of war and performed prodigies of selfless, devoted service for the men under their care. But of them all, it was Weary's feats of endurance on the Burma railway that most caught the public imagination. His men regarded him as a 'lighthouse of sanity in a world of madness'.

The whole terrible story of his prison camp years reads like *The Boy's Own Paper* and the denouement of heroism triumphant seems almost unbelievable. One can only marvel that Weary was not summarily executed for his defiance (as indeed almost happened on three separate occasions). It seems likely that he survived only because it suited the Japanese very well to have him there to preserve the morale of his troops so that they had at least some workers to build their railway. But perhaps they too realised that here was a rare example of the greatness of the vaulting human spirit.

There can be no doubt that Weary thoroughly deserved the label of a 'great man', in the best sense of the term. His richly merited knighthood puts him in the company of other great men (explorers, soldiers, sportsmen) who really deserve a special category of their own with a different mode of address. But to say that a man is great does not imply that he is perfect. Like other great men, Weary had his faults, which in fact were merely the obverse side of the very qualities which made him capable of such great deeds in the first place.

The fact that he was never a 'College' man is not only understandable but inevitable when one considers his contempt for authority and his complete unruliness; he could never have worked his way patiently through the councils of the College because he was the very archetype of the individualist. He regarded College and Hospital administrative meetings as much talk and many words, which promised much but achieved little, so he left them to others and went his own way.

His enormous self-confidence and egotism made it difficult for him to regard others as his equal and this applied to his surgery, just as it did elsewhere. He preferred, for example, to perform abdomino-perineal resection of the rectum single-handed, and clearly believed that the orthodox combined synchronous approach with another surgeon would have been an admission of weakness on his part and a betrayal of his duty.

He simply ignored the convenience and comfort of those who worked with him, although he also ignored his own. This made things very trying for his colleagues. The late Gordon Stanton, his permanent anaesthetist, often displayed the patience of a saint when kept waiting hours on end, but persisted for many years with total loyalty and dedication far beyond any reasonable call of duty, working on and on at all hours, day and night. Weary seemed quite unaware that anyone could regard his behaviour as other than completely normal and necessary.

During the 1930s and throughout the war, the Royal Melbourne Hospital was staffed by conservative general surgeons with little interest in the new surgical specialities that were emerging. None of them, except Edgar King, had ever attempted intrathoracic surgery, and Weary's surgical apprenticeship was served at a time when operations within the chest were in their infancy. It was only through the efforts of Sir Alan Newton that beds were made available in 1946 for three new departments: thoracic surgery, plastic surgery and neurosurgery. The returned servicemen who were appointed to the hospital over the next few years were all innovators anxious to expand the horizons of surgery. By the early 1950s, the scope of surgical expertise had widened enormously, particularly in the new specialities. John

Hayward, as a surgical resident, had pioneered the maintenance of negative pressure in the chest once it had been opened. The new Department of Anaesthesia, established in 1949 by Norman James, together with rapidly improving intravenous therapy, set the stage for oesophageal resection to become a practicable procedure. Weary was drawn irresistibly towards the new challenges posed by thoracoabdominal surgery.

His doggedness and his refusal to accept even the thought of defeat inevitably led him towards his enduring surgical interests (distressing and often incurable complaints such as carcinoma of the larynx, oesophagus and stomach, ulcerative colitis and even abdominal aortic aneurysm), all of them demanding major surgery at the limits of the possible. In his early days he treated many patients in partnership with John Hayward who taught him how to open and close the chest, while Weary for his part supplied the expertise relating to bowel resection and anastomosis. Together they pioneered oesophageal surgery at the Royal Melbourne Hospital after the war. As the years went by, Weary no longer felt the need for Hayward's assistance and his enthusiasm and self-confidence led him to undertake massive operations, which could easily stray beyond the bounds of prudence. His patients were greatly helped by the tireless ministrations of Melbourne's first specialist resuscitationist, the late Dr E.B. Drevermann, but even so there were disasters at times.

Laryngectomy, oesophagectomy, abdominal aortic replacement and total colectomy; these were hazardous procedures in those days and this made it inevitable that mortality and post-operative morbidity would be high in the hands of such an aggressive surgeon. It sometimes seemed that he almost welcomed intra-operative complexities for the problems they posed. He would, for example, resect part of the full thickness of an adherent aortic wall and patch the defect in the course of an oesophagectomy for carcinoma when a more cautiously orthodox surgeon would abandon the operation. These multiple procedures sometimes took an unconscionable time and stretched beyond reasonable bounds. Accordingly, his successes were punctuated by serious complications. But he continued, sparing neither himself nor others. I vividly remember one particular operating day at the Royal Melbourne Hospital with a proposed list of nine major cases booked for eight a.m. We started two hours late. The first operation took eight hours, the second seven. At one a.m. the next morning Weary was outraged that the theatre staff flatly refused to allow the third patient to be brought up! None of us had eaten since breakfast the previous day.

Despite its high morbidity and mortality, it must not be overlooked that this aggressive surgery did produce results. His five and ten-year survival figures for laryngectomy were easily the best in the world at that time. He was determined to give his patients a chance of 'cure'. Regrettably, this aim often proved illusory, as it so often does, today more than ever, but at times it could produce a brilliant success against the odds.

Weary's legendary contempt for time did not endear him to his professional colleagues, especially his fellow surgeons. He was apt to schedule massive operations at a moment's notice with a sublime disregard for his own or anyone else's convenience; consequently another surgeon due to operate in the session after Weary's might easily find himself cooling his heels for hours on end while he waited in vain for the theatre to become vacant. Some of his fellow senior surgeons made it quite clear that they regarded this as intolerable rudeness and thoughtlessness. And indeed they had a point!

He ate and slept at the most irregular hours and inevitably was chronically late for appointments. But he drove himself mercilessly and would embark on a full round of his patients at any hour of the day or night, whenever he had finished operating. He seemed baffled that others could regard this as unusual.

His post-operative care was thus exemplary; it was never too late and nothing was ever too much trouble. As a result, many patients almost worshipped him and gave him a surgical reputation to rival his image of 'Christ of the Burma Railway' during the war.

His remarkable personal qualities were really not well adapted to produce the 'ideal' surgeon of the post-war era. Such a man should display self-confidence, aggression tempered by caution, technical precision, deftness and delicacy, and should be a 'team man', even if he is the team's most important member. Weary's attributes were somewhat different; they were more appropriate to the 'hero-surgeons' of the 19th century when the surgeon really was a one-man band. He was reluctant to delegate responsibility and believed, above all, in his own powers.

He was therefore tailor-made for the Burma railway, both as commandant and surgeon, where his qualities made it inevitable that he would conduct himself as he did. No wonder those four years dominated his reputation for the next forty.

But the demands of improvised surgery in the jungle are different from those in civilian practice. Small wonder then, that Weary emerged in his surgical persona as the most rugged of rugged individuals and became something of a lone figure who took little part in hospital and College affairs. Instead, he chose to direct his energies to a multitude of committees concerned with former prisoners of war, returned servicemen, Legacy, the Colombo Plan and international relationships with South-East Asia. His war experiences thus became inextricably intertwined into his later life as an ambassadorial figure. He never forgot his ex-POW survivors and served them to the end of his days in many different ways.

One final anecdote will serve to illustrate Weary Dunlop the surgeon. He performed one of the first aortic grafts at the Royal Melbourne Hospital, but the patient was not originally his. Two other staff surgeons (one general, one thoracic) were embarking on the formidable procedure and it was necessary for the graft to be made on the spot. Weary volunteered to do this menial task, but an hour later he had taken over the entire operation while the original protagonists stood by and watched him. On this occasion, as on others, he moved on like some inexorable natural force.

All in all, Weary Dunlop was one of the greatest Australians of the twentieth century. It is doubtful if we shall see his like again. His surgery was the product of all his remarkable personal traits and was brilliant at times, but flawed by complications made inevitable by his uncompromising determination to succeed.

Those of us fortunate enough to have known him and worked with him were by turns stimulated, infuriated, instructed and exhausted.

He was the most remarkable man I have ever known.

4

IN THE SERVICE OF OTHERS

Weary Dunlop spent his life in the service of others. The number of local organisations in which he participated is astounding. Over the years, the groups to which he made a significant contribution included the Australian Asian Association, the Anti-Cancer Council of Victoria, the Victorian Foundation of Alcoholism and Drug Dependence, the Melbourne Council for Overseas Students and the Friends of Vellore. These and other groups vied for his time with the many commitments which sprang from his wartime experience, and included the Prisoners of War Trust, the Prisoners of War Association and the Ex-POW and Relatives' Association.

Of course Weary was a citizen of the world. He travelled for the Colombo Plan in India and Asia and welcomed into his home many overseas doctors who came to train in Australia. He was a member of the International Society of Surgeons and the James IV Association of Surgeons, and built on the extensive contacts he made through international medical conferences. He was recognised for his services to the medical profession in Thailand in April, 1993 when he was made a Knight Grand Cross (First Class) of the Noble Order of the Crown of Thailand by King Bhumibol Adulyadej.

His contacts with the ex-POWs were international, too. He travelled extensively to attend reunions and in 1991, he was made president of the Scottish branch of the Far East Prisoners of War (FEPOW) association.

Weary Dunlop's service to others lives on in a number of charitable endeavours and scholarships, most notably the Sir Edward Dunlop Medical Research Foundation, the Weary Dunlop-Boonpong Exchange Fellowship, the Asialink Dunlop Asia Fellowship and the Queen's Trust Sir Edward Dunlop Memorial Award.

The interviews that follow represent the tip of the iceberg.

On the advice of his superior, L.B.M. Joseph, in 1973 **Dr Phillip Nathaniel** *came to Australia from the Christian Medical Centre in Vellore, India, to train with Sir Edward Dunlop. On his return to India, he was professor of surgery at the CMC before migrating to Melbourne in 1979. He and his family now live in Essendon where I spoke to him about Sir Edward.*

I CAME TO Australia in August 1973. In fact, all I had from Australia was a telegram from Sir Edward addressed to the High Commissioner in India stating that Phillip Nathaniel would be working with him. I didn't even have a letter in my hand. With that telegram we went for our interview and I got my visa and I came alone in August. I left Madras and the temperature was forty degrees, and touched down in Melbourne where it was four degrees. I came in the early morning and I got to the customs and I said to myself, Oh gee, it's a new place, I hope Sir Edward is here, and then I saw him sitting wrapped in a blanket. He had had been there since about 5.30 a.m. and my plane touched down at 7.15.

After the formalities, we left the airport and he said, 'Phillip, would you mind scrubbing with me? I have four operations before I take you home.' So, straight from the airport, I went to the Mercy Hospital and scrubbed over there. There were four cases and we finished at about 11.30 p.m. I was almost feeling sleepy. (laughs) He took me home and I stayed with him for about six weeks until my family arrived.

Were you surprised to arrive and be put straight to work?
We are used to long hours of surgical work, I didn't mind. But I was surprised. Here I was coming into the country, I didn't have my registration, nothing at all, just straight into the theatre. Because no questions were asked those days. But he was as friendly as he ever was.

While I stayed with him, Lady Helen and I used to have such long talks in the evenings. He was home at about ten or eleven at night, so from tea in the evening both of us would sit and talk. She was such a gracious person, a very softly spoken lady. In the morning at seven o'clock, she would put out the breakfast things for us. She was very gentle, not ostentatious at all. We used to talk about various things, about what they did before they got married and all the troubles that she went through waiting for him to come back from the army. She looked after me like one of the family and it was nice to come to a different country where you didn't know a soul, a different culture, and then to be in a family like that. It was unbelievable.

Sir Edward had his rough edges too. He could be pretty strong in the theatres, the girls used to be frightened of Sir Edward. But there was an underlying kindness with all his activities. One day he was supposed to catch a flight to Adelaide. The plane was supposed to leave at seven o'clock and we left his office at quarter to seven. I remember sitting next to him and I looked at the speedometer and it was 160 kilometres on the Tullamarine freeway. That was the only time I got scared driving with him.

You were saying he actually frightened the nurses?
Well, not scared. Some of them used to complain. You see,

being a younger person, a junior person, they would unfold and tell you, 'Oh, I wish he would do this,' but then nobody would confront him. They used to look up to him as a father figure, so you can't really get angry with someone of that stature. I mean, it was good fun working with him. I initially learned a few tips from him about doing things, then as you analyse the things, you find that some of the things that you do are completely different to what he is doing. You stick to what you know is the better, easier way that you've learnt. But he had vast experience in many of the surgical things.

I used to assist him in most of his operations, especially in the first six months or so. I had the background, since I was the cancer surgeon at Vellore. Then I got a position as senior teaching fellow at Monash, at the Alfred, and I couldn't assist him as much because I had full time work and operating sessions at the hospital.

When did you go back to Vellore?

I went back to Vellore in 1976 and I became professor of surgery there. During that time, Sir Edward and Michael Long and Ian Russell came and stayed with us in our home and we renewed our friendship. Sir Edward had been in Vellore a couple of times earlier. He used to have contacts with a lot of people up north. Punjab University conferred on him an honorary degree. Up north, he was a legend as far as the Burma trail was concerned, and lots of people knew about him.

Really? He was known for his war reputation in India as well?

Before Bangladesh became part of Pakistan, Burma was just the other side of the Indian border. In World War 11, as the Japanese came in, quite a few refugees crossed over from Burma to India. So a lot of people knew about Sir Edward.

What sort of surgeon was Sir Edward?

He was a real complete general surgeon. I remember Weary operated on the Consul General of Japan in Melbourne and he had cancer of the oesophagus. I assisted him. It was not a curative, but he had relief. He could have flown back to Japan to have the operation done but he decided to have it done here, which was a great thing at that time. Sir Edward never held any bitterness ever, as far as I know, against the Japanese.

He seems to have been remarkably free of any sort of racism.

Well, here was I, an Indian who had just come in, and he took me into his own home without any questions. You can't have any better expression of non-racism. He used to help so many people from South-East Asian countries. I think Thailand was one of the other areas where he had a special interest, and he used to have people who came from Singapore, Malaysia.

Weary was renowned for the long operation.

I helped him with oesophagus cancer – we took about four to six hours for the operation. Once you're immersed, working with him, you don't feel the time pass by. Weary is well known for his slow, deliberate operating. He was very slow compared to these days. These days there's a lot of pressure, you've got to go fast.

He seems to have had an amazing relationship with his patients.

Oh yes. He used to have a lot of the old diggers come to his rooms. I remember the first week I was in his office, I was sitting and talking to one of the old diggers and he talked at length about his experience in the army and how Weary helped him, saved his life, etc, and then as he got up, he shook my hand and said, 'Doc, it was bloody nice meeting you.' And I thought Oh gosh! Bloody is a word that you never use in everyday vocabulary in India. It is a curse word. (laughs) Then I realised later on that it's the gentle way of saying it was nice. He used to get a lot of those very old patients, and they adored Weary. They almost used to worship the place that he trod.

Dr Davis McCaughey was the master at Ormond College when L.B.M. Joseph and Dr Phillip Nathaniel were in residence.

WE HAD A succession of people at Ormond from the Christian Medical College in Vellore, India. Weary had given a good deal of support to the college. L.B.M. Joseph was a leading surgeon at that hospital and eventually became head of the medical school there. I remember him saying to me that Weary was a great person for him to work with because, he said, 'He's so courageous as a surgeon. He'll take on things that other people might think are beyond doing anything about.' He said, 'This is very useful for us in India because, you see, an awful lot of our cases are brought to us really far too late and if you're going to operate, you've got to be pretty courageous about it and realise that really it is genuinely the last hope.' So it wasn't only his skill but his courage as a surgeon that he found very helpful in the Indian situation.

D. G. (Scotty) Macleish, a past-president of the Royal Australasian College of Surgeons, helped set up the Dunlop-Boonpong Exchange Fellowship which began in 1986. Mr Macleish was honoured by the King Bhumibol Adulyadej of Thailand in 1993.

WEARY VISITED THAILAND in 1956 as part of the Colombo Plan to help the developing nations up there. Like a number of other people, of whom Benjamin Rank is a good example, Weary worked in those countries, in particular India and Thailand.

Naturally he had an interest in seeing Thailand again because he'd spent three years there as guest of the emperor, but he went up there and worked and taught at several hospitals. In Thailand, he probably introduced some operations which had been little practised in that country. There was a notable story of an operation on a young man. People had taken a pessimistic view and had more or less felt that any operation would kill him, but Weary operated on him, and the patient survived. This impressed them enormously and so he became a surgical figure of some renown to the Thai surgeons of that day, particularly the people on the teaching staff of the Siriraj Hospital in the mid-1950s.

After the Dunlop-Boonpong Fellowships started in the mid-1980s, Weary made several trips to Thailand. Some were to return to Hellfire Pass and the River Kwai, and some were to meet people involved in the fellowship project. When Weary went up to Thailand, he had the capacity to meet the lofty or the poor, and he could talk to everybody. I think this is what the Thais liked about him. There was a bit of mysticism that accompanied him everywhere he went and he became a sort of cult figure. He behaved modestly, but he really was very pleased by all that sort of thing. He was recognised as a teacher of surgery and as a major figure.

The Thais regarded him as a very lofty figure and they revered – I think that is the proper word – him. People were keen to meet him and he attracted feelings of awe in those he met. They seemed to take pride in having met him. In April 1993, he was awarded the Knight the Grand Cross of the Order of the King of Thailand. I was honoured at the same time.

I saw a letter he wrote to notify the Royal College of Surgeons.

Well, he would let them know all right. I haven't written to the college to let them know what mine was (laughs), but Weary never missed an opportunity to let all his colleagues know. He had a good publicity machine working for him. I'm not saying that's good or bad but that's the sort of person Weary was.

Professor Thira Limsila is the chairperson of the Dunlop-Boonpong Exchange Fellowship in Thailand. Boonpong, a Kanchanaburi-based river trader, was part of the Thai underground movement that helped smuggle drugs, food and money to the prisoners of war. When the exchange fellowship was first mooted, Sir Edward suggested his name be used as a memorial to him and other like-minded Thais.

*In November 1995, Professor Thira gathered together some of the surgeon-recipients of the fellowship, and at the invitation of **Thanpuying Sumalee**, the wife of Professor Kasarn Chartikavanij, we met for a lunch at their home. Also present were members of the selection committee and Boonpong's grandson, Virawej Subhawat, a fellowship sponsor.*

Professor Thira Limsila is also the director of Siriraj Hospital and the vice-president of the Royal College of Surgeons of Thailand. He organised a Buddhist ceremony in Bangkok when Sir Edward died. He drove me to and from the lunch and we had plenty of time to speak in the car. 'To do surgery is better than driving in Bangkok,' he said.

MANY PEOPLE ASK me why I give myself utterly for this Dunlop-Boonpong Fellowship program. I'll give you some idea why.

I have very bitter memories of the cruelty of the war. I was eleven years old when the Japanese army invaded the southern part of Thailand. My home town was at the Ismthus of Krais. At first, at about four o'clock in the morning on 8 December 1941, we saw an awful lot of Japanese soldiers coming up. What would we do? Children were awakened to fight for their country. We had our provincial army but they were far, far away. Our little kids, aged about thirteen, fourteen, had to fight alongside our policemen. They had been fighting at least half a day when our government gave up and agreed to be allies with the Japanese. Then the fighting stopped and it saved a lot of lives.

The Japanese said, 'Oh, we don't want to do anything with you, we just want to be allowed to pass through Thailand to Burma, Malaya, Singapore.' We were afraid. The next day the Japanese went through my town. Up to the war, all through our part of Thailand, we had Japanese dentists, we had Japanese merchants, we had Japanese teachers, and when the war started, they suddenly had army uniforms.

The headquarters of the Japanese in that area was just next door to my home. All the women and children left for the jungle to get away from the fighting. For a year or two they were away. Though I was a little boy, my brother and I had to stay with others in the town. There I saw the cruel things that happened to people. With the Japanese army, if you stole from their belongings, they sometimes forced you to drink a salted solution of oil or petroleum. I saw a lot of what was done to the thousands of forced labourers, from Malaysia, the Philippines, from Singapore. It was bad and even though we were children, we remember.

Then I came to Bangkok to study. On the way to Bangkok by train, at the Nakom Patom station, there were prisoners of war. Even for our people, the sun is very, very hot. These prisoners were naked except for this small piece of cloth. It was so hot, their skin looked red. We threw some fruit and sweets to these people as we passed. It was unbelievable.

Terrible things have happened, so I just hate the war. The cruelty, the suffering, the inhumanity to man that happened to those forced labourers, to the prisoners. I don't blame the Japanese. I blame the war. People do anything to win a war.

When it finished, at first I heard nothing. I didn't know at all what happened in the camps until later. I think when we discovered what had happened, we had to thank Boonpong and the Boonpong family. The younger brother of Boonpong happened to be my schoolmate at secondary school in Bangkok. Boonpong, and many of the other natives of the Kanchanaburi region, are examples of man's humanity to man. They helped the prisoners in the camp even though the Japanese would have killed them if they had known.

Now it is the fiftieth anniversary of the war. I think Sir Edward followed the Buddhist way – that to forgive is the best medicine against cruelty and suffering. You forgive but you don't forget. During the war Sir Edward suffered a lot, for himself, for his fellow man, yet after the war he said, 'You are better to offer friendship and understanding.' It made men friends instead of enemies.

When did you first hear of Sir Edward after the war?
Sir Edward came to Thailand in 1956 and he was part of the first of the Australian medical mission, an unofficial ambassador. After the war our medical situation was not very good but many senior medical people were returning from England, like Professor Kasarn. Sir Edward spent seventeen days in Thailand, giving a lot of serious lectures, teaching and also doing ward rounds in our two teaching hospitals.

I was house surgeon at the Siriraj Hospital in 1956, and the first operation he did there is worth mentioning. It was an operation for what we call portal hypertension. The patient was a teenage boy who had congenital malformation of the portal vein, and liver cirrhosis. The boy had bled badly the night before and there was a difference between Kasarn and Sir Edward. Kasarn said, 'Operate? Oh no. We can't do this case. If the patient dies, it will be bad for the program,' because Weary had come as a goodwill ambassador. Sir Edward is a very strong man, strongwilled. He said, 'We must do it. If we don't do it, the patient will die. If we do the surgery, he will die or survive.' Weary is an expert on this kind of surgery. Kasarn assisted, and finally it was okay. The patient survived and lived for years.

I think Weary might be the first Australian to assist Thai surgeons. When I was studying surgery, I went to England. But now we are closer to Australia and we have to thank Sir Edward for that.

How did the fellowship come about, from the Thai end?
Kasarn was president of the Royal College of Surgeons of Thailand when I was secretary-general. If a senior surgeon came, Kasarn and I would try and have them visit the university teaching hospitals for two or three weeks. Scotty Macleish, the president of the Royal Australasian College of Surgeons, knows Thailand better than I do. He has visited many hospitals outside Bangkok. I would consider both he and Sir Edward unofficial ambassadors for Australia.

When the offer of support for this fellowship came through, Sir Edward came and asked me and Kasarn what we wanted the program to do. I told him I agreed that we needed surgical equipment, but in the short term the most important thing we needed was knowledge. I said it might be better to give us surgical training for our young surgeons. He over 100 per cent agreed with me and so did Kasarn. The Dunlop-Boonpong Exchange Fellowship gives opportunities for our young surgeons to get specialist training in Australia. Through it, thousands more lives can be saved. It is important to pass on to a new generation what Sir Edward has done, what Boonpong has done, how and why this long story happened.

Dr Chittinud Havanonda was the first of the Dunlop-Boonpong surgeon-scholars. He specialises in surgical oncology.

I WAS IN NEWCASTLE in 1988 for about ten months. The last few months I was in Australia, I went to Melbourne and met Sir Dunlop and he gave me a dinner at his home. He told me about his work during the war as a soldier at the Kanchanaburi Hospital, in the Kanchanaburi province. I think it was very helpful for me to work in Australia. I learnt a lot about cancer, but I should say that I learnt more about a system of work at the hospital, systems that I could then try to use in our hospitals. I am a teacher now at the university hospital in the Kanchanaburi province medical centre.

He was still very healthy when I met him. I went with a group of Thai people and he showed us his garden at the back of his house and he picked a red rose from his garden and gave it to my friend and she was very appreciative. (laughs) When I introduced myself, the first thing he said was, 'Oh, my first colleague. Our first fellowship.' I was very grateful.

Dr Athikom Supabphol furthered his training in the area of genito-urinary tumour surgery and renal transplantation at the Royal Melbourne and St Vincent's hospitals, in Melbourne in 1993.

I'M LUCKY BECAUSE when Sir Edward Dunlop returned to Melbourne after receiving his royal decoration, I accompanied him.

When I was in Melbourne, he invited me and another surgical scholar and Mr Macleish to a dinner at his house. It was fantastic. After dinner he took us upstairs to show us all the paintings, the many things there. At Melbourne I saw his way of life and I was really impressed. He still attended surgical meetings at the Royal Melbourne Hospital on Saturdays and he would still offer a comment on the topics that they were discussing. Even though he was eighty-five years old, he went to the Royal Melbourne Hospital by himself.

When he died, I read the Thai ambassador's speech at a meeting of the Australian Asian Association in memory of Sir Edward. I was really lucky to accompany him to Melbourne and to learn about his life.

Professor Kasarn Chartikavanij was very ill and joined the gathering briefly. He was unable to speak but nevertheless he was keen to contribute to what he saw as a tribute to his friend Sir Edward. Kasarn and Sir Edward met and became close friends during Sir Edward's 1956 visit to Thailand. Smiling broadly, he wrote shakily: 'He was a very good assistant' (It is not hard to imagine Sir Edward's response to that!) and 'He was a great drinker. We used to drink all night and start work early in the morning.' Thanpuying Sumalee Chartikavanij is married to Professor Kasarn. She had recently returned from the United Nations' Fourth World Conference on Women in Beijing.

PROFESSOR KASARN SPENT sixteen years in England. He went to public school there and university. That's why, I think, he and Sir Edward shared many sentiments and ideals together, because they were brought up on exactly the same standards. Both of them were not British or English, but were brought up in the British way. So they adapted the training to their own character.

They enjoyed each other's company very much and they tried to spend as much time together as they could. I think I first met Sir Edward after World War II, when he came back the first time to visit Bangkok again. Lady Dunlop was with him, too.

What do you remember of Sir Edward in those days?

I think first of all his sense of humour, his very straight-faced jokes. My English was not as good as his or my husband's so I was wondering, Is that what he really meant or was he just joking? Also, he was very much a gentleman in the old English way. He was very charming, especially to the Eastern ladies, who are not used to being treated like that. In Thailand the ladies are not ladies really, they are more or less companions, but he treated every woman as a lady.

He could also adapt himself to wherever he lived, even adapting himself to the prison camp during the war, that's the hardest test of any human being. He survived that – very well, too. When he was eighty, he still travelled a lot, carried his heavy luggage himself. Age seemed no problem to him at all, he wouldn't even think about it.

I do not know much about the work side because it was a separate world. But my husband invited many friends and visiting professors and he would spend a lot of time working through the night, especially through the early stage of thoracic surgery. I remember that he invited many famous doctors from abroad. They were put up at special apartments and quite often they would stay one or two months. They were from Denmark, from England, from the United States, Australia, New Zealand. My husband wouldn't come home sometimes for two days, working through the night and that is where they spent the night drinking – not in my house. (laughs)

Was Sir Edward's death a shock to you?
It was to many of us. The quickness with which he died seemed to many of us a blessing. Being very ill would have been completely out of the question for him. To all of us he is a symbol of strength, strong will and the willpower to survive as best as you can. Whatever he did, it was with the best intentions.

He received a very high honour in 1993?
Yes. In fact, we think he is even more high in our thoughts but that's the rules and regulations. So when he got the royal decoration, we were delighted but we feel if he had lived longer, he would soon be elevated to a higher decoration. Everybody appreciates what he did for Thailand.

Sir Edward wrote the following letter to his secretary, Vera Hart (Marquis) during his visit to Thailand, in 1956.

August, 1956   Flying from Chieng Mai to Bangkok

Dear Vera,
Life has been full of interest since arriving here to schedule. The Thais are too polite and considerate to permit me to work on the day of arrival – just courtesy calling – then a long weekend with a holiday on the Monday for the Queen's birthday.
    I have given some lectures and done a few operations

notwithstanding, oh Lord, how many dinners, lunches, receptions, and official calls. I feel rather like a film star with a girl with a Cine camera standing in front of me right through a luncheon.

You will be interested to know that I have met 'Miss Thailand' and 'Miss Chieng-mai'. My photograph was taken with the former, but fortunately it was far too dark for the film to record!!

This is a fascinating country as I found out long ago. It is exceedingly priest ridden with a standing clergy of at least 200 000, plus innumerable novices and 'hangers on'. One does not work after donning the yellow robe, and the only wants of this world are laid on c.q. monastery for contemplating 'the middle way', yellow robe for all occasions, and food by just pushing out your bowl – or Thermos flask to the faithful who wish to acquire merit by donating some nourishment. Today I visited a Shangri-La like monastery up on Chieng-mai mountain – where there was a priest, Phra Surmangalo – a perfectly good American Doctor of Laws who had been to Australia recently. He found the robe rather cold down there and on one occasion caught fire getting a bit too close to the fire.

Anyway the Bhuddist religion is a gentle affair and the most sincere devotees have nothing to do with killing in any shape or form, so that meat eating is regarded as aggressive. Some make a good thing out of caging birds and animals so that the faithful can acquire merit by buying them and releasing them!

Home and your letter to hand – rebukes noted – feel baffled and perplexed as I wrote one letter before leaving England at least entrusting you to buy flowers for Rhonda and another on the plane. I was groaning under the necessity to cough up for six kilos overweight due to instruments I bought in England. How I could be overweight after all the clothes and gear I sent home I really don't know.

You must forgive the writing as the flight was somewhat bumpy. Chieng-mai has been deep in flood with a foot or two of yellow water and all the debris of 800,000 people swirling through the streets.

Strange how, unlike nearly all Eastern countries everyone in Thailand seems well fed and happy, and the children gambol round in the most unsanitary drains and canals without seeming much the worse. This is a rich food producing country.

Dr Stanton was very far from well at Chieng-mai and has had a good deal of tummy trouble plus a bad throat. I have the local 'wog tummy' since I have already had all the diseases that can be got in that line, and have lived and eaten more primitively than most of the inhabitants – so I am carefree. . . I am doing my poor best to look after that wild devil Stanton.

I shall be home on schedule Thursday 13th Sept if still alive – which I gravely doubt. . .

God Bless. E.E.D. – Same to John.

*Sir Edward Dunlop joined the executive committee of the Anti-Cancer Council of Victoria in the early 1970s, and was chairman from 1974-80. The director of the council, **Dr Nigel Gray**, spoke about his role in the organisation which was very close to his heart.*

THOSE WERE THE early days when we were attacking the tobacco industry vigorously and there were really two things you knew about Weary and these were very real. One was that nobody was going to stick a knife in your back while Weary was around, or in your front, The second was that he was a lousy chairman, he couldn't chair a meeting to save himself. He muttered and mumbled. But he was a very useful counterpoint.

As many of his friends will have told you, he was a pre-war style surgeon but he had a very good mind, very intuitive, very sympathetic, and always took the courageous way out. I never saw him duck aside. That was instinctive and I think it was also part of his ego, which was not monstrous but he had a reasonable touch of it. Not in any sense overt, nor in any sense did it intrude on any of his relationships. If you left him off a list, he didn't get angry. If you forgot him, he didn't get angry. But he liked to be recognised and as life went on that became a bit more obvious and we all recognised him.

Weary went from being chairman to being president in 1980 because he was too valuable to lose, he was very well known and as our president he stayed until he was seventy-two, and then, because precedence suggested that he'd have to stand down, we made him deputy patron to the governor and he signed our fundraising letters for years. I remain of the view that he was a good puller as signer of the letters. But he was a sucker for a worthy cause and he didn't restrict himself to us. We were one of his major favourites, but the old digs always were his favourites and he would help anybody, without being unduly discriminating. In other words, despite his ability to tell the difference between right and wrong, he was a soft touch, a genuinely soft touch, especially in his later years.

While he was chair of the executive committee, I used to report to him every fortnight. We used to go to Frenchy's, which was the local restaurant. It was a good restaurant and he used to like that.

Those lunches are quite legendary within the council.
Yes, it was a lot of fun. We'd send him back to work late, usually, and Valda would have to simmer down the patients, who were always tolerant.

Of course I was extremely amused when he took on presidency of the Alcohol Foundation because I think he did think something needed to be done about alcohol use, but not about his. I can remember a number of occasions when Weary got into his car and drove home when he shouldn't have, as president of the Alcohol Foundation. I think he took the view that *alcoholism* was what he was president of, and a little bit of friendly drink-driving was neither here nor there.

At least half of lunch would be taken up with anecdotes. I have to say, you didn't get many of them twice. Some of his more famous ones I've had two or three times, but he had a rich fund. The reporting process was often a bit disjointed, but I'm a conscientious reporter to my chairs, I like them to know what the hell I'm doing, especially if it's something provocative. As time went on, we became more provocative. If you look at the history of the Anti-Cancer Council over the last twenty-seven years, you'd have to say it was a provocative, strong-minded organisation, and that wouldn't have been possible if we hadn't had Weary, number one, and the chairmen who followed him, extremely straight people who recognised that what we were on about was difficult. The tobacco battle was very unpopular in the early 1970s. We thought at that time that our fundraising was probably being adversely affected by our opposition to smoking, but it didn't occur to any of us to change that posture. It didn't occur to Weary, it didn't occur to me.

I guess, over those years, we had a very deep friendship. There was always humour. He probably didn't steer me much, he gave me advice when I asked for it. He generally waited for me to ask. All in all he was a fabulous companion and an integral force in the Anti-Cancer Council.

One of the other characteristics Weary had was to wheel in his veterans who were being dudded by the Repatriation Department. He and I shared the view that the bureaucrats in the Repatriation Department were a bunch of villains who were grinding the faces of the poor veterans, and they were. Doc Evatt had written the Repatriation Act after the war and in it he'd spelled out quite clearly that in cases where there was doubt the benefit was to go to the old digger. The Repatriation bureaucracy had this amazing tier of appeals and tribunals. At one stage I can remember that, by some bizarre reasoning, they accepted seventy-two per cent of lung cancer as war caused and rejected twenty-eight. Now how they managed that, I can't understand. The basic rationale was the war taught them to smoke, they were given free cigarettes by the army, and it was a war-caused disease in the sense that the environment of war contributed to it, and that's all you have to prove.

So Weary used to bring along these patients with chronic malaria and we'd try and get it straight that their leukemia had been caused by their chronic malaria or whatever. Mostly it was pretty difficult and Weary was prepared to bend the scientific evidence a lot farther than I was, or anybody else was. He didn't really give a bugger about it, his thing was that the veterans deserved what they'd been promised by Dr Evatt and they ought to get it. I took that same view, although I wasn't willing to put my name to such airy documents as he was.

So Weary was prepared to bend the scientific evidence?

Yes, I think that's true, but I know perfectly well why he did. I wouldn't – and didn't think I could afford to – bend science but I used to write strong-minded letters in support of Weary's which quoted the Act and generally pointed out we couldn't prove that this was cause and effect but that they couldn't prove it wasn't, and under these circumstances I couldn't understand why it was that they weren't accepting this claim. Weary would go a bit farther and try and stretch the evidence. Yes, you can criticise him for that. On the other hand, he was doing what was practical for the diggers.

Over the years he was involved with the council, were you aware of his growing reputation?
We contributed to it really. It wasn't a conscious process but we would have contributed to it quite a bit. His reputuation grew, and I think rightly so. Because he didn't aspire to sainthood but he was a very powerful force for good. The war made the man. You read his diaries – and I've never spoken to anybody who thought they're an exaggeration.

As a surgeon, I think he was a pre-war surgeon. They used to do those heroic things – rush in and rush out. But I believe I could discern his surgical philosophy, and that was that a lot of cancer patients were better off dead or cured. He was willing to accept a higher mortality than other surgeons. You can dispute that surgical judgment, it certainly wasn't a cautious surgical judgment. I happen to be in favour of the view that it is better to kill or cure in a lot of cases. I think we keep a large number of cancer patients alive far beyond the time when they're comfortable. Also, I think a lot of cancers produce deaths which are extremely unpleasant. It's not so bad now, but in the 60s and 70s it was extremely unpleasant and it was better to have a high operative mortality and take a risk than to leave them to the progress of their disease. Weary, I think, had that surgical philosophy, although I didn't ever hear him spell it out. You could see by the pattern of his behaviour and by the sort of patients he selected. He would do things that other people wouldn't. It's generally termed 'heroic surgery' and I think in those days, there was a case for that.

Did you have contact with him socially?
When his wife got sick and as time went on, we always made sure we included him in things at the Anti-Cancer Council, and I used to have him around for dinner every few months because it was clear he was getting lonely. Everybody wanted to look after him. He used to be remarkable. I can remember him turning up at the Melbourne Club cocktail party when Lady Helen had Alzheimers in the early stages. He brought her to the cocktail party and looked after her for a while and then he left us to look after her. His mates all did a stint. He had lots of mates. But he used to do things like that. One of the habits he had, Weary had a round of people he used to pop in and have a whisky with on the way home. In fact, I inherited one after his death who I visited for two or three times a week for one or two years while she was alive. She was a dear old lady, solitary, friendless and Weary used to pop in. He was a classless individual, and I must say that's a fairly Australian characteristic but he didn't have any sense of class.

***Adrienne Holzer** was with the Anti-Cancer Council of Victoria from 1975 to 1993 and had many dealings with Sir Edward.*

I USED TO go to his rooms in East Melbourne to get signatures on cheques. At four o'clock in the afternoon, he'd have a room full of people, and his secretary Valda would say, through gritted teeth, 'Look, he hasn't come back from lunch' or 'He's just come back from lunch.' (laughs) He was dreadful, he really was. But his patients just adored him and they'd wait until eight o'clock at night for him. It was just a measure of the man. But he'd drive you to distraction – how Valda stood it for all those years, I really don't know. They used to have the most awful arguments. He used to roar. He wouldn't come out of his rooms and say, 'Val, would you come in?' he'd roar, 'Valda!' out the door.

He was a very staunch friend and when Nigel [Dr Gray, director of the Anti-Cancer Council of Victoria] decided to take on the tobacco industry in the early 1970s, Sir Edward really stood behind him in all his efforts. When he was chairman of the executive he really stood up to be counted.

He had quite a wicked sense of humour. He wrote a letter to me when I retired and in it he mentioned a Thai honour he had received. He said something like, 'Now I'll look like a prize bull.' I thought he was quite a humble man actually, you'd never know that he was so decorated.

We used to go occasionally for lunch. He used to enjoy his food and enjoy his wine and he was a great raconteur. He was a great scribbler too. I'll always remember one evening, when I ended up next to Sir Edward at the Melbourne Club. Someone came up to him and Sir Edward was describing something, an operation that he'd done. He picked up this beautifully ironed white linen napkin and started doing this diagram. My eyes must have been out on the plate. I didn't like to say, 'Sir Edward, that's someone's table napkin.' Then someone who was next to me said, 'Oh, he always does that, don't worry.' And there he was just scribbling away. At the end of the dinner, he obviously realised what he'd done and he apologised to the waiter. They used to adore him, 'Oh no, that's quite all right Sir Edward, quite all right.' But he was so anxious to describe what he'd done, I don't think it occurred to him what he was doing.

I think he was impulsive, dreadfully impulsive. Probably less so in his latter years. He was a very convivial sort of fellow. He was always polite, except to Val, except to those people that he really sort of knew and that he was at home with, if you know what I mean. Then he didn't have to be.

He was very much a part of the establishment but he was very, very deeply Australian. His popularity seems to have grown along with Australian nationalism.

Was he very much a man's man?
Well, he was very much a ladies' man too. He could charm the pants off any woman. Oh yes, he'd only have to look at you and you'd melt. The twinkle in the eyes, he could get you to do anything. He would have been a bit of a devil in his day, I would think. (laughs)

Dino De Marchi, *a Vietnam veteran and solicitor, was chairman of the working party representing the ex-service community and the Department of Veterans' Affairs that established the Sir Edward Dunlop Medical Research Foundation in 1985. The foundation was set up to look specifically at veterans' health problems and funds medical research. He and Sir Edward met in the early 1980s when he was a member of the state executive of the RSL and Sir Edward was assisting veterans to prepare their cases for the Veterans' Review Board. We spoke in his office in Brunswick.*

WEARY WAS INVOLVED from the start and he was quite agreeable to giving his name to the research foundation. We started to fundraise and have little functions and Weary was always the initiator. Every week he'd be a guest speaker and he'd talk about the foundation and collect cheques and bring them in at the next board meeting or mail them to the treasurer. It was amazing, really, the amount of money he collected personally from week to week. He was the fundraiser, he was the patron and he was the prime mover, too, because if he felt the foundation wasn't going in the right direction he'd come along and he'd listen in at the board meeting, make pertinent comments and put people back on track.

There was a specific incidence where I was fairly keen in getting a study on POWs funded by the foundation and we had a fair bit of opposition to it because some of the members of the board felt that this was old history. I must admit that I was guilty of alerting him that the board didn't appear to be supporting that project, so he came along and by asking the right questions he put the thing back on track again. In fact that study, which was on morbidity and mortality in POWs, was very well received, it was a really important study. So Weary had his way, and he had a way of getting his way.

Did he use gentle persuasion?
Oh, very, very subtle. Almost inconceivable. But the fact that he was there and that he felt the study was worthwhile made all the difference. He was able to use his influence in many ways. In dealing with veterans' admissions to hospital, for instance, urgent admissions where there were no beds – it was amazing what a phone call from Weary Dunlop could do, and it happened so often. He was able to help a lot of people out that way.

Weary was very generous with his time and his house. He made no secret that any time we wanted the house we could always put on a function there, a cocktail party or whatever. Even after his death, his son continued to have an open house there for us. There was a great generosity there, in opening up his own personal life.

But he had no personal life, that was his problem. Essentially his life belonged to everybody else. Everybody that wanted to have Weary, it was just a matter of ringing him up and asking him to come along and he'd be there. I guess in that respect he was too generous. If it was a humane thing to do, he would be in it.

People would simply go to his rooms in Parliament Place and see him there, not because there was necessarily anything the matter with them but because it was a good thing to do and his secretary would make them a cup of tea. He was that sort of person, very generous and very kind-hearted. But nevertheless he wanted his medical research to go ahead and he was fairly strong in his pursuit of that.

He sacrificed himself, on the railway as a commanding officer, as a surgeon, and when he came back he cut back his own private operation to be able to expand into voluntary work, in areas of assistance to veterans and having also in the back of his mind the concept of the importance of future medical research, which to him was essential. That was exemplified, too, in the Colombo Plan that he was involved in and the sort of bridge-building he continued to engage in with Asia.

He was always a person of tremendous inquisitiveness – wanting to know beyond the current capacity. He often talked about the discussions he used to have with Macfarlane Burnet in relation to the causation of cancer. Obviously to him it was very important because a lot of veterans suffer from cancer. It's an old-age problem, but they were getting cancer a lot younger than you'd expect. One of the theories he had was that war service and the strain and stresses of war did in fact inhibit the immune system. I think it's proven that the degree of smoking that veterans were exposed to might have the same affect. That was his theory and he worked on that for many years before the foundation came on the scene. He was a patron of the Austin Medical Research Unit as well. Wherever he felt that people could utilise his name and his abilities, he would allow them to.

He really had no limits as I saw it. He was involved in other areas as well. The Australian Asian Association was a social, cultural type of association which created links with Asian students, and there was the exchange program, the Dunlop-Boonpong Fellowship. I can see some potential in the future for some sort of exchange in medical research projects between Thailand and Australia, in view of Weary Dunlop's connection. He has created a sort of a family over there in a way, hasn't he?

Did he have a private life in the end?
Very little that I could see. Even at a private engagement, he'd be having dinner, but still talking about what the foundation was doing for veterans, what was happening at the Veterans Review Board. The subject was always there.

How was Weary's pro-Asian stance and compassion, towards the Japanese in particular, accepted within the RSL?
I don't think it sat that comfortably with the RSL in the early years. There was a fair bit of antagonism there. Also with the Vietnam veterans. They'd just come back, they'd fought a war and lost their mates to the North Vietnamese. There was a bit of resentment there. I think Weary was above that. He didn't even hate the Japanese and the Japanese had done some terrible things to him personally and to his friends. He really treated people as individuals, it didn't matter what nationality you were. You were either a good bloke or you weren't a good bloke, he'd make up his mind, fairly quickly. He had a perceptive mind, he could see if you were going to fit in or weren't going to fit in,

and if you were on his side he was all for you and if you weren't on his side, well, he didn't like you. But generally speaking he was far more humane and understanding than a lot of our contemporaries, both in the veterans and RSL generally. I think he could overcome and rise above the petty prejudices of individuals. He was operating on a higher plane, I think that's really what it was all about.

He had respect for the Japanese because I think he was basically a samurai himself, deep down. He was of that mind and resolution and resolve. He could stand up to them, anyway. He was just as good as they were and he could hand out just as much as they could, if not more, and he tried to prove that, didn't he? I think that's what made him respected by the Japanese. It probably saved his life too.

He certainly had a way of inspiring people to do things. The foundation was very much his project. His commitments were such that he couldn't really get involved too much, but he did what he could by going out talking, collecting cheques for the foundation. He would talk about the foundation and people would write out a cheque. Today, it just keeps on coming in. Recently a chap died and left his house to us. We now have three properties, not large properties, but war service homes, and they left the house to the foundation. These are people who knew Weary or who knew of him and respected him. People are continuing to give to his memory.

Rajah Kannan came to Australia from Malaysia in 1982 to study engineering at the Footscray Institute of Technology. As president of the institute's Overseas Students' Organisation he automatically became a part of the Melbourne Council for Overseas Students (MELCOS), a group in which Weary Dunlop

*was involved from its beginning in 1979. He spoke to me on the
eve of his return to Malaysia, to take up a position as general
manager with an engineering firm.*

THE STUDENT MEETINGS were at about 6.30 at night. He
was old and he looked distinguished, because he always wore
the pinstripe suit and his handkerchief in his pocket and his tie,
and he'd sit and doodle a lot and sometimes you'd feel like he
was nodding off. Then suddenly, halfway through the meeting,
he would comment on what another person had said half-an-
hour ago when he'd appeared to be asleep. I was so amazed at
the intellect of this guy.

The people at this meeting were probably one-third or a
quarter his age and some of these meetings would be still going
at ten o'clock at night. The thing that kept coming to me is
what is this guy doing here? He understood our issues, and I
thought at first it was probably a front but he was so humble
and he never even raised the fact of who he was, and eventually
we all worked out that he was a fair dinkum guy. Everything he
did, he believed in.

In 1985, when the Labor government increased fees for
overseas students, Weary Dunlop was the president of MELCOS,
which received government funding, and he supported us when
we set up our own student body and campaigned against the fee
increase. We went to Canberra and we learned how to lobby people and we learned how to talk to senators. Coming from an eastern culture where a member of parliament is almost untouchable,
it was all very foreign to us, but we learned and to a large extent
it was because we were dealing with people like Weary Dunlop.

Somehow, for a man of his stature, he admired people. He
would admire the simplest thing in an overseas student. Like he
always said to me, 'You've come all this far, and you're paying

so much money and you're studying and you have to pass a degree, and you still have time to get involved and fight for your fellow man. That I admire.' He actually appreciated the fact that here these students were, in a foreign country, fighting for their fellow men. That gave us a lot of courage, because the number of students who were involved actively was a dozen or so and we did believe what we were doing was not for ourselves but for the masses.

It took us something like a year for the government to say yes, that Bill will be amended, those charges will not apply to students already in the country by a certain date. It was a big victory from our perspective, and to a large extent it was due to people like Weary who said, 'You've got to do it.'

After that my relationship with Weary became a bit more personal. We would have lunch in his rooms and we would get together for MELCOS dinners and things like that. What amazed me was that it didn't matter what time of the day it was, it could be eleven o'clock at night and we could be having dinner in this dingy Chinese restaurant and he'd be there. (laughs) And he didn't have to be. Another thing that always surprised me were his driving skills. We used to park underneath the World Trade Centre. When you come out of the carpark and turn right you are supposed to take the far lane, whereas he would take the closest, which is actually for oncoming traffic. He would always scare me.

We had a friendship then – but it wasn't a friendship, I suppose, it was admiration, because I admired him and he felt I was doing some good. We were extremely comfortable together. He would ask me to write his speeches for some of the Australian Asian Association and MELCOS events. When you write a speech, you always imagine the way you would present it, the places where you would stress and places where you'd pause. I would give him the written notes, he would make a few scribbles and he would present it and every time I was there, he would deliver it exactly the way I wanted.

Towards the end of my college years I became vice-president of MELCOS. Having Weary there in MELCOS was very useful because his name gave a lot of credence to what we were trying to do. He believed in the overseas student movement and in Australian education. He used to say there is no gift more valuable than knowledge. He fundamentally believed in plans like the Colombo Plan and in the fact that Australia was educating people from the region. In the long run he believed it was going to benefit Australia and the region as a whole, because the more people understand each other, the less chance of any form of conflict.

MELCOS had a very strong community back-up. The logic behind it was that when a foreign student came to Australia, one of the best ways of giving them a good impression of the country is to bring them off-campus. MELCOS played that role extremely well. Weary would actually tell his contemporaries why they should have overseas students in their houses and, in order to practise what he preached, he would have functions or barbeques where he would have students from all the campuses coming in and he would invite his friends and members of the Australian Asian Association and others of his contemporaries who had a similar outlook.

The government restructured the overseas student industry in the 80s, and after that they didn't see the need for organisations like MELCOS. Weary felt very strongly that if the government moved away from that sort of commitment – which was minuscule, financially – then what Australia was saying to the overseas students is 'we'll take your money for your degree, then you go back'. He was very passionate about it.

The Industries Assistance Commission held an enquiry at

the time Dawkins had turned the overseas students' program into a billion-dollar industry, to see whether or not the industry was doing the right thing, and Weary decided that MELCOS should put in a big submission. Weary and I spoke at the commission hearing. Personally I've always cherished the times that I've spent at the podium with him. Though we were good friends, he always remained a hero to me. He was an Australian hero, a contemporary hero and here I was, a no one from Malaysia, sharing the same themes with him. I looked up to him. He invited me as a guest to the Australian Asian Association monthly luncheon a couple of times. The Japanese consul was always there and he was extremely close with Weary.

Everything Weary did he was passionate about. At no time in the nine years that I knew him did I ever see him saying or expressing the feeling 'I have no time, I am too busy'.

When we were together, sometimes we would talk about the fact that I was still in Australia. What you have to remember is that we've come here to gain the knowledge to take it back to our countries. I used to say to Weary, 'I haven't fulfilled that yet,' and he'd say, 'You will. Give it time. What makes you say what you are doing in Australia is not useful to society as a whole?' That put me at so much ease. Weary said to me, 'What you are doing now, you are using your skills to develop some part of the human society – it doesn't have to be in Malaysia, it doesn't have to be in Hong Kong, it doesn't have to be anywhere. It just so happens at this point in time, you are helping to contribute to society in Melbourne. Down the track it will be in Malaysia or somewhere else. You are still doing it.' He made me feel so comfortable then, I realised that I was doing the right thing, so I didn't have to rush back. But of course I felt at some stage I would have to go back to my country.

What was it that made Weary so special?
He had an extraordinary intellect. He was extremely smart. He was like a sponge in picking up information. He would just take it and he'd understand it. Later on when he wanted to speak on a campus, he would ask me to come in and brief him, to put together a few notes and put it into context so that he'd understand who the audience were, what they were expecting of him or what the issues were. You'd give him about ten, fifteen minutes of briefing and then when he was presenting, he'd present it like he'd been doing it for twenty years.

*The Christian Medical College in Vellore had a number of links with Sir Edward and Australia, not the least was **Ted Gault**, his tutor in physiology at Ormond College. In 1944 he became Foundation Professor of Pathology at the Christian Medical College in Vellore, India and Sir Edward visited him in 1960.*

* **Louise Joy** is Ted Gault's daughter and one damp winter's afternoon we sat in front of the fire at her home in Warrandyte and talked. **Dr Stewart Joy**, the treasurer of the Friends of Vellore, was present and their son **Tim** wandered through the dining room and contributed during the interview.*

LOUISE: The Friends of Vellore had an annual dinner in April 1991 at which Weary spoke. Our daughter and other young people went up and spoke with him. They felt that while he was a distinguished person, his presence was benign. He had none of the aggression that obviously showed up in other aspects of his life. He had such twinkling eyes and gentle humour in this massive form. There was something almost Rip Van Winkle about him.

STEWART: At Ted Gault's seventieth birthday dinner, it was all men. He was sitting between Louise's brother John and me. At the end of the meal, we were talking with Weary about all sorts of things. I can't remember how the question of depression arose. He said to us that all his life he'd had the most fiercesome depressions, and that each time he was suicidal, but what brought him through it each time was the memory of how he'd got through every other one, and that it was only a matter of waiting. He'd had an accident on his farm and he was really recovering from that when he was talking to us.

LOUISE: One of our neighbours, Ian, is an ambulance officer who was called to Weary when he had that accident and he took the name Dunlop and Weary said, 'Oh, they call me Weary.' There was this modesty about him, but he was this great figure.

STEWART: He liked that picture of modesty but he also liked to be in the limelight.

LOUISE: He loved that, yes. He was very like my father. There was that generation who were young in the 1920s with this very positive Christianity and positive attitude towards helping. I don't know how strong Weary's Christianity was but his was certainly a very strong humanitarian impulse. But there was a dark side of that – because my father suffered from depression too – and I think possibly, they were so strongly positive all the time that there had to be some sort of reverse side.

He said he felt very privileged when we asked him to speak and launch the biography of my father. There was never a sense of self-importance about it. A lot of people admired my father, not just because he was a missionary in India but he had a sweetness of temper and a wonderful sense of humour. He wasn't an earnest sort of person, and he carried – and I think this is true of Weary too – this real responsibility and interest in world affairs lightly, and I think that's what made them such engaging people.

They both carried this legendary quality, and they both enjoyed it too. Let's say they enjoyed their fame but there wasn't an overweening pride about it. Certainly they enjoyed being the centre of attention. Weary enjoyed the company of young people at the dinners.

STEWART: He was keener to have them around than he was to make small talk with adults. He was prepared to make conversation that kept them enthralled.

TIM JOY: He seemed to be having a good time. He was very, very happy – I remember him at Grandpa's book launch and he was telling me about Grandpa. I was expecting him to be big bullocky war veteran and all of that but at the dinner, after he spoke, the waiters all sat around asking him questions.

STEWART: He had a very gentle manner.

TIM: Yes, that's what he was like.

STEWART: He wasn't like an army officer.

Or your average surgeon?

STEWART: No.

Eve Brunner was the bursar at Ormond College during the 50s and 60s and worked with Weary for the Friends of Vellore. She brought notes to our interview and referred to them from time to time. 'I've got here: he was "generous to a fault, with his time, with his actions and with his money". Too good, I think perhaps, the darling.'

I THINK MOST of time I was at Ormond, Weary was on the council, he was chairman of committees, he was on Ormond's appeals and building committees. He was also on the Ted Gault Trust Fund.

When Ted Gault retired as chairman of the Friends of Vellore, I thought of Weary, because he had been a foundation member. It was 1979 and I went to see him to ask if he would be chairman and he said, 'Eve, are you sure you want to ask me? You know, I'm not what they call a good Christian. I don't know that they'd want me.' I said, 'Neither am I but they wanted me.' Weary said, 'Yes, if you think that would be right.'

I was delighted, but unfortunately when we next had our meeting, someone else was put forward and appointed. I've always been very sorry, but Weary stayed loyal to us. Whatever we wanted, he would do. Never did he refuse any request I made of him. When he came on the Vellore Committee, knowing that he was such a busy man, I said, 'You don't have to come to all of the meetings, just the fact that we've got your name would mean a lot to the committee. He was in his seventies then.

Way back in the early days when I was working for Vellore, we decided we'd have an Indian dinner. We had it at Ormond College, and we invited Weary to come. We asked that every-body wear an item of Indian clothing. We all trotted in wearing our saris and eventually Weary lunged in and his Indian piece was a bottle of Indian ink in his lapel. So he did the right thing.

I often used to see Weary at Ormond College. He and I were standing out on the front steps one night in the 1960s, and I said, 'You look happy tonight.' He really did look glowing, and he said, 'Oh Eve, do you know what happened?' He had a little attache case and he opened it and took out three New Zealand newspapers and showed them to me. Across the top on those three newspapers was the heading 'Weary Dunlop to lead Anzac March'. On the three different papers. He was so thrilled.

I said, 'I think that's absolutely wonderful,' and he said, 'Oh, so do I.' I said, 'Have you ever been asked to do that in Australia?' He turned around to me with a real twinkle, and said, 'Eve, you know, a prophet in his own country. . .' This was before he became so well known and popular. I was so pleased, for his sake, that eventually they did take notice of him. But it was lovely the way he said it, with a real twinkle. I'll never forget that, the sweetheart.

Later on he had some wonderful accolades, and he wasn't too humble to want to show them to you. All sorts of things from kings and queens, and life memberships and honorary things. He wasn't – what do we call people like that – a shrinking violet, but he didn't throw them at you.

If you said, 'Please could we hold a function in your house for Vellore?' he'd say, 'Yes, yes, yes.' He never refused a request to speak or host a function at his home. We stopped doing it because I thought we were taking advantage of him too much, and after he was on his own there, I just thought it wasn't quite right.

Whenever he was a speaker anywhere, he was always surrounded by medical students and other young people. They would gravitate towards him – it was fascinating. Edna Gault and I used to watch it and we were amazed at what happened there.

His wife Helen developed Alzheimer's disease and I'll never forget the first time she looked through me. I thought, What on earth have I done? I couldn't believe it. That disease, it creeps up in such a funny way. Slowly her mind went and she didn't recognise people. He said that he stopped taking her out after the night the Concert Hall opened. He said that they were wandering around and the bells rang for the commencement and for some reason he let go of Helen's hand. He turned around to catch hold of her, and she was missing. The hall emptied and everybody went in and they searched the foyers. All the staff were looking for her, asking any odd person, 'Are you Lady Dunlop?' When she was found, she said, 'I'm Helen Ferguson.'

And that was the last time he ever took her out with him. So sad. I've never forgotten him telling me that. It was heartbreaking actually, she was such a darling.

Her funeral was a beautiful funeral – if you can say a funeral is beautiful – but it was so beautifully done and with such affection. It was lovely. They sang 'Jerusalem', that wonderful old hymn, because Weary proposed to Helen from Jerusalem during the war, and of course she said yes. They didn't see each other for eight years and when they got married the hymn they sang was 'Jerusalem'. There wasn't a dry eye in the church at the funeral. I get quite emotional when I think about it.

Dr Davis McCaughey arrived at the University of Melbourne's Ormond College in 1953 and took up the position of master of the college six years later, a position he held until 1979. He was Governor of Victoria from 1986-92. I spoke with him in North Melbourne, where he lives with his wife, Jean.

WEARY WAS A non-resident tutor in surgery when we arrived there, and he used therefore to be up and around the place. He didn't only come up to take tutorials. The students' club would put on a common-room dance – these were very decorous affairs, compared with what they might be now – and Weary and his wife Helen would turn up at these things.

He was always a great man for a party. Even then the noise level made hearing a little bit difficult, and Weary was so tall and he mumbled so much that Jean always said she never quite knew when he was making a comment on the weather or the state of the nation or asking her to dance. However you could be quite sure he would want to dance. He would throw himself with great energy into these occasions.

I take it that he'd been asked back fairly soon after he came back from the war. He belonged to a generation that had much stronger institutional loyalties than perhaps people did later on. People have quite strong personal loyalties but his loyalty to Ormond as an institution was great. He was very loyal to his hospital, too and if there was an annual golf match between the Royal Melbourne and the Alfred, he would turn up, probably late, and play with enormous zest and energy.

Towards the end of my mastership he came on to the council for a while. I had the feeling that if he was going to be on the council, he ought to have been on a bit younger. He always wanted to be helpful but some of his rather quizzical comments showed he wasn't quite where the discussion was. Yet they were worth listening to. The danger partly was that some of the older people there had such a veneration for Weary that they would perhaps take his contributions a little more seriously than they warranted, but I wouldn't want to exaggerate that.

I think it was part of his institutional loyalty that he was asked to go on and that he enjoyed coming on. He'd never have dreamt of refusing to do anything. Whether it was going to India to spend some time in a hospital operating there or coming to an Ormond dinner.

For many people as they get older, this kind of loyalty becomes exhausting, particularly if you've been associated with as many institutions as he was. But he had this terrific physical and psychic energy. (laughs) What people say about him is true. He was larger than life.

The Junior Strings of Melbourne were a group of young musicians, aged from nine to fifteen years old who gave regular concerts at the Toorak Uniting Church, next door to Sir

Edward's home. Sir Edward became patron of the group and maintained a lively correspondence with the young violinist **Lerida Delbridge**. *I spoke with Lerida and her mother,* **Natalie**, *at their home at Kangaroo Ground.*

NATALIE: We were at St Edward's house at a charity function in May, 1989 and there was a break in the music. Lerida, who was only eight then, sat down and started playing on the harpsichord.
LERIDA: I ran out of notes. My teacher was there and she said, Just keep on going, keep on going, make it up. Everybody knew.
NATALIE: And Sir Edward was there, and it was then that this relationship started.
LERIDA: I think you made me write a letter saying 'Thank you very much for letting me play on the harpsichord.' I remember him writing back. Oh wow. For him to write back was really just amazing, and it wasn't as if he wrote in six months time, it was within a couple of days.

I thought he was a very good letter writer – he was probably the sort of person who would get the letter and sit down and write immediately, so that he'd know he'd written.

Dear Lerida,
Outwitter of crocodiles! [Perhaps something to do with teeth? Lerida suggested.] Best wishes for school success although the daily routine sounds rather hectic for a promising young musician.
I can envisage you playing violin on buses!
Press on regardless my dear. As my Irish friend used to say in prison camps, 'There's nuthin stopping you.'
With love,
Edward

NATALIE: After that we saw him occasionally at his house and he became patron of the Junior Strings.

LERIDA: He always reminded me of a bear. I don't know why, he just did. He was very gentle. He used to fall asleep in the concerts and I used to look out and there he was. I thought it was funny. Dad used to sit next to him at every concert and sometimes he'd find himself dropping off. He'd say, 'Well, I'm not the only one. If Sir Edward can do it, so can I.' When you finished, you'd look out there and he'd come to life and he'd be clapping away as if he'd heard the whole thing.

NATALIE: My mother would wander to his place after a concert and have a chat with Sir Edward while I'd be tidying up and what have you. After the last concert we went in and got Nanna from his place, and here they are the two of them, having cups of tea in the kitchen and biscuits out of a packet. Nanna said, 'Isn't that lovely? Here he is making me cups of tea and opening packets of biscuits in the kitchen.'

LERIDA: His funeral was amazing, because I'd never been to a state funeral before. We sat and I thought, Oh this is really bad, I don't know why I couldn't get a better seat than this and these benches are so hard. When it finished we walked out and I nearly fell over. I didn't realise so many people would come. I think that's when it really hit me, what kind of person he must have been, because I never actually realised until I saw the people. That was amazing for me, because I had been feeling really bad, stuck in this corner of this huge church. He loved being made a fuss of. I think he would have loved to have been there to have seen the state funeral. I think that was the sort of person he was.

THE MAN, THE HERO

Alexander and *John Dunlop* *share a history at Smith's Gully, what is left of the Dunlop family farm. On the occasion we met, John had come up to the farm to visit Alexander and his family who now live there. As boys, they learnt to shoot here, clearing the rabbits which infested the property and shooting the occasional kangaroo to take home and cut up for cat food.*

'I learnt to see up here,' John said. 'It's something that never leaves you. If there are kangaroos in the bush, I'll see them before you do.' John strode ahead through the paddocks, and Alexander walked behind, rugged up with a jacket over his rugby jumper in spite of the hot sun.

'Remember when you picked up the snake?' Alexander said. They both laughed. 'It was when we were teenagers,' John said. 'I picked up a copperhead and Dad's Asian guests weren't impressed.'

Later, Alexander and John sat on the verandah overlooking the farm. We were joined midway through the conversation by Alexander's wife, Amanda.

Tell me, what was it like growing up with your father? I've been told several times that your father neglected his family.
JOHN: Well, people talk about their childhood in terms of what they remember and what they think is normal. These stories about childhood neglect are not about neglect so much, I suspect, rather than that our father led a very busy life. Now, if

you were to say that the Prime Minister neglects his children, well, he would say he doesn't, but he's not there very much. So if that's neglect, then all right, we were neglected. But we certainly did a lot of things together. For example, it would be true to say that we didn't do normal things. Some people pack up their camper and they go camping at the same place every year and probably fight like hell when they get there. But Alexander and I travelled all over the world, to many different countries and that was something that was part of the neglect, if you like, in that we were dragged along on what were otherwise business trips. I don't really see it as an issue of neglect, rather we were part of a family with a busy father. That's all.

Was it a case of his patients first, then his men and then his family?

JOHN: In terms of his priorities that may well have been the case, but I don't think that's necessarily a bad thing. He was still very proud of his family. He was very pleased that he had an elder son who was going to become a doctor and I think he was pleased at what I was doing, too.

I don't think his priorities were wrong. Look, I have three children. Two of them are in their mid-twenties and I never see them. They live in Melbourne, I live in Perth. I travel constantly, I'm probably home one or two or three days a month. So what are my priorities? My priorities are earn a living first, and family second.

Alexander, it would seem that your priorities are different.

ALEXANDER: Because I did training in medicine and was a doctor, I actually worked more closely with my father and I didn't have much time to settle down and have a family. I've only reached that point now. I think that we've had a lot of time together in projects such as the farm, and we used to go on journeys overseas and to Queensland and down the coast. I looked upon it more or less as an adjusted work program, in which we all took holidays at different times and learnt to find a bit of a balance between work and recreation.

Nevertheless, I would imagine you will spend more time with your children than your father spent with you.

Oh yes, I'm going to be allowed to. But I just don't feel we were neglected. It was just that we had a pretty long work program over a long period of time. It's just that you don't sometimes realise how much relaxation you can sometimes afford. I haven't been able to really sit down and relax for the whole of my university and working life, and I find it very relaxing to be able to do that.

But we used to go down the coast, staying with family friends and relatives, just for weekends and so forth.

Sir Edward is still a time-consuming father, isn't he?

(Alexander laughs.)

JOHN: Yes, he's time-consuming even when he's not alive. In the year after his death, the correspondence took about twenty to forty hours a week, which I did mainly on planes, with dictation machines, or at night. That gave way to a project of one sort or another. It might be Asialink or Queen's Trust or Anti-Cancer Council or the Research Foundation or the Australian Asian Association who wanted some continuity on committees.

Then there were projects like statues and war memorial fundraising. Gradually it dropped back to about twenty hours a week, now it's probably an hour a day. It will stay that way for the rest of my life, I'm sure, because you get a constant stream of phone calls and letters all the time. Most of the committee work, you've got to do some of that, but I've just about finished now with the war memorial, transferring papers and so on. But I'm still on some of the fundraising committees, still on Asialink, and Alexander does the Research Foundation.

AMANDA: Alexander, a sculptor rang while you were out.

JOHN: He's the one from South Australia. For example, yesterday I spent probably two hours with him trying to help him get his sculpture right. He was taking a whole lot of photographs – trying to take pictures of my head from different angles because he reckoned it would help him.

I'm not whingeing about it. You asked the question, I'm just giving you the answer. I have two faxes, a business fax and a private fax, and I go away for five or ten days, when I come back, there'll be anywhere between sixty and 100 pages of fax, and about fifty per cent relate to my father. It's full-on.

Every time a new project starts up, you're getting badgered all the time. If somebody decides they want to do a film documentary or something like that, you are going to have someone knocking on the door saying that they have got to have access to everything immediately and please stop what you're doing and help out. Soon someone will figure out that they want to make a film on the prison camps and then you can bet that it will start again. A lot of those people have started sending Christmas cards. Have you had that problem?

ALEXANDER: (laughs) My father used to get more than 2000 Christmas cards.

JOHN: It was the bane of the old man's life, he hated Christmas cards. He used to sit up all night writing Christmas cards and he had sheets of stamps, and he used to do hundreds and hundreds of Christmas cards.

AMANDA: We got a letter yesterday from Illinois with an American dollar in it. He wanted a signature of your father's. It's one thing a day, at least.

*I spoke with **John Dunlop** on the trip back from Smith's Gully to South Melbourne and the next business appointment in his hectic schedule. These days he is a Perth-based mining engineer whose feet rarely touch the ground.*

When we spoke to arrange this interview, you said that Alexander is one side of your father and you are another. What do you mean by that?

For example, he grew up on a farm, and he never lost his attachment to the land. I'm quite at home in the bush, whereas my brother has lived in the city all his life. Dad was hopeless mechanically. He couldn't drive. He thought he could but he was a hazard on the roads, and he'd have difficulty changing a spare wheel, whereas I don't have that sort of a problem. But my brother's hopelessly unmechanical. So there were many sides, and my brother and I share them.

Dad was very good at sport and he was extremely good scholastically so he could have done anything he wanted and been good at it. He could have been an artist or a poet or a writer, or he could have been a sportsman in any of a dozen sports. Now I was hopeless at sport, but my brother was very good at it and scholastically he was also very good. He did his matriculation twice. First year he stuffed around all year and failed and the second year he took it more seriously and did very well.

I didn't have the same scholastic ability. I got into engineering school and I inherited my mother's gift for languages, but I struggled all the way. But there were other things that I could do. I went into the Boy Scouts at school and I stayed with them right through senior school. I was a Queen's Scout and also did a lot of hiking, serious, high-level mountain climbing, and ice-climbing in New Zealand.

At university you went on to Ormond?

Yep, yep. The old man wanted me to go to Ormond because he thought that a residential college was a good thing to experience. I'd never have thought of it. He applied, I didn't, and he just said, 'You've been accepted,' and so I went to Ormond. It was good fun.

Do you remember when you became aware of your father's wartime experiences or was it something you always knew?

No, well, he didn't speak about them all that much. But you were really more conscious of other things. I mean you were conscious of the wartime experiences because you'd go to the prisoners of war picnic every year. Obviously you'd be aware of your father's wartime experiences if you went to this reunion and saw all these guys walking around with one leg or one arm. I was conscious of the fact that they seemed to hold him in pretty high regard, which I found hard to understand in some ways. For example, we drove down there one year, down past Frankston, and my brother and I were whingeing like hell because we wanted to stop and get an ice cream because it was a hot day. The old man hated stopping. If the radiator boiled, he'd just keep on driving. He had some fetish about driving from A to B without stopping. He got really annoyed and finally he agreed to stop in Frankston and get an ice cream. He found an angle park, nose in to the curb, and just as he was about to back up and drive in, a little sports car went in behind and took the spot.

He was in a foul mood and he jumped out of the car and we couldn't hear what was said. It was a sort of a convertible, from memory, and he lifted this bloke up from the steering wheel of this convertible and really socked him. I remember this because his head jacked back like a rag doll being shaken and I could see that this bloke was definitely out cold. (laughs) The girlfriend he had sitting next to him seemed to be pretty concerned as the old man slipped the gear into neutral and pushed the sports car back out into the traffic stream.

As he got back into the car to assume his parking place, we said, 'We don't want ice creams. We don't want an ice cream any more. We've changed our minds.' And he said, 'Well, you'll bloody well be getting an ice cream.'

Then we went down to the picnic and everyone revered him, but you'd be wondering whether this was really right or not.

Was the private man completely different to the public man?
No, it's just that he grew up on the farm and there was a certain amount of bold bravado that he carried through his life and right through into his seventies, maybe even into his eighties, he used to go out and have scraps. We used to dread going out in the car because we'd know something was going to happen. We'd go to the MCG and watch the cricket. He'd drive into the parking lot and there'd be a bloke in a white coat, saying, 'Over here, over here,' and the old man would just park where he wanted. This bloke would come up and say, 'Hey, you can't park there, you've got to park over here in a line with these other cars.' The old man would say, 'Look mate, I'll park where I want to park.' Because he was resentful of petty authority. He'd say, 'Look, you take your white coat and your bag and you go and annoy someone else, I'm parking here.' Anyway, there would be a great kafuffle. My brother and I would be thinking, Ah no, it's going to happen again.

Anyway, one time the bloke said, 'Now back up here.' There was one of those green poles and the bloke said, 'Plenty of room, plenty of room.' Crunch! He said, 'That should be about right.' So the old man got out and gave this bloke the workover, and there was another unconscious parking inspector with his bag stuffed down his throat.

Then we'd go on to the cricket. Now how could you sit

there and watch the cricket, and think, Oh, this'll be a nice day, when the old man's decked someone? I remember when we came out of the cricket and walked back to the car, I was looking around to see if the man was dead on the grass, (laughs) or if he'd been picked up and recovered.

He used to have scrapes. Like he was a terrible driver, and he'd pull in front of someone and they'd toot him and he might turn around at the traffic lights and say, 'Well what's wrong with you?' People would jump out of the car with an iron pipe or something. He'd quite often come home late at night and he'd be all bandaged up, and you'd know he had been in some altercation somewhere.

So he didn't always come out on top?
Oh no, sometimes he'd come off second-best. But usually if he'd come off second-best it was because he'd had an accident. He was quite accident-prone. He'd have some phenomenal falls. At the rugby dinner once, he had a colossal fall off a catwalk and he broke his nose and some arms and ribs and things and I remember he looked terrible. He reckoned he only missed one course at the dinner that night.

You said on the phone your father couldn't say no.
Well, more or less. If people could get around his secretary or if they rang at home, quite frequently he would just agree to do whatever they wanted him to do. Sometimes he agreed to do things that were rather unnecessary and made him late for something that he needed to do. He didn't have much time then to do other things he needed to do.

Was it when the diaries were published that he became such a public figure?
That probably had something to do with it, but long before

then it was difficult. I would come back from being away somewhere and he wouldn't be able to see you because he wouldn't
be free. He'd just have something on every night. He used to
have a schedule hanging on a nail in the kitchen, and there was
literally a nail driven into the mantelpiece, that's how sophisti-
cated it was. He stuffed the piece of paper on this nail and it had
what he had to do every night and every day and morning and
afternoon. So you'd come through and you probably wouldn't
be able to see him. That was a bit of a problem.

That is a bit of a problem, isn't it? How did you feel?
It's not so much 'how do you feel'. I'm sure the family of any
public figure would have that problem. You might feel resentful
– for example, how come we can't see our father – but realisti-
cally, it's just the way it is.

Your grandmother lived with you, didn't she?
She'd have been in her mid to late eighties when she died. I
think she owned half of the big house in Toorak and Dad owned
the other half. Her half passed to her daughter, who was my
mother, so Mum and Dad ended up with half the title each. It
was a big house. The mother-in-law, so to speak, had her master bedroom. Mum had a sitting room so she could do her
sewing. Dad had a sitting room where he could store all his
junk, his medals and uniforms and stuff like that.

*I'm told your father quite often arrived home with guests
he'd invited to tea without telling your mother. How did she
cope?*
Yeah. He wasn't a great communicator in that respect. He
would quite often do these spontaneous things and that was just
the way he was. It caused a few problems. If you tell a couple of

Japanese high commissioners that a Japanese rugby team – almost the entire team in this case – would be welcome to be billeted at home and they all show up unbeknownst to Mother, and one of them wants to eat the cat, it causes a few problems.

You're exaggerating! He didn't really want to eat the cat.
Well, that's the truth actually.

Your father was very close to your daughter, Isabelle, wasn't he?
Yes, he was. I would say she will probably turn out to have a lot of his abilities. She doesn't seem like she's seven when you talk to her. And don't overlook the fact that her grandmother was the captain of the school at Morongo. She was no dummy. She had a science degree. I think she was a microbiologist or something like that. I kept her degree as a souvenir for Isabelle. She might get some inspiration out of that.

Did your mother have any input into your studies?
She used to teach me French and she would give us coaching in chemistry and stuff like that. She took much more interest in our schoolwork than perhaps our father did. She certainly made quite an impression and contribution.

She seems to get lost in the story of your father.
Yeah, well, I can't remember exactly when she got sick, you see, but that was a major factor in the fifteen to twenty years before she died.

Were you and Alexander a couple of wild boys in the neighbourhood when you were growing up?
Well, we weren't very conventional. We weren't really well fitted to a staid private-school environment. I just simply didn't

like the way a lot of the young schoolboys there seemed to behave like they were to the manor born, and the same sort of guys would always get made into prefects and so on. I thought that they thought they were men amongst boys, but I saw them as boys amongst men in a wider community. For example, Jeffrey Kennett was a guy who was in charge of the cadets and was typically born to rule. He bossed everyone around and no doubt still does. He was an example of the conventional role model for prefects, whereas my brother and I were totally unconventional.

Alexander used to sometimes look a bit dishevelled and almost Chaplinesque because he was quite thin and spidery and cut quite a comic figure. At lunchtimes he used to amuse the schoolboys by grabbing the pole vault and running along the track and pole vaulting some astronomical height, well above the competitive level, and then not turn up for practice when they wanted to get him to do it, on the day.

I was probably thought to be a bit unreliable too. I hitchhiked to Cairns one weekend. I hitchhiked across to Perth about four times while I was still at school. At Scotch they used to tell me my attitude was wrong, which I thought was rather silly. Because it just made me think that it was a rather immature thing to say to an adolescent young man. Don't tell him his attitude is wrong. Show him which way he ought to go with positive reinforcement. But they said, no, you're attitude is wrong. What they needed to do, and what I think they probably do these days, is differentiate a lot more and say, 'Now, this student really wants to do bushwalking and outdoor stuff,' or this student wants to do whatever.

I don't have a hang-up about it, it's just that I had a view that was in line with modern times and they had a conventional view as to how they could educate you, and I didn't really fit into it very well. But still I got a good education basically, and haven't been ungrateful for that.

Did your father ever take you back to Benalla?

No, he never took us back there. Not much, anyway. And strangely enough, I never met his parents. I don't know if they were still alive when I was a child. I just simply don't know. His brother was a school teacher, and he got divorced and he had a second family. For some reason Dad was very pious about this and had perhaps an old-fashioned view about it so the second family was never really accepted.

I remember going along to Mum's funeral and there was this bloke there at the wake having a sandwich and a beer and I said, 'Well, who are you?' And he said, 'Well, I'm actually your first cousin.' (laughs) I said, 'Oh, are you? Good, right.' We see them quite a lot now. My brother and I have tried to mend those bridges. We got them to come along to the state funeral, and once we started to have a say in things we did the right thing, so to speak.

Your father was very upset when you were divorced, wasn't he?

I think for the same reason. He came to terms with it but it was a problem for a while.

Did you ever take your father hiking?

He did come on some trips. He asked me to take him into Pine Valley, in the Cradle Mountain Reserve, in winter and we ran into very heavy snowfall and it was pretty desperate. We had an Indian guy with us, nearly killed him actually. We were moving through at night up the Pine Valley and he said, 'We're history. We're never going to get out of this alive.' I knew we were in a pretty tough situation but thought it best that we kept going because I figured we weren't too far away from a hut that I knew. I'd been there many times before. I said, 'No, we've just got to keep going and we'll get shelter.'

The snow was kind of lumpy and wet and lying all over the ground and wasn't thick enough or hard enough to build a snow cave. We kept walking and I was starting to get a bit worried that this Indian fellow was going to collapse if we didn't get there pretty soon. I looked around and I saw this deciduous beech tree that I recognised. I said, 'Stop, go straight up through here,' and they followed me up. Sure enough, there was the ridge of the hut sticking out of the snow, just the ridge of the roof. They said, 'How in the bloody hell did you find that?' and I said, 'Never mind, start digging.' We dug down to the door and got in, and I'm sure we were pretty lucky.

The old man, I think he realised that there was bit of give and take there – that we'd shared a lot of things over the years and this was something he was getting back from me. So he enjoyed that. He always told his friends about this epic journey. (laughs) This epic journey when I nearly wiped both of them off.

11 May, 1993

Dear Chantal, John and Isabelle 3¼,
What a nice packet of photographs, snapshots, pictures and news cuttings.

Isabelle is becoming a clever artist after the style of Picasso!

I am pleased to hear that my small gifts arrived. Isabelle will have a big job unpacking hers as they are all individually wrapped.

Mephan [Jim Ferguson] reports that John [his grandson] has an assignment to handle over the next three months.

I could do with one myself as my income these days is a vast outgo. Still I'll be moving out of 14 Parliament Place fairly soon. I am now about the 'last of the Mohicans'.

One goes on with flagellation because you get used to it.

I'll think of John this week at the Melbourne Scots Annual general Meeting. Andrew [his grandson] is coming – 'Fathers and Sons Night'.

I believe that Sue will be out here for two or three weeks towards the end of the month. The Macedon house and grounds and garden are on a grand scale.

The Thais gave me a great reception and the 'Knight Grand Cross (1st class) of the most noble order of the crown of Thailand' carries a gorgeous cross body sash with two glittering insignia.

It is too grand to wear publicly unless I get into grand opera!

I've had about three major receptions and garden parties devoted to charity recently.

I hope to get to the British Isles later in the year – trusting that 'Republicans' other than French will be admitted still.

Well, we carry on. C'est la guerre.

With love,

Ompa.

P.S. Thank you for the Le Soeuf/Dunlop cuttings.

E.E.D.

Dr Alexander Dunlop and I spoke in Smith's Gully only days after he had given up possession of the family home in Toorak. Removalists boxes still crammed the rooms. While we talked, young Edward lay nearby, running through the vocal gymnastics of a seven-month-old. For a time he lay back crooning and gurgling in his father's arms, both father and son totally relaxed.

It must have been an enormous move for you from 605?
Well, we moved into 605 in the 1950s, and it's a long time to live in a home. You have great memories and everything, and then you realise that you've got a rather big place to look after and unless you've got a house staff of some description, it's too big. After my mother died, my father thought the family home might be a little too big and impractical to maintain. He did engage in some sort of transaction that was not completed. After that he was just resigned to the fact that he wasn't going to try and move.

Did you spend much time with your father when you were a child?
We always had time together. We used to come up here to the farm on weekends and we used to make some trips overseas when possible. We had our times away here and there – trips for three or four weeks at a time.

What was travelling overseas with your father like?
It was terrific travelling with my father. Always the hosts were the most wonderful people. We were always taken out to dinner. It was a mixture of business and relaxation so we visited some wonderful hospitals. It was very interesting to see and understand the work people were doing in other places.

We visited some extraordinarily interesting places. When I was about seventeen or eighteen, we made a trip that involved Malaysia, Sri Lanka, Madras and Vellore in Southern India. We went on to Bombay, New Dehli and then the Punjab, and parts of Thailand. We travelled on to Taiwan, the Philippines, Hong Kong and back home. We took about eight weeks.

Did your father influence your own interest in medicine?
When I first learnt to walk, he used to take me to see his patients, so I always had an understanding of medicine. I was quite happy to study medicine and I was always learning from him, dealing with common problems, so I had a slightly closer relationship with him than my brother, who is an engineer.

It did mean that I could sort of learn to undertake some common areas of practice and assisting, and I developed a liaison with a number of his medical colleagues socially. I found that I was very interested to pursue some areas of medical research that he was involved in.

Did you enjoy working with your father?
I was happy to assist my father. He was able to maintain a private practice until he died. He was only operating until possibly 1990 but he came to assist in operations. We always had a third person with us. I didn't actually find working with my father difficult.

When did you first become aware of your father's wartime experiences?
I found that he didn't personally speak very much at all about his war experiences other than to say that he'd had certain illnesses when he was a prisoner and that he'd faced confrontation on certain occasions. But he actually gave the impression of having incurred what you might call scarring. The experiences of the war do not leave you unscathed.

What do you mean by scarring?
It is unpleasant as a doctor to see a lot of preventable illness and injury. I think in his post-war career, he resolved in his mind to try and correct areas of imbalance and misunderstanding in a lot

of areas through medicine. He would look towards the experiences of war in trying to redirect goals for people. He used to set his own pace and his own goals.

Were you aware of your father's reputation when you were growing up?
He liked to visit schools and talk about a lot of things as guest speaker. I think that people found him very interesting because of his experiences and because he was always able to relate something of interest and try to bring it into a modern context.

Was that something you were very proud of as a child?
I was caught up in a very interesting area of activity and I found it was stimulating to be able to develop my own training and my own skills and just . . .

And be your own person?
Yes, sure. It's nice to have your own areas of interest but I actually found that we didn't get in each other's way at all. You can't say that it's easy. None of our lives were easy. Most of my life, my father used to work at least ten-hour days. I find I don't regret any of it, apart from the fact that I would like to have settled down and had a family earlier. I just found that I ended up spending quite a lot of time with my family – I was looking after my mother when she became unwell, and I suppose, my father came to depend upon me to look after the house and farm and other things. I couldn't get far away, you understand?

Your mother died in 1988. When were you first aware that she was ill?
My mother's illness first made itself apparent in the late 1970s. She went out to visit one of her friends in her car and she

couldn't remember where she was going. It became evident that she was just getting forgetful about things and she was losing her ability to think through things, so we took her in for all the routine investigations and assessment by neurologists and it became evident that she had a pattern of Alzheimer's that gradually reduced her capacity for ordinary daily functions.

It meant that we had to get a district nurse in to look after her. We managed her at home for as long as we could and when it was clear that we could not manage any longer, we found her a comfortable nursing home in Malvern where she was very happy. She grew very frail, like a delicate flower. She passed away very peacefully and I don't think she was uncomfortable. She wasn't unhappy, but she'd lost a lot of her memory.

It must have been very hard.
Well, it was pretty annoying. It's not very easy when you can't communicate with someone. It was just something we had to accept, that's all.

It must have been very difficult for your father.
I think he was very realistic in his appraisal of the situation. He came to accept the fact that he'd need to rely on me to help more than usual. I used to help do things around the place, look after her. I always got on very well with my mother, actually. She never disliked me. I actually felt we were very close. I did realise she'd had a few problems in the past. When you grow up in a medical family you tend to understand what people's problems are, and they are much happier having people around them who have some medical training.

The house is often described as an open house, with guests from many nations.

We had a large home and we had several guest rooms, so that we always had people who stayed for various lengths of time. It was rather interesting. We had doctors who stayed with us for periods of over six months, and other people used to call in at times.

Was that difficult for your mother?

My mother didn't complain very much, but you did feel that it was a lot easier when there weren't so many people around. That was a pretty big place for her to look after, but my mother used to have housekeepers and she used to take time off to play golf and pursue some other interests.

Does being Weary Dunlop's son carry with it many responsibilities?

Well, we make representations at certain RSL functions. There are certain representations that I am involved in, like the Queen's Trust scholarships. The medical scholarships and management of the research foundation are undertaken by other people and we still attend the Australian Asian Association functions and Asialink.

Is it very time consuming?

We've actually learnt to map out a bit of a program of what we're capable of doing.

How do you feel about your father's extraordinary hero status?

I feel that it's always a good thing if people are recognised for the work they've done and what they were able to achieve. I think he was able to achieve an enormous amount as an individual and it has been a very interesting thing to see how things have been taken over. Things do move on.

Sometimes you've just got to be aware of the significance of your own part in things and that it's nice that an individual should be recognised. People should understand what he was and what he tried to achieve here. He had very many interesting aspects to his life and I think he was able to breach great and interesting cultural barriers in Asia and internationally as a surgeon. He had some great charisma with his colleagues in Europe, Canada, America, Asia and Japan. He also took trips to Moscow, and he was very, very much at home in those surgical forums with colleagues from all over the world.

In dedicating a copy of his diaries to **Ray Parkin**, *Weary wrote 'To my time-tested dear friend'. Ray Parkin was reluctant to talk about his friend. 'It was always the private Weary that I knew,' he said. Nevertheless, he did offer these glimpses of the man.*

LAURENS VAN DER POST and I were talking about Weary, and Laurens said, 'He'll always be the eternal undergraduate.' And that's what he was. He never lost that boisterousness, his sense of fun. His lack of proportion.

Weary went along with being a public figure. He did enjoy the popularity and the good fellowship, but mostly it was advancing his causes, getting some justice done for various causes. It was actually doing himself an injury, because people could pick him for just being a show man and grandstanding and all the rest of it, but he only grandstanded for the causes he was working for, not for his own personal thing.

When he was in his practice, he'd have people coming down from the country, just ordinary people, not people who could afford big fees or anything and lots of times he wouldn't charge them. If they were marooned in Melbourne, say over Christmas or the New Year, you'd just as likely find them dining out with Weary for Christmas dinner at 605 Toorak Road.

He was really compassionate underneath but he never made a big show of that, it was all very private that he did that. His public acts were much more flamboyant. No, always he was a very, very simple man and a sincere man. He was using himself up for a cause – he didn't mind sacrificing himself. Well, originally he was going to work himself to death. He told me way back, I think it might have been 1960 or 1965, sometime like that. He was working like mad both at his profession and for this POW cause and so forth, and he was really battling, all out. He told me then he didn't expect to live much over sixty. He said, 'I'll be worked out by then.' But he was prepared to do that and he never spared himself.

He couldn't say no, because he couldn't live with himself if he did say no. You know, he couldn't have felt comfortable with himself, so he had to do it to satisfy himself as well as to satisfy the people who were asking. But he was used up, for all they say, he's been feted and everything. That didn't compensate for the way he was used up. The only compensation for that is that he did achieve a few things for the people he was working for. And I think, too, his big contribution was that he brought a bit of morality back into things. People could see that there was such a thing as altruism, where everyone was cynical of that with this economic rationalism – just do what you can get away with, that's the essence of that business, and the devil take the hindmost. Exploit, exploit, whereas Weary was prepared to be exploited. He knew he was being exploited, but even then, when he felt that, he'd silence himself, he'd say, 'No, these people are entitled.' (laughs) You see? He was like that.

Of course he still had his conditioned reflexes, being brought up on the ideals of the old British Empire and British sportsmanship. He was a real Biggles in many ways. Nevertheless, he was still the enquiring man, the person who was looking for answers. He could act very definitely but he was always willing to question. I think that's where his real qualities came out, through this inner core of wholeness of nature and things natural and anti-intellectual. Because although as a surgeon and a doctor and a chemist, he had a great intellectual capacity, he didn't rely on that. He was governed more vitally by his instincts and intuitions which he couldn't express himself. The only way he could express them was through the way he was acting.

Out at Smith's Gully, on his farm, he had these black Angus cattle and the Herefords and he was very proud of them. He used to get a lot of people – I suppose you'd call them VIPs – who'd come from overseas and he'd take them out to the farm for the day. On several occasions, I would go out with him. We crowded into two cars, we were stacked on our heads just to get in. We drive around until we came to the top of the hill and there was this paddock in front us and down below there were these great black Angus cattle. Weary would get out of the car and go straight over to the fence and start calling to them, bawling at them – literally bawling like a bull. And very slowly these great black Angus would come up and congregate. They just looked at him with these big eyes, chewing their cuds, and in the loudest voice, Weary would say, 'Hello, you black bastards.' (laughs) And that was Weary.

Gert Hutchins, *from Shepparton, was a regular visitor to 605 Toorak Road.*

WE USED TO go down and stay at 605 after Mike had his operation. One time Ern had a fall – he broke his wrist and broke his ribs – and the woman who was looking after him then rang and said, 'Could you and Mike come down and look after him? I'm not staying here.' She shot through for the week – she just didn't want the responsibility.

We used to go down, in the finish, and prune his roses for him. I got third prize in the Melbourne Rose Show once for him with his roses, but he was a devil, you couldn't depend on him. You'd go down there and you would have had them all ready, but he'd go along and pick them and take them to his patients.

James Mephan Ferguson returned to his home at 605 Toorak Road from war and days later, on Thursday 8 November, 1945, attended the wedding of his sister Helen to Lt. Col. E.E. Dunlop. The bridegroom had recently featured in the 20 October issue of the Australian Women's Weekly.

Jim and his wife Doreen now live in Torquay where their home is called the House of Mephan, after his father, Mephan Ferguson.

Did Helen and Weary have a big wedding?

JIM: Weary came home and he wanted to get married tomorrow and they had to pin him down. My mother was terribly hurt when my brother Boyd had married away from home during the war. She had no conception of the restraints of being in the army during the wartime.

So there was no way that Helen's wedding was going to be a quiet one?

JIM: No, no. Weary had so many army people that he wanted to be there. There were lots of people still away. I'd just got home. But Old Meph had a lot of friends he wanted to be there.

Did Weary come home a hero?

JIM: Oh yes, it came out pretty quickly. I was on a commercial plane coming home, coming down from Sydney, and there was a lady there who had a copy of the *Women's Weekly*. That was one of the first articles that indicated what he'd done when he was a prisoner of war. At that stage they talked of him as the Christ of Thailand.

How did you feel?

JIM: Oh, I just accepted him, I think.

DOREEN: Jim's brother Boyd was killed in the war and he was a very dearly loved, highly regarded young man, and probably Weary coming into the family was a good thing for them at that stage.

JIM: Weary met my brother in Palestine. He didn't know Boyd was killed until they were liberated. It was a great knock to him then. They'd have got on well together. Boyd was seven years older than me, Helen was nine years older. She was more a motherly figure to me in a way. We were very close.

Helen waited eight years for Weary, didn't she?

DOREEN: Weary wanted Helen to go to England. He wrote to her and asked her to come over and join him but her family wouldn't allow it.

What did Helen do during the war?

JIM: She worked with the Commonwealth Serum Laboratory right up till Weary came home. It was extremely important work. She was one of three scientists who set up the original production of penicillin in the south-west Pacific area.

What was life like at 605?

JIM: When we got married in 1950, my father had died, and that left my mother on her own in a great big house. She was immovable and that was a bit of a worry. But we said, 'Well, there's nothing we can do about it, we're getting married and that's that.' So then Helen and Weary moved in.

605 was always home and if ever I had anything in Melbourne and we wanted to stay a night, we'd stay there. That went right on until Weary died. We were always really close. Our son Bill did chemical engineering at RMIT and he stayed at 605 in his first year. At the time, the Ceylonese surgeon Jayasekera was there. He's a great friend of Weary's. He lived there for quite a while before his family came out and other doctors stayed there at Weary's invitation. He was hard on Helen in that respect. She put up with a lot. Weary would say, 'Look, something has gone wrong, I've got five surgeons from overseas, I'll bring them out to dinner in an hour.'

How did she respond to that?

JIM: She just did it. She was very sweet natured and placid, Helen. Mother dominated her to a great extent. She didn't flap terribly much, though she could stamp her foot down, as she did with the kids sometimes.

Weary left the kids to her. He would get up and go out and start operating at eight o'clock. Then when he got home at night they'd gone to bed. At the weekends he'd have so many commitments that he didn't spend as much time with the kids as he should have. I think he realised later in life that he should have spent more time with them.

DOREEN: You can't blame Weary in a way, because he came from all that prisoner of war business and was dying to make a career for himself. He wanted to be somebody, he knew he had the surgical ability and he wanted to have a good career in surgery in Melbourne. He realised it would take up all his time.

What did your mother, christened 'Tossie' by Sir Edward, think of her new son-in-law?

JIM: She probably was a little bit upper class and the fact that Weary was a celebrity, she was proud of that from the status point of view. If I came home from a night out somewhere, she'd say 'Who was there?' (fiercely) 'Oh,' she'd say, 'that would be the son of so and so.' My father didn't want to move from the old home in Royal Parade, Parkville. Tossie said, 'Oh, it's much better to have a Toorak address. Be close to all the –'

DOREEN: The up and coming suburb.

JIM: He'd have loved to have just stayed on in Parkville. It was a lovely old home and of course it was easier to get across to the works in Footscray than from Toorak. [Jim's grandfather, Mephan Ferguson, established the family pipe-making business, Mephan Ferguson Pty. Ltd. which was sold in 1950.]

DOREEN: As far as entertaining was concerned, Helen was superb at that. Yes, she was, she had a real skill for it. She'd done a course, Jim, hadn't she?

JIM: Helen went to Morongo in Geelong and what was a bit tragic was there was no science teaching there and she said she wanted to be a scientist. So she matriculated with English and French and History and Music. In those days you were admitted into any faculty in the university as long as you matriculated, it didn't matter how you did it. So she started off doing a science course in 1937 without having done any chemistry or physics or mathematics. So she fell by the wayside very badly in the first years and it took her five years at least to do the three-year course.

But when she first left school, my parents sent her to Invergowrie. She went there for a while then in 1934 my parents made a grand tour of the world and they took Helen with them. I suppose Tossie would think she would meet someone with a title over there.

DOREEN: Jim's mother had this daughter, Helen, first and she was a very pretty little child with curly blonde hair and the blue eyes that matched and she obviously worshipped her. Then they had a boy, Boyd. Then when Boyd was eight years old, Jim was born. He was a sort of 'change of life' baby, you know, not really wanted, from what you gather. Even to the extent that the house was left to Helen and Jim was left out of what might have been considered to be a fairer division in the family. Mother was just all Helen. But that didn't change Helen's character. She was always sweet and gentle and kind, but brainy. She could see people's characters. She was not naive.

And as for being Weary's wife, she was absolutely suited to be that. You would be proud of Helen, whatever company she was in. A lovely person to marry and she was very capable, too, as a housekeeper. She could put on beautiful parties because she had done that Invergowrie course. Very artistic as well.

You can see how Weary's thinking was probably, Helen, she's superb, she'll make a wonderful wife for me and I'll go up and up and up. That's what he wanted to do, I think. That was his goal. He wanted to make a real success of his career, and Helen could go with him in all that.

Was Weary a very charismatic figure in his later days?

DOREEN: I can remember Weary would look for a woman to take to the receptions at Government House. I got asked once, so I went. It was really quite an experience. All the women in the room were looking at me, looking me up and down to see who it was that Weary had brought. This young woman came in and she had on a beautiful dress and high heels. She saw

Weary at a great distance and she tottered over to him in these incredibly high heels and threw herself up onto his chest. Which was just typical behaviour. She wasn't the only woman who did that, that night. Then they'd look me up and down. Oh yes, I had a really interesting night.

He was proud of that social acceptance, I suppose, because of the sheltered life they'd had up on the farm. He could cope in any sort of situation. He met the most interesting people. I always think there was a bit of an affair or something when he met Lady Mountbatten in Thailand straight after the war. They must have been madly attracted to each other because they were both those sort of people.

In a way, Weary was a bit naive about those sort of things. You never rubbished him about it, it was just his way. He enjoyed that sort of social life. He was a bit of a social climber in a way that you might be scathing about but he was just superb with people from all walks of life.

JIM: He could just as easily relax with ordinary people. One time we took him up to Puckapunyal with our regiment. They were going to do the Beating of the Retreat, but a terrible storm went through and they had to cancel it. We were left on our own then and we went back to the motel room, just a few fellows, no high rank – they were all just sergeants and troopers – and we sat down in the motel room and out came bits of grog and bits of food and he just enjoyed just sitting there chatting away all night.

Were you involved with Weary in the Melbourne Scots?
JIM: My brother was in the Victorian Scottish regiment before the war and they started a highland dancing group in the Sergeant's Mess. All those people rose to high ranks during the war, then after the war they re-established that group.
DOREEN: Helen loved the highland dancing.

JIM: The Melbourne Scots are quite an institution. Weary enjoyed the dinners. He wore the Stuart tartan which he claimed. The Dunlops came from Dumfries in the Scottish lowlands.

DOREEN: Weary bought a kilt in Scotland and it was very much the correct thing, the one they wear for evening, when the women are wearing long dresses. Very formal. And of course he looked magnificent in it. Oh gosh, any woman would fall for him in that kilt.

JIM: I remember one year, it must have been in 1962, there was an election. Bob Menzies was re-elected and Bob was the president of the Melbourne Scots. Weary asked me to come up from Geelong and attend the Saturday night dinner as his guest. He said 'Meet me at 605 at half past five'.

Weary's story is something like this: Friday was a day on which he did his honorary surgeon's job at the Royal Melbourne Hospital and that went on till about eleven o'clock at night and then he came home. He had just come home and they called him back – it was a great emergency and he worked all night and then he went up to the farm. On the way back from the farm, in what he used to call his rabbiting clothes, he walked past a polling booth and saw people handing out cards and said, Oh, I thought the election was tomorrow. When I caught up with him at 5.30, he'd probably had about six hours sleep on the Thursday night, nothing on the Friday night, and off we went to the dinner. Of course there was a great amount of cheering and so on when the election result was announced.

On the way home he said, 'I've just got to call in to see a couple of patients at St Andrews Hospital,' and he went in there, full of whisky, to see if his patients were all right. And when he came out there was a median strip there and you are supposed to turn to the left to go round so Weary just turned to the right and took a shortcut.

DOREEN: That's typical Weary.

JIM: And when we got home, at about one o'clock he said, 'Well, I think I'd better have a nightcap,' and brought out a bottle of whisky and we sat up for another hour and chatted. He was unbelievable really.

Weary appears to have had a bad history as a driver.

JIM: My brother bought a little standard ten-horsepower car in 1939, I remember it had a double-A number plate, it was the first of the letter number plates. That was virtually a brand-new car after the war because of all the petrol rationing.

My brother left that to Helen, and Weary came home and he took it over. It didn't take him long to realise it won't go without petrol, but it took him a bit longer and was a more costly business to realise that you've got to check the oil and the water gauges. It became a wreck very quickly.

He had a standard excuse after every accident. It was Helen that had left a rolled-up umbrella under his feet and it had rolled through and he couldn't put his foot on the brake. That excuse came out time and time again. A lot of people wouldn't drive with him.

DOREEN: We didn't if we could avoid it. As he got older, too, he lost his peripheral vision, so he didn't know what was going on, on either side of him. He did seem to have someone up there looking after him. He could have easily got killed in those years, couldn't he? He wasn't an angel, by any means, but he thought he was a good driver.

JIM: He had a certain amount of understanding that he was a naughty boy with his driving. One time he drove my cousin Arthur down to the Peninsula Golf Club in Frankston. At one stage there, when you went round some back road, you crossed the railway line, and as they went there the lights started to flash and the bells rang and Weary just planted his foot down and whipped straight across in front of the train and he turned round to Arthur and said, 'That's quite good for your blood pressure.' (laughs)

DOREEN: He was very tough.

JIM: One time he came down to us when we were living in Geelong. He was about seventy and it was Christmas Day. I said, 'Oh, would you like to come down and have a swim in the river?' I had a little stretch of the river that was about 500 metres long and I said 'I'll go for a swim up there', and he said, 'I'll come with you'. Without any training at all, he swam that. He didn't swim with any style that would win races but he could swim long distances. He'd never drown. He was as game as Ned Kelly. He saw me ride a wave and he said, 'I can do that,' and he came down and plonked on his head. Talking of his toughness, at the age of sixty, he climbed Ayers Rock and for some unknown reason, he took his shoes and socks off in the bus and he climbed it in bare feet. There was a fair amount of blood around the place by the time he got back.

DOREEN: No wonder he could take all those things up on the railway, he really was tough.

JIM: He'd just press on doing what he was doing.

DOREEN: He didn't care what other people thought about him.

JIM: He had horrific stories of injuries when he was on the farm as a little boy. His father was a pretty brutal surgeon. He'd open up a wound and get a paintbrush out and slosh iodine into it.

You went to Thailand for Weary's memorial service, didn't you?

JIM: There was a fifteen-year-old piper from Scots College in Perth who played the lament there and it was really most moving. And when they launched the boat with Weary's ashes, there was an eddy that went around. Weary went upstream first and the idea was that he'd go out and catch the main stream and go on down, but being Weary, he went round and round and round. (laughs)

DOREEN: Everyone who was there that knew Weary said it was his character.

JIM: It was typical.

*A few days after this interview, a letter arrived from **James Mephan Ferguson.***

I AM A bit concerned about the story of Weary seeing patients after a Melbourne Scots' dinner. I would not like to give the impression of him seeing patients whilst under the influence. The story of that event is an example of his stamina and ability to press on without sleep.

His relationship with alcohol is interesting. On the occasional nights when he was not out at functions or entertaining at home, he would not drink. When friends called on him at home, his hospitality was generous, even dangerous!

He told me of a dinner held when he was the President of the Alcoholism and Drug Dependency Foundation. The police surgeon attended with a breathalyser. They had alcohol in different forms before, during and after the meal. I think Weary would have consumed enough to make common mortals have a blood alcohol reading well over 0.05. Weary blew 0.03 only!

His vital organs: heart, liver, lungs etc. were very large and enabled him to perform with outstanding strength and stamina, and handle alcohol. He would accept drinks or food when he did not feel the need, to avoid disappointing a host or hostess – even if he disliked the taste.

*Dr Tom Kemp who was taught by Weary at St Mary's in
1939 returned to England from service in the Middle East in
1947 and he and his wife Ruth moved to their present home
in Northwood, Middlesex.*

WEARY CAME OUT here and sat on that sofa many times and
in the late 1940s, early 50s, he would sit there and relate his
wartime experiences.

RUTH: Very hesitantly.

TOM: Very hesitantly and very fidgety, and obviously very, very
tense. He'd get to the edge of his chair. Emotionally, he was
recalling a very painful experience. Talking about it made him
very itchy and irritable and awkward. Gradually, over three or
four years, he'd sit further back in the chair and he eventually
became completely relaxed about it.

I was speaking earlier to Dr Cockburn [another St
Mary's colleague], and he mentioned it, too – the lasting
emotional effect it had on Weary and how it took years to
peter out. He must have been going through tremendous
emotions recalling all these events. It was something he'd do
his utmost to hide that it had affected him in any particular
way.

RUTH: Yet there was no bitterness.

TOM: He believed that if the world was going to be a safe place
to live in, bridges had to be built and they had to be built
between Australia and Japan. I think he was one of the few people immediately after the war who saw that. People still feel
very anti-Japanese, don't they?

RUTH: He understood the way the Japanese brain worked.

TOM: And the tradition of Japanese military: if you showed any
cowardice, you were shot.

Your daughter was married in Melbourne, wasn't she?

TOM: Yes. Weary came to Kathy's wedding and he was almost the life and soul of the party. There was dancing and Weary got up and danced round and jitterbugged and he thoroughly enjoyed that. He said we should have a reception in Toorak at 605. There were quite a lot of people there – our family would be about a quarter – there were all kinds of local people. After we'd had a nibble and a drink downstairs, I was thinking that it was about time to go home when Weary said, 'We will now go upstairs to the ballroom where we will have some champagne.' (laughs) So we went upstairs and he said a few words and I said a few words and it was really a very thoughtful thing to do for a young girl. It touched Katherine.

He was very supportive and nurtured everyone. I suppose that's what doctors are supposed to do when people are ill but Weary did it all the time, when people weren't ill. He did what he could for everybody.

What was he like at dancing?

TOM: Oh, he was bouncing up and down and sticking his legs out. It wasn't just a little step.

You and Weary first met at St Mary's but you managed to keep in touch over the years?

TOM: I don't think he came to London without getting in touch. One time Ruth and I went to a dinner in St James', some London club. There must have been a dozen or fifteen people for a dinner. All kinds of people, some prisoners, some medical, some rugger contacts – this was part of his way of living. He must have had a money factory somewhere. It must have cost him an awful lot. He was always off to Scotland and down to see somebody who had been a prisoner with him. The way he dedicated his life to his fellow prisoners, travelling the world to keep in touch with them, it was absolutely marvellous. Not many people would do that, I would have thought. When I was in Melbourne, he took me to have lunch in various clubs in Melbourne. He seemed to know everybody he passed.

RUTH: Weary was a good name for him too. He was always tired but he always sort of revived in the evening, then about one or two a.m., he'd fall asleep on your shoulder or something, and you couldn't say, 'Please excuse me, I must go,' because he was sleeping there. (laughs)

TOM: Have you got any ladies' view about Weary, Ruth, that I might not have spoken of?

RUTH: I don't know, I think he was so very nice to all the ladies. They all loved him in a nice genuine loving way. He was a very lovable person. I just wish Weary were here to enjoy hearing hear us talk about him. He spoke so marvellously at the end about the Japanese torturers and the Japanese people. He said there was no time in this world for hate. He was a pure Christian, if you like. Though he was very interested in Buddhism, wasn't he?

TOM: He was all for one world, there is no doubt about that. I think of him as a sort of modern day Paul Robeson.

The playwright Judy Bierwirth met Helen Ferguson during the war when their families became friends and she was friendly with Helen and Weary over the years. She saw less of Weary in later years and we spoke in Hawthorn of her regrets.

BOYD FERGUSON, HELEN'S brother was in my father, General Bierwirth's battalion in the war and after my father had moved on to some other job, Boyd was killed in a plane accident. When Dad came home on leave during the war, he went to see Mephan Ferguson to say what a beaut son he had and what a terrific officer he was and a lifelong friendship developed between those two old codgers.

Helen was a lovely woman. From the time Weary came home, she hadn't seen him I think for seven years and Weary had been through all the camps. They wouldn't be the same people. I thought Helen was terrifically courageous and full of integrity to marry this man. Maybe she was still in love but seven years is a hell of a long time. People change completely in that time.

Anyway she was lovely. It fascinated me because she had a beauty you couldn't quite catch. I mean she was beautiful to look at anyway but a bit tentative and vague and I was fascinated by her.

I was invited to the wedding and I was late. I turned up as they were piped out of the church and they only had to walk next door. The piper and everything, it was all exciting and she looked marvellous in her outfit. I met Weary's mother and father on that occasion and I remember they were very plain folk. Very plain country folk.

Helen was also very intelligent wasn't she?
I never thought of her as intelligent, I thought of her as beautiful. And I suppose when Weary was around, Weary was the centre of interest to some extent. Perhaps it was that the men were the ones who was always conversing, like my father and Mephan Ferguson.

After the war, I used to go regularly to Scottish dancing with Weary and Helen and a couple of other people I knew. They had a piper and I just loved it. And Weary was absolutely hopeless. He had no sense of rhythm. But everyone would love Weary to be in the set because he would sort of stand in the middle with this sweet smile and they would push him around. Come this way, Weary, that way Weary. Then he'd get into the centre and he'd do his thing. He wasn't good at it, yet he was the centre of everything. Weary wasn't a Scot but he delved back into the Dunlop name and loved the Scottish things.

What sort of relationship did Weary and Helen have? Was he attentive?

I remember once he'd been away to India or somewhere and Helen showed me a present he'd brought back and he bought her a beautiful blouse which fitted perfectly. I remember thinking that my father would be completely incapable of buying a blouse that would fit my mother perfectly, he wouldn't know where to go, but Weary – he was a romantic and he could delight her in that way.

Was Weary a handsome man?

No, but he had some indescribable charm. Very rare charm. He must have had it for men too. My father was a little jealous of him because the name Weary was always coming up in all sorts of things. And it's true that Weary had a higher profile than any of the others, like Coates and the other people there. But Weary was the god.

And he had a wonderful sense of humour?

Yes, but a little bit trying. He told long stories and you couldn't hear him very well. He didn't have to fight into the conversation because when Weary started talking, everybody listened. And he would tell this story and (she mumbles). And you would want to hear and he would be enjoying telling his story and he knew he was being listened to and everyone was listening. (laughs) He had us over a barrel.

Weary told me one story about my father that amused me a lot. My father had met Weary in Palestine somewhere. Weary said when he got to Australia there was a message from Bierwirth, something like Good luck, Weary, we're all looking forward to seeing you. Then he got to Brisbane and there was another message from Bierwirth: Well Weary, we are all looking forward to seeing you. I think he had three messages coming down. And when he got to Sydney, Weary just disappeared for a couple of days. He couldn't handle it. He must have felt he was being taken over or controlled or something and he said he just spent the time lying on the beach. He didn't put it into words but that gave it to me, that three messages from Bierwirth – We're waiting for you – were just too much for him.

Did you keep up contact with Weary and Helen over the years?
Helen of course got Alzheimer's and I'd seen Weary a couple of times after that and I went to Helen's funeral. Weary was surrounded by friends and dignitaries, and for a long time the hearse waited. It's illogical of course, but I felt disturbed and sad that Helen – in death – had to wait so long for Weary's attention. As maybe it was in life.

Weary came to my play in 1991 and he was bored. I spoke to him afterwards and said 'Well, did you like it?' And he said 'Oh well, I kept awake.' I thought well, I suppose that's a compliment. At that stage, him being taller than everybody else and being such a figure, people would come up and speak with him and you didn't have him at all. He just wasn't there. In the interval, we were just standing back and Weary's over there being talked to by all these people so you sort of lost him in later years, I think.

His funeral was most amazing. I'd more or less lost contact. And yet when he died, it was as if something had gone out of the world, it was quite strange. I went to the funeral, I stood at the back. I spent the whole time trying not to cry. Standing in the back – the silence in that packed cathedral, it was like a silence I've never heard before. It was so rich. Then you went out and the crowds! Mothers and little kids. I followed the gun carriage and the two sons walking right up to the Shrine and saw them put the coffin into the other vehicle.

I don't think I valued him enough. I thought Weary would live for ever. He's younger than my father and my father was still sitting in a corner and I was looking after him. It was just that when Weary died, it was a shock because although I hadn't seen him for probably for six months, Weary was always there. If I needed him, he was available. I know if Dad had said I'd like to see Weary, I would have rung up Weary and Weary would have come. Or if I'd felt unhappy with a doctor, Weary would look after me. Weary was always there. So when he died I felt terribly amazed at myself that I was so distraught and that the sense of loss was so amazing. Then I thought, Oh and I could have seen more of him, I wish this, I wish that. I expected him to go on forever. I didn't expect him to drop off the twig.

On the other hand, how marvellous for him that he did. Weary was not the person to be stuck away in a corner to go gaga.

Rowan Nicks was studying for his fellowship at the College of Surgeons in London at the outbreak of World War II, and spent the next six years in the British Navy. He retrained at the Brompton Chest Hospital after the war and returned to New Zealand in 1947 as a foundation member of the cardio-thoracic surgery unit at Greenland Hospital. In 1956 he took charge of the development of cardio-thoracic surgery at Prince Alfred Hospital and the University of Sydney.

He retired from the Prince Alfred in 1973 and in the remaining years he has worked in Africa, and in India, an interest he shared with Sir Edward. He invited Sir Edward to join the International College of Surgeons in the early 70s and the two became close friends.

When we spoke in Sydney, Rowan Nicks handed me a list of aspects of Weary he wanted us to cover.

WEARY BECAME FAMOUS with his diaries. He was just a marvellous personality whom we all loved and then it dawned on everybody that this was an extraordinary person, that he had not only kept a diary, but kept all the details of his men and what they were suffering. He guarded it with his life. Sue Ebury, I think, did a wonderful job on his diaries. I've seen them and they are bits of paper, bits of this and that.

What part did his wartime experience play in his life up until then?

It played a very big part. We always talked about it, and I think I knew all the stories of the guards, about Bill the Bastard and Hiramura the Lizard. He was always thinking of the chaps and how they were getting on and their wives and what was happening to them and their pensions. He was devoted to his men and he never lost it, it was always with him. His own personal career was nothing, it was secondary, and his family life was secondary to it.

One wonders if his family perhaps did suffer?

Yes, they did. They were living with their mother-in-law in their mother-in-law's house. Very difficult. Then Weary spent all his time operating, or with the soldiers, and I'd think, Poor Helen. I liked her very much, she was a very good friend of

ABOVE: *Weary takes a dip at Kinsayok Falls in 1987 (Quentin Fogarty)*

LEFT: *Weary and Kanit Wanachote at Hellfire Pass in 1987*

Weary revisited Thailand with his fellow prisoners of war for the first time in 1985 and then again in 1987.

TOP: *On a long boat down the Kwai Noi in 1987 with (front left) Blue Butterworth, (second row) Jack Chalker and Bill Haskell, and (back row left) Bill Wearne (Quentin Fogarty)*

BOTTOM: *With (from left) Blue Butterworth, Jack Chalker, Bill Haskell, Des Jackson and Keith Flanagan near Konyu (Hellfire Pass) in 1985*

OPPOSITE PAGE: *Exhausted, Weary is fanned by Bill Haskell during an attempt to find the Hintok Mountain Camp site in 1987. Leaning on a stick in the background is Bill Wearne, Weary's second-in-command at Hintok Camp (Quentin Fogarty)*

THE MELBOURNE SCOTS

MEETING OF THE COUNCIL TO BE HELD ON FRIDAY, 18TH JUNE 1993 IN THE BOARD ROOM OF FREEHILL, HOLLINGDALE AND PAGE, 48TH FLOOR, 101 COLLINS STREET, MELBOURNE AT 4 P.M.

AGENDA

To avoid security procedures, please arrive by 5:50 pm.

Robyn Ellis,
Hospitality Co-ordinator

If arriving late, please telephone 611 5444 from the Red 'Phone on the Ground Floor, so that you can be accompanied upstairs.

Weary was a great doodler. This selection shows self-portraits for his grandchildren; his recollection of the wartime Boonpong (middle right); and Rajah Kannan, amongst others, at a meeting (bottom)

TOP: *With children at St Michael's Grammar School, St Kilda, on the occasion of the Weary Dunlop Oration, 1987 (courtesy Herald & Weekly Times)*

BOTTOM LEFT: *With Jack Flannery (Dale Wright)*

BOTTOM RIGHT: *With Rowan Nicks at an international conference*

RIGHT: *Clifton Pugh's portrait of Sir Edward Dunlop, 1990 (Oil on canvas 182 x 121cm. The Dunmoochin Foundation Art Collection held at La Trobe University)*

OPPOSITE PAGE TOP: *Sitting for Donald Cameron*

LEFT: *The Ormond Students' Club dinner, 1987 (Martine Seccull)*

OPPOSITE PAGE BOTTOM LEFT: *With Melvie Barter (Dale Wright)*

OPPOSITE PAGE BOTTOM RIGHT: *On the occasion of the presentation of the Knight Grand Cross (First Class) in the Most Noble Order of the Crown of Thailand, April, 1983*

ABOVE: *The funeral procession in St Kilda Road, Melbourne, 12 July, 1993 (Colin Moss)*

RIGHT: *The Weary Dunlop statue by Peter Corlette in St Kilda Road, with (from left) Tom Uren, Martin Flanagan, Valda Street and Blue Butterworth*

mine, but one could do nothing about it. He was single-minded about everything he did.

Helen was a charming, nice woman. Utterly loyal to Weary. Fitted in, in every way to whatever he wished. He was the dominant figure and she was always coming behind him, as it were. She was a direct person, though. She liked life and she liked being with him. Enjoyed travelling very much. I think she felt a little neglected at times, but I never discussed that side with her or with him.

Was it on the trip to Japan in 1971 that the hotel refused to cash your travellers' cheques?
Yes, that was the funniest thing. The chap on the desk refused to cash both Weary's cheques and mine, and that evening Weary changed from his forgiveness of the Japanese to getting upset and hating Bill the Bastard or Hiramura the Lizard. I said to him, 'Weary, there must be another way out of this, let's go and talk it over.' So we left the chap with a grin on his face, and that's when I said, 'Why don't we entertain your friends here in the hotel?' The next morning we went down to this chap and he thought he'd won but then he saw the bill that we'd booked up the night before and he had to cash our cheques. So we won.

Weary told me, 'Rowan you've got to have face. The Japanese hate losing face, you have to outface them.' Our bus was waiting, but he took an enormous time to get his gear packed up. I said, 'Weary, you can't do this.' He said, 'We're gaining face, Rowan, we're gaining face.' So I put all his things together and got it all whipped away. He said, 'Did you put in my hair brushes? I had them all the way through the campaign, they're very precious.' I said, 'Yes, everything is away.' He said, 'Are you sure you put my hairbrushes in?' I said, 'Weary, we can't wait any longer.' He said, 'But we're gaining face, Rowan, we're gaining face. They won't go without us, I know the Japanese'. We found seats were left for us on the bus, and we'd gained face. (laughs) He understood the Japanese, he understood 'the face', and he understood the importance of never giving way to them. He was stubborn.

He was stubborn from the beginning. He used to tell stories of when he was boxing against the Sydney University champion after he'd been out to a party the night before with his friends. He got into the ring and the chap hit him in the stomach. He felt like vomiting, but he was determined he wouldn't give in. His nose was broken, there was blood, but he was determined he wouldn't give in, and he eventually won the bout. It was his sheer stubbornness and that stubbornness was part of what made him the man he was in the war. He would never give in.

Did that work against him sometimes in civilian life?
He always thought of the patient and himself. He was one-sided and his work was all-important, and he never thought of the other people who wanted to use the theatres or didn't want to be up all night.

He has been described as being always friendly, always affable, but impenetrable as a person.
I don't think he dropped any shutters. It's just that he was himself, and I think all great men have that facility of being themselves. They've got a private life and a public face. He was lonely in his private life but the phone was always ringing. In a way he was able to be what he was because he was lonely in his private life. He thought for himself. He liked to listen to other people's ideas and facts and see what the truth was and then he made his own judgment.

He seems to have been a good listener.
He would listen and then he would make a remark or a joke. He had so many appropriate stories, and you always felt better for them. They were never nasty.

His sense of humour seems to have been always present.
It was always there. And he had a sense of history. He loved the great men, the really great men. He loved poetry.

What great men did he admire?
He loved Churchill. He loved all the heroic figures of life. He liked Alexander. I can't remember his reaction to Napoleon – I think it was probably good. (laughs) Anybody who was heroic.

He might have reservations about Napoleon.
Well, I have the gravest reservations.

And poetry was important?
Poetry was very important to him and he carried his book of poetry all the way through the war. A.E. Housman was a very important part of his life. All the heroism of it, he liked. He liked the heroism of Shakespeare and the battles. He loved battles.

Did he like the military?
Yes, he loved the army, he loved the heroic figures and despised the people who did bad things. He despised the French surrender.

It's been suggested that he adopted the persona of an benevolent English gentleman, a hero.
I don't think he adopted anything. I just think he was.

Was he a driven man?

I think he would say no to anything he didn't approve of, and that's why he was a great man, because he would be kind and helpful but if there was something that was improper or he disapproved of, he'd have nothing to do with it.

I think his time was preoccupied in his latter years with the fact that he was growing old and that he ought to do what was asked of him and he ought to fill in his time. He didn't like not being active and if any patient rang him, he would always go and see them. I was rather sorry for him in a way. I could see that he was compulsive.

Was it a compulsion to do the right thing by others?

Yes, and he felt he ought to help the young generation. He wanted them to see that there was something in Australia that was great and grand and worth growing up for, that there was another side to life than the petty scramble for money and power.

He appears to have found it really hard when he was asked to stop operating.

Yes, I think he stayed on too long, myself, but then, he had the feeling that he was necessary. You know, it's part of growing old. We all have to give up, and his surgery was very important. He loved surgery, he loved the relationship of patients – and they loved him. So he did it for no profit, it was purely that he loved to serve them.

Did you discuss religion with Weary?

In the camps, they used the Bible for cigarette papers. He said the last one he smoked was the 'Sermon on the Mount'. (laughs) He thought that was the crux of Christianity, the 'Sermon on the Mount', and I do too.

We talked about religion but neither of us like hierarchies. The basis of Christianity is a way of life and thinking and it's beyond the priesthood. The Buddha appealed to him, and Christ appealed to him as a person talking in parables to the people. Christ was a great leader and he was a man, both of us agreed – and he had bones like we did.

Was his Scottish ancestry important to him?
Very important. He loved it, and he loved his mother. His mother was the centre of culture of his life and in my opinion, a lot of great men have great mothers. That's the source of their kindness and understanding and things.

But he wasn't really all that Scottish, was he?
Well, he cultivated himself as a Scot. How can you tell who is Irish? Well, they feel they're Irish. So that's Weary – Scotch. He thought they were great people. He liked the colour, he liked the sound of the pipes, and he liked their courage.

You have written here: 'Liked attractive women'.
Yes, he did. You would have a good friend who was attractive and you would introduce her to Weary and she'd forget about you and talk to him. Weary was very attractive to women. He just somehow charmed them all. He was so charming and nice and modest and full of stories.

He was a great kisser of hands and cheeks.
Oh yes, he had all the gestures of charm that are going.

Was he a womaniser?
Oh? No, I don't think so. He had affections, and old friends were very important. I remember several old friends. He'd go

and see them each week. I don't think he was a womaniser, he just liked female company. We both liked women and we liked the refinements and the talk. No footy. (laughs) No, I'm sure he was utterly loyal to Helen. He was in two minds about getting home in 1945. He spent two days in Sydney on his way home, wondering whether he could face up to marriage.

It's an extraordinary thing he and Helen did, to have married so soon after when they hadn't seen each other for eight years. Within a few days of returning. Well, it's an enigma. But he always stuck to his promise.

What sort of people did Weary like?

He didn't like any pretentiousness in any way. He liked real men and he liked courageous men and he loved courageous stories. He was very friendly but he had few real friends. They remained forever. I loved my friendship with Weary and I miss him very much, but he's so much a part of me that he's not dead in a way.

Honour was the great thing in life with him. Money didn't matter. He really did like all these write-ups in the paper. He kept a copy of them all and he was very fond of them. He loved honour and he loved his country and he was enormously patriotic. He always told the truth. Anybody told a lie, they were finished, he never forgave them. He didn't think the world of politicians, although he liked Bob Menzies.

He loved the Queen and the royal family. He just adored them and he liked his connection with them. Prince Charles would come and see him and the Queen and he had a great rapport with Lady Mountbatten, who was a particular friend and they talked of all kind of things.

She was an extraordinary woman.

She was an extraordinary woman and she had a penchant for Weary.

And handsome men.

He was a handsome man and an interesting man and there wasn't a love affair with Lord Louis, as you know. (laughs)

I think the war made Weary, and that he was terribly lucky. It made of a fine Australian, a great man. The prisoner of war experience brought out in him things that he never dreamed he had – all that feeling, and his intense compassion for people. He was a bit of a boxer and a bruiser in the university, a footy player, and his highest ambition was to become a surgeon in London and come back and practise and marry Helen. But the war changed him, so I think he was fortunate.

I loved the man for himself and I think of him in most decisions that I make in life. We shared everything, we shared life, poetry, books, people. He was a man of unending interest. To me he never varied. His word was his bond. I regarded him as a blood brother.

On the 5 July 1993, **Rowan Nicks** *wrote this poem in memory of Weary:*

Farewell

A mighty tree has fallen.
Besides its roots a stream flows on.
New sunlight floods a desolation
Where small life only grows.

A bastion of a nation,
  His living words say on,
Speaking courage and humility
  To growing life beyond.

Young trees in light press upwards,
  New roots entwine the life that's gone
And sturdy trees a'growing
  Will soon replace the old.

The ship of sunshine sets beyond horizon's rim.
  So dies their offspring's guardian
The lonely widow's friend,
  In rosy clouds of glory,
Their children and his friends.

On 29 May 1984, after a fall at his farm, Weary wrote to Rowan Nicks from the Freemason's Hospital.

My dear old boy,
Your letter of 20/5/84 received today – and for the first time in forty years I am abed, and, like a large turtle, on my back!

On Sunday eight days ago, was out on my own on the farm when my 'ratting tog shoes' slipped on the gravel and I crashed down right side onto a rocky outcrop, with a shocking smash of my right femur, with smash up of the intertrochanteric region and a spiral fracture running a foot down the bone.

The neck of the bone and hip joint look marvellously good for my age, and the bone good enough for a buffalo.

I got the leg straight by getting on my back, and pushing it down with my good leg and right hand.

Steady calling out eventually attracted help. My only movement an agonising thrust backward on my buttocks pushing with the unstable leg dragging after me. I needed eventually about six units of blood. The thigh and buttock very ballooned.

I made it here in six hours after being dropped at the Austin Hosp, pro temp, and then twelve hours later got into a theatre here for a 2½ hour operation. Now all loving kindness, the room full of masses of flowers including a spray of roses from the Governor, fruit and sweets and delicacies. And endless deluge of letters – telegrams, books, phone calls and visitors.

Pain and sleeplessness are my problem – the nights a horror. I've been out of bed for a short while, toilet etc with a walking frame. (three days now.)

Valda types most of my letters, Helen's nurse is coping somehow. A terrible suspension of purpose really. It is my Karma! I have a nail and large plate and very many screws. I say at least I am lucky to have 'the screws'!

Your letter saddened me. I would like to be with you. Please watch the food and the water. One gets run down. Now the Red Cross and Red Crescent. I'll try to alert the Victorian elements and through them our International division. Get the machinery working in Kampala. Let me know your worst needs. What a bloody mess this world – and so much of Africa is in semi starvation. . . .

Helen requires total care all day and night and gets worse. What a time to smash myself up! . . .

Alas, writing on the back is so difficult and it is now two a.m. I shall try to rest and watch the night drag on. This morning dawn was like Michaelangelo's *Creation* and Apollo drove splendid horses through the gate of my gleaming window.

So we fight on. Paris next year.

In great affection,

Weary

*I met **Father Gonzalo Munoz** in Dublin, where he was studying ecumenics on sabbatical leave from his position at St Francis Church, Melbourne. He met Sir Edward in 1968 when he was a chaplain at the Jessie McPherson Hospital. We spoke at the Blessed Sacrament Chapel on Bachelors' Walk.*

IN THE COURSE of my ministry I used to visit the Catholic patients and there was a lady there, she was an extraordinary woman. She was all of seventy-five, and very little, but with enormous vitality. Weary was her surgeon and he operated on her several times. I met him there one day in the room. One of the things that impressed me at the hospital, was that he used to talk. I saw him once talking to one of the newspaper boys who went around the wards selling papers to patients. He spent some time with him, and asked him many questions. I was very impressed, that such an important man was humble.

He invited me to have dinner one day and I felt honoured. I didn't know he was a big man like that. At that stage I could speak worse English than I do now. That shows the tolerance of the man, that he was able to accept someone – some wog – who wasn't able to speak English properly. I saw him again a few times at the hospital, visiting that lady. Doreen was her name and even recently, whenever I saw him, I'd remind him about Doreen. He'd say Ah, Doreen, Doreen, Doreen. (laughs)

I became a friend from then on. Well, friend – friend sometimes means many things. He wasn't a kind of very intimate
friend. I felt very honoured to be counted among the people
who participated in Christmas dinner for fourteen years. Apart
from his family, I was the only stranger there. Something I
always appreciated very much, when his wife Helen was alive,
he used to take me several times to the farm. Helen treated me
with a lot of affection. I always gave her a kiss. The later days
when she had Alzheimer's disease, it was very sad. It was very
hard for Sir Edward, too. I'm glad I saw her a few days before
she died.

Another thing, he took me two or three times, on Saturday
before he went to the farm, with him to visit some of his
patients and I was very honoured.

I went back to Spain in 1970 for three years. I think it was
in 1971 that Sir Edward went to Russia for a conference and on
his way back he passed through Madrid and I was his host there
for three days. I took him to the bullfighting. There were two
gentlemen behind us and one of the bullfighters was very bad,
so the people booed him. The two men they were saying, 'It's a
pity we haven't paid for the ticket so we cannot protest.' I trans-
lated that to him and he was very impressed with that kind of
ethic: if you don't pay, you don't have a right to protest.

The day he arrived in Spain, it was sometime in the afternoon. I was young at the time, and I didn't realise how tiring a
trip from Moscow to Madrid could be, and I took him to one of
those cafes where they perform flamenco. Everything is done at
night in Spain and it was ten o'clock when I took him there and
we had dinner and after the dinner came the flamenco dancing.
I remember him nodding like that, and I saw he didn't watch
much, it was very tiring for him. It was my fault.

But he was such a humble and unassuming man that he

never imposed his will. He could have told me, 'Look, I'm tired, I don't want to go,' but no, he just went along with what I asked him to do.

One thing I admired him for was his total forgiveness of the Japanese. When I was in Madrid, I asked him about when he was in the Japanese camp and all the feelings. He told me of the atrocities he went through. He was about to be shot two or three times and he had to stand his ground, otherwise the morale of the soldiers would collapse, so he was prepared to die for them. But he always impressed me with his forgiveness of the Japanese. I asked him a few times about the war and things like that and he wasn't a pacifist, but he was a compassionate man.

Sometimes I asked him about the monarchy and things like that. Of course he was for the monarchy, but he was also very Australian. I think Weary was an enormous contributor to Australia accepting Asians. I heard him once in a university, he gave a talk at a graduation ceremony. He defended the contribution of the Asians to the Australian life. He was very brave to do that.

It wasn't very easy making conversation with him. You meet people, it's very easy, the conversation flows very easily. It didn't flow with him. Sometimes you'd have to extract some from him, like when I asked him about the war, and I had to more or less extract from him some of the stories.

Shortly after I met him he took me to play golf at Sorrento. He was driving me to Sorrento and he had a Jaguar at that time. At Chelsea we were going across the railway gates. He stopped and the train was coming. Still quite far away. He said to me, 'Why not go across?' So he went. The train was quite close. He told me afterwards, 'I wouldn't have done that if I didn't know my car well.'

He took me to dinner at his clubs. He used to introduce me with a kind of a satisfaction that I was a Catholic priest. I used to notice how he would introduce me to some people and say, 'This is Father Gonzalez.' In private he used to call me Mon Pere.

When I was in Spain, I missed Australia a lot but I couldn't do much about it. So my sister-in-law in Melbourne went around and collected money from friends to bring me back to Melbourne for a holiday. Weary contributed a substantial amount of money and they organised a little party and Weary made a little speech. The day I arrived back, he asked me to sleep in his home. I treasure that very, very deeply, his hospitality.

Tell me about Christmas Day.

At Christmas dinner he was like the grandfather, he used to serve the meal. It was always a traditional English meal. We used to laugh a lot. He had a very distinct laugh. The lunch used to last from twelve to six, for a very long time. After that we used to go to the big sitting room and to open the presents. And there always was a present for me, too – a tie or something like that. The little children were there, the grandchildren, and Heather, his daughter-in-law.

Sir Edward seems to have kept to a punishing schedule.

Yes, even when he went to his farm to relax, I don't think he kept still. He was always very, very busy. He was Cancerarian – I'm a Cancer too. We don't keep still. (laughs)

It has been suggested that he didn't have many close friends.

He needed people to affirm him, and lot of people did affirm him, they loved him, really loved. Some women I have met really would do anything for him. Because of his stature and because of who he was, I think he attracted a lot of affection from people. I think he felt compelled to have to keep a kind of a distance. I think even if he wanted to be close, he wasn't. Because of what he was doing and what he was, he wouldn't open himself to people. He was involved with so many. If you start to give yourself closely and intimately to people, you can't. You are restricted. I have heard it said that Weary should not have been married, because he was a man for everybody. You can't be married to a person when you are for everybody.

There was a reverence people felt for him, more than a closeness. I have heard that POWs actually take their hat off and press it to their heart when they mention Weary's name. He became a mythical figure. You can't be close to heroes – you put them on a pedestal and you keep them distant, because if they come too close to you, maybe you see their things which are not so heroic, like the ordinary faults and mistakes that we all have. Then their hero begins to have feet of clay.

I never saw Weary like that. For me Weary was more than a hero. I didn't know he was a hero anyway, I met him as a caring person who impressed me because of the way he treated people. He never boasted about anything, and even when asked about the war, he didn't boast. He used to have that laughter, funny laughter, when talking about being ready to be shot by the Japanese. He laughed at it. I asked him about torture. He was in one of those bamboo cages, with the sun burning, he was there for punishment. He told me it was really tough, but he didn't make a big thing of it.

I think he was straightforward to everybody. I have seen him talking with the Governor and officials and I've seen him talking with children – he always seemed to be natural, never boasting of anything. Perhaps that's the greatness of the man, his humility.

All of us have an official part. When I'm in the altar there with those robes, I have to perform differently. You put on your role. I can't go in shorts to the altar, I have to put something on. And together with the vestments you use, you put on your own respectability. People probably think I'm very holy because they only see me at the altar, they don't see me in the private life. That's normal, I suppose. We all wear two personae.

You took part in the state funeral, didn't you?

When we were preparing the funeral, the family requested that I should take part. I did the opening prayer. I was impressed with John Dunlop. Because it was a state funeral, there were representatives of the army, and a circle of very important people preparing the funeral. Mr Keating's official organiser for functions from Canberra said, 'About the protocol' – and John interrupted him and said, 'I don't care about politics, I don't care about who is first or who is second, but I'm sure my father would be very pleased to have the POWs in the first pews.' And they were. Keating was in the fourth pew. Weary would have been very pleased.

I was proud to be involved. It was a tribute from me to him. I was very impressed with Jim Donaldson. His homily was excellent. So was Sir Ninian Stephen's. They were magnificent, the things they said of him were so true. Having known the family, knowing him for almost thirty years, the family also were fond of me. John said, 'We must keep on the tradition of the family Christmas,' but that hasn't happened. Christmas won't be the same.

Bill Haskell met up with Weary in Perth.

WEARY HAD INVITED Keith Flanagan and me to this big do in Perth. The Royal Australasian College of Surgeons was going to induct all their new bods, and Professor Kasarn from Thailand was going to receive an honorary fellowship. The Governor, who was to arrive at quarter to seven, was going to open proceedings and you had to be seated by half past six.

I was to meet them outside the hall. Half past came and went, quarter to seven came and went, the Governor came and went inside, and I thought, Oh strewth, this is crook. All I saw were people in these saffron robes, in their college garments, and I thought, I'm going to feel like a duck out of water in that place. I'd made up in my mind if they didn't come very soon, I'd just disappear, because I certainly wasn't going to go in there on my lonesome.

At ten to seven, along comes Flanagan with Weary and Rowan Nicks. They'd had a drink. Weary and Rowan cruise up the steps and Keith and I are bringing up the rear. We went into the great hall and all you could see was masses of doctors and surgeons. We're going down the aisle and I'm feeling smaller and smaller and smaller. I saw a couple of seats and I said to Keith, 'Here, quick' and we dropped into them. Weary and Rowan go right down the front. That's where they belonged and that's where they go. They get there and Weary looked around and he'd lost two of his troops, so he just turned around and he walked up that aisle until he sighted us and he said, 'Come on lads, we're all sitting together.' We went down the front in our ordinary suits, past all these blooming eminent surgeons, come from far and wide. We got down the front and Weary said, 'Move along a bit, please, move along.' We got the front seats! I just wished the floor would open and swallow me, but that was Weary. 'Come on lads, we're all sitting together.'

Bill Griffiths and Weary caught up each time he went to Britain.

HE WAS STAYING with us and one morning he said to me, 'Bill if you could see me now, you would be shocked.' I said, 'Why?' He said, 'Well, I've got a very, very colourful dressing gown on.' I said, 'Oh? Oh yes.' He said, 'You'd be shocked to hear actually it is a Japanese dressing gown.' I said, 'Oh dear.' He said, 'But you'd be pleased to hear that I nicked it from a Japanese hotel.'

The author Patsy Adam-Smith was a friend of Weary's. We spoke at length one morning at her home in South Yarra, interrupted occasionally by the little terrier Tinker, who was intent on helping the workmen who were building a deck onto the back of the house.

I WAS BROUGHT over from Tasmania in January 1970 to set up the manuscript field office in the State Library of Victoria. They had one of the usual bun fights, inviting prominent people to the library to meet me. I was very twitchy about this, thinking, It's not really what I want. It was a reasonably crowded gathering and along came a man who said, 'You're from the Western District family, aren't you?' and to my great delight, this very tall man with slightly stooped shoulders said, 'Good God, she's not from the Western District family. She's far too goodlooking for that.' I fell in love with him immediately. I thought, What a gorgeous character. From that day on, we were very good friends.

Weary began coming here to my home in the early 70s. He'd come across the road, waving a bottle of wine in front of all the people along here, unwrapped, on Sunday mornings after he'd taken his wife to church. He'd come in and we'd share a bottle and off he'd go back to his midday meal. He brought claret for a long time and then I said I couldn't bear claret, and so, quite to my horror, he began bringing two bottles, a bottle of claret and a bottle of chardonnay. It was a bit dangerous. It was taking a long time to knock a bottle of chardonnay off and I'd be usually jumping from foot to foot, thinking, I'm due out for lunch.

I suppose he was the greatest companion one could know. We went over overseas a couple of times with the old lags, as he called the POWs. It was great to see him in action, because he had a style about him which I think shows what a remarkable fellow he was. He could certainly walk among kings. The pity now is that people don't see the man.

I found when I was doing the book, *Prisoners of War*, it was very difficult to get them off Weary. I'd say, 'This other man who was captured –' and they'd say, 'Well, Weary, he really was a remarkable man.' He had charisma by the tonne. Sometimes Weary would be exasperated with all the war stuff around him. I know that many times he was just tired of it all, because there were just so many other interesting things he could get on with.

I had great joy with him when the POWs first began going across to Thailand in the 80s. He was always a delight. It was always as hot as hell in those places. One time we came across this exquisite little pool in the jungle. We were trying to tramp to somewhere and weren't getting there and here was this little pool, about as big as this room. Off went Weary's shirt, off went his trousers, and there he is in those old-fashioned knicks that those sort of men have, and in he goes.

'Patsy, come in, quick.' Well, I would have willingly, because it was so damned hot, but of course here were all the lady wives. Most of the blokes jumped in and the lady wives are saying, 'Aren't they naughty boys?' Weary kept calling, 'Get your clothes off and hop in, you've got no idea what it's like.'

That night he got stuck into me, 'Why didn't you get into that water?' So I said 'Don't you realise why?' And he said, 'Well, yes, I did but I thought you were greater than that.' Nothing great about me, he thought, if I didn't have the courage to leap in. (laughs)

He was extraordinarily gentle with fools. Lots of people can't accept fools, and there's probably more of us fools in the world than otherwise. But also he had a knack of getting rid of them. You'd realise that he'd just had enough, because they didn't leave him alone. They were always talking at him or with him, but he was always so nice about them.

We were in Singapore in 1985, and Weary sent a note down to my room to tell me not to worry about dinner but to come up right away, that there was somebody coming that I would really love. Well, it was one of the most delightful nights. Jack Chalker had arrived and it was quite a magic thing to see him with Jack, with them delighting in one another. I didn't have the tape going because I thought that would be an imposition but I've been sorry ever since because I think sometimes you need to cheat on those things. It was just gorgeous because they hadn't seen one another since 1945, and the stuff that was flying around! I felt that sometimes there were feathers lightly touching me. It was delightful light stuff, and beautiful. Other times there was a sombre mood and you'd sit quietly with them.

Even then there'd be the odd knock on the door. A woman and a man actually came straight in. She was a very difficult and odd lady and to my delight Edward said, 'Now look we've only got little glasses, have this little glass before you go.' Instead of him saying, 'Oh, hop it,' she had a couple of minutes with this little glass and then he took it off her and went to the door nicely, because it was just going to be the three of us.

He was great to travel with. He was great at picking up

interesting people and giving you the background. He could do quite a precis on background just walking across a room. Most people can't do that well, so you are left jumping from foot to foot, thinking where should I be in this situation?

Did Weary often stretch the truth?
He could pick out the choice piece in a story and he could stretch it. I don't think many of us tell a story without some of that.

He really had a knockabout humour. You could pick up his country boy beginnings from his humour, it was just magnificent. If anyone was putting side on, he was great but he wouldn't hurt anybody, he wouldn't attack anyone.

Was he very partial to honours?
A number of the decorations he had were tin-pot, that's the silly bit. He was a very vain man. He was vain in all ways. I think that is one of the cruel acts of fate, I suppose, one gets old. If one gets old and doesn't bother about it, that's okay, but some people worry terribly that the shoulders have gone or that the hair has either fallen out or gone grey.

I was watching him one day, Clive James and I were in the back of the car and a couple of officers were in front and I saw Weary coming down the street. We were to go to a breakfast and I yelled out, 'Oy', and to my surprise I saw Edward straighten and I thought, Yes, you do that most of the time. In one way it's a brave thing but in another it's that he was not accepting what most of us accept about life.

He was extraordinarily busy the weekend before he died.
I hadn't known that he'd gone to the Numurkah thing. He'd been there, you see, not very long before and so there was no

need. He seemed not to be able to say no. Sometimes he would be a bit cross about going to these things. He wasn't a saint in that way but then you think, Well, why did you go?

It seems almost as if he felt he couldn't say no because no one would love him if he did.
Oh, I do think there's a lot of that. I had to think a lot about him after he died. I suppose when he died I wasn't weeping and carrying on like everybody. A friend said, Why would you, you had the best of times with him. What do you want to cry about? I had done the things I would like to have done with him. I'm sure that was part of our friendship, because he knew I would say, 'I can't be bothered with that.' Whereas everybody did kowtow and I don't think that man really wanted all that kowtowing.

Right near the end he'd be so kind, though. I'd had a lot of operations, a lot of sickness, that he knew about. He was always driving me to things. I'd say I can get a taxi. 'No need to get a taxi. I will drive you.' And I would say, 'Yes, I'll be dead by the time you get there.' But he'd do that just out of straight kindness – that wasn't showing off. Nobody knew that it was him who drove me, it was nothing like vanity at all.

In the six months before he died, I was getting over a thing and he phoned on the morning of New Year's Eve and said, 'Now, you right for tonight?' And I said, 'No.' I didn't want to go. I'd been to these New Year's Eve things round there and I found them fairly boring. He didn't always know all the people there. They weren't so much gatecrashers, though I was never sure. He came round and picked me up and I sort of abused him. Well, he did the loveliest thing. He brought me in and it was getting towards midnight. They were dancing and they stopped to see the new year in. It just sounded the 'Auld Lang

Syne' time and someone grabbed me to get in the circle. Weary just stepped right in and got both my hands and he said, 'No, Patsy and I are going to sit and watch.' I wasn't well, but I knew that that wasn't the whole story – he couldn't have done it. We just sat there and kept clapping the rhythm and stuff, but he knew it was his last New Year.

When I came back, I sat and had a cup of tea and a long think. It's his last and he knows it. Because he had always got into it, I thought. He was a big lumbering sort of a dancer. No one seemed to notice or mind. But I thought then there won't be another 'Auld Lang Syne'. He knew all the words and I knew all the words. Very few people know:

> *We twa hae run about the braes*
> *And pu'd the gowans fine;*
> *But we wandered mony a weary foot*
> *Sin auld lang syne. (softly)*

We were singing this.

He was the most convivial fellow. The most convivial fellow. Edward loved to have not only beauty in his world, but ease and ambience. And he certainly didn't get it. But he loved gadding out, he loved people who wore good clothes, he loved all these things. One night we were going to the opera. I started off straight to my seat and I realised that he just wanted to stand, to be seen. I watched that many times. Or he'd lead you to somewhere where you would be seen. But then again, a lot of people wanted to see him, so why not?

He came from a very poor family. Well, many of us come from poor families, but he had poverty or near poverty, and for the first eighteen months of his life, his mother had puerperal psychosis, which I guess as a young boy he'd think of as lunacy.

He asked me once, how did I manage my life, seeing that I wasn't brought up with wealth. I was so startled. I said, 'But I've never thought of wealth, I haven't needed it, I've got it.' He went on then and told me about the hardships as a child. I said, 'Well, you have hardships as a child but you don't go on about it. You either make it or break it.' I was talking away like that and I found, no, he just wanted to continue to talk about it, and I realised he really hadn't gained that type of contentment most of us get.

I think that's why there was this great rushing around all the time. Never saying no to things he need not have gone to. The Ladies' Sewing Circles – it's a wonder they hadn't got to him. He did want to be admired. He would want to be admired on his deathbed. He needed it more than anyone I've known, man or woman, and I've known some very brave and some very great people.

Very few people knew he came here. I knew he felt it was the only place he could just sit back. He'd yarn away, sometimes he'd go off to sleep, have a little rest, and then start, 'Did I ever tell you about so and so', and he'd waffle on, never dull, always interesting, and I thought, Yes, you need this. He certainly liked all those things that his title and every other thing would bring him, but there was something else which he didn't have. It may have been his relationship with his sons. I don't know what it was. I don't know at all.

He had to have that other thing of holding the 'lags' together, the old men. That's what made many of the wives quite bitter. The wives wanted to get on with living, and indeed, if they hadn't got on with living, the men wouldn't have done so well after the war. But then when they got someone like Weary around them, the women were cut off. I used to see that and I used to feel very sorry. Someone said to me about her husband,

'I'm not married to him – my husband's married to Weary.'
That was a fault in Weary, he should not have permitted it to go
so far that it would affect the other person.

They felt he was holding them in the past?
In the past. Totally in the past.

I thought everything about the funeral was cold. I went to
see him because no one had seen his body, no one had seen him
since he left the house alone, with no family, and went to the hospital, then to the mortuary. I said, 'I feel eerie not to have done
this,' so I went. It was quite dreadful because I believe they took
a mask of him, a plaster cast. There was something not at all
right. They'd put a plaster on, I felt certain. Someone must have
thought, Well, they'll probably be doing a statue or something. I
just thought, The poor old boy, he deserved more. Because he
was a dear man, I always thought of him as an old man in a way.

He was certainly a great man, like people keep saying. And
I say, he was a great man, yes, but we've got to remember that
there are many other people who are great. Some are still alive
and they're great people. Magnificently great, generous, loving,
handsome – anything that Edward was. He's just another of the
great people we have. I think the only thing I ever had against
him, and it wasn't his fault in a way, was that people got around
to thinking that he was the person who saved all the men that
were left alive on the railway. I just always felt it was a pity that
it has to be one man drawn out from the many great men. I
guess it always has to be one. One covers the lot. People find it
easier. I don't know if other countries do this. I think we're big
enough to make allowances for all men.

Long before his death, they spoke of him as if he was a god
of old. They wouldn't have worried too much if he was a statue,
even then. That was what they were looking for. The figure.

That shouldn't be done to anybody, I don't think. Of all people, that shouldn't have been done to Edward, because he was a greater man than that.

Des Trowell was an ex-serviceman who sought Weary out in his retirement. He wanted to paint Weary's portrait and he and his wife became friends with Melvie Barter, Weary's housekeeper. While he was in the Caritas Christi Hospice, Des let it be known through Weary's former secretary Valda Street that he wanted to say a few words about his hero. We spoke on the phone in September 1995, shortly before he died.

I'D COME BACK from the war and I had been in the Heidelberg Repat. and I was rotten with malaria. They sent me to Stonnington, in Malvern, for rest and recreation. That must have been in early 1946, and while I was there, Weary came in to try and motivate the servicemen. That was the first time I met him, shook hands with him. Then we lost contact over the years until we met up again in the1980s.

One time Melvie Barker, his housekeeper, rang me at about one o'clock in the morning and asked if I could come over. She was very worried about Weary, who'd just come back from India with a very high fever. So we got over there and sure enough, there he is with a heck of a fever. We got some vinegar and hot water and we sponged him down. Melvie went to bed and I stayed with him. He kept asking me the time. 'What's the time, Des? I'm off to Adelaide tomorrow, I've promised the POW nurses I am going to speak over there.' In the morning we heard running water and, sure enough, there he is having a shower and off he went to Adelaide. That's another token of the man how honourable he was to everyone.

Clive Fairbairn, a life member of the Melbourne Cricket Club, is a veteran of Tobruk, El Alamein, New Guinea and Borneo. 'I wouldn't have missed it for quids,' he told me. 'There was always something doing in the army.' He used to take Weary as his guest to the football and the cricket.

YOU HEAR, 'Oh, we've got to be friendly with Japan.' It's no good talking to me about it. I admire it but I sometimes can't reconcile it. Weary wouldn't have much said against the Japanese. He'd stand up for them. I used to go berserk at him. He'd just give that smile. Whenever he saw the funny side, his eyes would half close and he'd have that smile. Tremendous smile. His words were he'd forgive but he'd never forget. How could you forget it? Gee whiz. I'm probably worse than I should be. My elder brother, he got a bullet just next to his spine, on the Kokoda Trail. It took him sixteen days to walk back and he carried a man. The things that happened then, they're not real. He passed away two years ago.

I'd invite Weary to a night game of football or cricket and he'd leave his car at Parliament Place and walk across the gardens. He loved walking. He was fit. Loved Australian Rules. I eventually got out of him that he was a Carlton supporter. I took him to the football a few times before he told me that. I asked him if he was keen on cricket. He said, 'What do you think of the one-dayers, Clive?' I said, 'Weary, one-dayers are for people who know nothing about cricket.' 'No wonder I like them,' he said. He always had an answer for you.

He was a character. He'd put those eyes half closed and he'd be thinking up something. He came up with a shocker about his rugby. He told me about a Test match he played against the Springboks. He named a chap and said, 'He broke a couple of ribs and broke my nose. But I think I got even with him. He came to see me before he went, and he was gloating over us, how they'd beaten us in the Test, how he was taking out one of my patients.' With his eyes half closed, he said, 'You know, I forgot to tell him I was treating her for VD.' He just had that smile.

There can be few closer relationships than that of the biographer and their subject. **Sue Ebury** *spent seven years working on* Weary, The Life of Sir Edward Dunlop. *Earlier she had edited* The War Diaries of Weary Dunlop. *We spoke at her home in Mt. Macedon. I asked her whether Sir Edward was ambivalent about the publication of his war diaries.*

NO, HE WASN'T. He was diffident about picturing himself as a hero. A lot of people have always said and continue to say that he pursued publicity far more than the other doctors. He didn't pursue publicity, it pursued him. He could never refrain from comment. It was the same character trait that meant that he could not say no to anything. It was a curious thing and I've never completely worked it out.

You mentioned that when you first met Weary he was at a pretty low ebb.
He was suffering from deep depression when I met him. That was in 1984 and it was a very unhappy time. Helen had Alzheimer's and she was still at home, and though she had a full-time nurse, he did a great deal for her himself. That's when he described it to me as a sort of black pain in the heart, knowing he could do nothing to help her. He was one of the last people to recognise that she had Alzheimer's.

***Am I right in thinking that you were fairly reluctant to take
on the biography?***
I was looking for a biographer for him. (laughs) Various can-
didates popped up and I suggested some names to Weary and
he wasn't keen. He came up with a couple, and I said, 'Oh,
for goodness sake, I can do better than that,' and he just said,
'Well, why don't you?' And I said, 'Yes,' then thought, Oh
my God, what have I let myself in for? Because it was a
huge job. I don't think I realised then how large it was going
to be, but then, luckily, one never does. So I don't suppose I
was reluctant, I was surprised. I wasn't preparing to be a
biographer.

That was in December 1986. I went back to Hong Kong
where I lived, but I came down to Melbourne about three times
a year, and I started photocopying the papers in the house. In
April 1987 I went to the Kwai with Weary. I also went to Java
and visited the various sites there and I went to Thailand on my
own again. I also went to the UK and did research there, and I
started the interviews.

In 1988 Helen died and I just left it because his mind
wasn't on it at all. I kept on with the interviews and research
but I left him alone. He knew Helen was dying and he lost
momentum. In a sense it was good because when he got his
momentum back he'd been contemplating his life with
Helen, and this let loose a floodgate in a way, so that after
1988 he was much more interested in talking and taking an
active part in the biography. Until then he'd been a reluctant
subject.

The role of the biographer is an incredibly close one –
It's a bit like being a psychiatrist.

Were there any areas in his life that he shied away from looking at initially?

His relationship with his children – it was one area which gave him distress and he didn't really know how to deal with it. Here was this father, who was larger than life both physically and in every other way. He said to me that it would be like a huge oak tree, with these boys struggling to get out from under the shade. Obviously it was difficult.

The house was full of former prisoners of war and people who had instant access to their father, and patients who had access to their father at all times, although that wasn't unique to Weary – that is the cost of being the son of a surgeon. The boys would be put in the back of the car and taken when he went off visiting hospitals.

And sometimes left in waiting rooms.

Well, he was pretty absent minded – no, he wasn't absent minded. He was so focused on what he was doing that he didn't allow anything else to intrude on it. The same thing kept him operating for such long hours. Once he'd opened up the patient, something would turn up that they hadn't expected and he'd fix that as well, and on he'd go, inexorably, into the night.

I gather that he had a shocking temper. Did you suffer from it?

No, never but I saw it in action. I've seen letters that he wrote if something went wrong – very terse letters went off. But he didn't usually lose his temper with women unless they were working for him. Weary told this story often, and he was very amused by it. This surgeon who Weary used to work with apparently said some disparaging remark about women to his nurse and she said, 'But Sir Alan, I'm a woman.' And he said,

'Woman? Woman? You aren't a woman. You are an instrument of my will.' Now, there was a bit of that in Weary. He told that story to me a number of times and laughed every time.

He seems to have loathed being called Ern.

Oh, he hated being called Ern, and he wasn't meant to be called Ernest either. Do you blame him? It didn't fit in with the image he created for himself. It's old fashioned. You see, he was meant to be Edward and because Alice had puerperal psychosis the birth wasn't registered for a little while. When his father went into register the birth he was a bit confused and it came out as Ernest Edward. He was meant to be Edward, after the king, and his grandfather, and Ernest after a favourite brother, Uncle Ernest, but it got twisted.

In his obituary (see page 263), Bob Marshall says Weary modelled himself on Clive of India or something like that. Well, that's not an unusual thing to do. Erikson, Freud, Jung – anyone – will tell us that the child establishes its personality and its ego identity very, very early in life after it's separated from the more immediate oral satisfaction. It first has ways of behaving imposed on it, then it decides to model itself on something. Weary first of all modelled himself on the fictional hero Deerfoot, and Gert Hutchins' mother [Lillian Steen], and then he moved on to other heroes. The only female mentor that he ever had was Gert's mother – not his own mother, because he felt stifled by her. He felt stifled by his whole background.

I said, I think in the book, that growing up in the country in a small town, and the fear that he might end up behind a shop counter and all the rest of it, was the grit in the oyster which compelled him to get on that train and go down to Melbourne. He waved to his parents on the platform and never looked back. He remembered, not only psychologically did he not look back, but physically he didn't turn around and look back. He was looking forward.

He told me he didn't like being called Weary but it was preferable to Ernie. As soon as he got to England, he became Edward, although he was Weary to his intimates.

His sense of humour seems to have been present throughout everything.
He had a great sense of irony. That was part of his persona, that irony, delivered in a quiet voice. A sting in the tail.

How does this sit with his love of honours?
He loved dressing up. (laughs) He absolutely adored dressing up. I mean, he's not a highlander, yet he had the full kilt. He always felt more Scottish than English. He got very upset at one stage when I said he was only half Scots.

He seems to have taken all those letters after his name so seriously.
He'd come from the country, he'd come from a small farm, he'd come from reasonably comfortable family circumstances but there was that passage in the book where I discussed how he hated their shabby clothes. He hated the shabbiness, and he hated being poor. The honours and everything were, 'Wow, look what I've achieved. Gosh, how have I managed to do that.' It was a very simple and naive and contradictory, in many ways, reaction. And yet he could make a joke about them as well.

He was keen to show people his latest honours.
That was often a substitute for conversation. How many people have you spoken to who have said that they sat down with

Weary and had a long conversation? With a few notable excep-
tions, usually it's *they* who had a long conversation with Weary.

Did he seek out intellectual stimulation?

I don't think so. I think he felt all the stimulation he needed, he
could generate himself. And he could. He withdrew into himself and read. Poetry, anything. Both Bob Marshall and I have
used the same phrase – he had a mind like a steel trap. He had
a very quick grasp intellectually of what he was reading or what
he was hearing and he could listen to something and he could
sum it up just like that. I envied him that capability.

To what extent was Sir Edward a man's man?

He was completely a man's man. He lived an almost monastic
existence, very much in the terms of the times, once he went to
Ormond. It was an all-male college, and in hospital, women
weren't much in evidence – it was all about single men, the
postponement of marriage and family in terms of career objectives. He faced the same sort of masculine segregation in
England as a doctor, and then the army. He loved the army, he
was made for the army. The excitement and the conviviality of
the mess, now that really suited him. So through all his forma-
tive years he was living in that kind of environment and then he
went into POW camps where he spent the whole of his war
with men.

He wasn't a man who I think was able to achieve close friend-
ships with women the way some other men do. I think probably
in the late 40s and the 50s and, a bit through the early 1960s, he
lived a much more normal life with private dinner parties and
things like that, but when I knew him, from 1984, his life was
almost wholly this sort of institutionalised existence of public dinners and cocktail parties. I guess that was part of the problem that

arose once Helen couldn't go out socially any longer. He had dinner parties sure, but as far as I can work out, they were never really dinner parties for many of his close friends. They'd be for people who were visiting. He was enormously hospitable. The Australian Asian Association had the run of the house practically, and a few other groups did as well. The quote given to me always was, 'Helen was a very gracious hostess,'

Did he regard women as equals?
I think he was stuck pretty much in the traditional mould.

He spoke of Helen as his princess.
Yes, I know. He would have liked her to continue her work, he told me, because he was working and away so much, but she wasn't interested, she wanted the traditional role of a wife and mother. I think he would have liked a bit more intellectual companionship and he didn't get it, for one reason or another. Perhaps he didn't give her much of a chance. But he had this very romantic view. Women were put on pedestals. It's very 19th century, but we've got to remember that he was a product of the 19th century and of Victorian mores.

You mentioned earlier how Weary would often go with the flow.
He would let it all go on around him. He let himself be moved from chair to chair, 'Now Sir Edward we'll do this, now Sir Edward we'll do that.' But he had the ability to withdraw while everything went on around him, although he could hear what was going on, so that he could go on writing letters or reading or doing something else. He'd just sit there and let it go on all around him.

I find his inability to say no extraordinary.
So do I, still.

What do you think drove him?
That small town, hating being poor, hating being shabby. Not
wanting to be a failure and the early imprinting by his two aunts
about the important family from which they came and how it
had gone down in the world – it was up to those two boys to
bring it back to what it ought to be. I'm sure that had a very
deep influence, because he was very interested in family and
background.

Weary had that naive, small-country town upbringing that
meant he was always very susceptible to titles, to important
people, to good wines and good food, and he could easily make
a joke about it in the next breath. He recognised that part of his
character and he could be amused by it but it didn't stop him
being impressed.

Was he vain?
He was vain about his appearance, yes, but not vain about himself. As he got older, he tended to not worry about it quite so
much, but there was a vast collection of club and institutional
ties that were always pulled out for the appropriate occasion.
He loved good tailoring, good clothes, and he liked his big
powerful cars, the appurtenances of success.

Was he a good surgeon?
He was much more respected overseas than he was in Australia.
He went to the Mayo Clinic in the United States and he lectured
in the United Kingdom. He was innovative in the late 40s and in
the early 50s. I think some of his character traits prevented him
from tailoring his career and procedures so that they would be

recognised by his peers, because he made no effort to get on with them. No effort. He didn't have a great deal of respect for many of them, and he didn't make any attempt to do anything in the Royal Australasian College of Surgeons.

He was a maverick. He was an outsider in every sense of the word, and I don't think I made any bones about that in my book. He was an outsider because he was born on an ordinary sort of little farm, his parents weren't members of clubs and they hadn't gone to famous public schools. He was an outsider because he worked in a chemist shop in Fitzroy, he was poor. He was an outsider because he had to put himself through that first year of university. He was an outsider at Ormond College because he didn't go to a public school and he was made to feel an outsider in those early initiations, and he remained an outsider all his life, despite all the honours and the honorary memberships of clubs, the honorary memberships of everything.

Whether he was a good or bad surgeon, his diagnostic abilities, I am told, were excellent. He was brought up in the pre-war medical educational system where they didn't have the back-up of technology that we have, so their diagnostic abilities were forced to rely on sight, smell, touch and taste – looking at a person's tongue, smelling their breath. And touch. He could tell a lot of things from feeling.

He had very beautiful hands. I always used to look at his hands and think they were very beautiful, even for an old man. His fingers were very long and very well shaped. And his face – the skin was always very smooth, very youthful looking, even though he was old.

Would he like to have become a diplomat?
Yes. When Lord Casey [the Minister for External Affairs from 1951-60 and Governor General from 1965-69] suggested he

might like to in 1965, Helen didn't welcome the idea at all so the subject was never raised again. But he was fed up with surgery at that stage and he'd have liked the change.

He loved the Colombo Plan, that was perfect for him. He was not only teaching, he was in Asia, which he liked, and he met a lot of interesting people and saw a lot of interesting things and it gave him a stimulus that life in Melbourne lacked.

If he had not been accepted by the Australian Army in 1939 before he was offered that job with the Royal Army Medical Corps, I'm convinced he would never have come back to Australia, except as a visitor. He himself suggested that, but fate decreed otherwise and he couldn't get Helen over there. I don't think he tried that hard because he was in awe of her parents and he realised that he didn't have any money. He was too proud to ask her to marry him at that stage, when he couldn't support her. If he'd come from a more moneyed background I suspect he would have asked her to marry him, whether he had money or no, but he was much too proud as a scholarship boy.

Did he always have that kind of pride?
I think so. He might have concealed it from time to time but you can't discard something like that.

Do you think he would have been a great man if he hadn't come back?
I think he was destined to be prominent if he'd stayed in England. He had the right mentors, he'd have become a powerful surgeon, and England fitted him like a glove. England is also very tolerant to colonials. They're allowed to get away with a lot more than an Englishman would be, and the fact that he was an absolutely marvellous sportsman was a major thing. A

rugby player, St Mary's, Arthur Porritt, Sir Thomas Dunhill – the doors were all opened for him. London House was the beginning. But he might not have been such a humane man, because the war was so significant for him, for all of them, and it changed his life irrevocably. He found his greatest sense of self-worth when he was on the railway.

Did he consider himself a Buddhist?
No. It's the usual claptrap talked. (laughs) He was truly ecumenical. He conceded dignity and worth to any religion whatsoever.

He continued to go to the Uniting Church next door.
I suppose it was routine, wasn't it? It was comfortable. He took Helen there as long as he could. It was part of his life, it was next door, it was a comfortable way of marking off the week – it was a social gathering. I'm not sure that he always listened. He was a great one for doing things for the continuation. That had been Helen's church and he was married there and the children were christened there, so there was a loyalty.

Loyalty to him was of paramount importance. Disloyalty was the ultimate crime. I was told very firmly in writing his biography that disloyalty was the ultimate crime and it was left to me to interpret it. I was meant to know what should and what shouldn't be put in. When he died, that became even more important.

Do you feel he knew he was dying?
Oh yes, of course he knew he was dying. I think he'd decided that it was time to go. He told me that when you reach a certain stage physically, if you decide to die, you can will yourself to die. I think he felt he'd had enough.

He rang you and was also able to speak to his grand-daughter Isabelle. He seems to have been very, very fond of her.

Well, she was the one who broke the drought. She was the first girl. Isabelle and her mother Chantal were staying with me in Hong Kong and as soon as I knew what was happening and that he was saying goodbye to me, I called them immediately so that he could talk to Isabelle, so that she could have a conversation with him.

Weary was a living myth in his own lifetime, wasn't he? He was larger than life. In some ways he'd been sanctified before he died.

He distrusted hero worship. Distrusted it very deeply. Didn't like it. And he became increasingly worried about it. I think it started after the diaries were published, and was something that moved him away from any degree of equality with people. The way he'd put Helen on a pedestal, now he was put on a pedestal.

I think he was a man who was innately shy in many ways, and quite introverted. Like most surgeons, he enjoyed performing. He enjoyed dressing up in his Knights of St John robes, or robes of the college, or anything like that, and he enjoyed being on stage. I watched him on a number of occasions in public places, usually at ex-POW or servicemen's things, when he was performing on a stage that he knew. Nonetheless, he would make his gestures larger than life. He'd 'wave' and he'd 'bow'. Always very slightly theatrical.

I've been told that he drove appallingly. Was it that he didn't care?

Of course he didn't care. What would he worry about that sort of thing for?

How about that he might die?

No, he was very cavalier about anything like that. The only place he was frightened of going was hospital as a patient. I said to him, 'But why?' He said, 'Oh well, you know, people die in hospitals.' (laughs)

Barbara Todd worked with Sir Edward in the early 1950s when she was qualifying as a nurse at the Royal Melbourne Hospital, and she took on the role of housekeeper at 605 Toorak Road in 1988 for what she thought was six months.

I CAME IN September because the house was being auctioned in the November and he was stuck having overseas visitors at that time. That turned out to be Jack and Helene Chalker. The sale of the house fell through and I ended up staying for fourteen months.

When I arrived at the house I don't think it had been really spring-cleaned since Tossie died. Sir Edward never wanted anything thrown out or moved. Any flat surface had to have papers or books on it. In the end I used to just move them.

I thought, Who is this man who is dictating! It just annoyed me. Having known him in the hospital and having known what honoraries are like, I was never really intimidated by him. Nor did I consider he was God. The POWs revered him, and anybody who came to the house respected him very much, but he was also a man. A man with human failings, the same as anybody else.

At one particular time when he was away in America, I started on the house and went through every room. I got into his bedroom and started from the ceiling and worked down. I was up in his wardrobe and I dragged down this box. It was a box of letters and I carefully lifted the top one. It was an airmail letter and I could see it was addressed to Lady Helen and it said, 'My dearest Helen' or something like that. I thought, Right, that's important. We were throwing a lot of rubbish out but Sir Edward didn't know.

That night he arrived home and I went into the sitting room with the box. I said, 'Sir Edward, whilst you were away, we did a big clean and I found this box of letters. I think you might appreciate having these.' He picked one up and said, 'They are the letters that I sent Helen during the war.' Then he stood there with the box in his hands and said in this very soft voice, 'I didn't really know she was a person who would keep my letters.' He hadn't thought that his wife would have thought enough to have kept his mail. I thought it was very sad.

Of course most surgeons, particularly in those years, didn't have much time for their family. He was making his way. He used to get a bit annoyed because people would make assumptions about wealth. He may have lived at 605, but he did say that he had paid his share of that house. It meant a lot to him to be independent, and it took him at least ten years after he returned from the war for his income to be in any way what you would call comfortable.

They always ate in the kitchen, which used to annoy me because I always liked to cook in the kitchen with nobody else around, but that didn't happen at 605. You'd have Alexander coming and opening the oven door and taking all the lids off the pots and everybody standing around having drinks. It irritated me. I told them, too, but they didn't seem to take too much notice.

One night we were on our own and Sir Edward had just had some function and he was telling me about it. I laughed and said, 'Well, Sir Edward, forgive me but the way you're lauded by everybody wherever you go, surely sometimes you must think about it a bit wryly? You're honoured so much, it's almost as if you're some spiritual figure.' He looked at me, he had this way of looking up. 'Well,' he said, 'sometimes they do sit me next to Moses.' I laughed and said, 'I suppose you could be sat next to Jesus Christ.' He grinned, and as soon as I said that, I said, 'Oh but of course you are Jesus Christ, aren't you?' and he laughed.

He was a man who wanted to please people. He had people he visited each week. For instance, Peggles [Margaret Gibson], who was his patient as well as a friend, he saw every Saturday. One Saturday he had a dreadful car accident and he wiped off his car. He had two Mercedes. Valda Street, his secretary, always said he had two because when he had a bingle, he could have it fixed and nobody knew because he had another white car to drive. But he was driven home after this, and I said, 'You've probably got fractured ribs there, Sir Edward and you're flying to America on Tuesday.' 'I'll be all right,' he said, 'I must go to Peggles.' And he did.

Jack Flannery was around the place in those days and Sir Edward would never ever make another arrangement if he thought Jack might be offended by it. Jack would come and mow the lawns and he wasn't well at the time, but we had to be very careful how we went about getting somebody else to do it. We didn't want Jack to feel he wasn't wanted. Sir Edward was very aware of the sensitivities, very. He was very protective of his old friends.

605 seems to have had such a personality.
Oh yes, and he loved it. There was this charisma around him, too. I was very careful while I was there to stay out of all the interpersonal stuff going around. I didn't feel it was my place to

get too involved in all the bits and pieces that went on around Sir Edward and I didn't encourage those that I knew were just deliberately ringing me because they wanted a bit of an entree to 605. I think in his own way he enjoyed all the stirring. He just padded through, never an action or a word that indicated he knew anything about what was happening. But he obviously must have known that people around him were perhaps discussing him. He just accepted that he was the central figure.

Jack Chalker and his wife *Helene* came to Australia for three months in 1988.

THE DAY WE arrived, Bill Griffiths was there with his wife, Alice. Weary got out of his bedroom so that we could have his bed. The house was always full of people coming in and out. It was very much an open house, and there was always a great welcome there. It was a happy house in that sense. He organised all those young students from elsewhere and they'd have these huge parties with about 200 students there, including Japanese and Chinese, and students from all over the world.

I thought that was a pretty generous gesture. Most of Weary's friends would come in the morning and they'd all bring food or cook or arrange this gargantuan rice meal that we all had. And things like that. It certainly was a centre for all sorts of activities, a meeting point for so many people. But Weary kind of drifted in and out of it. For all of us who were there, he just trusted us to enjoy the house and get on with it. On top of that, Valda had her finger on everything and so wonderfully organised everything that there were no hiccups. We were there at the time of the housekeeper Barbara Todd, who looked after him and was a very intelligent lady and very fond of Weary.

When we were there, the double bed we were given was so furrowed that Helene found it impossible to sleep in it. We lifted up the mattress and put pillows and blankets underneath to try and smooth it out a bit, but it was still very uneven. Then we found a mattress in the hallway that had just been standing there for years, so we hauled that in and put it on top of the other mattress. Then Barbara, the housekeeper, brought a mattress cover from home and that went on top and eventually Helene got used to it and was able to sleep.

All these characters were coming in. You'd be upstairs at 605 and suddenly this very loud voice would say, 'Hello.' Jack Flannery would yell at the top of his voice, this huge voice, and he was so funny. He was a dear. He was so dedicated to Weary and he was a real broad Aussie with a voice like a foghorn. He used to address Helene as one of his cobbers, and they had this marvellous, crazy relationship.

Jack had a great protective thing about Weary. He used to drive Weary about because everybody knew that he shouldn't be driving and it was Jack who came in to look after him all the time. He would appear, suddenly, saying, 'Well you're going to [somewhere] today, Weary, and I'm driving you,' and that was it. He was a real rough diamond. There was no messing about with Jack. If he was there, you heard his voice half a mile away, but he was as loyal and as kind and as good as they come.

There were all these ladies coming in with a proprietary claim to Weary, and Weary knew this of course and treated this with this kind of smile and like, Ooh, who's this coming in now? In a way, treating them with a little bit of distance but at the same time warming very much to them when they were there. A muddle of opposites and contradictions, with the women being slightly defensive with each other and some being nasty. It was funny.

It was a rather good time. Really, Somerset Maugham could have made a few stories of it.

So that was the mix of the house. Weary, with these very high-level satellites around, and these strange women coming in as well, and then there was Jack who came in like an explosion, and that sweet gentle lady, Gert Hutchins who used to bring boxes of oranges, and look after Weary's roses. She was a dear. But what a funny mixture because they all had a sort of free run on the house. It was a storybook house in a very strange way. I owe so much to that house.

Jack Flannery, an ex-prisoner of war, acted as Weary's driver in the last years of his life. A working class boy from Fitzroy, he and the esteemed surgeon were unlikely mates but they shared what Sue Ebury describes as 'the same devilry'. On 23 September 1994, he spoke at a tribute to Sir Edward held by the Kiwanis in Shepparton. Jack died later that year. These are excerpts from that speech:

GOOD EVENING LADIES and gentlemen, Mr Chairman, distinguished guests.

. . . Well, I'd like to tell you about Weary. I drove him for about forty-three years, and I had a ball. He was a character in his own little way.

He loved kids. He loved human beings.

If you never met the man, you don't know what you missed. I know it's a bit hard of me, but that's how I am. You've been with him for so long, it's just like losing your bloody right arm. I'm not too good at this speaking business. I'm a bit blunt, I'll tell you that much now, but I'll do the best I can for the time . . .

We had a party for him one night and how many turned up? Sixteen hundred. And I said to him, How the hell are you going to feed them? . . . He said, We'll do the best we can. I think they drank about 114 dozen bottles of beer with about sixty-five dozen bottles of champagne. Sixteen hundred people walked through that place. That was Weary. He enjoyed every minute and so did I.

He was a character to go out to the bush with. He loved kids. We were up at Euroa one time and we were standing waiting for the people to come, and he said to me, 'Who's using the big hall over there?' and I said, 'The kids, why?' He said, 'Come on, bugger this mob, we'll go over and get with the kids.' He sat on the floor with them for about an hour and three quarters. A bloke said to me, 'What about dinner?' I says, 'You don't worry about dinner, mate, when he's sitting there talking. It could be burnt black, we'll eat it, don't worry about it, we've had worse than that before.'. . .

We're down at Portland once, at a reunion. We had the reunion and we went to a party afterwards to about half past two in the morning. Six o'clock, he's hammering on my door. I said, 'What do you want?' He said, 'We're going for a swim.' I said, 'You are, but I'm bloody sure I'm not.' It was about four degrees in the shade. I sat in the hotel and watched him from the window. He dived in off the wharf and then he came in, mate, and he was blue. I said, 'You'll kill yourself.' He said, 'No, I won't. I'm used to it.' Well, I'm bloody sure I ain't. I never went with him.

It was kindness just to drive him because he was such a character. Why I drove him was this. He worked pretty hard, he used to operate pretty hard. You couldn't lose a man like that to an accident, so I took the job on of driving him and looking after him. I tell you what, it was worth thousands of quid, all those thousands of thing they could have in their life, the fun I had with him and just what a wonderful man he was to drive. That was life. . . .

Ladies and gentlemen, I'm not a good speaker. I'm pretty rough, I always have been. That's why I got on with Weary. He was a gentleman and he reckoned I was a man. . . .He was such a kind bloke you could not wish for anything else. He was a gentle giant, he could speak – beautiful! Don't kid yourselves. They used to say to me, 'He learns it.' It comes straight from the heart, every one he's done. It wasn't from papers. It's the way he spoke – a gentleman, a good fellow. . . .

In the camps . . . In the madness of the place, he was like a lighthouse. The more you walked towards him, the bigger he got.

Dr Jim Donaldson was the minister at Sir Edward's local church, and he delivered the sermon at the state funeral on 12 July, 1993. He had earlier delivered a memorial service for the ex-POWs at the Toorak Uniting Church. He was a friend of Sir Edward's and his neighbour. I spoke to him at his home in Hawthorn.

I FIRST MET Sir Edward Dunlop when I became the minister of the Toorak Uniting Church in 1983 and over the next ten years I got to know him very well, because I was not only his minister, I was also his next-door neighbour. We shared common interests – I had been an army chaplain in the reserve, I had a Scottish background, we shared the things of faith, and we shared a love of rugby union football. We spent many evenings at 605, talking.

I make a big distinction between the private Weary Dunlop and the public Weary Dunlop. The public Weary Dunlop travelled a thousand kilometres a week speaking at RSL clubs all around the place, whereas the private Weary Dunlop was, in many ways, lonely and isolated, and I think he valued the fact that I used to go in next door and we'd have a drink and share conversation. After Helen died, the housekeepers would ring us up if there was any medical problem and when he had his final collapse, my wife and I both went in there. We helped the paramedics carry him down the stairs and load him into the ambulance, so we felt his funeral was more than just a funeral for us. We had lost a friend, someone we admired and spent a lot of time with.

We were always invited in next door for what Scottish people call Hogmanay. That was every new year's eve. It was family and friends and we would sit and talk and drink, and then they used to have haggis and have The Ode to the Haggis, and stab it. It was really quite full of fun. Weary used to get dressed up like Young Lochinvar in his kilt.

We were both members of the Melbourne Scots, too, which is a kind of community group. They have bagpipe music and Scottish singing. They have poetry in Scottish, and they all clap politely at the end – I'm sure most of them can't understand it. On St Andrew's night, they get a telegram of congratulations from the Queen, from Prince Charles, from the Lord Provost of Edinburgh, the Provost of Glasgow, the Town Bailey of Dundee – it's absolutely mind boggling. (laughs) I used to think, here are people – they love their haggis, they love their whisky, they love their bagpipe music, they love their Scottish songs, they love their Scottish traditions – and every single member of the society has made a deliberate choice not to live in Scotland. (laughs)

I feel that the key to Sir Edward Dunlop is to understand that he was brought up essentially in the age of chivalry. If you read the very beginning of his war diaries, you discover that he was a bit saddened that when World War I came, he had been too young and had missed 'that adventure'. When Laurens van der Post writes in the introduction to the Diaries, of Weary leaving Java, ultimately to go to the Burma Railway, he describes Weary in terms that might be confused with *The Pilgrim's Progress*. When you listen to Sir Ninian Stephen's eulogy at the state funeral, the words are very typical of that – 'valiant knight', 'duty'.

I think in a sense Weary's upbringing was a bit like *Chum's Annual* with all the 'chivalry', with all the adages about 'doing one's duty', 'serving one's neighbour', 'God, King and Country'. My feeling is that Weary may have missed out on the opportunity for greatness, in that Chum's Annual sense, had he not become a prisoner of war. He was a sensitive man who had a good grip on English literature. He had a great memory for poetry and if you look at the poets that he liked, they reflect that kind of age. I think that in the back of his mind, Weary had the idea that to emulate the English gentleman was the means to attain greatness.

I used to wonder why a man needed to relive his wartime experiences for forty-five years, after most people wanted to forget. It can be explained by the fact that he wanted to serve his fellow POWs – he was always willing to stand up for the POWs, to look after the war widows, and there were always ex-prisoners of war staying next door – but I sometimes used to wonder how much of it was an ego trip, for his sake. I suppose everybody's got mixed motives, and in a sense when people give you a kind of image, you have to live up to it. I was very happy to see that all the names of the other doctors on the railway are given a place with Weary's statue in St Kilda Road. Weary wasn't saying he did it all himself, but in the public awareness and mythology, he stands like Goliath and there's nobody else about.

The public Weary really gave of himself. One night he fell down the stairs. He went to the Highland Games in Geelong the next day and he had to stand up in a Land Rover hanging on so he didn't fall over, with two broken wrists and a shoulder out of position. He was very gritty. Whether it was fixing his broken nose with a toothbrush or going to the Highland Games with two broken wrists – it was just incredible fortitude and grit.

He was a ball of energy. During the actual prison camp experience, he existed on three hours sleep a night, but even after the war he used to always visit people at ungodly hours of the morning. He was the only guy I could visit in my congregation at a quarter to eleven after a meeting, and he'd light the fire. And he'd pour you a tumbler full of whisky that you couldn't jump over. I used to try and make it last and he would say, 'You're not going home lopsided.' I'd say, 'Well, I can't drink another one like that. I'll be crawling on my hands and knees up the manse lane.'

I remember one afternoon I said to Weary, 'We haven't seen you for awhile, why don't you come in for a drink?' At one o'clock in the morning, we'd just finished watching the midnight movie, and I said to my wife, 'Well, we'd better be off to bed,' and the doorbell rang. It was Weary. He said, 'I've come for the drink.' He had tremendous energy. He used to drive as if he was in an armoured car. There was a saying that I made up: Weary was the only person I ever knew who could make a tramcar swerve.

The guy had tremendous charm. He would be very gentle with the little children, kiss the goodlooking ladies, a peck on the cheek for the older ones. Every time he came to church, he used to stay for morning tea, and he was so gracious to people. When Helen was suffering from dementia, she used to come to church and she would sing like a simple, little child. The Toorak congregation was very supportive and very sensitive to her need. It was lovely. Weary would come out and say, 'Sorry about the Luton Girls' Choir this morning.' He'd been married in that church, he was a member for forty-five years and Helen was buried there, so it was part of the family.

I always had the strong impression that had Weary wanted to be a writer, he could have done marvellously well. His letters are super – he's got a lovely turn of phrase. He was a real friend and I always see his frailties and whatever people criticise in the light of the bigger picture. He was a very sound all-rounder. He served his country, and there are a lot of prisoners of war and war veterans who revere what he did for them. I think that into that hellish situation came a man who happened to have the right attributes, qualities and characteristics, ready-made for hero status. It was that mixture of being a surgeon, a pharmacist, and an international sportsman. He was much more effective in charge than a Field Marshall would have been. He was a living inspirational figure and I think he rose to the occasion. I suppose, in a sense, legends grow out of people responding, out of recognition of that 'right man at the right place'. You become bigger than Ben Hur.

Was he a man that found it easy to be intimate?
I always found him a very warm character. Weary knew that we loved him, he knew we would look after him. We used to see him at a lot of dinners and he could just relax. On the private side he used to talk and share interesting things about his life. You almost felt at times that it was a kind of merry-go-round that he couldn't get off, whether or not he would have been happy to do that. I was always aware that a lot of conversations used to float back to the POW days. It didn't matter where you started, you'd be back up in the River Kwai Noi again. He also used to talk a lot of about Scotland and going to the Duke of Sutherland's grouse parties, about knowing Edwina

Mountbatten and how he used play poker with Alexander Fleming, the developer of penicillin. I found it fascinating. It was a bit like opening a door into history.

He was always very popular and as he became famous, he was regarded with great awe and majesty. To be chosen as one of the top 200 Australians in the centenary year, well, that's pretty unique, and he was Australian of the Year in 1977. Success breeds success and the figure gets bigger and the myth gets larger.

Weary sort of kept going as he got older. He was not willing to let go of his scalpel. This capacity to let go would have been quite difficult for him, and that related, in my opinion, to his inability to say no when someone in Timbuktu invited him to come up for a twenty-minute talk to the lady's auxiliary.

The state funeral must have been a magnificent event.
When the casket was transferred from the gun carriage to the funeral coach, and we drove out to Springvale cemetery, I was really quite touched – in fact, I had tears in my eyes – at the number of people who were standing in the streets. At Oakleigh, there was a bunch of drinkers, and they were standing with a beer in their hand. They'd actually come out of the pub to see it go past. There was an old man holding his wife's hand with his hat off, there was a postman who'd got off his motorbike and there was a mother with her three children, and I thought, Hey, in a normal funeral, everyone is cutting in on you and trying to cut off the hearse. What a fantastic mark of respect that the ordinary common people of life stood so reverently by the side of the road as this procession went past. That's one of the most memorable things about the funeral – not that the Prime Minister turned up, or that I was part of it or that 10 000 people stood outside, but somehow or other, ordinary people identified with this. I think that will be the one of the crowning things about

Weary Dunlop, his capacity to act as an inspiration for young people especially, on into future generations.

I felt there were two great aspects to Weary's life. One was his capacity to forgive. He could have been very bitter, and if you don't learn to forgive, the person who is really crippled by the wartime experience is not the Japanese you hate, but you. The other was his capacity to forget himself and to serve, and that's not a characteristic I see in a lot of Australians.

Kanit Wanachote met Sir Edward Dunlop in Thailand in 1985 and in the following years, they became close friends. Sir Edward often stayed at Kanit's property on the River Kwai not far from Hellfire Pass in the Kanchanaburi province when he visited Thailand. In the late 80s, this property was transformed into the Phu Toey Resort. Kanit also runs the English language school, the Home of English, in Bangkok.

IN 1985 I was sitting by the Kwai Noi. My wife and I and some of my workers were in our boathouse when along came a *hang yao*, a long-tailed boat. I saw that the people on it were respectable, they were foreigners and they were old. Because our boathouse is big and somewhat beautiful, they stopped. Somebody on board the boat asked me how much the beer cost here. I happen to like beer and I have a lot of beer in stock all the time (laughs) so I told them that no, we didn't sell beer here, but if you come up, you can have some. They were older than me and we usually respect the elders in our country, and they are very polite. There were about twelve of them all together. And then my wife happened to cook some curry – meat with some nuts – which we served and I wondered why they could eat such a hot thing.

After that another boat arrived, and the one who asked me how much the beer cost said, 'We drink beer here free.' On that second boat was Weary Dunlop. That was the first time we met. We drank and chatted and enjoyed ourselves. They spent about three hours here altogether. One of them said as they left, 'The last time we were here in Thailand, we were here as prisoners of war, we were tortured and we suffered. This time we have been made to feel so welcome.'

Since then we have been friends, and every year on Anzac Day when they came to stay at the River Kwai Village Hotel, I invited them to come here as my guests. Weary Dunlop came to stay with me every year. He would stay in another of our boathouses.

To me he was interested in mankind, not just the POWs or Thai people. All the people in the world know how good he was. One thing that I admired about him the most: what he did, he did without expecting any reward. Just for the goodness' sake. You can't find such people now in any country, you know. You want money, you want reputation, you want friends, you want higher position, something like that.

He had a great heart and he spoke his heart, he acted his heart and you could see his heart through his eyes. Every time he spoke, the greatness, the kindness came to his eyes. He looked into the eye of everyone every time he spoke, so everything flowed out smoothly. You don't have to add any colour or any layer – it came out from the heart without thinking. He was not thinking of the benefits.

Throughout the war, he fought all the time. He stood up for the people all the time, but the Japanese soldiers didn't dare to do anything to him because his eyes showed his heart.

His philosophy was one of moderation. What made him so great, I feel that he had really few things in his mind. Only some good, absolute good. At Kanchanaburi during the war, he didn't think of himself, he didn't think of his family, he didn't think of anything. He just thought, This is what's good, this is what's bad. So his thoughts went out quickly, and absolutely right, because very few things were in his mind. Very few people in the world can be like him, you know. He could do anything any time and whatever he did was right, good and perfect. Because it came from the perfect heart.

His simplicity was great. Here in Thailand we have a lot of monks. I tell friends here that if Sir Edward Dunlop happened to be a monk, he would be the most revered monk in the world. All the power was in him all the time, I think. He could drink whisky or he could drink ankavor up to any limit and it would not disturb him. (laughs)

Did you arrange the ceremony in April 1994 in which some of Sir Edward's ashes were launched upon the Kwai Noi by Sir Edward's sons, Alexander and John?
I offered to take care of everything when his friend told me that Sir Edward wanted his ashes in the River Kwai, because that is one thing that we could do for him. Here we built a boat about 130 centimetres long. We used jasmine flowers. About two hundred Thais and Australians were present and they put flowers and candles in the boat to pay their last respect to him. His sons, John and Alexander, carried the boat to float in the river.

Was it a traditional Thai ceremony?
No. For the boat to float on the river was just to do what he wished. We then punctured the boat so that it would sink. It was beautiful. With flowers and candles. It was already dark and this boat just kept coming around all the time. (laughs) Everyone said of Weary, he wouldn't like to leave.

In 1995, Kanit Wanachote was building the Sir Edward Dunlop Memorial Park on his property. The park consists of a re-creation of the prisoners' huts, the guardhouse, the cookhouse and other elements of the camp which once stood on the banks of the Kwai Noi.

'My friends ask me, "Why do you make a memorial to Sir Weary Dunlop? He's not a Thai." And I say to them, "I am not a Thai – I am a human being."'

Martin Flanagan's *father Arch was with Weary Dunlop as a prisoner of war. In 1985, Martin travelled to Thailand with Weary and they maintained contact on their return to Melbourne. He fondly remembers Weary's last words to him, written in a letter after the launch of his novel* Going Away: *'Up there Cazaly.'*

THE *AGE* DECIDED to send someone on the trip back to the Burma Railway that Keith Flanagan (who is no relation by the way) organised in 1985, and they offered it to me. My understanding of it all then was pretty vague. It was a fantastic opportunity to go back because Dad had been with Weary from Java through to Thailand and he'd been with him at Hellfire Pass at Hintok. We actually went back to Hellfire Pass. The jungle had reclaimed a lot of the railway, but this cutting that they'd had to cut out of stone, with pretty primitive, basic and inadequate instruments, that was still there. The jungle couldn't go over stone. That was a fantastic monument.

That night we stayed in a motel on the River Kwai and we watched the movie *The Bridge on the River Kwai*. They play that there every night, I think. I sat with Weary and we watched it together. Years ago my father, who hadn't said a lot about his experience in the prisoner of war camp, just saw the movie and said, 'Not true'. So I watched this movie that wasn't true that the world presumed to be true – about a bogus hero on the Burma railway, with the man who in fact was the hero on the Burma railway. That's the sort of profound irony that surrounded Weary to an extraordinary extent.

I used to go Weary's room up there and we'd drink whisky and talk. We'd talk till one or two o'clock in the morning, and he'd start telling me stories. He was the most fantastic story teller because his use of language was so good, so precise and descriptive. But when he'd tell me these stories, I'd have this enormous feeling of sadness and I never understood why. Later I realised that I sensed just how lonely a man he was.

To me he's like a figure out of a Greek tragedy. He's the man the gods gave everything. The only person that I've read about who seems to have been as gifted as him is Paul Robeson – scholar, singer, athlete, leader of men. Weary had all these gifts but the catch was that he never met anyone like himself, so he wandered through the world alone. He only ever met people who could share a part of him. I don't think – I could be wrong – but I don't think he met anyone who could share all of him. That's what I sensed. I think he was possibly the loneliest person I ever met.

He was intellectual, he was profoundly spiritual and he seemed to be completely familiar with eastern psychology and spirituality. I thought it was amazing when he died and the Melbourne Buddhists had the ceremony for him. I think in many of his views he was eastern, and that's what I thought about sitting up there with him watching this film about the experience he'd been in, and seeing how wrong it was and he's accepting it. It didn't make him angry. I'd read articles about him in newspapers and magazines that were just wrong, they were just completely wrong, all sorts of things, and he somehow understood that once you get the sort of fame he had, people do cease to be truthful about you.

When I sensed his loneliness, I thought, Well, should I try and do something about this? I'd try to take people to meet him who I thought might interest him. One was Mort Sahl, the American comedian. I'd told Mort Sahl a bit about Weary and he was really taken with him, but their conversation was unbelievable – grappling to find the right position of politeness. In the end they discovered a common connection, to do with a hospital in Los Angeles in 1938 that they both knew something about, and they constructed a conversation from there.

Weary was known but not known. I like that statue in St Kilda Road because that's how he was when I knew him. He was standing at attention while people walked passed him. That's exactly what he was like. One day up in Thailand I was with him in a bar and he started reciting Tennyson's *Ulysses*.

> '. . . *I mete and dole*
>> *Unequal laws unto a savage race,*
> *That hoard, and sleep, and feed, and know not me . . .*'

He just kept going and I thought, this sounds like he's Ulysses. It was incredible.

I thought, I've got to get this on tape, so when we were back here in Melbourne, I took my tape around but as soon as I put that on, he started performing and it wasn't nearly as good. But he got going and started reciting poetry. He recited Housman and Keats for two-and-a-half hours, and throughout, he'd look at me, watching to see if I was still with him, if I was still understanding him. In a way, I think that was probably the most honest or the most direct or the most open he ever was with me.

It was like a huge lament: for a sense of duty, for a sense of dignity and a sense of meaning, and a world that had passed and was his life. He was like a mammoth and the ices had melted. He was wandering round amongst a different sort of people.

For me, Weary was the finest expression I've met in my life of the values that were at the heart of what was called British civilisation. Before I met him I didn't even really respect those values, but in meeting him, I now understand it. Ultimately to describe him, as Laurens van der Post said, you had to go back to that archaic language which had words like 'steadfast' and 'valiant' and 'true'.

I liked the bloke. I liked him.

Whenever I was with him, I never really knew whether I should be there or not. After he died, Valda Street told me that I was one of his favourite young people. Well, I was never 100 per cent sure. I'd love to have done more for him but I didn't know what to do. Valda said to me, 'He loves you to come,' so I came. I tried to keep contact with him.

Was he a man whose time had passed?

Well, Ulysses set out with his crew on just one last voyage. It's like Weary wouldn't hand in his driving licence. God knows he should have. And if what one hears is true, he possibly should have retired as a surgeon before he did. But he was born for action.

There's a story he told me about a Keats poem. Weary was arrested by the *kempei* for having a wireless and they were going to bayonet him to death and they tied him to a tree. They started the countdown and they asked if he had a message and he said 'Not to be conveyed by a baboon like you.' They said,

'Cut him down, he'll suffer more before he dies.' He told me that story three times and he told it to me differently each time.

On the first occasion, he told me how they pulled him out of the cell and made him play quoits with the jailer. There was an old Dutch bloke whose hand quivered so much he couldn't hold the quoit. The second time he told me, there was an Asian bloke and they exchanged sign language. Weary went (draws his finger across his throat) and the Asian bloke nodded and they both had death sentences. The third time, he was alone and he found himself remembering this poem he'd learnt as a schoolboy, which is this Keats' poem. To my mind that summed him up, because he came from a culture that was so sure of its values, and at one stage probably the body of the culture really believed those values. He certainly did. They could sustain him in the moment he was fearing death.

These could be events that he had run together in his mind. Did the fact that he told you the story in three different ways cause you to doubt him?
No, that gives it more truth to me. I think when you start telling stories word perfect . . . Another time, he told me that when he was waiting for one of the Nips to take out his bayonet, he realised he wasn't as scared as he had been while waiting outside his headmaster's office. I find that amazing. He told me he was only scared twice in the war, and he liked the fact that war had made him run at full stretch. I imagine that's true, and I imagine it would take something like that to make him run full stretch. I think he did the rest so easily.

Were you involved in a proposed television series on Weary?
Because of the sort of person he was, I think people were able to use Weary to their own ends. At one stage I was involved in

this idea of getting a mini series up, and we had this night at his place and Weary wasn't interested at all. It was going whoosh, whoosh, whoosh, over his head. This was all being done in his name but he was totally uninterested. I felt there were so many situations where he met images of himself, that he seemed to accept it as being almost a part of his fate, that there was nothing that he could do about it.

Were you conscious of his sense of humour?

That's something van der Post wrote about in the foreword to the diaries, his sense of irony. It was absolutely fabulous. I remember him telling me a story about Ewan Corlette, who was one of the doctors with him in the camps. He was having trouble from this soldier who was ill. He said, 'Doctor, will I live?' and Corlette said, 'I haven't decided yet.' Weary loved that.

I was with him in Indonesia when the authorities had been notified to say we were coming and that we wanted to see the old POW complex. They mistranslated the message and thought we were penologists, so we arrived and were given an extensive tour of an Indonesian prison. At the end, a bloke got up and gave us a speech and Weary got up and responded.

He said, 'We see the great strides forward that have been made in prison conditions in Indonesia since we were last here.' It was just a hoot. Afterwards we came out and the prison band was lined up and played guitars for us and Weary danced. He danced like a big bear and the whole thing started breaking up and becoming slightly riotous. Some of the old diggers got involved, started shaking hands, and the prisoners started giggling, and it got so out of hand that when the party left, it was discovered that one old digger was still inside. They had to unlock the gates and go back and get him. And it was the wrong prison! We'd been to the wrong prison.

It's arguable that I might not be alive without Weary. My Dad had cholera and Weary was the one who controlled the cholera epidemic. Having said that, people probably think I'm biased because of my father. My father had and has profound respect and affection for Weary, but it wasn't something I was brought up with.

Stewart Noble was traced through a quickly scribbled note in an address book of Sir Edward's. Sir Edward had noted down Stewart Noble's name, his work phone number, and car number plate next to the words: 'car accident 9.20 19/Aug/89'.

YOU COULD SAY I knew him for a split second in my life, in August 1989 when I was twenty-six. I was driving up Williams Road early one Saturday morning and I saw this Mercedes pulling out of Bruce Street. I was doing about sixty kilometres per hour, and as I got closer I realised it was an elderly gentleman driving. He just didn't stop. I braked but I drove into him on the driver's side. It was pretty funny, he was doing donuts in the middle of Williams Road for about half a minute. Afterwards he said his foot got stuck on the accelerator. Then he stopped. We were both very apologetic. I recognised him immediately, and even though it wasn't my fault I felt quite guilty about hitting such a well-known and respected gentleman.

He went off to hospital and was out that afternoon. He was actually on his way to the airport, heading to Perth, when I hit him, but he didn't seem particularly fazed about missing his plane. Maybe because he knew he shouldn't have been driving in the first place. Because I hit him on the driver's side I really feared the worst, but he came out of it all relatively unscathed.

He was definitely tougher than most people, I'd think. My Commodore was a write-off.

Melvie Barter was Sir Edward's housekeeper from November 1989 until his death. She had just returned from a trip around Australia when I spoke to her in Croydon.

MY INTERVIEW FOR the job with Sir Edward was amazing really. Sir Edward said, 'Did you have much trouble finding the place?' I said, 'I must confess, I've never been to Toorak before but my sister came to show me the way.' So out he goes to the car and brings her in and he has quite a conversation with the both of us. Then he said, 'I suppose you'll want to see through the house.' So I started to go off with him and he turned to my sister and said, 'Come on, you come too, because you must approve as well.'

He showed me one wing of the house and said, 'Now you can have this. It's quite private away from everything else. Make it as homely as you can.' He took us out to see the backyard and picked us a rose each. We were chatting away and I said, 'You've got an appointment in Ballarat, haven't you, so we must go.' He said, 'I'll just show you where the external key is, dear and you just move in when you're ready.' I looked at him and said. 'Oh, I've got some references that I guess you'll want to see.' He said, 'No, no, no, I don't want to see your references.' He trots out to this old cupboard and pulls this sticky old rubber glove out and there was a key poked down in one of the sticky old fingers. He said, 'Move in when you like.'

It was a wonderful position. My association with Sir Edward, I haven't one word to say against my time with him. If he didn't have other engagements, he always had a lie-in on

Sunday morning. The first Sunday I was there he said, 'Melvie, we've got to be in church in ten minutes. We'll have to hurry.' He still had to have his shower and dress to go. So I skittled upstairs and I did a quick act, too, and off we toddled to church, the hand under the elbow and we get to the door and up to the family pew.

That's one thing I must say, he never ever made me feel any the less because I was his housekeeper. In fact I was a very important cog in the wheel. I was taken around and introduced to all the folk that he knew and they were people of rather high calling, a lot of them.

Sir Edward had an overwhelming amount of charisma. I used to tell him that he would charm the heart out of a wheelbarrow. One time his friend, Gert, was down from Shepparton, I had a friend over from Tasmania, and Sir Edward said, 'We'll all go into the Rose Show.' Of course we were all wanting to see the roses, but Sir Edward would take a few steps and he'd be halted by all these adoring women. The bowing and the handkissing that used to go on! It used to be a bit of a joke about how he kissed the various ages. The eighty-pluses got a kiss on both cheeks, sixty to seventy group, they got the handkissing, but the young ones got it right on the lips. Some of the old ex-POWs used to torment him about that. When we got home, we asked him which rose he thought was the nicest. Then we said, 'You didn't even see them, did you, you were so busy handshaking and kissing and all the rest of it.' It was quite amusing really and he loved it.

He would get hundreds and hundreds of birthday cards and Christmas cards and he would send a handwritten reply to everyone. It was amazing. He always ate his meal and looked at the mail at the kitchen table. He'd write half the night and I always waited until twelve o'clock at night to give him a cup of tea and a couple of biscuits. He'd leave the little plate and the cup and saucer on the dining room table and next morning I'd go in to get it and he'd have a great pile of letters there.

My grandson, Dylan, had a terrible accident and Sir Edward was very worried about him. Sir Edward had been to something in St Paul's Cathedral, with his grey top hat and his swallow tails and his grey striped trousers. Dylan was visiting me when he arrived home. As soon as he walked in, he said, 'Dylan my boy, come here,' and I'll never forget how, with the tips of his fingers, he ran them down his face, down his spine. He just stood there going all over and he looked at his mother and said, 'He'll be fine. He'll be fine dear, you won't have a worry in the world.' That was the one thing I wanted to know when the undertaker came: what did you do with his beautiful hands? (Melvie is visibly upset) They were magical hands.

I looked after him three or four times when he took ill. I hadn't been with him all that long and he went to India. The family he stayed with had children with gastroenteritis. Sir Edward came in on a very early flight and Jack Flannery went out to meet him. As soon as he walked in, he was just so stooped, he looked shocking. He said, 'I'm going up to bed.' Jack's eyes filled up and he said. 'First time I've ever had any trouble finding Weary, because he's usually head and shoulders over all the other passengers.'

Within a few hours, his hands had gone like claws, he was hallucinating, dehydrating, and he looked something shocking. I couldn't raise any of the doctors whose names he had in his book. I kept saying to Sir Edward, 'Can I get a doctor for you?' 'No, no, no, no, none of them are any damn good.' Finally the minister next door recommended David Kings who became Sir Edward's doctor. He said he would come down at once and it was with much fear and trembling that I accompanied him upstairs to Sir Edward's room. I thought, Will he go mad? And David said, 'I'm the NCO of the Dunlop Barracks.' That put David right up on the top rung of the ladder and they became good friends and David attended him each time he was ill after that.

David could be very firm. Sir Edward had a car accident and said no way was he going to go to hospital in an ambulance so David said, 'You'll come with me.' David and old Jack got him into the car, and took him into the hospital, got him patched up with crutches and brought him home to be nursed at home.

The thing was, he didn't want anybody to see him like that. He had that big shining countenance to uphold before all men outside the house and when he was ill, 'Just keep them away, dear, I don't want to see anybody. Only you and David.' He expressed that so much with that last illness.

I've heard you're a wonderful cook. Did Sir Edward do a lot of entertaining when you were with him?
He loved entertaining. He was the host with the most. He loved the table. He had beautiful table appointments and this enormous dining-room table and he liked to fill it. He loved all the beautiful silver and crystal, and he just absolutely loved flowers. He'd have a beautiful arrangement in the centre of the table and flowers all about inside.

He didn't like me to have anything wrong with me – either Valda or I. He needed us, so we weren't supposed to get anything wrong with us. I had the carpal tunnel done, which meant my arm was out of action, and if he told me once, he told me fifty times, that when Sister Gracey was his theatre sister, she had both hers done at once and she was back in the theatre in two days, assisting him with very intricate operations. (laughs)

It made me feel terrible. Here I was with my arm in a sling, in terrible pain.

But then I had some nasty falls and he'd say, 'Go to bed.' He'd be so concerned about me. I had several operations on my toes while I was there and he'd bring this injection home from work and come and see if I was all right before he went to bed. Things like that, he could be so concerned.

At the dinner parties, he would count the places I had set and often he would say he had invited two more and that would throw me into a bit of a flurry. He'd say, 'You're one short, dear. What about yourself? Where are you going to sit?' I'd say, 'Sir Edward, I can't be at your dining table and in the kitchen too. Not at the same time.' And even when the guests came, he'd take the time. I'd be making the coffee and he'd say, 'I'll come and have a cup of coffee with you.'

He would come out and escort me into the dining room and he'd find a chair at one end of the table and then go back to his place at the other end and then he'd make his little speech. What a gem I was, or what a treasure I was. 'Since Melvie came into the house, she's made a home – she's done the flowers and she's done all this cooking herself.' He'd usually end up saying, 'The thing that worries me most of all is that I might lose her to the Hyatt.'

After everybody had all gone, I'd say to Sir Edward, 'Now we can have a decent cup of tea.'

Those last couple of days, he was well aware that he was dying. On the Sunday he went to this Scots do down at Aspendale. When he went off in his kilt, he looked awfully, awfully tired. He'd had an awfully busy week. He'd been to Sydney, Mount Gambier. They got back from Numurkah at 3.30 on the Sunday morning and he had to be down there are Aspendale at about nine a.m. And it was tiring on old Jack Flannery, too. He'd picked him up at the airport and driven him to Numurkah and back again and then he came over on the Sunday morning to take him down there.

He went off to work on the Monday morning. He came home much earlier than he usually did and he walked in and said, 'I don't feel very well. I'm getting a cold.' 'Oh, you're not Sir Edward. Do you know, you have a cold every birthday? Well, you'll be over it by your birthday this year.' He said, 'I wouldn't be too sure about that, dear.'

That night I said, 'Why don't you have an early night, Sir Edward?' He said, 'I must finish this writing I have to do.' I persuaded him to take a couple of Panadol and made him a lemon drink and I said, 'Now, you wallop plenty of that good whisky into that.' Later I heard his faltering steps go up the stairs.

The next morning he came down looking something terrible. I said, 'Sir Edward, you don't look a bit well.' He said, 'I'm not.' I said, 'Go back to bed.' He said, 'Oh no, no, I've got this to do, I've got that to do.' I said, 'You were so late going to bed last night.' He said. 'I had that writing to do.' I went into the dining room and here was this pile of letters that he'd written.

I was making his bed and I heard the car start up. I thought, It couldn't be. Here he was trying to back the car out. He hadn't had time to have his breakfast. I stood there and I watched him. It took him so long. I went to the front bedroom and looked out and he'd got out on to the footpath. Usually he speared out of there, without looking, there'd be a screech of brakes and the tooting of horns. I used to tell him that he overworked his guardian angels every morning. This time the brake lights were going on and off, on and off.

At about three o'clock Valda phoned to say he was on his way home. 'I'm so worried,' she said, 'his speech seems slurred, his face is flushed and he just sat there with his hat pulled down over his eyes.' She said his mouth looked a bit twisted. He came in and he just said, 'Melvie, I'm ill. I'm going upstairs to bed straight away.'

He was so hot and feverish. Whenever he got anything wrong with him, it was like malaria coming back. He'd be yellow and he'd be shivering and yet he was so hot and clammy to touch. I rang David Kings and David came to him and he gave him an injection and got some tablets for him. That was on the Tuesday.

All day on the Wednesday, he'd sleep and he'd wake up and he'd be just ringing wet with perspiration. On the Thursday I phoned David and said, 'Sir Edward's a lot worse this morning,' and David came after surgery,

On Thursday night, I brought a chair and put it beside his bed. I said, 'Look I'll put your bottle and the jug there for you, they are easy enough for you to reach.' I put the bell there. I just got downstairs and I heard this crash. I thought, Whatever is it? For years I haven't been able to walk straight up the stairs, I've got to get both feet on the one stair, then on the next one. So I couldn't run up the stairs but I said, 'Sir Edward, what are you doing?' I went up and he'd got out of bed. Just in that three minutes, he'd got out, he was sitting on the chair with his elbow on the windowsill. And he was just frothing at the mouth and making a terrible noise. He was quite unconscious.

So I hurried back down and phoned Jim Donaldson. By the time I'd got to the front door, Jim and Joan were there. Two ambulances came and there were five paramedics there. They worked on him but he never regained consciousness.

It was so awkward getting this big man downstairs. It took the five of them to bring him down on the stretcher, two walking backwards, Jim was sort of guiding them down. I said, 'How bad is he?' They said, 'Very bad.' I remember after my mum died, my sister was told the very last thing they are conscious of is touch. As they carried him out, I said, 'It's Melvie, Sir

Edward,' and I went like that (stroked) down his arm. But I didn't think they'd bring him back. I didn't think he'd recover.

I went to the phone and I rang Valda. By this time it was one o'clock in the morning but I rang Valda and she came over. David Kings went to the Alfred Hospital and he kept phoning back about every quarter of an hour.

At about three o'clock they thought they had him stabilised. He had responded although he hadn't regained consciousness. At quarter past three David rang and said, 'He's gone.'

*Sir Edward 'Weary' Dunlop died on 2 July 1993. Ten days later, Melbourne stopped for his state funeral – thousands listened outside the cathedral, watched it on television or listened to the radio when **Sir Ninian Stephen,** the former Governor General and a fellow member of the Melbourne Scots, delivered this eulogy to Sir Edward.*

GATHERED HERE TODAY to pay tribute to Sir Edward Dunlop are not only his family, close friends and old comrades but the Australian nation itself, represented by the Prime Minister and the Leader of the Opposition and representatives of the Governor General and of the Governor of Victoria. Here too are the acting premier of Victoria, presiding officers of parliaments, and representatives of the judiciary together with representatives of associations and institutions Australia-wide; and the ambassadors and consuls of many nations overseas. All are here to pay tribute to Sir Edward, to express their sorrow at his passing, their deep respect for the man, their high admiration for his achievements and their sense of loss in his death. In doing so they represent the feelings of the millions of . Australians and of countless admirers overseas.

Sir Edward's family and his close friends mourn him privately and in their hearts; their great loss is intensely personal and no state funeral can attest that loss or adequately mark for them his passing. But by this service the whole nation mourns.

In this present age there is a dearth of heroes. And it is as a hero that we remember Weary Dunlop. He was virtuous, kind and immensely brave, utterly steadfast in the path of duty and invincible in his courage. We remember him not simply as the doer of some single deed of great bravery but as an immensely valiant human being who for years on end was consistently courageous under terrible stress, his sense of duty unshakeable and his compassion for his fellow men unfailing.

Having dedicated his life to the healing of others, he found himself tested as few have been before him. A prisoner among prisoners, all despised and all sought to be humiliated by their captors, he rejected humiliation. Through sheer strength of character and of purpose and strength of body too, he survived torture and vile treatment to continue his care for his men, caring for their disease-racked bodies, inspiring them with hope when hope was faint and with human dignity and self-respect when all outward dignity seemed gone and respect for self was sought to be starved and beaten out of them. As Laurens van der Post has written, he was both the inspiration and the main instrument of his men's physical survival.

Those of us who have in our lives been spared the extremes of brutality, starvation, disease and near-terminal exhaustion that he knew and, still worse, that he saw being suffered by those under his command and in his care, can only speculate on the despair to be overcome and the suffering to be endured by those Australian prisoners of war. We can only marvel at them, and at him, asking ourselves how we would have fared had we been one of them and knowing that, lacking the rare heroic qualities of Weary Dunlop, we might have survived but could never have quietly triumphed as Weary did.

For all his life was a quiet triumph, every test he put himself to, he passed; every task he set himself he fulfilled. As sportsman on the rugby field, as boxer in the ring, as surgeon, as soldier, as loving husband and father and as honoured friend to very many.

With perhaps only Douglas Mawson, of all Australians, he shares a lone eminence of sustained heroism and superb achievement.

His long life was an inspiration to us all. In death the inspiration remains, inspiring us to try as best we may to follow his example of courageous and unflagging nobility.

Bitterness never entered his soul, for he knew its corroding influence and forthrightly rejected it. Instead he gathered the strength to feel Christian forgiveness of the enemy, that coming to him, he said, at war's end when, seeing a wounded Japanese soldier slumped down on the floor of a railway truck full of Japanese prisoners and apparently in danger of being crushed, he went to help him up. Weary took him by the shoulders to lift him, only to find him dead. With that all his hatred of the enemy died too.

His life was filled with achievements, yet unaffected modesty and gentle good humour were always his traits. Innumerable honours were his, bestowed on him by governments, by professional colleagues, by universities here and overseas, by learned societies, by service clubs, by cities and whole communities and, of course, by his old comrades, ex-servicemen and former prisoners of war, many of whom feel that they owe their lives to him.

A country boy, he was born on his father's farm near Stewarton, out of Benalla, as it happens exactly eighty-six years ago today. He attended Stewarton primary school and then

Benalla High. Tall, raw-boned and shy, a good scholar, he was then apprenticed to a pharmacist in Benalla, began his pharmacy course and topped his first year. Then he moved to Melbourne and there completed his course while working for a pharmacist in Melbourne. He was gold medallist in pharmacy in his final year. Then inspired by the example of Sir Thomas Dunhill, who had also begun life as an apprentice pharmacist and lived to become surgeon to King George V, he too determined to become a surgeon, enrolled in Melbourne University's Medical School and gained a scholarship to Ormond College. But he knew no Latin, then a prerequisite for medicine, and in six months of cramming at Taylor's night classes learnt his Latin while at the same time studying medicine.

A brilliant student, he had an extraordinary memory, which did not fade with age. He loved poetry, especially Tennyson and the Romantics and could, and did in the most unlikely places and at the most unlikely times, recite faultlessly whole cantos and long passages of Shakespeare. He was also a great sportsman in the boxing ring and on the football field; first, as a schoolboy, playing Australian Rules and then, at Ormond, where he was introduced to rugby and soon was an international, playing for Australia with the Wallabies. Ironically, his studies prevented him from joining the Wallabies on their tour of Japan.

On graduation he served at the Royal Melbourne Hospital for some years, then, to gain his fellowship, sailed to England as ship's surgeon, worked at St Bartholomew's Hospital, took his London FRCS at first attempt and in 1939 was working at Hammersmith Post Graduate Medical School until, with war looming, he was posted to St Mary's, Paddington, as a specialist surgeon to the Emergency Medical Service under Lord Porritt.

To this point all seemed set on a civilian career of high

achievement as a surgeon. However, before the war, he had been, in turn an enthusiastic cadet and a citizen forces volunteer attending annual camps and had been commissioned in the Royal Australian Army Medical Corps after completing his medical course. When war was declared he was determined to serve with the AIF and, with a deal of wangling, managed a unique enlistment through Australia House, London. He was more successful in enlisting at Australia House than in being outfitted there; no up-to-date Australian uniforms were on offer and he had to make do with a World War I digger hat, emu feathers and all, and a generally picturesque, if antique, Light Horse uniform, to the delight of passing Londoners in the Strand, until he could buy more orthodox gear. He embarked, on New Year's Eve, 1940, for the Middle East as Captain Dunlop VX 259. There he served as medical officer with the AIF until the Balkan campaign took them, and him, to Greece. He was Medical Liaison Officer between the Australian forces and the British throughout the Greek campaign, much astride his motorbike between the Australian front line and Athens, bearing unofficial military intelligence as well as medical liaison details.

In the retreat south to the Peloponnese he narrowly evaded German paratroopers at Corinth and was finally evacuated to Crete where, after further hardships and danger, he was again evacuated, this time to Egypt. He arrived, ragged and sick with hepatitis, was hospitalised and, impatient to serve, deserted his hospital bed against medical orders, leaving a note on his pillow reading 'Sorry – gone to Tobruk', which he did, being ferried in by destroyer to the beleaguered town and joining the 2/2 CCS there, living in a cave and caring for the men of the 6th Division.

Then, after further service in Egypt and Palestine and with Japan now in the war and threatening South-East Asia, he sailed for Sumatra and Java with the 2/2 CCS, which was to form the nucleus of the 1st Allied General Hospital at Bandoeng. There he was promoted to Lieutenant-Colonel.

Singapore had fallen and in the chaos of the time he brilliantly organised a working general hospital in Bandeong. In March the Dutch forces in Java capitulated and thus began Weary's almost three years in captivity.

It was as if all his life to that point had been lived so as to prepare him for his new role. His great physical strength and fitness, his training as a surgeon, his knowledge of men. His ability to lead and inspire others to follow, to deal with his captors and to organise the foul, disease-ridden camps the Australians found themselves in: all this his thirty-three years of life had taught him. That and much more; a love of humanity, an ability to suffer appalling hardship yet never swerve from the path of duty towards others, a soundness of judgment and decisiveness of action combined with an unfailing sense of humour and deep compassion. These qualities he took with him to the hell of prison camps and there saved countless lives.

In Java he had been promoted to full colonel but he did not assume that rank as it would have risked separation from his men. Instead he stayed with them, serving both as a CO and as medical officer at prisoner of war camps both in Java and later, in Changi until sent to Thailand to labour on the Burma railway, in charge of some one thousand men. He was at one and the same time their commanding officer, fighting every inch of the way with brutal captors for his men's rights and indeed for their very survival and this at constant risk of his own life, and also their doctor, sharing with two other heroic medics their medical care. And all the while, in common with his men, systematically humiliated and inhumanly abused.

The unbelievable horror of those times lives in the pages of Weary Dunlop's prisoner of war diaries, the deaths, the beatings, the starvation, the sheer inhumanity of it. Throughout he was an inspiration to all, his own suffering ignored in the service of others. I can't attempt to describe the experiences of those times; nor should I, only those who have endured them, those whom Weary wrote of as part of 'the timeless, enduring, special brotherhood shared by all survivors of prison camps', many of them here at this service today, know and fully comprehend that experience. The diaries tell it all; and the tales of these survivors are the best testimony to the heroism of this man. Those diaries he wrote as a military duty, never intending publication and for over forty years they remained unpublished until he was persuaded that they should at last see the light of day.

He was a legend already on his return at war's end to Australia and to home. His sweetheart of many years, Helen Ferguson, he married very soon after his return and their long and happy marriage, blessed by two sons Alexander and John and now by three grandchildren, ended tragically with Helen's death in 1988 after a long illness lightened by their love for each other and by Weary's devotion to Helen.

His career after the war was that of a great and gifted surgeon in an extraordinarily busy practice, interrupted only by service in Vietnam, leading a surgical team. With his practice, he managed to combine a continuing and devoted care and concern for all his comrades of the camps and their families and an expanding interest in Asia. Through his friend Richard Casey he played an active part in the development of Australia's role in the Colombo Plan. He lectured, taught and operated in Malaysia, Sri Lanka, Thailand and India and thereafter never stopped working for closer relations with our neighbour nations to the north; few if any Australians have been as active in promoting the exchange of knowledge, skills and culture with Asian countries and none as honoured as he was by Asian nations and by Asian medical and other professional bodies.

Here at home in Melbourne he was active over a vast range of community activities and organisations, all the way from a host of ex-servicemen's associations to the Anti-Cancer Council and the Council for Overseas Students. I knew him as a member of the Melbourne Scots, he was very proud of his Scottish ancestry and very dashing he looked in his eighties in kilt and green velvet dress jacket, with an elegant flourish of lace at neck and wrists; others knew him as a Rotarian, a Lion, as a distinguished fellow of colleges of surgeons in many lands, as the patron or honoured member of almost every Australian association having links with Asia and of course as an eminent consultant surgeon at the Royal Melbourne and other of the great hospitals in this state. There was little that was for the welfare of Australians in which he was not active.

He was loved and respected at a distance by millions and intimately by his family and those fortunate enough to be his dear friends, themselves numbering many thousands at home and overseas.

It is lives such as his that teach us that man can aspire to and achieve true nobleness of character and by doing so can inspire us all; Weary Dunlop would have been surprised to hear himself described as saintly, but to many his dedication to all that was good and his own sheer nobility of character seemed saintly; they set him apart, although he would have laughed and gently teased whoever told him that.

His death does not leave us the poorer; instead, because it concentrates our thoughts on him and his life and example, we are enriched and inspired. If we cannot emulate him, his great gifts of mind and of character eluding us, we can at least try to guide our actions by the pre-eminent standards that he made his own and by which we will remember him.

INDEX

PENGUIN – THE BEST AUSTRALIAN READING

Keating: The Inside Story **by John Edwards**
The Man
The Myth
The Record

What kind of person is Paul Keating? The inside story of
Keating's years in power is a fascinating one, recounted in
colourful detail. At the forefront of Australian political life for
some thirteen years, both the man and his methods have
remained mysterious. This is the definitive biography, written
by economic journalist, John Edwards, who was also a key
member of Keating's personal staff.

PENGUIN – THE BEST AUSTRALIAN READING

Glass After Glass: Autobiographical Reflections
by Barbara Blackman

'One life has many autobiographies.
It depends how one sinks one's
shaft of remembering . . .'

Barbara Blackman, essayist, librettist, letter writer, was married
to painter Charles Blackman for thirty years. Caught up into the
Barjai art/literary group of the Forties, the Melbourne
Contemporary Art Society of the Fifties, and the Australian
wave in London of the Sixties, her gift for the feel and weight
and place of words, the music of words, draws us into her life as
daughter, lover, friend, wife, mother, grandmother. Her
portraits of family and friends, many to become among
Australia's finest artists, reveal both a delightful sense of the
absurd and a great capacity to love.

'Brightness and sunshine pour from every page of this book . . . you will
be a happier person than you were before you began it!'
Peter Bowler, Canberra Times

PENGUIN – THE BEST AUSTRALIAN READING

A Fortunate Life
by Albert Facey

This is the extraordinary life of an ordinary man. It is the story of Albert Facey, who lived with simple honesty, compassion and courage. A parentless boy who started work at eight on the rough West Australian frontier, he struggled as an itinerant rural worker, survived the gore of Gallipoli, the loss of his farm in the Depression, the death of his son in World War II and that of his beloved wife after sixty devoted years – yet felt that his life was fortunate.

Facey's life story, published when he was eighty-seven, has inspired many thousands as an award-winning bestseller, a play and a television series.

'I am stunned by the horror this man endured in his childhood. I am humbled by his gentle acceptance of the good and bad ... This is an extraordinary and moving book.'
Adelaide Advertiser

PENGUIN – THE BEST AUSTRALIAN READING

A Fence Around The Cuckoo
by Ruth Park

Written as vividly as any of her novels, this first volume of
Ruth Park's long-awaited autobiography is a moving,
passionate, often funny account of her curious early childhood
in the remote rainforests of New Zealand and her teenage
years of convent education and first steps into journalism. In
1942 she came to Australia to meet and marry D'Arcy Niland
and to continue the writing which has made her one of
Australia's best-loved authors.

Fishing in the Styx
by Ruth Park

Fishing in the Styx, the second volume of Ruth Park's
autobiography, is not only a candid portrait of a marriage and
industrious literary partnership. It is a passionate, humorous
and realistic account of a writing life: the sometimes
acrimonious dealings with publishers and agents, the uneven
financial rewards and the hard work of matching deadlines
with creative output.

Ruth Park's life is rich in experience and achievement.
Writing was, and is, at the core of her being and her work
continues to delight new readers. Of this book she said, 'I
want it to be full of joy for that is what my life has mainly
been about.'

PENGUIN – THE BEST AUSTRALIAN READING

The Anzacs
by Patsy Adam-Smith

Gallipoli was the final resting place for thousands of young Australians. Death struck so fast there was no time for escape or burial. And when Gallipoli was over there was the misery of the European Campaign.

In *The Anzacs* Patsy Adam-Smith tells of the men who gave birth to a legend. Winner of the Age Book of the Year Award when it was first published, it remains unrivalled as the classic account of Australia's involvement in the First World War.

'If you have not read **The Anzacs** *there will always be a part of Australia you will never understand.'*
Les Carlyon, *Australian*

9